Administration
in Zambia

Administration in Zambia

edited by William Tordoff

Manchester University Press

University of Wisconsin Press

© Manchester University Press 1980

First published 1980
by Manchester University Press
Oxford Road, Manchester M13 9PL

British Library cataloguing in publication data

Administration in Zambia.
    1. Zambia – Politics and government
    I. Tordoff, William
    354′.689′40009   JQ2824

    ISBN 0–7190–9785–2

Published in North America by
the University of Wisconsin Press
114 North Murray Street, Madison, Wisconsin 53715

ISBN 0–299–08570–8

Library of Congress cataloging in publication data

Administration in Zambia.

    "A companion volume to Politics in Zambia."
    Bibliography: p. 278.
    Includes index.
    1. Zambia—Politics and government—Addresses,
essays, lectures.   2. Local government—Zambia—
Addresses, essays, lectures.   3. Rural development—
Zambia—Addresses, essays, lectures.   4. Government
business enterprises—Zambia—Addresses, essays,
lectures.   I. Tordoff, William.
JQ2826   1980.A35   320.96894   80–52300
ISBN 0–299–08570–8

Computerised Phototypesetting
by G.C. Typeset Ltd., Bolton, Greater Manchester

Printed and bound in Great Britain by
Redwood Burn Limited
Trowbridge & Esher

Contents

Preface

This book is a study of administration in Zambia in the post-independence period (1964–78) and is a companion volume to *Politics in Zambia* (Manchester, 1974). It examines the changing political and socio-economic context in which the administration operates and, though the focus is on domestic administration, some attention is also given to the inter-action between internal and external events.

Following an introduction which reviews those forces which have shaped Zambian administration both before and after the introduction of the one-party state in December 1972, ensuing chapters discuss the economy, the public service and parastatal sector, party and administration under the one-party state, urban authorities, and rural administration and development. The conclusion assesses the performance of the Zambian Government and points to some of the problems which confront it.

Though conceived at the same time as *Politics in Zambia*, the preparation and publication of this volume have been delayed for a variety of reasons. Charles Elliott and Robert Molteno are among the original contributors who have had to drop out because of other commitments; unfortunately, Mr Molteno's withdrawal of his projected chapter on 'National Security and Institutional Stability' came too late to find a replacement. For reasons of space it was also not possible to include chapters on topics which it would have been desirable to have covered, such as the administration of foreign policy. While December 1977 is the cut-off date for most of the chapters, ch. 4 on 'The parastatal sector' extends into 1978 and ch. 3 on 'The public service', the latest submission, includes material from early 1979. I have incorporated recent changes briefly in the introduction and conclusion, and in ch. 8 on 'Rural administration'.

With the exception of Mr Alan Greenwood, all the contributors to this volume have been closely associated with the University of

Zambia, which generously made research and other facilities available. Our greatest debt is however to the many persons in Zambia, including university colleagues, politicians, civil servants and local government employees, who so willingly gave us the benefit of their knowledge and opinions; we remain, of course, solely responsible for the use which we have made of both.

In addition, Dr Sheridan Johns wishes to acknowledge support from the Duke University Research Council which facilitated the preparation of his chapter. I am personally indebted to the Social Science Research Council, London, for a research grant which enabled me to visit Zambia in October-November 1977 and to Dr Roger Tangri of the University of Zambia for his warm hospitality during my stay in Lusaka and subsequently for assisting me to keep abreast of political and administrative changes in Zambia.

I also benefited from discussions with Dr Morris Szeftel, now of the University of Leeds, who kindly allowed me to draw upon the rich body of material in his PhD thesis on 'Political conflict, spoils and class formation in Zambia' (University of Manchester, 1978). As editor, I would like to thank Professor Colin Leys of Queen's University, Kingston, Ontario, for his perceptive comments on a very early version of this volume and Mr Ralph A Young of the University of Manchester for his helpful suggestions and advice. I am also grateful for the encouragement and assistance of Mr Martin Spencer, the Publisher, and Messrs Ray Offord and John Banks, the Editor and Assistant Editor respectively, of Manchester University Press. Finally, the authors and the editor owe thanks to several secretaries for the typing and in particular to my secretary, Mrs Caterina Paleorouta, who has been mainly responsible for preparing the final typescript.

William Tordoff
University of Manchester, 1979

Notes on contributors

William Tordoff, Professor of Government at the University of Manchester, was seconded to the University of Zambia as Professor of Political Science, 1966–68. He is the author of *Ashanti under the Prempehs, 1888–1935* (London, 1965) and *Government and Politics in Tanzania* (Nairobi, 1967), and editor and co-author of *Politics in Zambia* (Manchester, 1974).

Michael Bratton is Assistant Professor, Department of Political Science and African Studies Centre, Michigan State University. He was Research Affiliate of the Institute for African Studies and Lecturer in Political and Administrative Studies, University of Zambia, 1973—76. His publications include *Beyond Community Development: The Political Economy of Rural Administration in Zimbabwe* (London, 1978) and *The Local Politics of Rural Development: Peasant and Party-State in Zambia* (Hanover, New Hampshire, forthcoming 1980).

Dennis L. Dresang, Professor of Political Science and Associate Director of the Centre for Public Policy and Administration at the University of Wisconsin-Madison, was a Research Associate at the Institute of Social Research, University of Zambia, 1967–69. He is the author of *The Zambia Civil Service* (Nairobi, 1975) and articles on development administration in Zambia.

James Fry, Director of Research, Commodities Research Unit, London, was Lecturer in Economics, University of Zambia, 1969–75. His publications include *Employment and Income Distribution in the African Economy* (London, 1979) and several studies of the copper market.

Cherry Gertzel, Reader in Political Science at the Flinders University of South Australia, was Professor of Political Science at the University of Zambia, 1969–75. She is the author of *The Politics of Independent Kenya* (London and Nairobi, 1970) and *Party and Locality in Northern Uganda, 1945–1962* (London, 1974), and co-editor of *Government and Politics in Kenya: A Nation Building Text* (Nairobi, 1969).

Alan F. Greenwood was Town Clerk, Leamington Spa, and an Assistant Secretary in the British Civil Service before becoming Adviser and later Permanent Secretary, Ministry of Local Government and Justice, Ghana, 1951–63. He subsequently served as United Nations Adviser on Local Government in Uganda, 1964–66, and Zambia, 1966–70. His published articles include 'Ten years of local government in Ghana', *Journal of Administration Overseas*, vol. 1, No. 1 (January 1962).

John Howell is Research Officer, Overseas Development Institute, London, and was Senior Lecturer in Political and Administrative Studies, University of Zambia, 1974–77. He is the editor and co-author of *Local Government and Politics in the Sudan* (Khartoum, 1974) and has published a number of articles on politics and administration in the Sudan and Zambia.

Sheridan Johns, Associate Professor of Political Science at Duke University, was Lecturer in Political Science at the University of Zambia, 1968–70 and 1974–75. His publications include *From Protest to Challenge: A Documentary History of African Politics in South Africa, Volume I, Protest and Hope, 1882–1934* (Hoover, 1972) and articles in numerous scholarly journals.

Dr Ian Scott, Lecturer in Political Science, University of Hong Kong, was Lecturer in Political Science at the University of Zambia from 1967 to 1970 and from 1974 to 1976. He is the author of a forthcoming book *Party Politics in Zambia* and has written a number of articles on Zambian politics and administration.

George K. Simwinga, Director of Training at the African Centre for Monetary Studies in Dakar, Senegal, was Senior Lecturer in Political and Administrative Studies, University of Zambia, 1977–78. His PhD thesis on 'Corporate Autonomy and Government Control' (University of Pittsburgh, 1977) focused on three state enterprises in Zambia. He has also published a number of essays on various aspects of public administration in Zambia.

Ralph A Young, Lecturer in Government at the University of Manchester, was seconded to the University of Zambia as Lecturer in Political Science, 1968–70. He wrote the chapter on 'The 1968 general elections' for D. H. Davies (ed.), *Zambia in maps* (London, 1971) and contributes the sections on Zambia and Malawi for *The Annual Register—World Events*. His major study of urban local politics in Zambia is nearing completion.

Notes on currency and copper prices

Currency

The kwacha replaced the Zambian pound in January 1968; two kwacha were worth one old pound, which was at par with sterling before the British devaluation. One kwacha then equalled 58p, but its value fell to 54p when the kwacha was pegged to the United States dollar in December 1971. Since the floating of the British pound the sterling value of the kwacha has varied widely; for example, it stood at 70p in May 1972 and 64p in December 1978. There are 100 ngwee in one kwacha.

Copper prices

Between 1939 and 1953 the price of Zambian (then Rhodesian) copper was controlled by the British Government. Thereafter, apart from interludes between 1955–57 and 1964–66, Zambian copper has been sold at prices determined daily on the London Metal Exchange (LME). The average daily price per tonne in March 1970, just three months after the Zambian Government had acquired a 51 per cent ownership interest in the copper mines, was K1,241 (£720). However, by the end of 1970 the average price for the month of December had declined to K740, and the average annual price remained below K800 per tonne for each of the next two years. In 1973 political threats to the Zambian transport system, among other causes, resulted in a sharp rise of the price level to a record peak of more than K2,150 (over £1,400) in April 1974. Thereafter, the price plummeted, reaching K766 in January 1975. Despite a slight rise in the intervening period, the price, at over K1,200 per tonne in December 1978, was still not high enough to meet mining production and transport costs.

Zambia adopted the metric system under the Metric System Act in 1970. There are 2,205 lb in one metric ton, compared with 2,240 lb in one long ton, and 2,000 lb in one short ton.

Miles 10 0 10 20 30 40 50 60 70 80 90 100 Miles

Provincial Boundaries . . . .
Provincial Headquarters . . . . ●
Towns . . . . ●
Roads . . . .
Railways . . . . +++
Aerodromes . . . . +

ZAIRE

ANGOLA

Mwinilunga

Solwezi

Ch

Chingola

West Lunga

Kabompo

West Lunga Nat. Park No. 14

N O R T H   W E S T E R N   C O P P E

Zambezi

Kabompo

Kasempa

Liuwa Plain Nat. Park No. 15

Zambezi

Kaoma

Kafue

Mumbwa

C

LUS

Kalabo

Kafue National Park No. 11

Mongu

Kafue

Lochinvar Nat Park No 13

Mazabuka

W E S T E R N

Monze

Gwembe

Senanga

S O U T H E R N

Choma

Sioma Ngwezi Nat. Park No. 16

Kalomo

KARIBA

ANGOLA

Sesheke

NAMIBIA

Zambezi

Mosi-Oa-Tunya N.P. No. 17

Livingstone

BOTSWANA

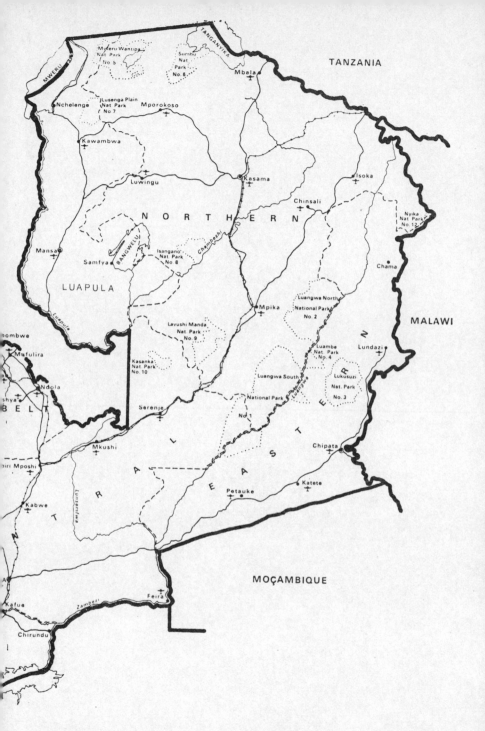

The Republic of Zambia (*by courtesy of the Ministry of Development Planning and National Guidance, Lusaka*)

1. Introduction

William Tordoff

Several writers have questioned the relevance for Africa of Riggs's development model.[1] Yet Riggs taught one lesson which is of universal application – the need to take environmental factors into account in studying the bureaucracy in developing countries. This introductory chapter assesses the importance of such factors for the Zambian administration in the period since Zambia became an independent state on 24 October 1964. An additional focus is provided by Fred Burke's argument that a legitimatising ideology is 'critical to the success of institutional transformation', that is the argument that a new state polity which seeks to transform, and not merely to modify slightly, the inherited political and administrative institutions must be capable of developing a supporting ideology.[2] We shall assess the power of Zambia's ideology of Humanism which was officially adopted in 1967.

In surveying the post-independence scene, it becomes at once apparent that the context within which Zambia's administration now operates is very different from that of the 1960s. It is tempting to explain this change by the introduction, in December 1972, of a one-party State. This constitutional innovation, which President Kenneth Kaunda justified by arguing that it would enable national energies to be focused on development instead of being dissipated in factional conflict, was certainly important. However, a rigid division into the first and second Republican periods is avoided since it obscures the elements of continuity in Zambia's political and socio-economic life that are at least as important as the elements of change consequent upon the introduction of the single-party State. We therefore identify those forces which have shaped Zambian administration, both before and after December 1972, and preface this discussion by a brief review of Zambia's legacy at independence.

Colonial rule – its consequences[3]

The British South Africa (BSA) Company which, chartered in
London, was initially a South African enterprise ruled Northern
Rhodesia from the 1890s to 1924. For mainly economic reasons, it
then handed over its administrative role to the British Colonial
Office. The Company continued, however, to receive mineral royalty
payments under dubious treaty arrangements; 'these purely
parasitical rights of ownership' were eventually eliminated by
African leaders shortly before they attained independence for
Zambia.[4] Though Britain retained ultimate control of the 'protected
territory' until independence, in 1953, despite loud protests from
Africans in the two northern protectorates, she did permit the
creation of the Central African Federation. This united Southern
Rhodesia, Northern Rhodesia, where rich copper deposits had been
discovered and exploited since the 1930s, and Nyasaland. For a
period of almost 10 years Northern Rhodesia became the milch cow
of predominantly Southern Rhodesian white interests. The African
agricultural sector was neglected and Southern, rather than
Northern, Rhodesia was purposely developed as the manufacturing
base of the Federation.[5]

The unsuccessful anti-Federation struggle of the early 1950s was
led by the African National Congress (ANC), founded in 1948.
However, the ANC suffered from indecisive leadership, weak
organisation and internal dissension and a more militant offshoot,
the Zambia African National Congress, itself succeeded by the
United National Independence Party (UNIP) in 1959, emerged to
spearhead the final stages of the struggle for independence.[6] The
migrant labour system, which compelled a circulation of workers
between country areas and town, greatly helped UNIP to mobilise
certain of the rural provinces against colonial rule. As Rasmussen
has written:

Many UNIP supporters in Zambia received their political education on the
Copperbelt, and there was considerable social interaction between the
Copperbelt and those provinces (Northern and Luapula) which supplied
the bulk of its manpower. Workers on the Copperbelt were socialised into
UNIP politics, and they spread the UNIP message to their kinsmen when
they returned home.[7]

Migration itself was a pointer to the most profound consequence
of colonialism – Northern Rhodesia's incorporation into the
international capitalist economy; this occurred through the medium
first of commercial and secondly, and more important, of mining
capital. The result, as Morris Szeftel has pointed out, was a highly

distorted and uneven local economy:

In being willing to respond to settler and mining pressure beyond their
apparent or actual needs, the colonial state accelerated the process of
uneven development and sharpened the combined character of that
development; it created a territory characterised by a patchwork of
advanced capitalist industrial areas, isolated pockets of commercial
agriculture, scattered and often backward commerce, areas of African small
capitalist and peasant farming, and regions incapable of yielding a bare
subsistence and dependent on migration and the rewards of wage labour to
supplement village production. The adaption of the indigenous population
to colonial penetration therefore necessarily varied considerably, and with it
the degree of change and stagnation in traditional forms of technology,
culture and ideology. Colonialism and capitalism thus integrated all
elements of the society into a single mode of production and a single social
formation; but it did not do so evenly or equally.[8]

Northern Rhodesia's industrial heartland was the Copperbelt,
where the copper mining industry was controlled by two groups of
foreign-owned companies, the Anglo-American Corporation Group
and the Roan Selection Trust Group.[9] Commercial agriculture was
undertaken almost entirely by white settlers along the line of rail,
while commercial activity in the urban centres was dominated by
South African- and Rhodesian-owned firms, though the
contribution of locally-based white entrepreneurs was not
insignificant. A tiny African petty bourgeoisie owned small shops in
the towns and larger villages, entered the commercial farming sector
on a modest scale, and constituted a salaried stratum mostly made
up of clerks and school teachers. A growing proletariat worked for
wages in the central regions of the country mainly as miners,
agricultural labourers and domestic servants. The bulk of the
African population (estimated at $3\frac{1}{2}$ million in 1964), however,
worked as peasant farmers. In the Central and Southern Provinces
they grew cash crops and reared cattle both for their own needs and
to meet the demands of the urban market. Away from the line of rail
farming was less profitable, though groundnuts and tobacco were
grown successfully in the Eastern Province. Until the early 1950s,
fish farming constituted an important source of wealth for many
Luapulans. However, villagers in the outlying rural areas faced
formidable marketing problems – infrastructure during the colonial
period was almost solely geared to the needs of the mining industry.
In short, the rural sector off the line of rail was badly neglected
during the colonial era and there was a wide, and widening, gap
between rural and urban dwellers.[10]

Given that gap, Zambia inherited at independence features of what is often referred to as a 'dual economy'. The reality however was much more complex: within a framework of uneven development there coexisted a relatively advanced modern sector and rural zones marked by *varying*, but usually substantial, degrees of underdevelopment. This point is of considerable political importance for, as Robert H. Bates shows in *Rural responses to industrialization: a study of village Zambia*,[11] the main competition for a share in national resources in Zambia has been between the outlying rural provinces (and between districts within a particular province) rather than between these provinces and the urban centres.[12]

In his book, which extends well beyond the colonial period, Professor Bates demonstrates that the greater the distance of rural production areas from the line of rail, the lower the profits from cash cropping; that the higher the level of rural prosperity, which was often linked to cattle owning, the lower the level of emigration; and that migrants gravitated to the towns nearest their homes – to the Copperbelt in the case of the Luapula villagers with which he is primarily concerned. Emigrants, who were predominantly young adult males often with some education, sought urban employment both to escape themselves from rural poverty and, through remittances, to ease the lot of those who stayed behind in the village.[13] In the same way as Luapulans – and also Northerners – were attracted to the Copperbelt, Nyanja-speaking people left the Eastern Province for the national capital, Lusaka, and Lozi-speakers from Barotseland were drawn to Livingstone.

This migratory process resulted in an acute urban problem which the independent Zambian Government was to try mainly to solve through its rural development policies. Newcomers to town wanted jobs and houses, as well as schools for their children.[14] Urban residents in employment wanted better wages and working conditions and, for this purpose, joined trade unions in preference to the earlier tribal associations which the mining companies had imposed as a control structure to regulate their work force.[15] Those unable to secure employment looked to their kinsmen for accommodation and support or eked out a precarious existence in the overcrowded and insanitary slums which ringed Lusaka, the capital, and to a lesser extent Kitwe and the other Copperbelt towns.[16]

There have been other consequences for Zambia of Northern Rhodesian colonialism. The latter was an extension of the white south. It was South Africa and Rhodesia which were the sources of most of Northern Rhodesia's white immigrants, resulting in a European population of some 75,000 by 1960. Europeans monopolised managerial, professional and skilled artisan occupations and were deeply committed to a private enterprise economy; so, too, was the much smaller Asian minority which dominated the country's middle-range retail commerce.[17] The racialist practices introduced by the European minority against the African majority[18] created a convenient target for the nationalist movement (for example, the boycott of butchers' shops in the 1950s) and served as a spur to the formation of the powerful African Mineworkers' Union in 1949. But racialism also created a series of post-independence problems, including some of an administrative kind. Many Europeans left precipitately after 1963, before citizens had been trained to replace them, and wage negotiations on the Copperbelt were often soured. As Gupta comments: 'In an industry in which the expatriate standard of living sets the norm, it is natural for the miners to shape their aspirations according to that norm rather than in accordance with the living conditions of the average Zambian.'[19] High wage settlements in the mining industry resulted in 'upward pressures on wages in other sectors', both private and public.[20] Again, the economic cleavage between Africans and other racial groups continued at least throughout the First Republic: 'despite the vigorous efforts of UNIP and the government,' wrote Bates in 1971, 'racial inequity still prevails in the mining industry.'[21] This cleavage diverted popular attention from the evolving intra-African class formation which took place as independence paved the way to African entry into the private sector and domination of the public bureaucracy.[22]

There were other features of Northern Rhodesia's orientation to the south. It was through Rhodesia that Northern Rhodesia's first and major railway outlet to the sea ran – the route lay through Salisbury, the Rhodesian capital, to the port of Beira in what, until 1974, was Portuguese ruled Mozambique. As a result of Federation, by 1964 Northern Rhodesia had become dependent on Southern Rhodesia for a very large proportion of her manufactured imports, while essential foodstuffs were already being imported from the south in large quantities. Moreover, Northern Rhodesia's copper exports were transported to Beira via Rhodesia Railways. These southern trade links have created vast problems for Zambia since 1964 and have led to the construction of immensely costly alternative routes through Tanzania to the seaport of Dar es Salaam.[23]

The impact of colonialism on national integration was fundamental in the sense that the Zambian nation would not have existed in its present form without colonial rule. Moreover, colonialism, and especially the imposition of Federation upon a reluctant people in 1953, evoked a nationalist response and was therefore itself functionally integrative. But the colonial authorities also took certain measures whose effect was to retard the growth of national consciousness; thus, indirect rule was introduced after 1929 and cemented some degree of loyalty to the pre-colonial governmental authorities.[24] Moreover, the deliberate withholding of secondary education until the 1940s, and of locally based higher education throughout the colonial period,[25] both retarded the emergence of a nationalist leadership and meant that Zambia entered independence with only a small pool of educated manpower.[26]

Training facilities for Africans within the civil service were poor prior to the establishment of a staff training college in 1963 and little progress was made in localising the civil service until 1962, when, with the dismantling of the Federation now certain, it was decided to introduce a constitution which would make majority rule possible.[27] Artisan training had been neglected under the Federation and until 1959 no African in Northern Rhodesia could be apprenticed. The result, as President Kaunda has stated, was that Zambia '. . . entered Independence without a single African technician in one of the most highly industrialised societies on the Continent.'[28]

There were further factors which weakened Zambia's administrative legacy. Almost to the eve of independence, the Northern Rhodesian administration tended to be preoccupied with law and order functions – though never exclusively, because of the nature of the economy. Again, while Ministers had been created in the 1950s out of a loose amalgam of departments, the latter were not fully integrated into the Ministries. Their organisation was often not based on rational principles, and inter-ministerial co-ordination was weak. Further structural disruption was caused in January 1964, when the formerly federal government departments were handed over to the Northern Rhodesian Government. This necessitated extensive reorganisation, including the amalgamation of hitherto racially segregated Ministries such as African Education and European Education. In general, the institutional legacy was weak: a difficulty facing the Zambian Government in 1964 was

the inadequacy of economic and politico-economic institutions inherited from the federal era alike in the government, private and parastatal sectors. Very few civil servants were experienced in the formulation and implementation of policies for rapid economic development. In the private sector, local managers had hitherto been entirely dependent upon policies originating in Rhodesia or South Africa. Almost by definition, the parastatal organisations were federal in character and management. Thus upon independence, parastatal institutions from the Agricultural Rural Marketing Board to the Bank of Zambia had to be created *ex-nihilo* in a very short space of time.[29]

An unusual feature of the Zambian situation at independence was that those who, through the policy of Zambianisation, were promoted rapidly to senior posts in the civil service, tended on aggregate to be less well educated than political leaders who became Cabinet Ministers.[30] On the other hand, while most of the new senior civil servants had learned civil service procedure in a junior capacity,[31] President Kaunda and his colleagues had been in office for less than two years and had next to no experience of operating a governmental system on a national scale.

At independence, too, the Zambian Government inherited the wide-ranging and arbitrary powers exercised by the Governor of Northern Rhodesia and this fact, coupled with the weakness of the institutional legacy, contributed indirectly to the advent of presidentialism in Zambia – in other words, to the institutionalisation of what one Zambian Minister boldly described in 1968 as the trend towards the 'Divine Right of Presidents' in new African states.[32] As we shall see, the consequences of concentrating so much power in the hands of Zambia's President have been immense.

Finally, the nature of the nationalist struggle, which was itself affected by colonialism, has also had important effects on the political culture, structure of political conflict, and party and State institutions of the independent Republic. The unevenness of the nationalist impact – it was profound in Northern and Luapula Provinces, but minimal in parts of Western and North-western Provinces – as well as the short duration of the anti-colonial struggle within a culturally and linguistically fragmented society, meant that the unity which UNIP established was fragile; it was to be severely strained after independence as different parts of the country competed with each other for a share in the limited economic resources available for distribution. This gave rise to the problem of factionalism, as the leaders of a particular faction deliberately encouraged sectional identifications among the masses and sought to manipulate the political process in the interests of themselves and their supporters.

The political setting: factionalism

At independence Zambia, unlike most Commonwealth African States, immediately became a republic, with a President who was both head of state and government. The latter was formed by UNIP, which had been returned to office in the pre-independence general election of January 1964. The ANC, the parent nationalist party, continued in being until the one-party State was inaugurated in December 1972 and drew its main support from among the Ila–Tonga people in Southern Province and parts of Central Province. In the general election of December 1968 it won twelve out of fourteen seats in Southern Province, three seats in Central Province, and most of the seats in Western (formerly Barotse) Province, as a result of the efforts of the United Party (UP), which had been formed in 1966 and was proscribed by the Government following UNIP–UP clashes on the Copperbelt in August 1968.[33]

Until the December 1968 general election, when UNIP won eighty-one out of 105 seats, the ruling party was tested less by external opposition from ANC or UP than by division within its own ranks. These divisions came to a head at the Central Committee elections at Mulungushi in August 1967: though expressed in the idiom of tribalism, with a Bemba–Tonga alliance pitted against a Nyanja–Lozi combination,[34] the competition between these regional–linguistic groups was really over access to political power, jobs and development money. As Robert Molteno has shown, these sections were interest groups competing for scarce economic resources.[35] The Bemba-speaking group triumphed in 1967 and in December of the next year rural Lozi voters expressed their discontent by turning against UNIP and voting predominantly with ANC. By 1970, however, the political pendulum had swung away from the Bemba in favour above all of the Easterners. Simon Kapwepwe, close associate of President Kenneth Kaunda and a former Vice-President of UNIP and Zambia, broke with UNIP in 1971 and became leader of a new party – the United Progressive Party (UPP) – dominated by Bemba from the Northern Province. Whatever the reason – perhaps alarm at the open eruption of factionalism represented by the UPP or possibly a fear that UNIP might be defeated by a UPP/ANC alliance at the next general election – UNIP over-reacted, detained most of the UPP leadership and, in February 1972, proscribed the new party. Then, in response to what was claimed to be a demand from all sides, President Kaunda tooks steps to create 'a one-party participatory democracy'. This was a significant departure from his previous assertions – that a one-party State would not be legislated into existence but would emerge through the ballot box.

Though factional conflict did abate under the one-party State, it never disappeared and the approach of a UNIP general conference and a general election, to be held in 1978, stimulated renewed factional activity. However, the context within which such activity now takes place has changed, for a number of reasons. First, the present scarcity of national resources (itself the result of the mounting economic crisis which Zambia has faced since 1975) makes competition between the outlying rural provinces less meaningful than it was ten years ago, though not necessarily less intense. Secondly, a disaffected linguistic group or province can no longer use as a bargaining counter the threat of switching its electoral support from UNIP to another party. The most it can do is to express its disapproval of government performance by abstaining from voting; this is a lesser sanction than backing the opposition but one not without its effect on a government concerned at the poor turnout (39.8 per cent) in the first one-party election in December 1973. Thirdly, UNIP has declined in both vigour and effectiveness since the one-party State was established, up-country party officials at constituency and branch levels being particularly demoralised and disgruntled.[36] Finally, the formation of classes within Zambian society has accelerated in recent years, giving rise to the possibility that factionalism, reflecting the division of society along vertical rather than horizontal lines, will no longer be a major determinant of political behaviour.

The creation of the one-party State

Under the independence constitution, Zambia's presidency was modified by elements of the British parliamentary system and certain concessions with regard to British property, citizenship and the political position of local Europeans.[37] Parliament comprised the President and the single-chamber National Assembly, to which all Ministers had to belong. The primary responsibility of the Cabinet however was to the President, to whom it was advisory. From 1968 especially, President Kaunda used his constitutional powers to the full and took major policy initiatives in both domestic and foreign policy without the prior concurrence of the Cabinet or UNIP central committee; prime, early examples were the economic reforms of 1968 and the take-over by the State of a 51 per cent capital share of the mines in 1969.

Faced with what was fast becoming a doctrine of presidential infallibility, the broadly-based Chona Commission, which was set up to consider what form a one-party participatory democracy in Zambia should take, recommended in its 1972 report that while the President should exercise specified executive powers, responsibility for government administration should be vested in a Prime Minister. This proposal was not acceptable to the Government, which announced in a White Paper that the President would retain executive power, with the Prime Minister as his senior Minister. The Government also rejected proposals that the tenure of office of the President should be limited and that his veto powers should be curtailed.[38] It was above all the powers of the President which were increased under the one-party State constitution. The latter assigned administrative decision-making to the Cabinet and overall policy direction to the UNIP Central Committee. However, the President himself continued to preside over both these bodies and to act in his own discretion on a wide range of issues, which from 1973 included the sensitive Angolan and Rhodesian situations. While President Kaunda deserves the highest praise for Zambia's post-independence achievements, the effect of his intervention, which has by no means been limited to issues of the first magnitude, has had far-reaching and sometimes undesirable consequences for the conduct of government and administration. His intervention helps to explain the abrupt changes which have periodically been made in Zambia's rural development strategy, leading (for example) to the introduction of Intensive Development Zones in 1971–72 and the Rural Reconstruction programme in 1975. It also forces MPs and other critics to attack government policies on most occasions through Ministers who are only nominally responsible for them and who are powerless to change them. There is a marked, understandable, but unhealthy reluctance to criticise policy proposals emanating from the President's Office, where Dr Kaunda has created a corps of personal assistants and advisers,[39] or even from Ministers housed within it.

An important reason which has led the President to take major policy initiatives has been the factional divisions among the political leadership. Convinced that UNIP's structure was responsible for its problems, Kaunda appointed a commission to review its constitution.[40] In May 1971 the UNIP general conference approved a new party constitution which, in essentials, was retained when single party rule was legalised. Against the wishes of the Northern Province faction, the constitution provided for equality of provincial representation at future conferences and a Central Committee of twenty-five members – the Secretary-General (but no Deputy), twenty other members elected by the general conference, the Prime Minister and three nominated members.[41] The holding of high office in the party no longer carried the automatic right to appointment to the corresponding post in government (as it did in 1967[42]) and in the one-party State an incompatibility rule was adopted by which no person, except for the President himself, the Secretary-General of UNIP and the Prime Minister, could simultaneously be a member of the Cabinet and the Central Committee; however, this rule was never formalised and has subsequently been breached.[43] There was nothing in either the 1971 UNIP constitution or the 1973 one-party state constitution about the provincial equality of representation on the Central Committee to which Kapwepwe had objected vigorously in 1969–70. Nevertheless, Kaunda has used his influence to make sure that the Central Committee, like the Cabinet which he himself appoints, encompasses Zambia's leading factions. Before examining the composition and roles of these two bodies, we look at the 1973 general election.

The 1973 general election

The one-party State constitution provides for a National Assembly comprising a Speaker, 125 MPs elected from single-member constituencies in a two-stage process (a party election followed by a popular election) and up to ten members nominated by the President. Though the UNIP Central Committee vetted the candidates who were allowed to stand (and disqualified twenty-six of them), the centre did not entirely control the outcome of the elections: twenty-nine out of seventy-two sitting MPs lost their seats, including three Cabinet Ministers and ten Ministers of State. Nevertheless, by exercising his nominating powers the President was still able to determine the character of his Administration – he appointed all ten of his parliamentary nominees to government office.[44]

There were other significant features of the election. Since local issues were dominant, candidates who would otherwise have belonged to the same faction stood against each other; however, following the election, 'a re-aggregation of regional factions occurred in Lusaka as groups vied for access to resources'.[45] Secondly, the low poll (39·8 per cent) was a pointer to the decline in UNIP's ability to get out the vote and meant that the one-party State rested on 'an uncertain mandate'.[46] This apparent decline in the legitimacy of the UNIP Government may explain the increased use in this decade of the State's coercive machinery: examples are the wholesale detention of UPP leaders and supporters in 1971–72, the detention of some twenty-one University of Zambia students, as well as five members of staff, and the closure of the University in 1976, and the take-over by UNIP of the Lonrho-owned *Times of Zambia* and the *Sunday Times of Zambia* the previous year.[47] It may be significant, too, that Mr Wilted Phiri, the country's head of Intelligence, was made Minister of Home Affairs in August 1977 and that the military was not only 'decentralised' (by posting a middle-ranking officer to each provincial headquarters) but also placed in charge of the national airline, the mechanical services branch, and the rural reconstruction scheme which seeks to settle young people on the land.[48] On the other hand, though the mass media as a whole is now subject to increased government control, the press is not muzzled;[49] the judiciary remains independent of the executive and the verdicts of the courts have been respected;[50] and the device of Ombudsman has been instituted to protect the individual against party and government.[51]

The National Assembly

While the peasant farmer, worker, and trade union interests continued to be under-represented, significant numbers of what Baylies and Szeftel have called 'indigenous entrepreneurs' entered Parliament for the first time in 1973:[52] over 40 per cent of successful candidates were businessmen or small traders or had business interests. Though they were mostly engaged in small-scale commercial activity, as owners of shops, bars and restaurants, a third of them were involved in large productive enterprises (including commercial farming), thereby conferring a disproportionately high level of representation on what is still a very small section of the Zambian community.[53]

Thus, the new Assembly included some able backbenchers whose occupational background made them more independent of the Government than their backbench predecessors; they challenged the Government on a number of issues. Three main themes in this parliamentary debate can be distinguished.[54] First, MPs consistently raised the needs of their constituents, pointing for example to rising prices, inadequate housing, unemployment, and the requirements of farmers and businessmen; some of them, particularly members from the Northern and Luapula Provinces, also complained of provincial neglect. Thus Mr Valentine Kayope, MP for Bahati (Luapula), stated early in 1974 that Luapula Province had not received its fair quota of posts 'in the civil service, in parastatals and indeed in the foreign service',[55] while in December 1977 Mr Peter Chanshi, MP for Mwansabombwe (Luapula), expressed the growing resentment at the allocation to Easterners of key positions in the bureaucracy and the coercive machinery of the State, alleging that people 'have had to change their names to Bandas, Zulus and Tembos' in order to be employed.[56] Secondly, backbenchers criticised government performance in a variety of ways: they probed, especially by means of the Public Accounts Committee, into government financial management and charged the Administration with tribalism, nepotism and inefficiency; they also pointed to party weaknesses as contributing to the lack of rural development. Thirdly, the backbench criticised government policy, particularly in the economic sphere and over Southern Africa, and called into question the Government's overall development strategy. Thus, despite the sharp rebuke administered to MPs by President Kaunda in June 1975, when he told them to desist from 'their anti-party and anti-government mouthings',[57] and the amendment of parliamentary Standing Orders to authorise UNIP's disciplinary committee to censure MPs for statements made in the National Assembly, backbenchers returned to the attack in February 1976. This was a very difficult time for Zambia: basic commodities, such as cooking oil and soap, were in short supply; prices, especially of mealie meal (the staple food), were rising sharply and there was a threat of increased unemployment; Zambia's Southern Africa policy, particularly towards Angola, had misfired; and the copper export route via the Benguela railway to Lobito was blocked.[58] MPs expressed their concern in unequivocal terms, but from different ideological standpoints. One MP even made bold to suggest that 'The Party and Government's shift to socialism was scaring away would-be investors and if not relaxed the economy would collapse . . .'[59]

Such criticism – in contrast to that expressed in Tanzania – was directed at fundamental tenets of government policy.[60] Part of the explanation is that the circumstances early in 1976 were abnormal and the widespread public concern over the prevailing situation was expressed also by students and trade unionists. No clear left–right spectrum had emerged and the critics were not agreed on the alternative policies that should be pursued. Nevertheless, in 1976–77 the Government showed signs of moderating its policy towards Southern Africa, and sought both to attract foreign capital into the country and to propitiate the consumer by restocking empty shelves; it also launched an anti-corruption drive. In this way, it was responding as much to pressures in society and reacting to external events, such as the reality of the Angolan situation, as it was yielding directly to parliamentary criticism. Again, the political challenge posed by Kapwepwe in the 1978 presidential election and economic considerations explain Kaunda's decision, in October 1978, to reopen Zambia's border with Rhodesia (Zimbabwe).[61] The trend, which is likely to continue in the Fourth National Assembly, has been to restrict the freedom of speech of backbench MPs more than the Chona (One-Party State) Commission had intended.[62] The UNIP parliamentary caucus still exists and MPs continue to be subject to party whips and disciplinary regulations. Moreover, if one takes specific issues in the law-making process, MPs do not obviously change the content or direction of government policy. Few government bills have been amended as a result of backbench pressure under the Second Republic, though four instances did occur in the first year of the 1973–78 Parliament.[63]

Government in Zambia is characterised by executive dominance. The National Assembly, like the press, cannot check or restrain an executive determined to have its way. It is to a further consideration of the executive that we now turn; we begin by looking at the Cabinet.

Table 1.1: Regional balance in Cabinet under the one-party system, 1973–77

Individual's Province of origin	All ministries			Central ministries		
	1974	1975	May 1977	1974	1975	May 1977
Central	2	2	2	2	2	1
Copperbelt	–	–	–	–	–	–
Eastern	3	4	5	2	3	4
Luapula	2	3	3	1	2	2
Northern	5	4	5	3	2	4
North-western	3	4	4	1	1	1
Southern	2	2	4	2	2	4
Western	4	3	3	2	2	1
Other	1	1	1	1	1	1
Totals	22	23	27	14	15	18

Note
In each case the Northern Province total includes two Ministers holding seats in Copperbelt Province. The Minister listed under 'other' also represented a Copperbelt constituency. The President and UNIP Secretary-General are excluded in all cases.

The Cabinet

In general, as Table 1.1 shows, President Kaunda has sought to maintain a regional balance in allocating Cabinet posts to UNIP leaders.[64] Taking the 1977 figures, it is clear that the main factions competing for power – Northern and Eastern – score highly both overall and in their control of central Ministries; the latter are the key Ministries to hold in the sense that they determine the allocation of national resources. The Southern Province also comes off well since all its Ministers serve at the centre.

A number of points, which are not apparent from the table, require emphasis. First, the size of the Cabinet has increased steadily since independence, as have the number of central Ministries. Excluding the President, the Cabinet numbered fifteen both in October 1964 and in December 1966, sixteen in December 1968, and – following the first general election after independence – eighteen in January 1969.[65] The major reorganisation of government which was then undertaken entailed the appointment of a Cabinet Minister to each of Zambia's eight provinces and a drastic reduction in the number of central Ministries; this was made possible by the creation of omnibus Ministries. The latter however soon proved unwieldy and were mostly split up into smaller units, resulting in the appointment of additional Ministers. At the end of 1972, the Cabinet had twenty-five members, of whom eight served in the provinces.[66] There was a further increase in size under the one-party State, as the Table reveals, rising to twenty-seven (excluding the President and UNIP Secretary-General) by May 1977; nine Ministers then served in the provinces.[67] However, this increase has not been sustained: following the 1978 general election, President Kaunda abolished the post of provincial Minister and this has resulted in a considerable pruning of the Cabinet.[68]

By enlarging the size of his Cabinet in this way President Kaunda has extended his patronage network and has used it to accommodate new claimants – the disgruntled Luapula and North-western Provinces, for example, from mid-1969. The reorganisation of government earlier that year and the appointment of provincial Ministers gave him greater leverage in assigning portfolios since he now had a second tier of ministerial posts to fill. It is significant, too, that with the partial exception of the Lozi-speaking faction's defeat in the 1967 Central Committee elections, defeats in party elections or defection into opposition (notably of Northern Bemba MPs in 1971) have not permanently deprived a faction of its allocation of Cabinet positions. The President, supported by political leaders not

closely tied to a particular faction (examples are Grey Zulu, Mainza
Chona and, until his suspension from office in 1977, Aaron Milner),
has sought to placate the grievances of disaffected factions. Thus, in
the period before the formation of the UPP, he gave one extra
Cabinet seat to the Northern Province; this seat has subsequently
been retained.[69]

It is not inevitable that an increase in the size of the Cabinet, as
between December 1972 and December 1978, will reduce its
effectiveness provided that established Cabinet procedures are
followed and committees are used to facilitate, rather than defer,
decision-making. As compared with the First Republic,[70] there has
probably been a modest improvement in the latter respect and, by
concentrating on major policy issues, the Cabinet now handles its
business more expeditiously – it normally meets once a month
instead of weekly, as before. Cabinet procedure continues to be
based on the Downing Street model, and a civil service Secretary to
the Cabinet is again in charge of the Cabinet Office, having replaced
the political Secretary General to the Government, appointed in
February 1969. However, since the Cabinet no longer includes the
strong political personalities of an earlier period (Kapwepwe,
Chimba, the Wina brothers and Sipalo, for example) and since it is
also more technocratic in composition than previously, the effect has
been to increase the President's dominance over it. The changes in
the composition of the Cabinet have been very frequent – by the end
of the First Republican period less than one third of the Cabinet had
been Ministers since 1964, while three Cabinet Ministers were
defeated in the 1973 general election – with the result that only the
President and a handful of Ministers can provide continuity in
policy-making. Moreover, the President's frequent reshuffling of
portfolios between Ministers has both disrupted policy-making
within Ministries and in some cases lessened the authority with
which a Minister can speak in Cabinet on departmental matters.[71]

While the Cabinet under the Second Republic has tended to lack
political weight and is privately characterised by some of its critics
(often themselves ex-Ministers) as a body of 'yes-men', it is
technically competent and well equipped to undertake those
administrative and policy-implementation tasks constitutionally
assigned to it.[72] Though himself taking key decisions, the President
still consults it on a wide range of issues, including some aspects of
general policy, budget proposals, and draft legislation. The Cabinet
also discusses matters on which Ministers disagree and which have
not been resolved at official or ministerial level.

The Central Committee

In the one-party State, the Central Committee is established on a full-time basis and assigned the overall direction of policy: the Cabinet is relegated to the subordinate role of policy implementation and administrative decision-making. Constitutionally, the Central Committee is the superior body, reflecting the supremacy of UNIP over the Government.[73] Thus, the Secretary-General of UNIP takes precedence over the Prime Minister and acts for the President when the latter is out of the country; similarly, a chairman of a sub-committee of the Central Committee outranks the Minister (or Ministers) whose portfolio falls within the competence of his sub-committee. The Central Committee occupies spacious office accommodation in the centre of Lusaka and has a substantial bureaucracy of its own, including a Secretary, who (in late 1977) was a former Secretary to the Cabinet, and a Director of its Research Bureau.

UNIP has avoided a repeat of the divisive Central Committee elections of 1967; instead, the general conference has merely endorsed the list of Central Committee members submitted to it by the outgoing committee. The President's influence has been dominant in presenting a slate of candidates representative of Zambia's leading factions. Thus, in August 1973 four seats were allocated to the Eastern Province, two to Central Province, and three to each of the remaining provinces. Since one of the Copperbelt representatives was originally from the Northern Province, the two main factions – Northern and Eastern – were equally represented.[74]

The Committee operates through eight sub-committees established in 1973[75] and enlarged early in 1974 'to facilitate consultation on a broad basis'.[76] Full members are either members of the Central Committee (MCCs) or MPs, and several of them serve on more than one sub-committee; in April 1974 MPs outnumbered MCCs on four sub-committees, while there was equality of representation on a fifth. Advisers include the permanent secretaries of relevant Ministries, as well as citizens with a special knowledge of, or interest in, a sub-committee's field of work; a sprinkling of students is included.[77]

These somewhat large sub-committees – in April 1974 they ranged in size from ten to twenty-six – have the right of access to all government papers and can summon Ministers before them. In practice, these powers are rarely exercised and a sub-committee mainly relies on its permanent secretary adviser(s) to provide essential background information. Though clashes between the

Cabinet and Central Committee have occurred, it would be wrong to assume that they are perpetually or even frequently at loggerheads. Several channels of communication exist and help to remove potential conflict: Ministries are represented on relevant sub-committees; the sub-committee chairman will normally consult with the Minister before his sub-committee discusses any matter of importance affecting that Ministry; and joint meetings of the Central Committee and Cabinet are held approximately every two months. Moreover, the Secretary to the Central Committee and the Secretary to the Cabinet work closely together. Again, friction is avoided by not channelling instructions direct from a sub-committee chairman to a Minister. Instead, the sub-committee reports to the full Central Committee and, if its recommendations are accepted, the Secretary-General of UNIP, acting on behalf of the Central Committee, directs the Minister through the Prime Minister.[78]

A possible compensatory advantage of this Cabinet–Central Committee tandem is that by widening the scope of the President's patronage, it has enabled him to appoint a new-style Cabinet, with a high proportion of technocrats; it may also serve to insulate the Cabinet from direct political pressure. Significantly, while it was the Central Committee which stepped in to revoke highly unpopular major price increases of a number of commodities, including bread and cooking oil, in November 1974, the decision to remove consumer price subsidies in the first place was taken by the Minister for Commerce, presumably with Cabinet backing but certainly without prior consultation with the Central Committee. The 'bread crisis' seems in fact to afford an isolated instance of the Central Committee asserting its control over the Cabinet, at a time when the President was out of the country.[79] As far as public (as distinct from party-political) policy-making is concerned, the Cabinet at least retains its primacy in advising the President. Szeftel notes: '. . . despite the nominal supremacy of the Central Committee over the Cabinet, real resources and thus real decisions lie with the latter and with the President'.[80]

To suppose that members of the Cabinet can be confined to implementing policy determined elsewhere is unrealistic. Yet the whole Cabinet-Central Committee relationship is based on the fallacy that it *is* possible to divorce policy-making and policy-implementation – at this level of government they are opposite sides of the same coin. The relationship represents a most unsatisfactory arrangement, wasteful of human and material resources. Not only does the Central Committee have little impact on policy, except in the broadest sense, but it also causes embarrassment by interfering in minor matters – for example, on one occasion it concerned itself with the arrangements being made for a cultural dance group to welcome a visiting dignitary at Lusaka airport! At provincial level – in January 1976 a MCC was posted to every province, where he outranked the Minister – the arrangement placed a premium on good personal and working relationships between the Minister and MCC; where these were not forthcoming, confusion was sometimes caused through the issue of conflicting instructions.[81]

Nor do the Central Committee and Cabinet represent such sharply differing interests that it is essential for them to be accommodated in two separate bodies, the one formulating and the other executing public policy. Specifically, there is nothing in the suggestion that the Central Committee serves as an ideological pep group which is pushing a conservative-inclined Cabinet in a socialist direction – several of its members share the middle-class values of their Cabinet colleagues.

In 1977 especially the arrangement was the subject of adverse comment in the press and National Assembly. A number of MCCs were believed to favour the recommendation made by a parliamentary select committee in November 1977 that the Central Committee should be reconstituted on a part-time basis.[82] Several of them admitted privately that they had little to do; this fact, coupled with the run-down of the party machine, may have contributed to what then seemed to be a low state of morale among senior party members. However, the position of the Central Committee remains substantially unchanged. When, in December 1978, the President decided to end the duplication of senior political figures at provincial level, it was (unexpectedly) the post of provincial Cabinet Minister which was abolished rather than that of the provincial MCC.[83]

Ministries

The constitutional supremacy of the party notwithstanding, real power does not lie with the Members of the Central Committee but with their Cabinet colleagues who are in charge of central Ministries. In the First Republican period, ministerial organisation was characterised first by the vast increase in the size of the Office of the President – in 1967, it was divided into seven separate divisions, each under the administrative control of a permanent secretary.[84] Secondly, whereas most Ministries retained the same Minister between 1964 and 1966, a ministerial game of musical chairs was begun early in 1967 and was repeated at frequent intervals. Thirdly, considerable structural reorganisation took place – in 1967 when the machinery of government was 'streamlined' (according to the official claim) in order to implement the First National Development Plan (1966–70)[85] and especially in 1968–69 when President Kaunda initiated sweeping changes in the organisation of government with the aim of accelerating development of the rural areas.[86] The essence of the latter reforms was the placing of a Cabinet Minister in every province, where he was supported politically by a Minister of State and District Governors[87] and administratively by a permanent secretary and other senior civil servants. A corollary was the drastic reduction in the number of central Ministries – apart from the Offices of President and Vice-President, only eight Ministries were retained initially at the centre.[88] However, the experiment with 'umbrella' Ministries largely failed and by the end of 1972 only two of the original seven remained in existence.[89] Nor was this all. The responsibilities of the President's own office proved so manifold and time-consuming that he progressively gave certain of his portfolios, notably Provincial and Local Government and Defence, to Ministers outside his office. The President's decision in August 1969 to acquire for the State a controlling interest in the copper mines led to the splitting up of the umbrella Ministry of Trade, Industry and Mines into a Ministry of Trade and Industry and a short-lived Ministry of State Participation. The latter remained in the Office of the President. Its very small staff handled the take-over negotiations with the Anglo-American Corporation and Roan Selection Trust Groups in late 1969.[90] The Ministry became responsible for the newly formed parastatal body, the Zambia Industrial and Mining Corporation (ZIMCO) – which in turn controlled the Industrial and Mining Development Corporations (INDECO and MINDECO) – as well as for certain other statutory boards. The rapid growth since independence of the parastatal sector, particularly in the aftermath of the Rhodesian UDI and the economic reforms of 1968–70, has had profound effects on the organisation of government as a whole. State-owned companies and statutory bodies, operating to a varying extent independently of civil service and parliamentary controls, continue to extend the long arm of the State into the most vital areas of Zambian economic and political life.[91]

The pattern of ministerial organisation has not changed significantly under the one-party State. Few of the recommendations on decentralisation made by a Working Party in 1972 have been implemented[92] and, as the Mwanakatwe Commission reported three years later: 'Effective decentralisation of the decision-making process has not yet been achieved, but is vital to the morale and efficiency of the service.'[93]

Unfortunately, too, President Kaunda has not adhered to the commitment which he made in November 1969 to 'really minimise the movement of Ministers and officials from now on'.[94] The practice by which he undertakes major Cabinet reconstructions once or twice a year represents part of his continuing search for a solution to the seemingly intractable problems which face his government in the economic and social spheres; it is sometimes, too, the inevitable sequel to political events such as the general election of December 1973, when three Cabinet Ministers were defeated. Further structural change in the arrangement of Ministries has also been undertaken. In 1974 the Ministry of Development Planning and National Guidance[95] disappeared as a separate entity and the Development Division was reabsorbed by the Ministry of Finance (as in the 1970–72 period), which became the Ministry of Planning and Finance. In December of the next year, however, a separate Ministry of Development Planning was created. Further change followed in May 1977 when a National Commission for Development Planning was established in the Prime Minister's Office.[96]

This arrangement was retained in December 1978, but the merger of the Ministries of Finance and Economic and Technical Co-operation was one aspect of the reorganisation undertaken in the wake of the elections.[97] The reason for certain of the other changes made is less obvious. Thus, in 1974 some of the parastatal organisations previously controlled by the Ministry of Rural Development were transferred to the Ministry of Commerce, only to be handed back in 1975.[98]

The civil service[99]

Such frequent transfers of departments and agencies among Ministries, the general reallocation of subject responsibilities, and the frequent movement of Ministers and civil servants[100] have adversely affected the quality of administration. Chains of command at senior levels have been disrupted, resulting in serious delays; votes have had to be changed; and resources have been wasted both because of the lack of cost-consciousness in the public sector and inadequate financial control inside Ministries, which, like the Ministry of Finance itself, are short of qualified accounting staff. The staff shortage is general and the number of vacant posts in many grades of the civil service is alarmingly high, as Table 1.2 reveals. One reason why so many vacancies remain unfilled is that, as the Mwanakatwe Commission found in 1975, 'Appointments procedures are cumbersome and time-consuming. Much greater delegation is required.'[101]

Table 1.2: *Number of vacant posts as a percentage of the total approved establishment in 1975 (professional superscale posts excluded)*

Grade of posts	Total approved Establishment	No. of vacant posts	Approximate percentage	Approximate 1974 percentage
Superscale	1235	316	25·6	21·9
Professional	1322	423	32·0	25·3
Technical	4208	980	23·3	31·1
Technical education	792	260	32·8	N.A.
Administrative & executive	5429	978	18·0	19·0
Clerical & related	5489	364	6·6	7·6
Secretarial	1389	253	18·2	22·4
Medical & related	3979	1384	34·8	37·3
Nursing	1733	762	44·0	47·1
Teaching	17645	118	0·7	0·6

Source: *Zambianisation in the Public Service: Progress Report, 1975* (Lusaka, mimeo., n.d.), Summary, pp. ii–v.

The relationship between the Public Service Commission and the Personnel (formerly Establishment) Division has been unsatisfactory for much of the post-independence period. The overlap and even duplication between the functions of the two bodies, on which the Staff Inspection Unit of the Personnel Division reported in 1967,[102] continued into the 1970s and in 1971 the O'Riordan Salaries Commission went so far as to recommend the abolition of the Public Service Commission and the delegation of the President's powers of appointment to the permanent secretary, Personnel;[103] however, Government Paper No. 1 of 1971 rejected this recommendation. Four years later, as overlapping persisted, the Mwanakatwe Commission looked at the question afresh: it disagreed with the O'Riordan Commission and urged that the Public Service Commission should be retained;[104] Government accepted this recommendation.[105]

The Mwanakatwe Commission found that personnel administration procedures were 'generally archaic and must be radically overhauled'; that there was not enough delegation of authority by the Service Commissions in respect of appointments, promotions and discipline; that facilities for civil service training were both too limited and too centralised; and that personnel were transferred much too frequently. Government accepted in principle the Commission's recommendations for tackling these problems, though it ruled that promotions should continue to be dealt with by the appropriate Service Commission; it also modified in some instances the way in which the recommendations should be applied.[106]

Though civil servants were granted substantial salary increases as a result of the Mwanakatwe Commission's recommendations,[107] their morale was adversely affected by the continuing poor quality of personnel management and the failure of government policies to halt Zambia's economic decline. Many joined the boards of foreign companies, entered business on their own account,[108] or transferred to the parastatal sector, which had grown enormously since independence. Government continued in the Second Republic to interfere with the pricing and investment policies of the parastatal organisations, often to the detriment of their commercial performance. It also tightened financial control: in January 1975 Mr A. B. Chikwanda, the Minister of Planning and Finance, announced his decision 'to form an Inspectorate within my Ministry whose duty will be to ensure that financial discipline and propriety are strictly observed by these organisations.'[109] In the same year the Mwanakatwe Commission, alarmed at the 'great disparities in conditions of service among parastatal bodies' and noting also 'many disparities in salaries within the parastatal sector and between parastatals and the Civil Service', recommended that a Parastatal Bodies Service Commission should be created with statutory powers to control salaries and conditions of service. Government accepted this recommendation in principle, subject to a full review and assessment of the Companies Act and other legislation governing the operation of parastatal companies and statutory boards.[110] In November 1977 the parliamentary select committee appointed in response to President Kaunda's address on the economic crisis facing Zambia, recommended that parastatal bodies should be allowed 'flexible pricing policies and stable management terms'. It favoured, too, the creation of machinery which would allow the private sector to play 'a major and meaningful advisory role' in the formulation of government policy.[111]

Policies and ideology

Thus, Zambia has changed rather than transformed the institutions which she inherited at independence. Change has been piecemeal rather than the result of a comprehensive review of the machinery of government. Moreover, some of the reforms undertaken – such as the decentralisation of government – have fallen far short of the rhetorical flourish with which they were announced. While the bureaucracy has accommodated itself to the one-party situation, too many of the values, attitudes and behavioural patterns inherited from the colonial era have been retained for the bureaucracy to become that innovative force which Bernard Schaffer rightly argues is essential for development.[112] Fred Burke has identified ideological weakness as a prime reason for the failure of many new states to dismantle the inherited political and administrative institutions and their supporting ecology, including physical plant such as house and office.[113] This leads to the question: how strong ideologically is Zambian Humanism? As well as answering this question, we consider in the following sections the impact which Humanism has had on the socio-economic policies pursued by the Government since independence.

Humanism, an eclectic ideology combining capitalist, socialist and populist strands, was first elaborated by President Kaunda in April 1967.[114] It projects a man-centred society, in which men are valued as human beings and not according to their economic position and power. It therefore rejects capitalismn which spells an exploitative economic system based on individualism and competition, a social system characterised by class conflict, and a political system based on a number of different parties representing different class interests. Instead, it seeks to create a just and equitable society, with the rural standard of living raised to the urban level; a society where one man's wealth is not another man's poverty and which, therefore, will not accommodate the domestic capitalist any more than the foreign capitalist. Humanism, in short, involves a rejection of imported Western capitalist values and a reassertion of traditional, communal values.

Humanism also rejects communism which entails governmental regimentation,[115] results in human suffering and 'falls into the same trap as Capitalism, measuring a man's importance by his social class'.[116] It favours a 'mixed economy', with State-controlled companies such as INDECO, private firms and co-operatives all working side by side.[117] As Sklar has pointed out, a non-doctrinaire strategy of development, relying upon such a combination and under the auspices of a managerial bourgeoisie and in partnership with multinational corporations, is unlikely to build socialism.[118] This is not in any case Kaunda's intention: 'Zambia's destination', he has said, 'is neither capitalism nor orthodox socialism.'[119] Despite a number of statements in *Humanism Part II* suggesting the contrary,[120] a humanist State would not be a socialist State. For Kaunda, socialism has a purely instrumental value – it is 'an instrument for building a Humanist society'.[121] His intention is 'to socialise the economy by the instrument of State control in order to bring this important sector of our life closer to the people who now own it'.[122] This is part of a strategy subsequently launched by the President in September 1976 under the title of 'Communocracy – a Strategy for Constructing a People's Economy under Humanism'.

Politically, Humanism is to be achieved through participatory democracy, 'a state predicated on the reality of popular power'.[123] This means that the people must be involved in the day-to-day running of government and that tolerance and free discussion should be combined with responsible leadership.[124] Ironically, no one emphasises the virtues of participatory democracy more than the President himself, yet his own style of increasingly personalised decision-making renders its realisation difficult.

Humanism, judged by the terms of Edward Shils's exacting definition,[125] is ideologically weak since it lacks explicitness, systematisation and comprehensiveness. It is sometimes even contradictory, as well as fundamentally ambivalent in its attitude to the private sector.[126] Kaunda is its principal, indeed virtually its only exponent, and there is no 'ideological primary group' dedicated to spread humanist values.[127] Humanism is a philosophy, and for Kaunda almost a creed, rather than an ideology in any strict sense.

While it is true that Kaunda cannot match Julius Nyerere in the incisiveness of his thought,[128] Morris Szeftel is right to suggest that Kaunda's writings show a clear understanding of the problems which he faces and that Humanism has to be wide enough, or sufficiently imprecise, to accommodate all the interests which go to make up the coalition over which Kaunda presides.[129] Perhaps this point can be put, no less accurately, another way round by referring to Kaunda's conception of the State: for him the State is not an instrument by which one class oppresses another class, but a broad umbrella under which all the people, irrespective of race, colour, religion or class, can shelter and from which all should benefit equally. This, he believes, would be impossible in a State which rests on a narrow ideological base since all except the devotees of that ideology would be alienated from it.

Humanism, it is claimed officially, is 'the basis of all the policies and programmes of the Party and Government'.[130] This is an extravagant claim since Humanism has always had a high rhetorical content and it is not easy to state categorically that government policy has invariably flowed from it. However, in so far as Kaunda is himself both the creator of Humanism and the chief architect of his Government's major policies, it can be said that Humanism has informed a considerable action programme. We begin with domestic policy.

First, Humanism is 'a decision in favour of rural areas',[131] and since independence the Government has sought to develop a productive African agricultural sector and to improve the rural standard of living. A difficulty facing it was that to concentrate resources in the outlying rural provinces, where the bulk of Zambia's newly enfranchised electorate resided, would make political good sense, but would yield revenue returns that were 'relatively small, uncertain, or long term'.[132] In the event, the Government spent substantially more than it had planned in promoting non-mining enterprises in the urban provinces; these provinces received over two-thirds of government capital investment in the first plan period (1966–70).[133] Fortunately, however, the abnormally high prices paid for copper between 1966 and 1970 provided the Government with abundant resources, thereby enabling it at this time to avoid having to face up to difficult policy choices in both domestic and foreign policy. It was able not only to invest heavily in the central region of the country but also to pump as much money into the outlying provinces as weaknesses in manpower made it possible for them to absorb – over K14 million was invested in the co-operative movement within a period of six years,[134] agricultural credit was provided on a massive scale,[135] and marketing facilities were extended to the remoter rural areas.[136]

The Second Plan (1972–76)[137] stressed rural development and the need to promote simultaneously Zambia's industry and agriculture. From the outset this plan proved to be an unrealistic document both in its estimates of resources available and in its targets for development. It was launched in the most inauspicious circumstances, mainly because of the sharp fall in the copper price from mid-1970. Not only was it becoming increasingly difficult to find money for new projects, but there was also a disgruntled private sector, rising unemployment, and a widening urban–rural income gap. Unexpectedly, however, the economic situation was eased when

an artificial boost was given to the price of copper by the closure of
the Rhodesian–Zambian border in January 1973; copper fetched a
record £1,410 per tonne on 1 April 1974. The dramatic increase in
revenue in 1973–74 meant that hard decisions could again be
deferred and old policies continued. However, from mid-1974 the
price of copper declined and entered a long downward spiral.[138] As
the economic crisis mounted, the Government called in 1976 for an
all-out effort 'to turn the tragedy of our economic situation into a
blessing by developing our agricultural potential'.[139] The Intensive
Development Zone programme – a capital-intensive rural
development programme which had been introduced in 1971–72
and was heavily dependent on overseas technical and financial aid[140]
– was for all practical purposes abandoned and in October 1977
President Kaunda launched a programme of 'Production for one self
and export' throughout the country.[141]

Thus, Zambia has made repeated attempts since independence to
achieve rural development; these efforts have not yet been successful,
but are continuing. Humanism has not provided firm guidelines for
action and the President himself has been responsible for initiating
major shifts in rural development strategy. The emphasis has tended
to be on increasing agricultural output, for example through the
IDZ programme, without considering adequately the need also to
expand rural employment opportunities and to reduce income
disparities between the rural and urban sectors and within the rural
sector itself.

A second stage in the institutionalisation of Humanism was the
steps taken to secure Zambian control of the economy which, though
averaging a remarkably high rate of growth in the post-1966 period,
was still dominated by foreigners at the ownership and managerial
levels. In 1968 the State took over, on a 51-per-cent shareholding
basis, twenty-six large firms mainly in the construction sector,
commerce, and road transport; the mining companies followed in
1969 and the insurance companies and building societies (but not
the banks) in 1970.[142] Three years later the Government terminated
the sales and management contracts awarded to the mining
companies and, on payment of further compensation, redeemed the
outstanding ZIMCO bonds and loan stock;[143] however, the fact that
the key technical production positions were still held by non-
Zambians in both mining groups diminished the reality of public
control.[144] In a series of measures between 1968 and 1972 the
Government also progressively excluded foreigners from
participation in retail and wholesale trading.[145]

The effect of these reforms was to increase the State's

participation in the national economy, as well as to extend State control over economic policy. However, the reforms also had certain negative consequences. First, Government had taken over the mines at a time when the copper price was high; by the end of 1977, when the price had slumped, the mining industry, from being the main source of government revenue, had become a drain upon it. In these circumstances, the Third National Development Plan was deferred and the Government was forced to re-think its economic and social policies. It not only attempted to boost agricultural production, but also sought salvation in an external infusion strategy, symbolised in a successful approach to the IMF for assistance and in the passage of the Industrial Development Act in 1977 to attract private foreign investment.[146] In November 1977 a parliamentary select committee, set up at the prompting of the President, favoured more help for the private sector, reduced governmental interference in the pricing and investment policies of the parastatal sector, and cuts in social welfare expenditure.[147] The second main consequence was social: the economic reforms enormously facilitated the growth of an entrepreneurial and State bourgeoisie, whose values ran counter to those which Humanism was trying to inculcate. We return to this issue subsequently.

The third stage in implementing Humanism was the curbing of domestic exploitation by a series of measures which have included the abolition of fee-paying schools and fee-paying sections of hospitals from 1 January 1971; the nationalisation of private nursing homes and the abolition of freehold land tenure, both in 1975; and the introduction of a steep income tax system, price control, workers' participation in industry, and a code of behaviour to be adhered to not only by UNIP leaders at all levels, but also by senior civil servants, employees of parastatal bodies, and army and police officers.[148] It is easy to criticise some of these measures – on the ground, for example, that their effect has been to strengthen rather than weaken Zambian capitalism – and to deride the slow or half-hearted way in which several of them, such as workers' participation and the leadership code, have been applied.[149] Nevertheless, since they undercut to some extent the economic and social power and privileges of Zambia's elite, it has required courage on President Kaunda's part to go as far as he has done, particularly in view of the external difficulties which Zambia has faced and the fluctuating state of her copper-based economy.

Turning to external policy, Humanism's assertion of the dignity of man and its rejection of racialism have been reflected in support for the Southern African liberation movements. This has been questioned by some writers who have argued that 'Zambia's diplomacy in Southern Africa is a reflection of the interests of its new ruling class in its maintenance of its own affluence and control,'[150] and that Zambia's support for the liberation movements has been lukewarm.[151] While conceding that Zambia does now possess a substantial middle class and that some of its members have a vested interest in the performance of the foreign-owned companies on whose Boards of Directors they serve, such statements take insufficient account both of nationalist sentiment and the strong streak of idealism in President Kaunda's character. They also ignore the post-independence record which shows, moreover, that Zambia's support has not been limited to the moderate liberation movements – she gave early backing, for example, to the Popular Movement for the Liberation of Angola (MPLA).[152] As Douglas Anglin has written: 'Class interest is undoubtedly present in Zambia, and growing. What is so surprising is that, at least to date, it has been so impotent in diverting the government from its liberationist goals.'[153]

While Zambia won widespread admiration in Africa and beyond for her bold, yet realistic response to the Rhodesian unilateral declaration of independence, she has been taxed in recent years with compromising her ideals both in her policies towards Angola and Rhodesia.[154] Certainly events in Angola, following the April 1974 coup in Portugal, proved embarrassing to Zambia, especially as a result of South Africa's military intervention on the side of the UNITA/FNLA[155] alliance which President Kaunda was thought to favour. He protested against foreign intervention – of Cuba and the Soviet Union, as well as the United States and South Africa – in the internal affairs of an African State and worked hard to secure a government of national unity. However, Zambia was accused of giving material support to UNITA and the victory of MPLA meant that a potentially unfriendly government was now installed in Angola, leaving an economically crippled Zambia exposed on her southern and western flanks. It was not until April 1976 that the Zambian Government recognised the government of Dr Agosthino Neto, not least in the expectation of being able to resume copper exports through Lobito.[156]

President Kaunda also sought to achieve black majority rule in Rhodesia through negotiation rather than armed conflict, but was criticised for his willingness to work with Mr Vorster, the South African Prime Minister, to achieve this end. Major setbacks in Zambian foreign policy in 1974–76 were probably caused by tactical miscalculations, but it was Dr Kaunda's misfortune that they coincided with a period of grave economic difficulty, resulting from the world energy crisis of 1973, the plummeting of the copper price from mid-1974, and the blocking of Zambia's trade routes. Subsequently, the President has stepped up his support of the Patriotic Front, led by Joshua Nkomo (whom he is thought particularly to favour) and Robert Mugabe. Together with the other 'front-line' Presidents, he has condemned the 1977 'internal' Rhodesian settlement.

Looking back on the post-independence period as a whole, it can reasonably be claimed that the Zambian Government has successfully mixed the pursuit of revolutionary principle with *realpolitik* – 'the realistic pursuit of one's narrowly defined national interest'.[157] The result has been that, despite a colonial legacy of extreme dependence on the south and vulnerability to its pressures, as well as a worsening economic situation since 1974, Zambia has been constantly in the forefront of the struggle to liberate Southern Africa. That this is so is due above all to President Kaunda, upon whom revolutionary idealism continues to have a powerful claim[158] – some of Zambia's political leaders, even including Cabinet colleagues, would have shied away from a policy of confrontation with the white minority regimes.[159] However, to state that, to a considerable extent, the Humanist principles of human dignity and racial equality have been upheld in Zambia's African policy is not to minimise the importance of *realpolitik*: 'To a degree', as Sklar wrote, 'the norm of *realpolitik* has prevailed',[160] and it is no doubt Kaunda's conviction that a negotiated settlement in Rhodesia and the establishment there of a friendly, and desirably non-Marxist, black African government would be in Zambia's national interest.

In both domestic and foreign policy, then, the links between Humanism and the policy pursued by the Zambian Government are somewhat tenuous and, as was stated earlier, Humanism can perhaps be said to have informed a considerable action programme only in the sense that President Kaunda, its formulator, is Zambia's principal policy-maker. Moreover, while Humanism may have served to restrain blatant expressions of self-interest on the part of Zambia's incipient middle class, it has not been able to check the growth of that class or the spread of the materialist ethic in Zambian society. It is to a consideration of this question that we turn in a final section.

The emergence of classes

In the colonial period conditions were not conducive to the emergence of an indigenous bourgeoisie. Independence, however, not only enabled Zambia's political leaders to pressurise the State for resources on behalf of their own particular faction, but also gave them an opportunity to advance their individual material interests. Noisy faction-fighting at a vertical level obscured a steady process of horizontal integration as top members of UNIP and the Government, as well as senior public officers, bought farms along the line of rail, became directors and shareholders in private companies, and launched businesses on their own account. This process was facilitated by the policies of economic nationalism pursued by the Government after 1968. Zambian citizens were given a monopoly in retail and wholesale trading, building material industries and transportation, while restrictions on commercial borrowing were imposed on expatriate businessmen who had hitherto dominated these fields of enterprise.[161] Senior parastatal executives were also brought into close working contact with foreign companies, and these companies appointed Zambians to their boards of directors. While former Ministers, permanent secretaries and parastatal directors were among those who entered the private sector on a full-time basis, many others defied the leadership code[162] and combined public office-holding with the pursuit of private business interests. Morris Szeftel records that

of 46 former or current parastatal personnel . . . who could be identified as having business interests or land-holdings, almost three-quarters (34 or 73·9 per cent) appear to have become involved in their private interests during the period in which they held parastatal positions. The same trend occurs with regard to senior civil servants.[163]

Even Mr John Mwanakatwe, a long-serving Minister and incumbent Minister of Finance, has retained throughout his strong business connections.

Given these overlapping links between public position and private interests, the two groups – business and government – do hold certain views in common. Thus, the business community favours by and large continued ties with external capital and markets and, despite public statements to the contrary, many government policies serve to reinforce an external dependency without however sacrificing Zambia's national interests.[164] In Professor Sklar's formulation of the 'managerial bourgeoisie' – the ruling class in an underdeveloped country that maintains a market economy and comprises businessmen, bureaucrats, leading politicians and members of the learned professions – this is to be expected since 'Within a host country for foreign investments, the managerial bourgeoisie consists of a local wing, which is normally nationalistic, and a corporate international wing that tolerates and patronizes local nationalism'.[165] However, Sklar also points out that the Zambian bourgeoisie – of which the managerial bourgeoisie is the apex – 'is no less diversified than is the proletariat'.[166] It is this diversification that gives President Kaunda some room to manoeuvre between the various 'middle-class' interests involved and allows UNIP to project itself as a mass party out to improve the lot of the common man through State welfare and other policies. This diversification leads Szeftel to differentiate the bourgeoisie by dividing it into two broad categories – on the one hand, State personnel who control State resources or State-owned companies and on the other, private entrepreneurs who seek to pressurise the administration to pursue policies favourable to the business community.[167]

The evidence put forward by Szeftel shows clearly that, despite its dependence on the State for public support in the form of subsidies and loans, the indigenous entrepreneurial bourgeoisie is today a considerable force in Zambian politics. Though its members do not yet hold political power or dictate State policy, they can often influence policy formulation. The influence of the property-owning class can be seen at work in the Industrial Development Act, 1977, which sought to attract foreign capital into Zambia, and in the November 1977 report of the parliamentary select committee, which was set up at the prompting of President Kaunda to consider how best to deal with the economic crisis facing the country. In its report, which was unanimously adopted by Parliament, the select committee recommended that 'capital expenditure on social services be slashed since this is also a way of restraining the growth of recurrent expenditure.'[168] This was one of several recommendations which gave the report a 'clear class bias'.[169] The fact that three Cabinet Ministers served on the Committee (alongside backbenchers with professional and business interests) and signed the report may point to an increasing identity of viewpoint between politicians and businessmen, thereby reducing the President's manoeuvrability.[170]

Members of the entrepreneurial bourgeoisie can also often block policies which they conceive to be inimical to their interests. Examples are the delay in implementing the leadership code and workers' participation in industry, for which provision was made in the Industrial Relations Act, 1971, and the failure to pursue the socialist course of action projected by President Kaunda in his 1975 'Watershed' speech. Again, in 1977 the parliamentary select committee turned down, for all practical purposes, the President's suggestion that redundant party and State personnel should be resettled on the land.[171] To the extent that this blocking process occurs, there is periodic tension between the business community and the Government, and this seems to Szeftel of more significance at present than the conflict between the local and corporate international wings of the managerial bourgeoisie, forecast by Sklar.

The evidence prompts Szeftel to draw a further, and at first sight (in view of the increased strength of the entrepreneurial bourgeoisie) unexpected, conclusion: 'If individuals articulate class interests in their capacities as members of the bourgeoisie, they must nevertheless continue also to articulate geographic interests in their capacities as politicians and leaders of factions.[172] As Szeftel points out, UNIP is not the organ of a single class and individual members of the party who seek election to public or party office must still appeal to local and regional interests. Their success will be measured by their ability to obtain State resources for their faction, as well as preferential access to State spoils for its members.[173] Thus in the immediate future, the entrepreneurial bourgeoisie is likely to use both class and factional forms of interest articulation – after all, there is 'no necessary contradiction' between them.[174] Moreover, we are dealing with an emergent and dependent class which, while becoming increasingly important politically, does not yet possess the strength, stability, or cohesion to impose its will upon a reluctant executive. What, then, of the rural peasantry and the urban proletariat?

As we suggested above,[175] rural dwellers from different parts of the country away from the line of rail have competed with each other for a share in national resources; they have not banded together to assert a peasant, as against an urban, class interest. In relation to the peasantry as a collectivity, Bates is therefore right to argue that 'Instead of class action in the countryside, we find internal division'.[176] However, as is shown by Bates's example of the Katofyio Building Co-operative,[177] as well as by studies of the ward development committees in Kasama by Michael Bratton[178] and of the co-operative movement in the Eastern Province by Stephen Quick,[179] the rural development programmes have had a differential impact on individual incomes, tending to benefit those who, as UNIP or Government leaders, are already advantaged.[180] In other words, while it is true to say that an identifiable peasant class interest has not yet emerged, social stratification *within* the rural sector has increased substantially since independence.

Workers on the Copperbelt, in Lusaka and the other main urban centres have a much stronger sense of identity than the peasantry: thus, domestic servants in towns as far apart as Luanshya and Livingstone are members of the same trade union. Class consciousness is most developed on the Copperbelt, where a high proportion of the settled labour force belongs to the Mineworkers' Union of Zambia. Though mine-workers resisted attempts by UNIP to secure the election of its own nominees to union branch offices, they remained predominantly loyal to UNIP throughout the 1960s[181] and, with the exception of Mufulira West (which Kapwepwe won for the UPP in a by-election in December 1971),[182] probably in the early 1970s also. But as the present decade advanced and Zambia's economic condition deteriorated, several UNIP leaders expressed privately their fear that ambitious politicians would exploit an explosive situation to their own advantage.[183]

There is no doubt that urban workers have experienced increasing hardship in recent years: essential foodstuffs – including maize meal, the staple diet – have been in short supply and the cost of commodities has soared, while wage levels have lagged behind. Moreover, with the copper industry now operating at a loss, they face the prospect of massive unemployment. Yet it is by no means certain that urban workers will show political solidarity as a class. For the proletariat is not monolithic, being divided into skilled, semi-skilled and unskilled workers, the first category being itself subject to many gradations. Urban workers as a whole have benefited from State subsidies – they reacted strongly when the wheat subsidy was withdrawn in 1974, permitting bread prices to rise dramatically[184] – but in other respects State rewards have advantaged most those who are already well-to-do. Thus, even on the Copperbelt there is no evidence at present to suggest that class will become the sole, or even the main, determinant of political action. Factional as well as class interests are likely to be invoked by politicians bidding for urban support. All in all, the proletariat appears at present to be a considerably weaker force in Zambian politics than the bourgeoisie.

Notes

[1] F. W. Riggs, *The ecology of public administration* (London, 1961) and *Administration in developing countries: the theory of prismatic society* (Boston, 1964). The best critique is by N. Kasfir, 'Prismatic theory and African Administration', *World Politics*, vol. 21, No. 2 (January 1969).

[2] F. G. Burke, 'Public administration in Africa: the legacy of inherited colonial institutions', paper presented at the World Congress of the International Political Science Association, Brussels, 18–23 September 1967.

[3] See *inter alia* L. H. Gann, *The birth of a plural society: Northern Rhodesia, 1894–1914* (Manchester, 1958) and *A history of Northern Rhodesia: early days to 1953* (London, 1964); and A. Roberts, *A history of Zambia* (London, 1976). The standard work on the terminal period of colonial rule, written by a political scientist, is D. C. Mulford, *Zambia: the politics of independence, 1957–1964* (London, 1967). For a brief discussion of the imposition of colonial rule and a fuller review of its consequences, see W. Tordoff and R. Molteno, 'Introduction', to W. Tordoff (ed.), *Politics in Zambia* (Manchester, 1974).

[4] R. L. Sklar, *Corporate power in an African State: the political impact of multi-national mining companies in Zambia* (Berkeley and Los Angeles, 1975), p. 37.

[5] Among works on the federal period are E. Clegg, *Race and politics: partnership in the Federation of Rhodesia and Nyasaland* (London, 1960); C. Leys and R. C. Pratt (eds.), *A new deal in Central Africa* (London, 1960); and P. Keatley, *The politics of partnership: the Federation of Rhodesia and Nyasaland* (Harmondsworth, 1963).

[6] See especially Mulford, *Zambia: the politics of independence, op. cit*, chs. III-IV.

[7] T. Rasmussen, 'The popular basis of anti-colonial protest', in Tordoff (ed.), *Politics in Zambia, op. cit.*, p. 55.

[8] M. Szeftel, 'Political conflict, spoils and class formation in Zambia' (Ph.D. thesis, University of Manchester, 1978), p. 59.

[9] See Sklar, *Corporate Power, op. cit.*, pp. 30ff.

[10] For a discussion of the colonial economy, see especially R. E. Baldwin, *Economic development and export growth: a study of Northern Rhodesia, 1920–60* (Berkeley, 1966) and W. J. Barber; *The economy of British Central Africa: a case study of economic development in a dualistic society* (Stanford, 1961). Particular aspects of the economy are studied by J. A. Bancroft, *Mining in Northern Rhodesia* (London, 1961) and J. A. Hellen, *Rural economic development in Zambia, 1890–1964* (Munich, 1968).

[11] (New Haven and London, 1976).

[12] Bates, *loc. cit.*, chs. 10 and 11.

[13] *Ibid.*, ch. 3.

[14] The massive increases in urban wages in the 1950s and the consequent strong incentive for management to make labour more efficient combined to produce a more settled labour force. While the mining companies increased the availability of married housing and encouraged men to bring their families from the villages to live in the 'mine townships', wage-earners outside the mining industry were obliged to look to the State and urban local authorities to satisfy their needs. *Ibid.*, p. 177.

[15] See A. L. Epstein, *Politics in an urban African community* (Manchester, 1958) and R. H. Bates, *Unions, parties, and political development: a study of mineworkers in Zambia* (New Haven and London, 1971).

[16] Many wage-earners also lived in these peri-urban areas. The administration of the latter is discussed in ch. 7, below.

[17] F. and L. O. Dotson, *The Indian minority of Zambia, Rhodesia and Malawi* (New Haven, 1968).

[18] See *inter alia* J. W. Davidson, *The Northern Rhodesian legislative council* (London, 1948), Mulford, *Zambia: the politics of independence, op. cit.*, and R. I. Rotberg, *The rise of nationalism in Central Africa: the making of Malawi and Zambia, 1873–1964* (Cambridge, Mass., 1966).

[19] A. Gupta, 'Trade unionism and politics on the Copperbelt', in Tordoff (ed.), *Politics in Zambia, op. cit.*, p. 317.

[20] *Report of the Commission of Enquiry into the Mining Industry, 1966* (The Brown Report), 1966, UNIP submission, pp. 40–1.

[21] Bates, *Unions, parties and political development, op. cit.*, p. 199.

[22] See R. Molteno, 'Cleavage and conflict in Zambian politics: a study in

sectionalism', in Tordoff (ed.), *Politics in Zambia, op. cit.*, ch. 3.

²³ R. L. Sklar, 'Zambia's response to the Rhodesian unilateral declaration of independence', in Tordoff (ed.), *Politics in Zambia, op. cit.*, ch. 9.

²⁴ W. M. Hailey, *An African survey* (London, 1957), *passim*.

²⁵ J. M. Mwanakatwe, *The growth of education in Zambia since independence* (Lusaka, 1968).

²⁶ See *Manpower Report: a report and statistical handbook on manpower, education, training and Zambianisation, 1965–66* (Lusaka, 1966).

²⁷ W. Kirkman, *Unscrambling an empire – a critique of British colonial policy, 1956–66* (London, 1966), ch. 7. The slow rate of localisation in the pre-1964 period is discussed by K. H. Nkwabilo, 'Remarks on manpower and Zambianisation' (Lusaka, mimeo., 26 June 1969). See also ch. 3, below.

²⁸ Speech to UNIP National Council at Mulungushi, 9 November 1968, ZIS Background Paper No. 84/68, 8 November 1968.

²⁹ C.M. Elliott, 'The Zambian economy' (Lusaka, 1968, mimeo).

³⁰ University graduates constituted half the Cabinet in 1964, a considerably higher proportion than was to be found among top civil servants at that time.

³¹ There were some exceptions in the early years after independence: these were predominantly recent university graduates who were appointed to superscale posts in the civil service on the strength of their formal educational qualifications and despite their lack of administrative experience.

³²The Minister (then of Agriculture) was Munukayumbwa Sipalo. *Nat. Ass. Deb.*, Hansard No. 13, 5 March 1968, col. 603. For a good, general view of presidentialism, see B. O. Nwabueze, *Presidentialism in Commonwealth Africa* (London, Enugu and Lagos, 1975).

³³ R. Molteno and I. Scott, 'The 1968 general election and the political system', in Tordoff (ed.), *Politics in Zambia, op. cit.*, ch. 5.

³⁴ The distribution of these regional–linguistic groups is – Bemba: Northern, Luapula and Copperbelt Provinces; Tonga: Southern Province and parts of Central Province; Nyanja: Eastern Province; and Lozi: Western (formerly Barotse) Province.

³⁵ 'Cleavage and conflict in Zambian politics', *op. cit.* For this paragraph as a whole, see W. Tordoff and I. Scott, 'Political parties: structures and policies', in Tordoff (ed.), *Politics in Zambia, op. cit.*, ch. 4, and J. Pettman, *Zambia – security and conflict* (Lewes, 1974).

³⁶ See ch. 6, below.

³⁷ S. V. S. Mubako, 'The presidential system in the Zambian constitution' (M. Phil. thesis, University of London, 1970).

³⁸ *Report of the National Commission on the establishment of a one-party participatory democracy in Zambia* (Lusaka, 1972), pp. 10–14, 23, and *Summary of recommendations accepted by government*, Government paper No. 1 of 1972 (Lusaka, 1972), pp. 4–6.

³⁹ These include Mark Chona, brother of Mainza Chona, the present Secretary-General of UNIP, and Dominic Mulaisho, a former permanent secretary, Ministry of Education.

⁴⁰ The Chuula Commission, named after its chairman, Mr F. Chuula, the Attorney General.

⁴¹ See Tordoff (ed.), *Politics in Zambia, op. cit.*, pp. 117–8.

⁴² Thus, following his election at Mulungushi as national treasurer of UNIP, Mr E. H. K. Mudenda was appointed Minister of Finance in place of Mr Arthur Wina, the defeated candidate, who was transferred to Education.

⁴³ Thus, in November 1977 Mr D. M. Lisulo (now Prime Minister) was a Member of the Central Committee (MCC), as well as Minister of Legal Affairs and Attorney General.

⁴⁴ Szeftel, 'Conflict . . . in Zambia', *op. cit.*, pp. 387–8.

⁴⁵ *Ibid.*, p. 388.

⁴⁶ R. A. Young, 'Zambia', *The annual register: world events in 1974* (London, 1975), p.

266.

[47] R. A. Young, 'Zambia', *The annual register: world events in 1975* (London, 1976), p. 239. The *Zambia Daily Mail* and the broadcasting services were already State-controlled.

[48] Szeftel, 'Conflict . . . in Zambia', *op. cit.*, p. 398. The Government may of course have used the military in this way as a means of pre-empting a coup.

[49] Though, with some notable exceptions, its editorial comment tends to be restrained, it carries speeches critical of the Government made by backbench MPs and others.

[50] In the Second Republic there have been no instances of significant tension between the judiciary and the executive to parallel those which occurred in 1967 and 1969. See Tordoff (ed.), *Politics in Zambia, op. cit.*, p. 368.

[51] See Robert Martin, 'The ombudsman in Zambia', *The Journal of Modern African Studies*, vol. 15, No. 2 (1977).

[52] C. Baylies and M. Szeftel, 'Control and participation in the 1973 Zambian one-party election', forthcoming in a volume on Zambian politics edited by C. J. Gertzel.

[53] *Ibid.*, and Szeftel, 'Conflict . . . in Zambia', *op. cit.*, pp. 433ff.

[54] I have drawn heavily at this point on C. J. Gertzel, 'Dissent and authority in the one-party State: parliament, party and president in the Zambian one party participatory democracy' (unpublished paper, 1975).

[55] *Nat. Ass. Deb.*, Hansard No. 35, col. 690, 30 January 1974, quoted by Szeftel, 'Conflict . . . in Zambia', *op. cit.*, p. 392.

[56] *Times of Zambia*, 2 December 1977, quoted by Szeftel, *ibid.*, p. 394.

[57] *The 'Watershed' Speech*: President Kaunda's Address to the UNIP National Council, Lusaka, 30 June 1975 (Lusaka, 1976).

[58] See W. Tordoff, 'Zambia: the politics of disengagement', *African Affairs*, vol. 76, No. 302 (January 1977).

[59] *Times of Zambia*, 6 February 1976, quoted by Gertzel, 'Dissent and authority in the one party State', *op. cit.*

[60] For a comparative assessment, see W. Tordoff, 'Residual legislatures: the cases of Tanzania and Zambia', *Journal of Commonwealth and Comparative Politics*, vol. XV, No. 3 (November 1977).

[61] See p. 263, below. Since this book went to press, the country has been designated 'Zimbabwe–Rhodesia' by Bishop Abel Muzorewa's government; the former legal designation has been retained throughout.

[62] Report of the National Commission (1972), *op. cit.*.

[63] These included bills on legislative drafting, fishing licence fees, and compensation for detainees. See *Times of Zambia*, 17 February 1974, and *Sunday Times of Zambia*, 11 August 1974.

[64] I am indebted to Morris Szeftel for allowing me to reproduce here table XXVI in 'Conflict . . . in Zambia', *op. cit.*, p. 390 and also to draw upon his chapter VI.

[65] See Tordoff (ed.), *Politics in Zambia, op. cit.*, pp. 244ff. The discrepancy in the figures is because the President is excluded from the above count (as he is in Szeftel's table), but included in the earlier count in *Politics in Zambia*.

[66] The President is again excluded. Tordoff (ed.), *op. cit.* pp. 244–6.

[67] A ninth province – Lusaka Province – was created in 1976.

[68] See p. 189, below.

[69] Szeftel, 'Conflict . . . in Zambia', *op. cit.*, ch. VI; Tordoff (ed.), *Politics in Zambia, op. cit.*, ch. 7.

[70] See Tordoff, *ibid.*, pp. 249–53.

[71] *Ibid.*, pp. 244ff. and 253–5.

[72] Szeftel observes that thirteen of the twenty-two members of the Cabinet in January 1974 had high educational qualifications or experience of University or some parallel institution; others had extensive experience of administration in various organisations. 'Conflict . . . in Zambia', *op. cit.*, p. 395.

[73] See 'The constitution of the United National Independence Party', n.d. [Lusaka, 1973], s. 12(3). Legal supremacy was conferred on UNIP by the Constitution of Zambia (Amendment) Act, No. 18 of 1974.

[74] Szeftel, 'Conflict . . . in Zambia', *op. cit.*, p. 389.

[75] Constitution of UNIP, s. 16. The sub-committees are: defence and security, chaired by the President; social and cultural; youth and sports; strategy, elections and publicity; appointments and disciplinary; economic and finance; rural development; and political, constitutional, legal and foreign affairs.

[76] 'Deliberations, proceedings and resolutions of the Fourth National Council of the United National Independence Party held in Mulungushi Hall, 20th–25th April 1974' (Lusaka, n.d.), p. 17.

[77] *Ibid.*, pp. 8 and 17.

[78] Based on discussion in Lusaka with senior civil servants and MCCs in November 1977.

[79] This incident is discussed by Gertzel, 'Dissent and authority in the one party State', *op. cit.*

[80] Szeftel, 'Conflict . . . in Zambia'. *op. cit.*, p. 395.

[81] See pp. 192–3, below.

[82] See *Sunday Times of Zambia*, 4 December 1977.

[83] Addresses by President Kaunda at the official opening of the first session of the fourth National Assembly, Lusaka, 18 December 1978, as reported in *Times of Zambia*, 19 December 1978.

[84] 'Ministerial reorganisation: division of the Office of the President', Cabinet Office circular No. 91 of 1967, 18 December 1967. For a fuller discussion of ministerial organisation in the first republican period, see W. Tordoff and R. Molteno, 'Government and administration' in Tordoff (ed.), *Politics in Zambia, op. cit.*, ch. 7, and ch. 3, below.

[85] Address by President Kaunda, 3 May 1967; ZIS press release, 3 May 1967.

[86] President Kaunda's speeches to UNIP delegates at Mulungushi, 9 November 1968, ZIS background paper No. 84/68, 8 November 1968, and to Ministers, Permanent Secretaries and District Governors at Lusaka, 30 December 1968, ZIS press realease No. 2223/68, 30 December 1968.

[87] The President appointed a District Governor to head each one of the fifty-three districts and sub-districts into which the country was now divided for administrative purposes.

[88] ZIS press release No. 2214/68, 23 December 1968, and *Government Directory*, April 1969.

[89] Thus, in January 1971 President Kaunda abolished the Ministry of State Participation (created in 1967), which had by that time become a huge affair responsible for the majority of the Government's vast undertakings in industry, commerce, mining, and transport; he divided its responsibilities among five Ministries. S. W. Johns, 'Parastatal bodies in Zambia: a survey' (unpublished paper).

[90] The substantial literature on the economic reforms of 1968–69 includes: Sklar, *Corporate power in an African State, op. cit.*; M. Bostock and C. Harvey (eds.), *Economic independence and Zambian copper* (New York, 1972); C. Elliott (ed.), *Constraints on the economic development of Zambia* (Nairobi, 1971); M. L. O. Faber and J. G. Potter, *Towards economic independence: papers on the nationalisation of the copper industry in Zambia* (London, 1972); and A. Martin, *Minding their own business: Zambia's struggle against Western control* (London, 1972).

[91] The State-owned company is created by executive action and incorporated under the Companies Ordinance like any private company; the statutory body is established by Act of Parliament to carry out certain specific functions. See ch. 4, below.

[92] *Report of the working party appointed to review the system of decentralised administration* (The Simmance Report) (Lusaka: Cabinet Office, May 1972).

[93] *Report of the Commission of Inquiry into the salaries, salary structures and conditions of service of the Zambia public and teaching services, the Zambia police and prisons service, the defence forces and staffs of local authorities, including casual and daily-paid employees, and of personnel employed by statutory boards and corporations and by companies in which the State has majority or controlling interest, Volume I: The public services and the parastatal sector* (The Mwanakatwe Report) (Lusaka, 1975), p. 18, paras. 3.21 – 3.23, and p. 20: Summary (6). Unless stated otherwise, all subsequent references are to Volume I of this Report.

[94] Speech by President Kaunda, October 1969, ZIS background paper No. 77/69, 1 November 1969.

[95] The tiny Ministry of National Guidance had been created in March 1969 to implement the national philosophy of Humanism; it came under the President's Office until 1972 when it was linked with Development Planning.

[96] Based on discussions with planning officials in Lusaka, November 1977.

[97] *Times of Zambia,* 19 December 1978.

[98] The parastatals were the Dairy Produce Board, National Agricultural Marketing Board, and Cold Storage Board of Zambia. *Review of the Working Group: Ministry of Rural Development* (Lusaka, 1977, mimeo.), p. 2.

[99] For a fuller discussion of the civil service in the first republican period, see Tordoff and Molteno, 'Government and administration', *op. cit.,* pp. 264ff., and ch. 3, below.

[100] In the August 1969 changes alone the President altered nine of the twenty-seven permanent secretaries in government.

[101] Mwanakatwe Report, *op. cit.* p. 78, paras. 10.8 and 10.13, and p. 119: Summary (1).

[102] Staff Inspection Unit, 'Review of establishment and personnel work' (Lusaka, 1967, mimeo.).

[103] *Report of the Commission appointed to review the salaries, salary structure and conditions of service of the Zambia public service (including the Zambia police) and the defence force: Government Paper No. 1 of 1971* (The O'Riordan Report) (Lusaka, 1971).

[104] Mwanakatwe Report, *op. cit.* p. 77, para. 10.7 and p. 119: Summary (1).

[105] *Summary of the main recommendations of the Commission of Inquiry into the salaries, salary structures and conditions of service, together with the party and government reactions to the recommendations, Volume I: The public services and the parastatal sector* (Government Paper No. 1 of 1975) (Lusaka, 1975), p. 16: H, 88(a).

[106] *Ibid.,* p. 1: A, 1–4.

[107] *Ibid.,* pp. 34–50: Annexures 'A' and 'B'.

[108] Examples of those who have prospered in the private sector are Emmanuel Kasonde, a former permanent secretary in the Ministry of Finance and managing director of FINDECO, and Elias Chipimo, also a former permanent secretary as well as High Commissioner in London. Szeftel reviews many other cases: 'Conflict . . . in Zambia, *op. cit.,* ch. VII.

[109] Budget address by the Hon. A. B. Chikwanda, MP, Minister of Planning and Finance, delivered to the National Assembly on 31 January 1975 (Lusaka, n.d.), p. 8.

[110] *Summary of the main recommendations of the Commission of Enquiry* (1975), *op. cit.,* p. 27: K, 148; p. 29: L, 163; p. 31: M, 167.

[111] *Sunday Times of Zambia,* 4 December 1977.

[112] B. B. Schaffer, 'The deadlock in development administration', in C. Leys (ed.), *Politics and change in developing countries: studies in the theory and practice of development* (London, 1969). pp. 191ff.

[113] Burke, 'Public administration in Africa', *op. cit.*

[114] K. D. Kaunda, *Humanism in Zambia and a guide to its implementation* (Lusaka, n.d.). Further elaboration followed in August 1967: 'Address by His Excellency Dr Kenneth D. Kaunda, President of the Republic of Zambia, to the Mulungushi Conference and a guide to the implementation of Humanism in Zambia', presented to the annual general conference of UNIP at Mulungushi, 14–20 August 1967 (Lusaka, n.d.).

115 K. D. Kaunda, *Take up the challenge* (Lusaka, 1970), p. 50.

116 *Humanism in Zambia*, with narration by President Kenneth Kaunda (Lusaka, n.d.), pp. 22–3.

117 *Ibid.*, pp. 33–4.

118 Sklar, *Corporate power in an African State, op. cit.*, p. 213.

119 Kaunda, *Take up the challenge, op. cit.*, p. 49, quoted in *ibid.*

120 For example: all the means of production and distribution must be 'totally owned by those who labour to produce'. *Humanism in Zambia, Part II* (Lusaka, 1974), p. 100.

121 Address by President Kaunda to the Ninth National Council of UNIP, 20 September 1976, in *Communocracy (A strategy for constructing a people's economy under Humanism) – Addresses by His Excellency the President, Dr K. D. Kaunda* (1976), p. 9.

122 *Ibid*, p. 10.

123 Sklar, *Corporate power in an African State, op. cit.*, p. 215.

124 *Humanism in Zambia* (with narration by President Kaunda), *op. cit.* pp. 28–9.

125 E. Shils, 'The concept and function of ideology', reprint from vol. 7 of *International encyclopedia of the social sciences* (New York, 1968), pp. 66–76.

126 For a fuller discussion see Tordoff (ed.), *Politics in Zambia, op. cit.*, pp. 391–2.

127 Shils, 'The concept and function of ideology', *op. cit.*

128 Cf. R. Hall, *The high price of principles: Kaunda and the white South* (London, 1969), p. 49.

129 Szeftel, 'Conflict . . . in Zambia', *op. cit.*, ch. VI. pp. 375, 404.

130 *A Humanist handbook: how to understand and practice Humanism* (Lusaka, November 1976), p. 6.

131 K. D. Kaunda, *Zambia: towards economic independence* (Lusaka, 1968), p. 14.

132 Bates, *Rural responses to industrialization, op. cit.*, p. 109.

133 *Ibid.*, p. 105; *First national development plan, 1966–70* (Lusaka, 1966).

134 Bates, *Rural responses to industrialization, op. cit.* p. 114.

135 Through the agency of the Credit Organisation of Zambia, established in 1966 and wound up in 1970, when it was replaced by the Agricultural Finance Company. *Ibid.*, p. 116.

136 The Agricultural Rural Marketing Board was established in 1965. See *ibid.*, pp. 116–17.

137 *Second national development plan: 1972–76* (Lusaka, 1971). Difficulties in implementing the FNDP had forced a postponement by one year of the Second Plan.

138 *The year ahead* (Lusaka, 1976), p. 7.

139 *Ibid.*, p. 3.

140 *Zambia, 1964–74: ten years of achievement* (Lusaka, n.d.), pp. 26–7; J. Finucane, 'Intensive and experimental approaches to rural development: Zambia's IDZs', University of Zambia Correspondence Lecture No. 41, PA 410/73/26. See ch. 10, below.

141 Address by President Kaunda to the First Emergency Meeting of the National Assembly, Lusaka, 11 October 1977, ZIS Background Paper No. 93.

142 See Tordoff (ed.), *Politics in Zambia, op. cit.*, pp. 26, 29, 31, and *passim*. The banks successfully resisted being taken over.

143 Sklar, *Corporate power in an African State, op cit.*, p. 61.

144 R. T. Libby and M. O. Woakes, 'Nationalization and the displacement of development policy in Zambia' (Lusaka, November 1977, mimeo.), p. 16, diagram 1.

145 See Tordoff (ed.), *Politics in Zambia, op. cit.*, pp. 26, 366.

146 The Industrial Development Act, No. 18 of 1977, embodied backbench amendments designed to increase the attractiveness of foreign investment in Zambia.

147 *Sunday Times of Zambia*, 4 December 1977; supplemented by discussions in Lusaka, November 1977.

148 For a fuller discussion, see Tordoff (ed.), *Politics in Zambia, op. cit.*, pp. 388–93.

149 The leadership code was first outlined in very general terms in August 1969 and

in more concrete form in November 1970. It was the subject of an Address by President Kaunda to the UNIP National Council on 2 December 1972: *The leadership code and responsibilities of the leadership in the creation of a new social order* (Lusaka, 1973). A majority of leaders have not complied with the Code's requirements, leading the Government to postpone its implementation from time to time. Szeftel records that though the leadership code prohibits leaders from having private business interests, other than small-scale enterprises or smallholdings of land, the study of business ownership undertaken by himself and Carolyn Baylies indicated that 'an overlap of public position and private interests is characteristic rather than exceptional'. Szeftel, 'Conflict . . . in Zambia', *op. cit.*, ch. VII, p. 425.

[150] T. M. Shaw and A. T. Mugomba, 'The political economy of regional détente: Zambia and southern Africa', *Journal of African Studies*, 4 (winter, 1977).

[151] *Ibid.*, and T. M. Shaw, 'Zambia and southern Africa: from confrontation to co-existence', in O. Aluko (ed.), *Foreign policies of African States* (London, 1976).

[152] D. G. Anglin, 'Zambia and the Angolan civil war' (April 1977, mimeo.).

[153] D. G. Anglin, 'Zambian versus Malawian approaches to political change in southern Africa', Conference on African Responses to Colonialism in Southern Africa, California State University, Northridge, 10 January 1976 (mimeo.), p. 31.

[154] These policies are discussed more fully in Tordoff, 'Zambia: the politics of disengagement', *op. cit.*

[155] UNITA – National Movement for the Total Liberation of Angola; FNLA – National Front for Liberation of Angola.

[156] This was important to Zambia because of congestion at the Tanzanian port of Dar es Salaam.

[157] Sklar, 'Zambia's response to the Rhodesian UDI', *op. cit.*, p. 362.

[158] Cf. Sklar, *ibid.*

[159] Anglin, 'Zambian versus Malawian approaches to political change in southern Africa, *op. cit.*, p. 31.

[160] Sklar, 'Zambia's response to the Rhodesian UDI', *op. cit.*, p. 362.

[161] Sklar, *Corporate power in an African State, op. cit.*, p. 210.

[162] The leadership code specifically prohibits leaders from having private business interests, other than small-scale enterprises or smallholdings of land. See p. 28, above; Szeftel, 'Conflict . . . in Zambia', *op. cit.*, ch. VII, *passim*; Constitution of Zambia Act No. 27 of 1973, Part IV; and '*The leadership code and responsibilities of the leadership in the creation of a new social order' – Address by his Excellency the President, Dr K. D. Kaunda*, to the National Council of UNIP on 2 December 1972 (Lusaka, 1973).

[163] Szeftel, *loc. cit.*, p. 425.

[164] Cf. Szeftel: ' . . . it is important to emphasise that Party and Government policy are not inimically opposed to capitalism'. *Ibid.*, p. 438.

[165] Sklar, *Corporate power in an African State, op. cit.*, p. 201.

[166] *Ibid.*, p. 206.

[167] Szeftel, 'Conflict . . . in Zambia', *op. cit.*, pp. 414–15.

[168] *Sunday Times of Zambia*, 4 December 1977.

[169] Szeftel, 'Conflict . . . in Zambia', *op. cit.*, p. 452.

[170] The Cabinet Ministers were John Mwanakatwe (Chairman and Minister of Finance), David Lisulo (Minister for Legal Affairs and Attorney General), and Lameck Goma (Minister of Education). The first two were lawyers and businessmen, while Dr Goma was formerly Vice-Chancellor of the University of Zambia and a poultry farmer. Only one member of the committee did not belong to the 'managerial bourgeoisie' as defined by Sklar. *Ibid.*, p. 453.

[171] *Ibid.*, pp. 441ff.

[172] *Ibid.*, p. 455.

[173] *Ibid.*

[174] *Ibid.*, pp. 456–7.

[175] See p. 4, above.

176 Bates, *Rural responses to industrialization, op. cit.*, p. 259.

177 *Ibid.*, pp. 133–6.

178 See ch. 9, below.

179 S. Quick, 'Bureaucracy and rural socialism: the Zambian experience' (Ph.D. thesis, Stanford University, 1975), esp. ch. VI.

180 Supporting evidence for an earlier period is to be found in G. C. Bond, *The politics of change in a Zambian community* (Chicago and London, 1976). However, a different view is taken by J. K. van Donge in 'Independence at the grass roots and dependency theory: a case study in decolonisation and privilege from Mwase Lundazi, Zambia'; Graduate Research Seminar paper, University of Manchester, 17 May 1979.

181 Bates, *Unions, parties and political development, op. cit.*, ch. 7.

182 C. Gertzel, K. Mutukwa, I. Scott and M. Wallis, 'Zambia's final experience of inter-party elections: the by-elections of December 1971', *Kroniek van Afrika*, vol. 2 (June–July 1972).

183 They had in mind particularly Simon Kapwepwe, the former UPP leader who was readmitted to UNIP in September 1977 and who tried, unsuccessfully, to contest the 1978 presidential election.

184 There were angry demonstrations in Lusaka and the Copperbelt, some of which were articulated in class terms. Szeftel, 'Conflict . . . in Zambia' *op. cit.*, pp. 455–6.

2. The Zambian economy

James Fry

The fourteen years since Zambian independence have witnessed very substantial changes in the structure of the Zambian economy. Because these changes have occurred far from smoothly, it would be misleading to try to encompass the entire post-independence period in one wide sweep of analysis. Fortunately, the framework adopted for government planning divides the period under review neatly into two segments of equal length, the first running until the end of the First National Development Plan[1] (FNDP) in 1970, and the second lasting until December 1976, when the Second National Development Plan[2] (SNDP) was due to terminate. Not only does this provide us with an extremely convenient way of comparing administrative and political efforts to plan for economic development with the actual pattern of growth, but, as we shall see later, 1970 may be viewed as marking a distinct turning point in Zambia's fortunes, separating a period of rapid economic growth from another of much slower growth.

Accordingly, the present chapter will be divided into two parts, covering 1964–70 and 1971–77 respectively. One further point of clarification to be made at this stage concerns the statistics quoted in the text. Many of these are drawn from Zambian government publications, which have a disconcerting, if understandable, tendency to revise and improve their methods of data analysis. The effect of this is often to cause the value of a certain economic variable given in one table to be different from the value of exactly the same variable quoted in another table. I have tried to resolve this conflict by ensuring that all the statistics in any one table are fully comparable with one another, even if that necessitates some manipulation of the published data.

1964 to 1970

Zambia became independent in 1964 after a decade in which little economic progress was achieved. It is true that the country's Gross Domestic Product had increased in real terms (i.e. after appropriate adjustments to allow for price changes) by over 45 per cent between 1954 and 1963, when Zambia was part of the Federation of Rhodesia and Nyasaland. However, a large part of this income accrued to foreign companies in the form of profits and royalties, especially from mining, and a proportion of one-sixth of GDP in 1954 (a proportion which had fallen only to one-eighth by 1963) was remitted out of the country to foreign investors.

African and non-African wage earners both enjoyed substantial wage increases during the federal era, but the numbers benefiting from these increases actually fell. African wage employment[3] was 241,000 in 1954, and rose to a peak of 273,000 in 1957 before falling back to stand at only 224,000 in 1963. The effect of cutbacks in mine expansion programmes in the late 1950s, when copper prices were low, was heightened by the poor investment climate when the end of Federation was in sight. In 1964, therefore, the omens for the newly independent nation were inauspicious. In particular, the economic structure of the country was most ill-suited to the requirements of a country striving for self-sufficiency. Over sixty per cent of GDP originated in the mining sector, which sold all its output on the export market. Only 6.6 per cent of GDP was produced by the small manufacturing sector that throughout the colonial period had competed unsuccessfully with imported products from Southern Rhodesia and South Africa, and only 4.6 per cent of GDP was contributed by a commercial agriculture sector that was dominated by a few hundred expatriate farmers along the line of rail.

The reliance upon expatriates and foreign sources of supply imposed a tight straitjacket upon Zambia's freedom of manoeuvre in developing the domestic economy. At the start of 1964, there were a mere 961 Africans who had obtained a Cambridge School Certificate or 'O' Level passes, and barely one-tenth as many African university graduates. Accordingly, education was given a very high priority in the first serious attempt to plan the economic future of an independent Zambia, described in the 1963–64 UN/ECA/FAO-sponsored report of the mission led by Dudley Seers.[4]

(i) Planning objectives

The Seers mission had a difficult task. Independence gave the Zambian Government control over the considerable revenues from mining that had formerly been used mainly to finance the economic development of Southern Rhodesia, but the distorted nature of the economy prevented the Government from being able to do much quickly to remove the distortion. The first dilemma that Zambia faced, and one that continues to beset her, was that she required foreign exchange to finance development and diversification, but the foreign exchange had to come mainly from copper exports. Hence, the short-run need to increase foreign exchange earnings seemed to imply continued investment in copper mining, yet this served only to reinforce the lop-sided structure of the Zambian economy.

A similar dilemma arose in agricultural policy. The majority of marketed agricultural output came from a few hundred commercial farmers, most of whom were expatriates. The Zambian Government would have liked to see a higher proportion of agricultural sales coming from peasant farmers, but would also have liked total agricultural sales to have been considerably greater. The latter objective was most easily achieved by encouraging existing large-scale farmers to increase their output, but this conflicted with the former objective.

The final dilemma facing the Seers mission, and still not entirely resolved, was how to bridge the unacceptably wide gap between local and expatriate wages without creating either severe inflation or an equally unacceptable gap between rural and urban incomes.

In the event, the preferred strategy of the Seers mission, and of the Transitional Development Plan of January 1965 to June 1966,[5] as well as of the subsequent First National Development Plan, running from July 1966 to December 1970, was something of a compromise. For example, as can be seen from Table 2.1, it was proposed that copper mining output and investment should be expanded, but at a slower rate than the manufacturing, agricultural and service sectors. The compromise in the case of agricultural policy was that peasant agriculture should be encouraged, but that the required volume of production targets should be attained by means of a judicious combination of large-scale commercial agriculture and State-encouraged co-operative mechanised farms, modelled upon a prototype cotton farm at Chombwa.

Wage policy was to prove the most tricky of the major issues facing the planners. The Seers Report spelled out carefully the dire consequences of conceding excessive wage awards. However, given the prevailing background of considerable resentment, particularly in the key copper mining sector, against racially determined pay scales, it was perhaps understandable that machinery for implementing an incomes policy was given a low priority in planning documents in the mid-1960s.

(ii) The performance of the economy
The plans for the economy were overtaken by events, in the form of Rhodesia's unilateral declaration of independence, after little more than a year of Zambian independence. However, it is not entirely clear in which way UDI deflected the development of Zambia from its planned course. On the one hand, UDI, the subsequent campaign of economic sanctions, and the closure of the Rhodesian border to Zambian foreign trade, raised the cost and disrupted the supply of vital imports such as petrol to Zambia. On the other hand, UDI, by excluding Rhodesian products from the Zambian market, granted infant Zambian industries some protection from their main rivals (this may help to explain why the manufacturing sector performed better than the FNDP predicted).[6] Thus, while the net impact of UDI on the Zambian economy during the 1960s was indubitably unfavourable, it was unlikely to have accounted for more than a small proportion of the failure of the economy to reach the targets set for it in the FNDP, and summarised in Table 2.1. The shortages of inputs caused by UDI tended to have a slowly-growing, cumulative impact upon output. By contrast, the three factors described below caused serious problems for producers within a short period of time.

Wages
As we have just mentioned, there are at least three other major reasons for this failure to reach the FNDP targets, a failure whose magnitude is quantified in Table 2.1. One reason was that the process of eliminating from local and expatriate wages and terms of service the most unpalatable relics of the colonial pay scale proved to be considerably more traumatic than had been anticipated. It was not until 1967, when other sectors followed the lead of the Brown Commission in the mining sector in granting pay rises of over 20 per cent, that the heat was taken out of the issue of wage determination. In the meantime, wages had risen 108 per cent above 1963 levels; and, by 1970, average African wages were 190 per cent above 1963's value. Inflation halved the increase to 93 per cent in real terms, but a near doubling of the real cost of African labour within seven years without any comparable rise in labour efficiency caused Zambian

Table 2.1: Monetary GDP by industrial origin (K million in producers' values at 1965 constant prices)

Industrial origin	1964	1965	1966	1967	1968	1969	1970 Actual	1970 Planned
Commercial agriculture	19.3	18.3	20.0	18.8	19.2	20.5	24.0	33.0
Mining	251.5	291.8	243.5	229.9	222.0	254.9	221.9	408.9
Manufacturing	27.7	48.0	57.5	66.8	72.7	74.2	81.0	68.2
of which: Food	4.4	6.6	6.6	6.1	8.1	10.4	12.2	9.3
Beverages & tobacco	5.9	13.0	17.4	18.5	24.0	22.6	27.5	12.5
Textiles & clothing	1.3	3.9	3.9	7.0	5.5	7.0	7.6	4.9
Wood & furniture	2.1	2.4	3.0	2.3	1.9	4.0	3.9	7.0
Paper & printing	1.5	2.1	2.1	3.0	4.3	3.0	3.2	3.0
Rubber & chemicals	1.5	3.6	3.7	6.0	6.5	9.4	7.5	4.4
Non-metallic minerals	3.8	6.1	5.1	5.1	5.5	4.9	6.7	10.8
Metal & machinery	6.8	10.2	15.4	18.5	16.6	12.6	12.2	15.0
Other	0.4	0.1	0.3	0.3	0.3	0.3	0.2	1.3
Construction	21.6	40.9	44.8	38.4	34.3	39.9	34.8	64.2
Electricity & water	7.2	5.4	7.3	7.5	10.4	14.6	16.2	11.0
Commerce & finance	39.6	95.2	89.5	91.9	115.1	91.7	113.7	86.2
Real estate	11.2	11.6	14.6	18.5	19.8	31.8	33.1	23.5
Transport & communications	21.8	32.8	30.1	42.5	40.3	35.5	34.6	41.5
Government services	39.2	30.4	36.0	36.3	39.4	34.0	47.1	113.9
Domestic services	7.4	9.0	8.2	8.5	8.4	8.3	12.1	11.6
Other services	16.1	34.1	33.2	46.1	50.1	50.5	60.9	37.3
Total	462.6	617.5	584.7	605.2	631.7	655.9	679.4	899.3

Note
The 1964 and FNDP 1970 figures have been derived from the estimates given in the FNDP document (which are in 1964 prices) by multiplying by a factor of 1·06, representing an estimate of the rate of inflation between 1964 and 1965.

Source: FNDP, op. cit., p. 6, and Monthly Digest of Statistics, April/May 1975, table 58.

products to be less competitive than had been hoped for. Furthermore, where, as in the government sector, products were not actually sold to consumers, high wages had the effect of reducing the growth in employment well below target. As Table 2.2 reveals, African wage earners in every sector enjoyed large wage increases, with the mining sector retaining its position as the sector paying the highest wages. Expatriates' earnings, however, grew much more slowly, rising at an average rate of only 3 per cent per annum in real terms between 1960 and 1970. Nevertheless, the average wage for non-African employees still vastly exceeded that of African employees in every sector. The ratio of non-African to African average wages varied from nearly 4:1 in the transport sector to 13:1 in agriculture.

Agriculture

The second reason for the failure to achieve FNDP targets lies in the particular problems of the agricultural sector described in Table 2.3. The Chombwa mechanisation schemes were found to require more managerial expertise than was available; therefore, the volume of production hoped for from this source failed to materialise. Despite the successes achieved in the two agricultural activities – sugar cane and poultry – that most readily lent themselves to industrial farming methods by a small number of large private enterprises, those agricultural activities that relied heavily upon the production of several hundred commercial farmers suffered as a result of the steady exodus of such farmers. This adversely affected tobacco, milk, beef and maize output.

Peasant-marketed output did grow respectably over the period, and even in the bad harvest year of 1970 was fully one-third higher than it had been in 1964, but its growth was insufficient to allow output targets to be achieved. The collapse of the Credit Organisation of Zambia, whose extreme generosity in granting agricultural credit in the mid-1960s made the allocation of rural credit difficult for many years afterwards, was one factor behind the relatively slow growth of peasant output. The equally dramatic rise and fall of the co-operative movement was another factor. However, the particular factor I should like to emphasise was government policy regarding producer pricing in agriculture.

Throughout the 1960s the Zambian Government was torn between using agricultural producer prices as a means of controlling inflation or as a means of stimulating farmers to produce more output. The barter terms of trade measure how agricultural producer prices move relative to the cost of living. If the cost of living rises faster than

Table 2.2: Average earnings of African workers, by sector (1960–70) (Kwacha per annum)

Year	Sector									Low[2] income cost of living index (Jan. 1962= 100·0)	Average earnings in Jan. 1962 constant prices	Public sector	Private sector
	Agriculture	Mining	Manufac- turing	Constr- uction	Electr- icity	Comm- erce	Trans- port	Services[1]	Mean				
1960	120	570	236	236	210	232	292	256	272	100·3	271	–	–
1963	132	596	346	276	254	314	426	328	320	101·3	316	–	–
1964	176	732	406	286	320	388	482	392	382	104·5	366	–	–
1965	172	826	486	322	388	464	486	458	428	113·0	379	–	–
1966	190	934	478	332	456	488	688	526	480	124·5	386	476	482
1967	248	1322	676	500	795	679	934	690	666	130·7	510	646	676
1968	352	1248	635	549	689	744	946	720	713	144·9	492	689	727
1969	360	1412	744	560	721	801	1034	793	765	148·4	508	690	788
1970	348	1543	802	609	816	795	1211	789	928	152·3	609	724	1048

Notes
[1] Excluding domestic service
[2] Up to 1969 the indices were calculated from a 1962 base. For 1970 the published indices use a 1969 base year.

Source: Monthly Digest of Statistics, various issues.

Table 2.3: Marketed output of main agricultural commodities (tonnes unless otherwise shown)

Commodity	1964	1965	1966	1967	1968	1969	1970 actual	1970 planned
Maize	194,010	254,320	377,580	374,680	249,240	253,140	124,370	361,100
Groundnuts	3,630	6,740	11,530	14,810	5,390	7,820	3,270	19,500
Raw sugar	–	–	–	–	21,500	30,400	40,100	36,900
Beef	12,600	12,400	10,800	9,700	8,600	8,800	11,800	18,400
Pork & bacon	690	680	870	910	920	930	1,150	2,000
Poultry, dressed	880	1,230	1,920	2,860	4,350	5,170	5,440	2,950
Eggs (thousands)	17,400	22,800	27,000	36,000	54,000	93,000	99,000	42,000
Milk (thousands of litres)	20,500	19,800	19,000	18,300	18,400	16,200	15,300	31,400
Tobacco: Virginia	10,970	6,610	6,570	4,590	6,290	5,020	4,790	16,060
Burley	1,700	1,990	860	270	290	240	250	2,090
Oriental	300	530	210	130	110	75	29	1,000
Seed cotton	1,650	2,270	2,780	1,830	4,250	6,920	5,610	8,490

Source: SNDP, op. cit., p. 14.

producer prices, this means that the purchasing power of a typical unit of a farmer's produce has fallen, and that the farmer has to increase his output merely to maintain his spending power. This is precisely what happened after 1964. A peasant farmer who produced the same output in 1970 as he had produced in 1964 would have found he could have bought only 85.8 per cent of the goods he could afford to buy in 1970.[7] Consequently, it is not surprising that peasant output grew only slowly after 1964, since the incentives for increased output were weak.

Zambianisation

It was inevitable that, after the neglect of the colonial era, the assumption of local control over key aspects of the economy should have caused some disruption. In practice, there was little freedom of manoeuvre for the new government; many skilled expatriates made it abundantly clear that they would not remain long in the independent State. Hence, the Zambianisation of jobs at all levels had to proceed apace. In terms of the distribution of skilled jobs among different races in 1963, one rough estimate is that by 1970 local workers were performing over twenty thousand jobs which before independence would have been held by expatriate workers.

From Table 2.4 one can observe that total African wage employment (other than in domestic service) rose from 190,000 to 310,000 between 1963 and 1970, while expatriate employment fell from 32,500 to 27,400 over the same period. Although employment growth of this order would be considered exceptional in most contexts, it left employment in 1970 well short of the FNDP target. Part of the failure to achieve this target must be blamed upon the unexpected upsurge in wages that encouraged employers to seek methods of economising in their use of labour; but the speed with which Zambianisation occurred probably reduced employers' abilities to absorb a large increase in their labour forces.

Zambianisation did not only apply to employment. The Mulungushi and Matero economic reforms of 1968 and 1969 saw Zambian control extended over a wide range of economic activities. In commerce this took the form of restricting most areas of retail trading to Zambian citizens, but where, as in manufacturing, transport, mining or supermarket chains, the sums of money involved were too great for any single individual, it was the Government, through the acquisition of a majority stake in the enterprises concerned, that acquired control on behalf of Zambian interests.

In the longer term, this extension of Zambian control over the

Table 2.4: African formal sector employment (1960–70)[1]

Year	Sector Agriculture	Mining	Manufacturing	Construction	Other[2]	Total[2]	of which Public sector	Private sector[2]
1960	37,000	42,700	17,900	36,000	65,400	209,000		
1963	36,000	40,800	15,900	23,400	73,900	190,000		
1964	34,350	42,500	18,000	29,100	77,900	202,000		
1965	31,020	44,730	24,730	44,740	87,540	232,760		
1966	31,540	46,570	26,180	58,130	85,880	249,480	84,470	165,010
1967	36,060	48,480	28,500	60,580	101,030	274,650	102,710	171,930
1968	36,280	49,150	31,390	67,420	106,560	290,800	108,820	181,980
1969	37,520	49,420	32,730	57,470	114,490	291,630	117,890	174,740
1970 (Actual)	33,480	51,060	33,920	66,740	125,120	310,320	126,990	183,330
1970 (Actual)[3]	33,930	56,510	36,810	69,490	141,010	337,750	134,750	203,000
1970 (Planned)[3]	47,000	57,000	40,000	75,000	188,000	407,000	N.A.	N.A.

Notes

[1] The figures until 1964 are yearly averages; thereafter they refer to the June quarter.

[2] These figures do not include any allowance for African workers employed as domestic servants.

[3] African + non-African

Source: Monthly Digest of Statistics and FNDP, op. cit.

Zambian economy has been, and will doubtless continue to be, of considerable benefit. Yet, in the shorter term, some disruption, particularly in the retail sector, followed the economic reforms and this must have adversely affected the performance of the economy in the FNDP.

The price of copper

In view of the many problems that faced Zambia during the first years of independence, the degree to which FNDP targets were achieved can be considered creditable. Furthermore, the planners could take pride in the economy's success in meeting all the optimistic targets laid down for fixed investment. Private consumption and government consumption both grew only half as rapidly as had been forecast, but the former still managed to grow by 50 per cent, and the latter by 85 per cent. Fixed investment actually trebled as planned, in the course of only six years. However, one cannot evaluate the growth of the Zambian economy during the 1960s without acknowledging the unexpectedly favourable trend in copper prices that occurred in the same period. If some allowance is made for the effects of inflation, the price of copper was unusually high, on a historical basis, during the late 1960s.

The high copper prices of the late 1960s provided the planners with an unexpected bonus. While *output*, which is measured by GDP at constant prices, grew much more slowly than the planners had hoped, *income*, in the sense of the purchasing power of the same output, grew nearly as fast as the FNDP had predicted. The difference between output and income existed only because the price of the output (i.e. the price of copper) rose at a different rate from the prices of the goods being bought by Zambians. In Table 2.5 the magnitude of the boost to incomes from high copper prices, known technically as the adjustment for changes in the terms of trade, is described. In 1969, the peak year, Zambian *income*, at K1032.9m, was well above FNDP forecasts, even though *output*, at K677.4m, was considerably below FNDP predictions.

The main impact of these high copper prices was felt on Zambia's balance of payments, which went from strength to strength. But it was natural that the rapid growth in Zambia's income, even though it was due to a fortuitous upsurge in the copper price, should have caused many people to view the economic record during the FNDP in a more favourable light than was justified by the underlying trend in output.

Table 2.5: Monetary GDP (K million in purchasers' values at 1965 prices)

	1965	1966	1967	1968	1969	1970
FNDP Projections	632·0	705·8	788·5	880·6	983·7	1098·9
Actual	632·0	602·7	636·7	654·8	677·4	701·1
Adjustment for changes in the terms of trade	–	+126·0	+125·5	+139·0	+355·5	+175·0
GDP at 1965 prices adjusted for changes in the terms of trade	632·0	728·7	762·2	793·8	1032·9	876·1

Note
The FNDP forecasts are made in terms of 1964 prices. For simplicity it is assumed that the FNDP predictions for 1965 were correct.

Sources: FNDP, op. cit., p. 6, and *Monthly Digest of Statistics*, April/May 1975, table 57.

(iii) The situation in 1970

The entire discussion so far needs to be put into its proper perspective. Until now, we have implicitly been considering only the so-called 'modern', monetary sector of the economy. Yet only 310,000 adults out of approximately two million adult Africans in 1970 were employed in the modern sector. Approximately 150,000 were employed as domestic servants or worked in the urban informal sector as marketeers, sellers of charcoal and firewood, shoe repairers, tailors, casual builders etc.[8] Around 650,000 people were classified as 'working proprietors' in traditional agriculture in the 1970–71 Census of Agriculture,[9] with 120,000 people dependent upon paid employment in traditional agriculture. The largest group of all, some 800,000 strong, consisted of housewives, students, unemployed workers and people not seeking work.

While incomes outside the modern sector varied significantly, it would probably be fair to state that the vast majority of households in rural areas had annual incomes (including the value of their subsistence output) which would have been comparable to an income in urban areas of only K250.[10] The rural population probably received some benefit from the social services introduced by the Government after independence, but in purely economic terms the lot of the majority of Zambia's population improved little between 1964 and 1970. It was the urban wage earners, more than anyone else, who enjoyed the 'fruits of independence'. In 1963, the typical wage earner in the modern sector was perhaps twice as well off as his rural cousin; by 1970, he was nearly four times as well off. At the same time, the economic position of Africans within the modern sector was transformed. Whereas in 1963 the total wage bill of non-African workers (K100.5 million) was 43 per cent higher than the total wage bill of African workers (K66.4 million), by 1970 it was 56 per cent lower (K141.4 million as against K320.5 million).[11]

Looking at the distribution of income nationally, the overall impact of the upsurge in African wages was twofold. At the top of the scale, the gap between the very highly paid and less highly paid workers narrowed. I only have data for 1959 and 1970 for comparison, but Table 2.6 indicates that the share of national income received by the richest one per cent of households fell from 16 per cent in 1959 to 13 per cent in 1970. However, lower down the

Table 2.6: Household income distribution (in 1959 and 1970)

Share of total income received by the given top percentage of all households	National income distribution (%) 1959	1970	Urban income distribution (%) 1970
1	16	13	8
2	25	19	13
5	38	33	24
10	45	48	36
20	57	63	51
50	79	80	80

Source: Fry, *Employment and income distribution, op. cit.*, and Baldwin, *Economic development and export growth, op. cit.*

scale, the gap between the moderately well paid and the poorly paid actually grew larger. The share of national income accruing to the poorest 80 per cent of the population fell from 43 per cent in 1959 to 37 per cent in 1970. Since the table reveals that the income of urban workers was much more equally distributed than that of the population as a whole, one can reasonably deduce that the rural–urban gap must take much of the blame for income inequality in Zambia in 1970, as now.

1971 to 1977

The copper price may have helped to put a better light on the performance of the economy during the FNDP, but the role it played over the next seven years proved to be a source of very serious concern to the Government. 1971, 1972 and 1975 were all years in which the average copper price was lower than in any year between 1965 and 1970. With an appropriate allowance for the effects of inflation, one discovers that only in 1973 and 1974 of the period under review were copper prices high enough to earn the mining companies (which in 1970 became 51 per cent government-owned) a reasonable return.

(i) Planning objectives

The Second National Development Plan did not commence until January 1972, since the Government set aside 1971 to complete outstanding projects from the FNDP. However, the delay did little to dampen its expansionary enthusiasm. The rate of growth of output between 1971 and 1976 was planned to be 7.5 per cent per annum, with the manufacturing sector intended to achieve a remarkable 14.7 per cent annual rate of output growth. Alongside an aggregate 43.5 per cent increase in output between 1971 and 1976, wage employment was to grow by 100,000, or 27.0 per cent. The real wage, it was hoped, would rise at only 1.5 per cent per annum, supported by machinery for the implementation of a prices and incomes policy.

The Government's assumption, towards the end of the FNDP period, of control of the main mining, manufacturing, transport and financial companies in Zambia meant that the financing of the SNDP depended very heavily upon the financial resources of the central government. In agriculture, however, the SNDP aimed to continue to balance carefully the desire to stimulate peasant agriculture against the need to rely upon a large volume of production from a few hundred commercial farmers. Direct government involvement in agricultural production during the SNDP, like the FNDP, was planned to be confined mainly to the very large scale plantation cultivation of crops linked to industrial processing; but, unlike the FNDP, the SNDP was opposed to any encouragement of Chombwa-style mechanisation schemes, favouring instead the rather ill-defined concept of Intensive Development Zones, areas of high agricultural potential upon which government resources would be concentrated.

(ii) The performance of the economy

The targets set for the SNDP proved to be just as excessively optimistic as the targets for the FNDP had been. As Table 2.7 makes clear, the failure to achieve SNDP targets was common to all but three of the sectors listed in the table, the exceptions being

Table 2.7: Monetary GDP by industrial origin (K million in producers' values at 1965 constant prices)

Industrial origin	1970	1971	1972	1973	1974	1975	1976 actual	1976 planned
Commercial agriculture	33·7	35·8	46·2	47·4	43·6	49·8	55·0	47·7
Mining	232·6	202·7	217·6	227·2	231·8	211·4	232·0	273·0
Manufacturing	82·3	86·2	101·0	106·0	117·2	112·3	107·5	171·5
of which: Food	12·2	13·5	13·8	10·7	42·5	41·5	41·0	19·0
Beverages & tobacco	27·5	27·3	31·3	29·4	12·6	12·6	12·8	16·4
Textiles & clothing	8·1	7·1	8·9	10·6	} 4·6	} 3·4	} 3·0	19·0
Wood & furniture	3·3	2·1	3·0	3·8				7·4
Paper & printing	3·7	3·8	3·9	4·3	} 4·4	} 5·0	} 3·9	8·2
Rubber products	2·5	3·8	3·9	4·9				3·0
Chemicals & plastics	5·0	5·2	11·2	15·6	24·6	22·1	21·0	21·7
Non-metallic minerals	6·8	6·0	6·4	6·1	6·9	7·4	6·6	13·0
Basic metal products	1·8	1·5	1·9	1·8	2·2	1·7	1·7	24·6
Fabricated metal products	11·2	15·6	16·6	18·4	19·0	18·2	17·1	31·5
Other	0·2	0·3	0·1	0·4	0·4	0·4	0·4	1·0
Construction	52·1	51·1	56·6	61·0	59·1	70·1	66·5	75·7
Electricity & water	16·0	19·8	27·2	30·4	38·0	39·2	40·5	32·2
Commerce & tourism	103·3	99·8	101·3	107·1	132·0	121·6	117·5	153·0
Finance & real estate	43·0	48·9	45·4	50·4	53·8	58·6	60·5	63·5
Transport & communications	39·8	47·5	43·9	45·1	44·0	42·1	41·5	67·4
Government services	110·0	116·9	126·6	110·7	112·3	123·8	132·8	142·2
Domestic services	14·8	14·9	15·3	15·2	17·2	17·4	17·8	18·7
Other services	17·0	20·5	23·9	27·0	26·7	25·9	25·9	31·5
Total	744·6	744·1	805·0	827·5	873·7	872·2	897·5	1076·4

Note
In 1970, the basis upon which national income statistics were collected was altered. This table, using the new convention, is therefore not consistent with Table 2.1.

Source: Monthly Digest of Statistics, various issues.

commercial agriculture, the manufacture of beverages and cigarettes, and the distribution of electricity and water. The most important single factor behind this failure was undoubtedly the behaviour of copper prices.

Copper prices
The depressed level of copper prices during most of the SNDP affected national income and output adversely in at least three separate ways. The immediate impact was upon export earnings. Table 2.8 reveals that the value of exports in 1976 was slightly below the value recorded in 1970. In the meantime, inflation had increased the cost of imports. The Government was, therefore, obliged to introduce import controls to ensure some sort of respectability for the balance of payments statistics. In 1973 and 1974, when copper prices were historically high, the Government did not allow the improved circumstances to boost the country's foreign exchange reserves; instead, it redeemed the bonds issued at the time of the take-over of 51 per cent of the capital of the copper mines and negotiated compensation for acquiring the mine management contracts from the former private owners.

When they were applied strictly after 1974, import controls disrupted production in virtually every sector, as imported inputs and spare parts became scarce. Furthermore, the reduced supply of imported staple items made the recruitment and retention of skilled expatriate workers difficult, particularly in the mining sector, and this further disrupted production.

Another problem created by the low copper prices of the SNDP period was that they caused both profits and the tax revenue available to the Government from profits to fall far short of expectations. While total wages outpaced inflation, more than doubling between 1970 and 1976, profits, which provide the bulk of investment funds and of government revenue, actually fell nearly twenty per cent between 1970 and 1976. Despite this, government consumption nearly doubled between 1970 and 1976, with as much as half of the rise alleged to have been accounted for by military expenditure. But higher government consumption meant that capital expenditure bore the brunt of the cutbacks in government budgets in 1975 and 1976 and, combined with the drop in company profits, caused real investment to fall by one eighth between 1970 and 1976, instead of achieving the hoped-for increase of one half.

The full impact of low copper prices on national income, however, is brought out most clearly by the divergence between the trends in output and income. With the exception of a slight hiccough in 1975,

Table 2.8: Balance of payments (K million)

	1970	1971	1972	1973	1974	1975	1976
Exports	710.4	479.2	543.2	733.5	898.2	523.1	705.0
(of which, Copper)	681.4	450.2	490.9	698.3	838.5	471.1	650.0
Imports	340.7	401.3	404.5	349.4	508.6	599.6	490.0
Balance of trade	374.3	77.9	138.7	384.1	389.6	−76.5	215.0
Balance of payments surplus on current account	66.5	−176.5	−148.8	93.4	48.5	−392.5	−103.0
(of which, Invisibles)	−307.8	−254.4	−287.5	−290.7	−341.1	−316.0	−318.0
Capital account balance	47.4	−10.8	45.5	−102.6	−40.3	248.3	−2.0
Overall balance of payments surplus	113.9	−187.3	−103.4	−9.2	8.2	−144.2	−105.0
Net foreign assets at year end	300.1	186.2	78.5	67.2	76.6	−75.0	−180.0

Source: Monthly Digest of Statistics, various issues.

output grew steadily until 1976, albeit much more slowly than had been planned. GDP at 1965 constant prices rose from K783.1 million in 1970 to K995 million in 1976. This was in sharp contrast with the trend in *income*, which suffered from a marked deterioration in the terms of trade. Real income in 1976 was lower than in any year since 1967, and was over one third below the income level set as a target in the SNDP. Whereas real income at 1965 constant prices was K958.1 million in 1970, it had fallen to K771.5 million in 1976, compared with the SNDP target of K1,168.8 million.[12]

Agriculture

Against the background just described, the performance of the agricultural sector in surpassing SNDP targets is especially commendable. As Table 2.9 indicates, the performance of different crops was somewhat patchy. Oilseeds and wheat, whose cultivation was a new venture during the course of the SNDP, were, with sugar cane, the most successful crops; all three were produced almost entirely by large-scale commercial farmers. The successes achieved with maize and poultry farming also depended heavily upon production by commercial farmers. There were, however, some agricultural commodities, notably milk, beef and virginia tobacco, where commercial farmers reacted to bureaucratic interference in marketing and pricing by switching their energies to the production of other commodities.

Pricing policy was undoubtedly responsible too for the relative lack of success in schemes designed to promote peasant production of groundnuts, beef, virginia and burley tobacco, cotton and rice. Preliminary calculations indicate that government agricultural pricing policy during the SNDP continued in the tradition of the FNDP period by allowing the price of agricultural commodities to rise less rapidly than the cost of living for peasant farmers. Hence, prices did not provide much of an incentive for the transformation of peasant agriculture, and since neither Intensive Development Zones nor the militarily-managed Rural Reconstruction Centres established during the SNDP proved successful as catalysts for the long-heralded rural revolution, 1977 found the agricultural sector still uncomfortably dependent upon the activities of a few hundred, largely expatriate, commercial farmers.

Manufacturing

If agriculture recorded the most impressive success of the SNDP, the other glamorous sector – manufacturing – fell the furthest short of its objectives. The manufacturing sector did manage to grow during the

Table 2.9: Marketed output of main agricultural commodities (thousand tonnes unless otherwise shown)

	1971	1972	1973	1974	1975	1976	1976 planned
Maize	340.0	616.6	300.2	495.0	558.4	729.6	575.0
Groundnuts	6.8	6.6	2.9	3.0	6.5	8.4	11.0
Sugar cane	330.7	397.0	460.0	520.0	768.2	860.0	600.0
Beef	11.8	13.1	16.3	14.4	10.9	10.0	16.0
Pork & Bacon	1.3	1.7	1.8	1.9	2.4	2.6	3.3
Poultry, dressed	4.4	9.1	10.2	12.5	15.0	14.0	9.5
Eggs (million)	108.0	115.0	123.0	130.0	150.0	140.0	155.0
Day-old chicks (exports only) (millions)	0.9	1.1	1.3	1.3	1.5	1.4	N.A.
Milk (million litres)	16.0	16.6	16.8	16.8	12.2	11.3	32.5
Tobacco: Virginia	5.9	5.5	6.2	6.2	6.5	6.3	11.0
Burley	0.3	0.4	0.5	0.4	0.5	0.2	0.7
Seed cotton	12.7	8.3	5.2	2.5	3.1	3.9	11.5
Sunflower	0.0	0.0	1.0	3.3	9.8	13.6	} 7.0
Soyabean	0.0	0.0	0.0	0.1	0.7	1.1	
Wheat	0.0	0.0	0.0	0.1	0.7	3.5	–
Paddy rice	0.2	0.3	0.4	0.7	1.0	1.8	2.6

Note
Many of the 1976 figures are estimates.

Source: SNDP, op. cit., and Economic report, 1976 (Lusaka, 1977).

SNDP, but some of the larger projects upon which the SNDP's targets were based were found to be ill-conceived and poorly planned. One large-scale example is the 300,000 tonnes per annum copper fabricating plant, producing copper products such as copper tubes or sheet for export, which was included in the SNDP and was intended to contribute over one quarter of the entire growth in manufacturing output planned in the SNDP. Not only was it extremely doubtful whether Zambia could profitably produce and export copper fabricated products on this scale (because transport costs and damage to goods in transit would absorb any gain to the Zambian economy), but Zambia would also have to overcome tariff and other barriers to trade which would make the entry of Zambian copper fabricated exports into most markets extremely difficult.

In the event, the problems caused by the low copper price and import controls prevented the Government from realising many of the feasible industrial projects listed in the SNDP. After 1974 policy regarding the manufacturing sector had to concern itself more with ensuring full utilisation of existing manufacturing enterprises than with building and opening new ones.

Wages and employment
The failure to achieve manufacturing sector objectives or investment (and, hence, construction sector) objectives proved particularly serious for the attainment of employment targets. As Table 2.10 reveals, employment creation in the SNDP period fell far short of the declared target of 20,000 new jobs each year. Only the mining sector surpassed the SNDP's targets, but in view of the slow growth of copper production, it is doubtful whether the performance of the mining sector is to be hailed as a great success.

If one turns back to Table 2.4, one will note that the mining sector's employment creation record in the FNDP closely parallels its record in the SNDP. Where the SNDP period differs markedly from the FNDP period is in the effect of wages upon employment. Unlike the FNDP, when wages grew much more rapidly than had been anticipated, the SNDP saw the average real wage of African workers fall significantly, in contrast with the forecast that a slight rise would occur. With the single exception of transport workers (whose average earnings estimate for 1975 looks extremely improbable), all the main groups of African workers appear to have suffered a fairly large drop in their average real wages between 1970 and 1975, since their wage increases far from kept pace with inflation. (See Table 2.11)

Expatriate workers avoided having their average wage reduced in

Table 2.10: African/Zambian formal sector employment (1970–75)[1]

Sector Date	Agriculture	Mining	Manufacturing	Construction	Other	Total	Public sector	of which Private sector	Parastatal sector
African employment									
June 1970	33,480	51,060	33,920	66,740	125,120	310,320	126,990	183,330	
June 1971	37,390	52,380	37,680	67,470	136,900	331,670	136,490	195,180	
June 1972	37,690	52,090	39,840	66,220	142,910	338,750	138,580	200,170	
Zambian employment[2]									
December 1972	29,640	49,470	40,020	68,230	146,430	333,790	140,640	193,150	
December 1973	30,330	50,420	40,460	66,630	152,210	340,050	141,630	198,420	
December 1974	32,160	54,270	40,970	66,270	157,920	351,590	146,710	204,880	
June 1975	34,960	56,510	41,680	69,220	162,960	365,330	121,690	123,490	120,150
Planned for December 1976[3]	46,000	66,000	63,000	108,000	187,000	470,000	N.A.	N.A.	N.A.

Notes

[1] Domestic servants are not included in these figures.

[2] In 1972, African employment exceeded Zambian employment by approximately 9,000, the difference being accounted for, largely, by the employment of 10,000 alien African workers.

[3] These SNDP targets are for the combined total of Zambian and non-Zambian employment.

Source: Monthly Digest of Statistics, various issues.

Table 2.11: Average earnings of African/Zambian workers by sector (1970–75) (K)

Date	Sector Agriculture	Mining	Manufacturing	Construction	Electricity	Commerce	Transport	Finance	Other services	Mean	Low income cost of living index (1969=100)	Earnings in 1969 prices	Public sector	Private sector	Parastatal sector
African workers' earnings															
1970	348	1,543	802	609	816	795	1,211	1,121	756	928	102·6	904	724	1,048	
1971	383	1,636	1,005	707	829	836	1,424	1,217	884	1,033	108·8	949	899	1,108	
1972	407	1,554	910	718	822	883	1,348	1,100	871	1,017	114·6	887	914	1,056	
Zambian workers' earnings															
December 1972	434	1,601	1,025	703	825	1,081	1,204	1,298	129	1,014	114·6	885	990	1,079	
December 1973	419	1,685	1,064	724	922	1,147	1,292	1,328	318	1,135	121·9	931	1,144	1,129	
December 1974	445	1,701	1,071	716	803	1,019	1,397	1,356	299	1,122	132·1	849	1,096	1,141	
June 1975	425	1,982	1,130	688	1,038	1,087	1,835	1,594	267	1,199	145·5	824	1,104	869	1,635

Source: *Monthly Digest of Statistics*, various issues.

real terms, but this did little to boost the recruitment of expatriates. Other problems, such as delays in being allowed to remit money abroad and shortages of consumer goods in Zambia, upset short-term expatriate recruits considerably. As a consequence, the annual rate of turnover among expatriate miners in 1976 rose for the first time ever above thirty per cent and the mines were obliged to operate with an expatriate labour force well below establishment.

(iii) The situation in 1977

One unexpected result of the sizeable drop in African real wages during the SNDP was that there was some reversal of the trend that had occurred in income distribution during the previous decade. While the incomes of the highest paid workers kept pace with inflation, the vast majority of wage earners experienced a narrowing of the gap between their incomes and those of people in the rural sector. However, it would be unwise to draw any conclusions about the long-term trend in the structure of income distribution from developments during the period of the SNDP, since urban wage earners are still in a position where their conditions of employment are extremely sensitive to slight changes in the economic climate. Indeed, one can go further than this: Zambia's present economic difficulties and their repercussions upon the internal economic structure of the country illustrate all too well that the economy has not yet achieved the degree of diversification that will allow it to shrug off depression in the copper sector.

The copper sector is gradually declining in importance, but it still accounts for over ninety per cent of export earnings. In the past two years, the copper mines have contributed very little to government revenues; however, this matters much less than it would have done in the past because the Government has deliberately sought to widen its revenue base. Unfortunately, in an economy as dependent upon foreign trade as Zambia's, it is ultimately foreign exchange earnings that determine the pace of development. If the export revenue from copper falls, imports of industrial inputs and capital goods have to be cut back unless alternative sources of foreign exchange can be developed.

There can be no doubt that in many respects the Zambian economy has progressed considerably since 1964. The economy is much more diversified than it was; Zambians are at last assuming positions of responsibility in key sectors; and even the agricultural sector, so long the laggard and a disappointment to policymakers, is showing encouraging signs of sustained growth. But the benefits of Zambia's development remain, much as they were in 1964, confined to a small section of the population. In the towns, a growing proportion of the labour force is employed or is self-employed at relatively low incomes in the so-called 'informal sector', all too frequently despised and harried by the authorities; in the rural areas, the growth in agricultural output appears to have been the result of the efforts of a small number of medium- and large-scale farmers, with the standard of living of the vast majority of the rural population little changed from the level of ten or twenty years ago.

While there are many reasons that might be advanced to explain why the benefits of economic growth have been so unevenly distributed among the population, I should like to finish this chapter by focusing upon one of them – the objectives of national planning. Planning has always tended to be undertaken in terms of broad economic aggregates. It was not a desire for simplicity that caused all the targets of the FNDP and the SNDP given in the tables above to be listed as aggregates; the planning office has never interested itself much in attempts to direct the benefits of development to particular target groups. Hence, it has been virtually impossible to identify the implications of a national plan for individuals in the economy; and, instead of presenting a plan as a series of visible, tangible aims, such as uniform minimum standards of housing or sanitation throughout the country, to be achieved by a certain date, plans are presented as extremely abstract percentage growth rates that mean little to people. The planning office has always proclaimed its desire to ensure popular involvement in the process of planning, and both the FNDP and the SNDP have been disaggregated on a regional basis. Unfortunately, the disaggregation goes no further than this, with the result that, having persuaded local personalities to become involved in planning at a local level and in the determination of local objectives, the latter are rarely translated into tangible goals that will be meaningful to individual families.

In theory, the structure already exists, through village productivity committees, for local communities to plan their own futures in great detail. However, the actions of central planning authorities, and their preference for dealing in broad aggregates, fail to give local planning units the support that they need. As long as this state of affairs persists, it will continue to be total output, rather than the distribution of output, that will dominate policy, and development in Zambia will remain as uneven as ever.

Notes

[1] *FNDP, op. cit.*
[2] *SNDP, op. cit.*
[3] These estimates of African wage employment include domestic servants in the totals.
[4] *Economic survey mission on the economic development of Zambia: report of the UN/ECA/FAO Mission* (Ndola, 1964). This is hereafter referred to as the Seers Report.
[5] *An outline of the transitional development plan* (Lusaka, 1965).
[6] See Table 2.1.
[7] F. J. M. Maimbo and J. Fry, 'An investigation into the change in the terms of trade between the rural and urban sectors of Zambia', *African Social Research*, No. 12 (December 1971).
[8] These figures come from J. Fry, *Employment and income distribution in the African economy* (London, 1979).
[9] *Census of agriculture, 1970–71: first report* (Lusaka, May 1974).
[10] This represents the costs that an urban worker would have had to incur to purchase the goods and services consumed by a rural household. See Fry, *Employment and income distribution, op. cit.*
[11] These estimates are derived from the tables on employment and earnings in the *Monthly Digest of Statistics*.
[12] The SNDP targets are expressed in 1969 constant prices; an appropriate adjustment has therefore been made to them.

3. The public service

Dennis L. Dresang and Ralph A. Young

The demands for trained personnel confronting the new UNIP Government at independence were formidable. In its staffing requirements, the administration was faced with dual imperatives – organisational and political – of managing the timely replacement of departing colonial servants and of ensuring that Zambian officials had visible occupation of strategic public posts to buttress a substantially inexperienced UNIP Cabinet. The rapid expansion of the African electorate – from eleven in 1958 to over 7,600 in 1959, 99,000 in 1962 and nearly 1,380,000 by the January 1964 election – promised an irreversible shift in the concerns and scale of public policy. Though this shift was to require a half decade and more to become fully crystallised, it was evident that UNIP's post-independence commitments would entail both expansion of the administrative apparatus and a marked increase in its functional complexity as the State machinery became geared to a developmental role. Apart from Government's own requirements, personnel were needed to sustain key economic sectors hitherto dominated by expatriate skills – the commercial agriculture which had developed particularly in districts straddling the line of rail; the growing sectors of commerce and manufacturing; and Zambia's vital copper industry, the most technologically sophisticated industrial complex in black Africa.

Yet in 1964, there were only 109 Africans with university degrees and just over 1,200 with secondary school certificates[1] – roughly 0.08 per cent of the registered African electorate. In 1965, the year after independence, 40 per cent of the established posts in the civil service were vacant; and of the occupied positions in Divisions I and II (clerical officer and above), only 38 per cent were held by Zambian citizens.[2]

Though Africans had been employed by the administration since the imposition of European control in the early 1890s, they remained confined to junior positions until August 1955, when all service posts were opened to suitably qualified inhabitants of Northern Rhodesia. This reform brought a first, tentative step towards the creation of a unified public service to displace the existing racially stratified divisions comprising the European and African Civil Services.[3] Not that access to posts would be on precisely equal terms: the circular announcing the change stated that Africans with paper qualifications equivalent to those of Europeans in positions to which they aspired would need additional years of training 'to acquire the necessary experience and develop the qualities of character to fit them' for posts in the European Civil Service.[4] Accordingly, a new set of positions graded between the two Services was introduced to provide this training.

The breaching of so sensitive a barrier to African political advancement had limited immediate impact – a consequence of the dearth of qualified Africans available and also of the conflicting political pressures emanating from European settler and African nationalist leaderships, the Federal Government in Salisbury (Southern Rhodesia), and from within the colonial administration itself.[5] Initially, eight Africans gained appointment to the new intermediate posts; by 1960 there were still only fifty in this grade (another forty-five positions were vacant through lack of qualified candidates). The first African attained a 'European' post in 1958; there were nine blacks in the European Service by 1960, nearly all in departments specially concerned with African affairs. While the first eight reaching the intermediate grade in 1955 were all university graduates and included five direct entrants to the Service, only four of the fifty holding intermediate posts in 1960 had degrees, and only four had less than fifteen years' Service experience.[6]

At the time the decision to introduce a unified and localised civil service was announced in 1959, Northern Rhodesia's future was still officially recognised as a constituent member of a larger, multiracial unit, the Central African Federation; a government memorandum explained:

The changing circumstances of Northern Rhodesia arising from the general and constitutional development of the Territory, the advent of Federation, the growth of a settled European community and the accepted policy of African advancement have all contributed to make the present organisation of the Civil Service outmoded . . . . The Government has, therefore, decided that, subject to the preservation of the rights of serving officers, the present division of the Civil Service on the basis of colour must end and a single non-racial Northern Rhodesia Civil Service be established and that terms and conditions of service suitable for 'locally-based' officers of all races must be provided.[7]

The formal introduction of the Local Civil Service in November 1961, however, was clouded by an atmosphere of uncertainty due to the strongly running tide of African nationalism; amidst the heightened political tensions and with the apparent prospect of eventual African majority rule, many European officers were reluctant to transfer to the new non-racial Service.

Another factor discouraging Europeans from accepting local conditions of service was the introduction in 1961 of the Overseas Service Aid Scheme (OSAS) by the British Government. This programme had two principal aims: to provide colonial officials with compensation for loss of career resulting from decolonisation, and to provide inducements to attract persons with needed skills to serve the former British dependencies on a contractual basis. The terms of the Scheme as it applied to Northern Rhodesia were announced in a Secretariat circular in early 1962 – some three months after publication of conditions for the Local Civil Service.[8] Individual compensation was to be calculated on the basis of chronological age, years in the Service and current annual pensionable emoluments.[9] The formula used in determining compensation maximised benefits for those around forty, when a new career might be difficult to begin; awards could be as high as £13,500. On the other hand, the Scheme included generous inducement features. The OSAS salary was initially set at five per cent above the 1960 salary schedule resulting from acceptance of the Shone Report. In addition, the Zambian Government paid officers on OSAS terms a variable inducement allowance, generally around five per cent of the OSAS salary. The British Government in turn provided a tax-free payment of approximately thirteen per cent of the combined OSAS salary and local inducement allowance.[10]

The formally localised Service introduced in 1961 contained four divisions. The first consisted of all officers with superscale, administrative and professional rank as well as other senior personnel earning more than £1200 per annum. Division II incorporated most technical, field and works officers and also those Africans who were serving in the two highest of the three scales in the African Senior Service.[11] In Division III were placed cadres in the lowest scale of the Senior Service – various low-skilled personnel such as co-operative and veterinary assistants, court interpreters and game scouts – and also district messengers. These latter apart, all members of the former African Junior Service were placed in Division IV.[12] With the new structure, as under the old, Europeans were predominant in the upper ranks while Africans monopolised posts in the lower. In October 1963, the racial composition of

Divisions I and II was as in Table 3.1.

Table 3.1

	Europeans	Africans	Others	Totals
Division I	1,256	39	3	1,298
Division II	2,692	1,882	11	4,585
Totals	3,948	1,921	14	5,883

Note
  Under 'others' came public servants from the Asian and Coloured (or mixed-race) communities. For a discussion of official policy concerning recruitment from these groups before independence, see Dresang, *The Zambia civil service, op. cit.*, pp. 28–30.

Source: Report of the Commission appointed to review the salaries and conditions of service of the Northern Rhodesia public and teaching services and of the Northern Rhodesia army and air force (The Hadow Report) (Lusaka, 1964), Part I, p. 14.

The foundation of a Zambian public service

The objectives that were to guide the new UNIP Government's programme for Zambianising the civil service required a difficult compromise among priorities. At the outset 'Zambianisation' was dealt with primarily as a matter of personnel management rather than institutional adaptation – indeed, given the scale of the problems faced here, the initial phase of restructuring which the inherited institutional framework underwent in 1968–69 was unexpectedly far-reaching. Of the four significant areas of institutional change – the decentralisation reforms affecting provincial and district administration, the creation of large 'umbrella' Ministries at the centre, the substantial expansion of the parastatal sector, and the first steps towards a degree of formal politicisation of the State apparatus – the effectiveness of the reforms made in the first three was to prove very sensitive to the manpower constraint.[13] Furthermore, Zambianisation was not simply a matter of replacing departing colonial officials but also of coping with rapid growth under the impact of the first two development plans and the unexpectedly sharp increases in public revenues.[14] Between 1963–64 and 1969 the service more than doubled in size – from 22,561 to 51,497 – at a time when severe shortages of experienced personnel made it difficult to maintain existing levels of operation, let alone assume new commitments.[15]

In addition, official statements on Zambianisation frequently predicated an urgency which threatened to conflict with the need to ensure that posts were localised on the basis of appropriate qualifications and experience. The former concern was understandable in view of the political necessity of being seen to respond forcefully to the feelings of racial deprivation which formed for many Zambians an essential ingredient of the colonial heritage. It was necessary also to assert the new State's political identity and economic independence, enhance its ability to promote broad-scale national development, and secure its integrity in a troubled Southern African context.[16] Yet none of these objectives might be meaningful if the State's effective capacity was undermined. As President Kaunda observed in a speech opening the First National Assembly:

I must say ... that while my Government intends to advance Zambian officers to high positions in the civil service – and recent promotions to senior administrative and professional posts are positive proof of our intention – we shall require of these officers and those who follow them the same high standards in the performance of their duties as were required of their predecessors. Advancement will continue to be dependent on qualification, ability and efficiency, and those who aspire to higher positions must acquire the knowledge and experience to enable them to discharge their responsibilities.[17]

Government leaders also recognised that localisation in the public services was necessarily linked with the formidable task of indigenising other economic sectors. At the beginning of 1966 there were still over thirty-four thousand non-Africans (and mostly non-Zambians) in a civilian labour force of 306,000 – 99.7 per cent of them holding jobs in skilled labour categories; among Africans, by contrast, 92.1 per cent were in jobs requiring primary education or less.[18] But if for private employers Government might be a source of pressure (or at least a pace setter) in the creation of job opportunities, it was also a potentially vigorous competitor for skilled manpower – what President Kaunda could term 'Zambia's scarcest resource'.[19] Ironically, this competition only began being keenly felt after the Government had carried through its far-reaching nationalisation programme between 1968 and 1970, and it was the public service, on balance, which suffered through the departure of middle- and senior-level personnel attracted by the higher emoluments available in the greatly expanded parastatal sector.[20]

There were yet other issues complicating the Government's Zambianisation strategy. One was whether the administrative apparatus should be used as a means of rewarding loyal party service, especially during the independence struggle. The Government was subject to intense pressure from the outset, both from grass roots UNIP cadres and from centrally-based politicians, and the needs of party patronage were to make significant inroads on official policy in this sphere. Admittedly it remains difficult to document the precise extent to which this may have been the case. Concern was certainly expressed over the degree of effective insulation which the personnel machinery could maintain against political and other types of intervention. One Cabinet Minister, Justin Chimba, warned of ministerial interference in the case of the Public Service Commission: '. . . I can frankly admit that Ministers do influence . . . appointments through their recommendations',[21] while the Mwanakatwe Commission observed 'that the selection machinery does not always operate with the objectivity for which it was designed'.[22]

Yet among the central Ministries, only one experienced any marked politicisation of its personnel – Foreign Affairs, and specifically the Foreign Service; here, though, patronage needs in themselves would represent only one (and potentially a secondary) factor influencing the political appointment of diplomatic staff. At local level, on the other hand, the evidence suggests that UNIP activists were recruited to the police, certain posts in the district administration, and parastatal bodies like the Zambia Youth Service (since 1971 the Zambia National Service) and the Credit Organisation of Zambia, before its demise in 1970. Local authorities, especially in rural areas, may have experienced particular difficulty in resisting such pressures, at least before the introduction in 1975 of a unified local government service with a Local Government Service Commission. On balance, it appears that positions at lower levels (Divisions III and IV in the civil service, and equivalent posts in local authorities and parastatal bodies) were most readily prone to conversion for patronage purposes.[23]

A second and related issue was whether any formal tests of political identification, either with the ruling party or with publicly proclaimed national goals, should be incorporated into the recruitment process. This concern was only crystallised by developments associated with the 1968 general election. Following UNIP's election reverse – for despite the 4 per cent swing in its favour nationally it failed to eliminate the opposition ANC and suffered the defection of much of the politically sensitive Western Province to ANC ranks – President Kaunda told a seminar of Ministers and senior civil servants that henceforth loyalty to the ruling party would be a prime criterion in all senior appointments within the service.[24] Possibly in anticipation of a UNIP election victory paving the way for the introduction of a one-party State 'through the ballot box', President Kaunda had invited permanent secretaries to the UNIP National Council meeting in November 1968; they were made formal members in March 1969, a significant change in the role allowed civil servants under Article 69 of the existing Standing Orders. As well as the open invitation which was issued after the election to all civil servants to join UNIP, local level officials who were suspected of ANC sympathies were threatened with dismissal and, reportedly in some instances, actually sacked.

Along with the appointment of a political head of the civil service – the new post of Secretary General to the Government, with Cabinet rank, was created in the 1969 administrative reforms – these steps helped weaken the political neutrality of the public service and damaged service morale:

Top civil servants can no longer be certain that they can count on a career in the civil service, while those below them wonder whether proved political loyalty will be a more important criterion for promotion than administrative or technical efficiency. In the circumstances it is not surprising that many civil servants have either resigned from the service to join private companies or have transferred to the parastatal sector.[25]

There was a question also as to the appropriate balancing of sectional interests under the embracing 'national' rubric of Zambianisation. The possibility of ongoing inter-racial friction over access to public employment had largely disappeared with the advent of the first African-controlled government in December 1962; early in 1964 the Hadow Commission could recommend that official recognition be given to the fact that localisation of the civil service was in practice becoming Africanisation.[26] With the political salience of racial cleavage receding, another basis for group competition quickly became manifest – that between the numerous ethnic communities of which the African populace was comprised. In national politics, ethnicity as a basis of group demands and conflict asserted itself with the formation of the first UNIP Cabinet in January 1964 and resurfaced at the bitterly disputed UNIP Central Committee elections of August 1967 – by which time concern had already crystallised in public forums over the role of 'tribalism' in civil service appointments.[27]

The subsequent escalation of factional conflict over the control of State resources continued with little apparent moderation under the Second 'one-party' Republic. The linkage of ethnic and regional interests with employment opportunities in the public sector frequently had an explicitness which could hardly fail to sensitise interpersonal relations within the service. This was the more so during a period when a weakening of institutional cohesion – due to opportunities for rapid upward mobility, with attendant fluidity of career patterns, problems of inexperience and inadequate training, and absence of long-standing familiarity among service colleagues – would tend to encourage such sensitisation even without external stimulus.[28] A survey undertaken among Zambian civil servants in mid-1968, not long after the divisive UNIP Central Committee elections, is suggestive here. Fully a quarter of the respondents claimed to have directly experienced mistreatment within the service because of their ethnic affiliation; asked whether appointments and promotions should be based wholly on merit or whether a deliberate effort should be made to maintain an ethnic balance within the service, some 45 per cent felt the latter to be essential in the Zambian context.[29]

At a practical level, the Zambianisation programme proceeded by several methods. With many established posts already vacant or expected to become so soon after independence, much localisation occurred simply by the identification of qualified Zambians willing to accept available positions (either by promotion or on direct entry to the service). Use was also made on occasion of a constitutional provision permitting the compulsory retirement of expatriate officials before expiry of their contracts.[30] A third technique – employed in Zambianising many senior posts – entailed the appointment of Zambians in a supernumerary role to understudy expatriates for a period before they were confirmed in their substantive posts.[31]

Though the civil service might represent a strategic pool of qualified manpower, employing in 1966 no less than half of all degree holders in Zambia, it was also among the most demanding of economic sectors in terms of its skilled manpower requirements.[32] And while Zambia's educational facilities were expanding at a sharply accelerated pace after independence,[33] it was not anticipated that even by 1980 Government's own manpower needs would be satisfied from local sources.[34] Furthermore, most positions in Divisions I and II required some degree of special training, particularly since, given the scale and pressing nature of public sector manpower demands, Zambianisation strategy could place little premium on experience.

A Staff Training College[35] for administrative and executive personnel was only established in 1963. Yet across the whole field of civil service operations an impressive variety of training centres was available at independence. The *Manpower Report* listed two hundred separate training schemes (of varying duration) as already functioning or due to come into operation before 1969.[36] Roughly one in ten involved purely on-the-job training, and two in ten entailed part or all of the training being done overseas; the rest were based on local training facilities. In 1965, over 2,700 officers completed the 95 courses actually available;[37] Jolly estimates that in 1966 perhaps fifty per cent of all civil servants in jobs requiring secondary education or above received some training, while by the end of 1969 the cumulative total output was expected to be over 23,000.[38]

It remains difficult to assess the actual impact of training schemes, either for the short or the longer term. Certainly at senior levels, both Zambian and expatriate officers had reservations about the effectiveness of the 'understudy' approach.[39] The *Manpower Report* itself expressed concern on several points: for example, that the selection procedures used for administrative and executive training courses tended to discount experience as against educational qualifications – hence narrowing the pool from which recruitment could occur – and also that the generally low level of basic education encountered among applicants at some levels meant considerable wastage from many programmes.[40] Another, and likewise serious problem of wastage arose from the difficulty of ensuring, given the general scarcity of qualified personnel throughout the economy, that training experience became applied in due course to the posts intended.[41] In addition, there was a question as to whether enough was being done to meet the training needs of the rural sector.[42]

In sheer numerical terms, the transformation which was effected in the composition of the civil service was remarkable. Whereas less than 20 African officers had occupied posts in Divisions I and II in 1956, there were some 4,500 Zambian citizens in these divisions by 1966, and over 14,500 by the beginning of 1976.[43] The rapidity with which the Zambianisation programme was carried forward is indicated in Table 3.2.

Yet Zambianisation also proceeded at markedly uneven rates, according to the qualifications and experience required to staff different levels and sectors of the public service; and many manpower categories which had not proved susceptible of rapid changeover in the initial phase of Zambianisation experienced only gradual localisation thereafter. Overall, while the level of Zambianisation for established posts in Division I and II had nearly doubled between 1965 and 1968, the following seven years brought much reduced change, even though there had been a sharp falling off in the expansion of the public service;[44] in early 1976 Zambianisation in Divisions I and II still only accounted for

Table 3.2: Zambianisation in Divisions I and II

Year	Establishment	Strength	Zambians	% estab. Zambian	% estab. posts filled
1965	9,652	5,873	2,462	25·5	60·8
1966	11,589	8,269	4,507	38·9	71·4
1967	15,226	9,958	6,556	43·1	65·4
1968	15,198	11,469	7,662	50·4	75·5

Note
The above figures do not include the police, the prison service, defence forces, or the teaching service.

Source: Public Service Commission, *Annual reports* for 1965 and 1966; *Establishment registers*, 1965–69; *Government Gazette*, 1964–68; and records maintained by the Establishment (now Personnel) Division.

approximately seven in ten of the established posts.[45]

When localisation as an aggregate process is broken down according to the various functional bands of which the two divisions are composed, the extent to which the creation of a national public service has been more readily carried forward at junior than at senior levels, and in administrative rather than in professional and technical grades, becomes at once apparent. In Table 3.3 these bands are ranked according to the degree of Zambianisation achieved by the end of 1975.[46]

Table 3.3: Zambianisation in Divisions I and II: by position

Category	Establishment (31 Dec. 1975)	% Estab. Zambian
Clerical & related	5,489	93·0
Administrative & executive	5,429	77·5
Secretarial	1,389	69·8
Technical	4,208	66·9
Superscale	1,235	41·4
Professional	1,322	14·4

Notes
Among the administrative bands, the hierarchy in salary terms would be (with some overlapping): superscale, administrative, executive, secretarial and clerical. Of the other two categories, the technical ranks below the professional.

The grouping of the administrative and executive grades by this table's source obscures the line of demarcation between Divisions I and II, but reflects a broad functional similarity in the positions involved. In other sources, the administrative grades are sometimes grouped with the superscale.

Source: *Zambianisation in the public service, op. cit.*, pp. vii–ix, xi–xiii.

From the outset the Government had placed considerable emphasis on the early localisation of strategic – and publicly visible – points of authority within the State apparatus. Though at independence none of the Ministries was headed by a Zambian permanent secretary, by 1968 only two of these posts had not been Zambianised; and only one of the district secretaryships. On the other hand, expatriate personnel were not only numerous in the superscale and professional grades but continued to occupy many key posts; in 1968 expatriate officers still headed over two-thirds of all departments and agencies – a figure which, if greatly diminished by the end of 1975, still stood at more than a third.[47]

Progress of localisation by ministerial sector underlines the achievements of Zambia's independence decade while making clear the severe constraints – a combination of persisting manpower shortages and the substantial growth in public sector establishments – which Government faced in pursuing its Zambianisation objectives. Indeed, technically it remained possible that in particular cases (the Ministry of Health provided an actual example) the Zambianisation level might even decrease significantly during this phase. At independence the degree of Zambianisation by Ministry had been markedly variable, though in no instance very high. As of 1965–66, according to the *Manpower Report*, the establishments of only two of the fourteen Ministries were over fifty per cent Zambianised – Foreign Affairs (61·3) and Health (55·0); on the other hand, there were three Ministries – Transport and Works, Commerce and Industry, and Education – where Zambian officers occupied one in six of the established posts, or less.[48] Initially, Government proceeded with Zambianisation neither on a broad front nor with special stress on development-oriented Ministries; rather those sectors relating to the new State's internal and external security received priority[49] – a set of concerns whose influence was still apparent in the mid-1970s, along with the expansive 'levelling-up' which had occurred in the case of most Ministries.

When judged according to ministerial sector, the expatriate presence by 1975 appeared largely of incidental character (apart from two Ministries and two of the specialist services). Yet some 57 per cent of the 1,958 non-Zambians still serving in Divisions I and II were employed at senior levels, where they represented 61·4 per cent of the combined strength of the superscale and professional grades.[50] Moreover, when the staffing figures for individual units – Ministry headquarters, departments and other types of agency – are examined, a significant clustering of such personnel is evident in a variety of bodies, and particularly those with a specialised technical

Table 3.4: Zambianisation by ministry and specialist service (1975)

Ministry/service	% estab. Zambian	% estab. Expatriate	% estab. vacant
Prison service	99.9	0.1	0
Provincial mins. (average)	96.2	2.1	1.7
Police service	94.0	3.5	2.5
Labour & social services	90.4	3.7	5.9
Commerce	90.0	7.5	2.5
Legal affairs	89.4	5.3	5.3
Home affairs	88.5	0.7	10.8
Teaching service	87.7	11.6	0.7
Information & broadcasting	86.4	3.3	10.3
Education	80.6	5.0	14.4
Lands, natural resources & tourism	80.5	8.1	11.4
Foreign affairs	80.3	1.8	17.9
Local govt. & housing	76.8	8.2	14.9
Rural development	70.9	10.4	18.7
Power, transport & works	68.4	11.3	20.3
Planning & finance	68.1	9.1	22.8
Medical service	58.7	6.5	34.8
Mines & industry	54.8	36.5	8.6
Health	35.7	30.1	34.2
Nursing service	26.8	29.2	44.0
Technical education service	26.5	40.7	32.8

Notes

The Police and Prison Services came under the Ministry of Home Affairs; the Teaching and Technical Education Services were under the Ministry of Education, and the Medical and Nursing Services under the Ministry of Health. For the purpose of this table, these services have been subtracted from the establishments of their parent Ministries.

The eight provincial Ministries are not given individual mention because of their identical structure and close similarity in manpower patterns.

The estimates which exist for Zambia's military establishment are insufficiently detailed to allow inclusion here. The General Post Office was converted into a parastatal corporation during 1975 and so was omitted from the data on which this table has been based.

On 1 December 1975, the Planning Office of the Ministry of Planning and Finance was reconstituted as the Ministry of Development Planning. Because the source used here did not take account of this change, it has been necessary in this and subsequent tables to treat these Ministries as still a single unit.

The 1965–66 figure for Zambianisation in the Health Ministry mentioned in the text included the medical and nursing services, here treated separately. The equivalent 1975 figure for Health would be 45.5 per cent, which is still considerably below the level of Zambianisation occurring in 1965–66.

Source: *Zambianisation in the public service, op. cit.*, pp. vii–xviii.

role. Altogether there were seventeen units where the expatriate presence was in excess of the combined superscale and professional average noted earlier; within this group, non-Zambian staff represented 84·3 per cent of actual strength in the two grades.

Table 3.5: Superscale and professional expatriate staffing in selected public agencies, 1975

Agency	Expat. % of superscale/prof. strength
Water affairs	100·0
Survey*	100·0
Geological survey	95·1
Mines safety	94·7
Roads branch	89·5
Indust. plantations project*	88·9
Buildings branch	87·1
Min. health hospitals	85·2
Veterinary & tsetse control	84·8
Judiciary (except local courts)*	83·3
Forest	82·6
Land use service section	82·4
Agric. research	81·5
Public health labs.*	77·8
Town & country planning*	69·2
Planning office	66·7
Min. health hdqtrs. & provincial hdqtrs.	63·2

Note
Of the seventeen units mentioned, ten were departments, one was a departmental section and one a development project; the other five were, strictly speaking, functional categories comprising more than one unit. To avoid inclusion of various small-scale units which might be of only secondary policy significance, a minimum establishment of ten superscale and/or professional posts was set. Those units with a star were of medium to small size, with establishments in these grades of less than twenty-five; the rest were of medium to large size, with establishments between thirty-one and 746.

Source: Zambianisation in the public service, op. cit, passim.

Ministerial organisation

Modern ministerial organisation has been a consequence of a complex of factors, of which the foremost have been the stage-by-stage accretion of governmental functions, the institutionalising of the executive's political accountability to local public opinion, and a colonial legacy which has left its clear imprint on Zambia's administrative system in terms of organisational format, nomenclature and operating style. The first institutions looking recognisably 'ministerial' appeared as recently as 1949, when two elected European members of the Legislative Council were granted portfolio status within the Executive Council (the colonial counterpart to today's Cabinet).[51] In view of the uncertain constitutional future of the then Northern Rhodesia Protectorate, this reform was only extended in 1959, when, following the territory's first experiment with multiracial elections, all six elected members in the Executive Council were given portfolios.[52]

In itself the introduction of such a mechanism for establishing political accountability had a major influence upon the nature of ministerial organisation. The requirement that a politically manned cabinet body retain a sufficiently intimate size to deliberate and take policy decisions precluded direct representation of individual government departments. Insofar as their grouping became necessary, the fact that Ministers were both responsible to a legislative majority and might be answerable to possibly shifting congeries of social and political 'interests' meant that the process by which grouping occurred would be governed not simply by considerations of administrative rationality or convenience but also by concern over the political management of linkages with these broader publics – a fact apparent with the creation of the first portfolios in 1949, as with those since independence. Moreover, the combination of previously separate departments into ministerial structures entailed the elaboration of the administrative apparatus for purposes of co-ordination and control – in turn providing an organisational nexus which facilitated the creation of yet further departments. Partly for these reasons, the growth of administrative positions – as opposed to those in professional/technical and secretarial/clerical grades – has been marked, from roughly 16 per cent of all established posts in Divisions I and II in 1953 to 27 per cent by 1976. Yet again the presence of political managers at the top of Ministries helped infuse a range of administrative relationships (from policy formulation to personnel management) with political ramifications, and undoubtedly widened the access permitted outside groups to both policy making and implementation.

Since independence the number of central Ministries has, save for one relatively brief period, varied within fairly narrow limits. At Cabinet level, central representation has fluctuated between fifteen and nineteen, including the Office of President and Prime Minister

(or, under the First Republic, of Vice-President), which have
frequently had significant portfolio responsibilities.[53] The creation of
eight provincial Ministries in the decentralisation reforms of
January 1969 was effected by cutting the central Ministries to nine –
seven of them large-scale 'umbrella' bodies – and swelling the
President's Office to considerable dimension. But these enlarged
units proved administratively cumbersome, and with intensified
factional strains within the ruling party adding to patronage
requirements, five of the seven umbrella Ministries had been broken
down into smaller units by late 1972, and the Cabinet size (with the
provincial Ministers) allowed to climb to twenty-five.[54]

Following the December 1978 elections a considerable pruning of
the Cabinet occurred. The post of provincial Minister was abolished
(though the Central Committee members assigned to each province
were retained). Accompanying this change, however, the number of
central Ministries was permitted some upward drift. Defence
matters were detached from the President's Office and placed under
a new Secretary of State for Defence and Security. Within the
Cabinet announced in January 1979, there were three Ministries of
far smaller scope than had characterised those in its predecessor –
Youth and Sport, National Guidance, and Tourism.[55]

Ministry size in the period since the experiment with the umbrella
agencies has exhibited vast disparity in organisational scale; at the
end of 1975 the range among central Ministries extended from the
relative giants like Education (over 21,000 personnel), Home Affairs
(over 12,000) and Health (over 8,000), to quite modestly
proportioned units like Commerce, Foreign Affairs, and Mines and
Industry (with two to three hundred each).[56] Counting Division I
and II personnel alone, the average establishment among the
fourteen central Ministries was 1,249; some ten were more than fifty
per cent above and below the mean.[57] The eight provincial
Ministries existing then[58] had an average establishment of eighty-
one, only that for Southern Province deviating significantly from the
mean. In terms of personnel structure, the contrasting patterns
among Ministries revealed by Table 3·6 overlay important
similarities which emerge when attention is focused on the key
superscale and professional grades, neither of which (when certain
exceptions are allowed for) had more than a marginal, if strategic
presence within the total establishments. For the superscale
category, eleven of the fifteen Ministries[59] allocated only 8 per cent
or less of their posts to this senior level; the average among these was
4·3 per cent.[60] For the professional posts, twelve of the fifteen had
under 8 per cent, with the average in fact as low as 2·3 per cent.[61]

Table 3.6: Personnel structure of central and provincial ministries, 1975 (%)

Ministry	Superscale +admin./exec.	Professional +technical	Clerical + secretarial
Foreign affairs	72·5	0·5	27·1
Planning & finance	70·5	1·7	27·7
Labour & social services	62·0	3·5	34·5
Home affairs	45·0	5·4	49·7
Commerce	42·5	9·6	48·0
Education	38·9	10·6	50·5
Local govt. & housing	38·2	26·0	35·8
Information & broadcasting	36·3	26·5	37·3
Provincial mins. (average)	34·2	1·2	64·5
Legal affairs	29·1	3·8	67·1
Mines & industry	28·4	51·3	20·3
Health	24·8	43·7	31·5
Rural development	19·0	61·5	19·5
Lands, natural resources & tourism	17·4	55·6	27·0
Power, transport & works	9·4	60·0	30·6

Note
Because of their close similarity in internal organisation, the eight provincial Ministries have been grouped as a single entry.

Source: *Zambianisation in the public service, op. cit.*, pp. vii–ix, xi–xiii.

The size and structure of ministerial establishments, however, may show little correlation with expenditure outlays – as is apparent, for example, when the levels of recurrent and capital funding announced in the January 1976 Budget are related to the establishments existing at the end of 1975. On a per capita manpower basis, many of the least sizeable Ministries proved vigorous competitors in the spending league table. The provincial Ministries, which are smaller than many central departments, received substantial capital allocations and registered, on average, the fourth highest level of budgeted expenditure – a situation noteworthy in view of their small size, the virtual absence of technical and professional staff at their disposal, and the typically minor nature of development projects initiated from this level.[62] Among the central Ministries, Foreign Affairs, with its costly overseas infrastructure, closely competed with Rural Development in overall spending per unit of staff, and actually did head the list for recurrent expenditure. On the other hand, large-scale Ministries like Education and Health, despite their own heavy infrastructural requirements, fell near the bottom; Home Affairs, with its responsibility *inter alia* for internal security, was at the bottom.

Table 3.7: Ministerial spending allocations per unit of skilled manpower (1976) (K)

Ministry	Budget allocation per established post		
	Total	Recurrent	Capital
Rural development	31,161	26,696	4,465
Foreign affairs	30,916	29,081	1,835
Local govt. & housing	28,981	20,914	8,067
Provincial ministries (average)	27,205	8,115	19,090
Power, transport, & works	23,329	8,880	14,449
Mines & industry	15,945	8,488	7,457
Planning & finance	10,295	9,902	393
Lands, nat. resources & tourism	9,065	8,144	921
Infor. & broadcasting	6,946	5,128	1,818
Labour & soc. services	6,270	5,881	389
Health	5,670	4,838	832
Commerce	5,197	5,197	–
Education	4,764	3,940	824
Legal affairs	3,566	3,566	–
Home affairs	2,842	2,534	308

Note
The establishment figures used here cover Divisions I and II, but omit Division III. The figures for the Ministries of Health, Education, and Home Affairs include the establishments of the various specialist services attached to these agencies; for details see Note to Table 3.4. The capital budget figures omit certain loan funds disbursed by central Ministries to local authorities and parastatal bodies.

Source: Estimates of revenue and expenditure (including capital, constitutional and statutory expenditure) for the year 1st January 1976 to 31st December 1976 (Lusaka, 1976), pp. 2–5, 207–8; and Zambianisation in the public service, op. cit., pp. vii–xviii.

If Zambia's administrative system since independence has been marked by reliance for reform upon strategies of piecemeal change – as opposed to comprehensive review and overhaul – its institutions have also been characterised by processes of piecemeal alteration which, *in toto*, have reshaped the ministerial landscape to significant degrees. One such process has already been alluded to – the growth in the administrative establishment since the early 1950s, and particularly since independence. The Mwanakatwe Report itself called attention to the steady expansion of the superscale sector – from 184 posts in 1962 to 573 by 1967, 865 by 1971, and 1,299 by 1975:[63] in effect, a growth rate per annum of seventy-eight posts in the period spanning the ending of Federation[64] and the phase of initial post-independence expansion, dropping to seventy-three posts at the next stage but accelerating to 108 posts annually after

1971. By way of contrast, the civil service as a whole increased by nearly 130 per cent between 1963–64 and 1969, but by under 13 per cent in the following six years. What applied in this sector was true of other administrative categories, relative to the professional and technical grades. If the personnel structure of Divisions I and II at the end of 1975 is compared with that obtaining at the time of the *Manpower Report* in 1966,[65] the differential levels of growth are pronounced: (in percentage terms) superscale, 191·9; clerical and secretarial, 180·7; administrative and executive, 162·3; professional, 132·7; and technical, 53·7.

Bearing on this first process of change was a second – the progressive elaboration of the administrative apparatus with the addition of specialised units having responsibility for specific policy tasks. Over the past twenty years this growth has been impressive, though most rapid around the time of independence. The ministerial system of government introduced in 1959 had been constructed of just nine Ministries, most having two departments, though the largest, Transport and Works, contained five. By early 1976 there were seventeen central Ministries, including the Offices of President and Prime Minister; the two latter in turn contained five divisions (units capable of subdivision into departmental agencies). At this stage there were nine provincial Ministries, and seven further commissions and special offices (five being service commissions covering the various branches of government service). At a lower level, and excluding the parastatal sector, there were over seventy departments and under these another thirty-one sections.[66] In addition, there were at least thirteen separate training institutes either partly or wholly devoted to the training of government personnel.[67]

Certainly initially, this proliferation of operating units occurred upon an insecure foundation of ministerial organisation. Existing ministerial units, which had been evolving since the early 1950s, had tended to remain amalgams of constituent departments – still the basic building blocks of ministerial structure – lacking in cohesion at Ministry level and with the departments retaining a significant degree of autonomy. Moreover, in the period preceding independence, the beginnings of substantial expansion of the administrative machine had coincided with the exodus of experienced European personnel, the first major efforts at Zambianising the two top divisions of the public services, and the successive 'settling in' of the UNIP–ANC coalition government after the December 1962 general election and of the UNIP 'independence' government following that in January 1964. This period also saw the return to territorial level of departments federalised during the ten year tenure of the Central African Federation and the integration of services (such as those in education and agriculture) which had been previously administered on a racially segregated basis; inevitably, considerable administrative disruption resulted.[68]

Yet the persisting tendency towards departmental autonomy since independence – and the underlying strain it has created towards administrative fragmentation – has had other roots, notably in the lack of continuity of senior ministerial personnel. At political level, the ministerial merry-go-round, which began in modest terms early in 1966 and on a more serious scale the following year, continued at a heady rate during the first five years of the new one-party system. Amidst the mounting economic and political problems which faced the Government after 1974, but also reflecting ongoing factional divisions inside the ruling party and a seemingly unrelenting drift towards embourgeoisement within the political class, the Cabinet experienced five major reshuffles as well as several minor changes, all between January 1975 and June 1978. Five Ministers were sacked (including a Prime Minister), another was suspended indefinitely, and a Foreign Minister was sent on 'study leave'. Altogether some fifty-one Cabinet-level posts changed hands, and if the reshuffle following the December 1978 elections is counted, the number rises to seventy.

At senior official level the periodic movement of key personnel in some agencies gave a distinctly migratory character to an otherwise sedentary occupation. To be sure, among permanent secretaries turnover was uneven. Between 1968 and 1976, eighteen to twenty-four months appeared a rough norm for tenure in positions at this level, and some officers experienced longer postings – twenty-two of more than seventy permanent secretaries serving then had held a post spanning three to four years.[69] Moreover, following the volatile 1968–71 period, greater stability was evident among top decision-makers. On the other hand, the changeover in these positions, overall, remained considerable. There were only nine permanent secretaries in 1976 who had occupied similar posts in 1971; only three had been permanent secretaries in 1969. Half the provincial Ministries had had five or more permanent secretaries in seven years, while at central level there were seven Ministries with six or more permanent secretaries in nine years.[70] The planning office, responsible for preparing and overseeing the implementation of Zambia's ambitious development programmes, had seven permanent secretaries between 1964 and 1970 – four of them in a single twelve month period during 1969–70[71] – and four more in the following six years. Nor were other examples lacking: among superscale Foreign Service officers working abroad, the rate of transfer on home assignments threatened to cancel out the practical benefits of government training schemes for diplomats.[72]

High levels of staff mobility were in fact a common phenomenon throughout the public service. In view of the continuing personnel shortage in many grades and the unevenly developed pool of trained manpower outside the service from which further recruits might be drawn, frequent movement through transfer or promotion was a matter of organisational imperative, and a problem not readily amenable of correction. The staff turnover at top levels initiated by presidential directive thus occurred in a context where concern over the consequences for efficiency and morale of staffing instability was already marked.[73] The President himself publicly acknowledged the problems in this regard: 'It is important that people get settled in their ministries so that they will learn the intricacies, the problems that are involved in their respective ministries. And so I want to say that I will really minimise the movement of Ministers and officials from now on'.[74]

That such a commitment has proved in practice impossible to sustain has resulted from various factors – evidence of incompetence or corruption, as the President has argued;[75] possible policy differences;[76] the need to administer remedial shake-ups in the face of serious economic slump since 1975 and in response to declining public confidence in the Government's performance;[77] and undoubtedly, the necessity of accommodating the fluctuating pressures of strategic provincial and other interests over senior appointments.[78]

Staff instability in turn exacerbated other problems traceable to the relative newness and untried character of the Zambian public service at independence and the formidable functional load it was required to assume thereafter – thus helping to ensure that what were largely initial 'teething troubles' remained prominent among shortcomings over a decade later. Frequent movement of senior personnel might broaden experience. However, it also inhibited the development of expertise and the effective working command of ministerial or departmental domains; in addition, senior administrators had difficulty in familiarising themselves with the external milieu by reference to which ministerial programmes had to be formulated and implemented. Politically, a Ministry's viewpoint at Cabinet level might perforce be muted. Administratively, chains of authority within Ministries were weakened and networks of organisational communication disrupted, thus encouraging the

tendency towards ministerial fragmentation noted earlier. Where
Cabinet reshuffles entailed the restructuring of Ministries,
considerable administrative costs were incurred in the shifting and
renumbering of files.[79] The resulting arrangements might force
individual departments to adapt to greatly altered and less
supportive organisational bases – as suggested by the odyssey of the
Department of Community Development, which during a five year
period was attached successively to the Ministries of Native Affairs
(before independence), Labour and Social Development, Mines and
Co-operatives, Youth, Co-operatives and Social Development, and
Rural Development. The turnover in senior administrators was an
added burden upon the machinery for inter-ministerial co-
ordination; the latter was a persisting weakness of the governmental
apparatus. It appears also to have lowered morale and promoted
insecurity among officials, and hence a proclivity to executive
indecision. Following the June 1978 Cabinet reshuffle, the *Times of
Zambia* could complain of 'people who will not take a decision on the
smallest matter until the President has been consulted and has given
permission', observing:

During the height of the shortages of essential commodities, it reached a
stage when [the] President asked if he was personally expected to supervise
the parastatal companies involved. It has been the same in the Party and its
Government, with people not making decisions because of insecurity in their
jobs, or out of sheer spinelessness.[80]

Ministerial operations were affected by yet other staffing
problems. The Ministry of Foreign Affairs – albeit an exceptional
instance – suffered from the absence of firm lines of authority; some
heads of foreign missions were themselves of permanent secretary
rank, while the presence of politically recruited personnel among the
diplomatic corps meant a disposition to look to State House rather
than Ministry headquarters for guidance.[81] In the case of some
agencies – with varying seriousness, the Departments of Community
Development and Social Welfare and the Ministry of Information
and Broadcasting were examples – a failure to develop satisfactory
grading and salary structures could impair commitment and agency
effectiveness, as the Mwanakatwe Commission noted.[82] There was
also evidence that while competition among Ministries over
available personnel might be less severe than at the time of the
Whelan Commission in 1966, the attendant pressures for the
upgrading of individual posts had become a regularised feature of
organisational behaviour.[83] Staff shortages remained a significant
constraint on performance, especially insofar as these had an impact

on key departments or categories of personnel. In the Ministry of Power, Transport and Works, for instance, the vacancies among established professional and technical positions in the Buildings Branch stood at 45 per cent in August 1974; among equivalent posts some 33 per cent were unfilled in the Roads Department and 27 per cent in the Mechanical Services Branch.[84] The effects of the earlier shortage of qualified accountants, which had contributed to a marked decline in financial control and cost consciousness at Ministry level, continued to be felt.[85] Though requests for supplementary funding fluctuated considerably (and reflected other pressures as well), there was only one year between 1970 and 1976 when they failed to make a substantial addition to the intended expenditure authorised by the annual budget – an ingredient in the persisting budgetary deficits of which the International Monetary Fund was critical in negotiating the tough stabilisation programme for the Zambian economy announced in March 1978.

Table 3.8: *Annual supplementary estimates as a share of total recurrent expenditure*

Year	Supplementary estimates (K)	% of total recurrent expenditure	% expenditure heads affected
1970	72,887,141	22.5	53.8
1971	21,985,218	5.4	35.7
1972	56,727,137	19.1	57.7
1973	39,429,983	11.1	37.2
1974	54,643,453	12.5	55.2
1975	111,957,078	21.7	43.1
1976	78,819,282	14.6	61.3

Note
The figures above include constitutional and statutory, as well as normal recurrent, expenditure. The constitutional and statutory heading, which formally covers payments for pensions, debt servicing, the salaries of offices stipulated by the Constitution, and certain other minor matters, has also included defence expenditure since Government ceased to make this public in 1970. Spending under this heading is not subject to parliamentary debate when the annual budget is presented for approval.

Source: *Annual Financial Reports*, 1970–76 (Lusaka).

Conclusion

The civil service, which since independence had been accorded a primary role in engineering the conditions leading to Zambia's eventual economic 'take-off' into self-sustained development, has itself been among the economy's leading growth sectors. It has maintained a rate of expansion far exceeding that for employment in the economy as a whole. During the period between 1963 and 1968, four new jobs were created in the public service for every one created elsewhere in the economy; even during the following six years, when public sector expansion declined considerably, the general slowdown of economic growth meant that this ratio remained at two-and-a-half to one. By 1975, as the Mwanakatwe Commission observed, the central civil service had overtaken the copper industry to represent the single largest labour force in Zambia.[86]

Against a background of wavering economic performance since the end of the First National Development Plan in 1970 and with a significant decrease in the surplus public revenues that could be devoted to developmental investment, the size of the service and the burdensome costs of maintaining it had become a matter of official concern even before the effects of the Western industrial recession struck the Zambian economy in 1975. The warning in the Mwanakatwe Report that expenditure on the personal emoluments of civil servants had trebled between the 1964–65 financial year and 1975 was technically true,[87] but was expressed in terms that were not wholly fair, for it was also the case that as a proportion of total recurrent spending, civil service salaries had actually dropped substantially over this same period – from 30.1 per cent to 19.5 per cent.[88] Of greater importance in this regard were the rising funds required by the defence establishment as the marked escalation of violence in the troubled Southern African arena since 1970 continued to threaten Zambia's borders.[89] In any case the Mwanakatwe Report recommended, along with appreciable salary increases, 'judicious pruning' of civil service manpower to curb 'an over-inflated recurrent budget'.[90] In the January 1977 Budget stringent guidelines regarding civil service recruitment were introduced, and have been maintained by successive Budgets in 1978 and 1979; no new posts were to be created unless they provided new services, and all vacant non-professional and non-technical positions were to be frozen.[91] In October 1977, in a major speech on Zambia's deepening economic crisis before an emergency session of the National Assembly, President Kaunda proposed the redirection of surplus public servants into commercial agriculture – a potentially radical proposal to which, however, the select committee appointed by the Assembly to formulate more specific recommendations for legislative action gave only guarded support.[92]

Concern has also arisen over the service's reduced efficiency and dependability. This has been caused in turn by the problems of indiscipline which, if unchecked, threatened to reach intractable proportions, by nagging difficulties over corruption and, not least, by organisational shortcomings arising from the failure to evolve an effective institutional framework (and procedures) to cope with the service's largely altered role after independence. Precise details that would permit the proper gauging of the nature and scale of any of the three problems are difficult to assemble. Certainly as to the first, the catalogue of weaknesses by which the service had become afflicted was considerable; the Secretary General to the Government and Cabinet Minister responsible for the civil service listed them as disobedience, drunkenness, laziness, lack of commitment to the public service, and irresponsibility.[93] Tracing a root cause of the problem, the Mwanakatwe Commission was moved to comment:

No one is more conscious of the need, as the Party Manifesto puts it, 'to strengthen the disciplinary machinery' than the senior public servant who is inhibited in the exercise of his supervising functions by the lack of any effective powers of discipline over his subordinates and who must often wait months for the determination of a single case. There is a general consensus ... that the process is overcentralised, too complicated and too remote ....[94]

Figures published by the Public Service Commission in the circumstances are suggestive rather than determinative of the general contours of this problem. They record, for example, details of the types of disciplinary action administered but not of the total cases referred to the Commission for review, and give no indication of the offences for which sanctions have been incurred; further, it seems likely, as the quotation above would imply, that misbehaviour meriting disciplinary action was not always brought to the Commission's attention. As Table 3.9 makes evident, instances in which the most serious sanction – dismissal from the service – were applied have not been unduly high, given the size of the service and its expansion during the 1969–75 period. Another tendency worth noting is that the preponderant share of disciplinary action has fallen to a narrow range of Ministries. Such evidence of contrasting ministerial practice in enforcing discipline suggests differing disciplinary problems, in turn deriving perhaps from divergent recruitment policies or a variable 'opportunity' factor for breaches of discipline stemming from the nature of a Ministry's operations.

Some shortcomings of the service might prove more receptive to remedial action than others. With evidence of mounting disciplinary problems, Government showed its concern by bringing in the

Table 3.9 Dismissals from the public service (1969–75)

Year	Number of dismissals	Ministries with three highest dismissal levels	% of total dismissals accounted for
1969	185	Power, trans. & works; Legal affairs; Rural development	56·8
1970	267	Power, trans. & works; Legal affairs; Presidential office	49·4
1971	198	Power, trans. & works; Judical; Prov. & local govt. & culture	52·5
1972	179	Power, trans. & works; Legal affairs; Rural development	52·5
1973	154	Power, trans. & works; Pres. office; Lands, nat. resources & tourism	57·8
1974	197	Power trans. & works; Provincial admin., national guidance & culture; Legal affairs	61·4
1975	141	Power, trans. & works; Provincial admin., national guidance & culture; Legal affairs	61·0

Note:
Ministries are listed in descending order of reported dismissals. Other types of disciplinary action for which figures are available – viz, reductions in rank and reprimands – have not been used in this table since the PSC's reports do not contain a complete record of disciplinary action taken; these powers were shared with permanent secretaries at Ministry level.

By way of comparison, the three Ministries having the highest dismissal levels in 1975 accounted for only a quarter of all Division I and II staff. Figures for Division III personnel, had they been available to the authors, would have been unlikely to alter this proportion radically.

Source: Annual reports of the Public Service Commission, 1969–75 (Lusaka).

Finance (Control and Management) Act in 1969 to enable losses of public funds or damage to public property to be recovered from the officers responsible, though this Act was slow to be implemented and in fact proved sometimes difficult to apply.[95] The Government also experimented with the delegation of limited disciplinary powers to permanent secretaries and department heads after 1968, but the Mwanakatwe Commission felt a far more radical delegation was necessary if sanctions against poor discipline were to become a meaningful deterrent.[96]

If what President Kaunda termed 'the cancer of indiscipline' appeared so resistant to curative measures, the virus of corruption might seem essentially ineradicable since the symptoms were so much more difficult to detect, and its overall dimensions impossible to discern. Apart from the Lusaka City Council,[97] only one public institution – and that of minor status – has been the subject of probing public inquiry over corruption.[98] The Public Service Commission has noted the increasing numbers of corruption cases referred to it for action,[99] but its published figures on disciplinary action do not separate the one category from the other. On occasion senior public servants have faced prosecution over corruption charges: in 1972 two former permanent secretaries in the Ministry of Home Affairs were convicted of marketing citizenship to Asian businessmen affected by the economic reforms which restricted business opportunities to Zambian citizens;[100] and in 1976 the Governor of the Bank of Zambia was charged with involvement in the case of receiving stolen goods.[101] But to judge by the record alone the heavier burden of prosecutions has fallen upon the ranks of relatively junior public officials. The recommendations of public service review commissions might close loopholes facilitating the abuse of public office for private advantage,[102] and the eventual recruitment of adequate numbers of trained accountants would by itself inhibit many forms of petty malfeasance which have proved otherwise difficult to control.[103] But with corruption in particular, corrective action must be selected with care; a containable level of corruption may well prove preferable to the administrative (or political) consequences of absolute cure.[104] For the sake of argument, the ambitious leadership code introduced in 1973 may be taken as a case in point.[105] It was designed to enforce a civic commitment upon Zambia's political and administrative establishment and to prevent those holding positions of public trust[106] from using them to acquire a simultaneous base in commerce or commercial agriculture. The possibility remains, however, that its effectiveness to this end may exacerbate the harmful results of other corrupt practices by forcing the capital thus illicitly created into luxury consumption or encouraging, through currency smuggling, its export abroad.

The question of administrative reform and of the suitability for the post-independence setting of an institutional framework inherited from the colonial period is no less complex. In fact substantial institutional change has occurred, notably in the case of the 'decentralisation' reforms of 1969,[107] though in other spheres as well. While at no stage has Zambia's administrative system as a whole been subjected to critical review, the obstacles to a wide-ranging overhaul are not inconsiderable, or so the experience of attempts at piecemeal reform would suggest. The introduction of a political head to the civil service in 1969 – in the form of the Secretary General to the Government – was never fully accepted, despite the fact that the first incumbent of this office had formerly been a civil servant, and the arrangement was abandoned with the introduction of the one-party State.[108] The 'decentralisation' experiment itself had mixed results, in part through the reluctance of central Ministries to accommodate themselves to the working requirements of the new system.[109] And although the efforts at institutionalising an effective planning machinery were badly disrupted by the Rhodesian UDI and the subsequent imposition of UN-sponsored economic sanctions upon that country, Zambia's chequered performance in the planning field has also resulted in no small measure from the difficulty of establishing a niche for a planning agency within the administrative apparatus that would prove acceptable to vested ministerial interests.[110]

Moreover, any comprehensive reform programme would necessarily require a complex blend of components whose precise relationship even under the existing structure could prove difficult to disentangle. While in general terms it was evident that a considerable shift in administrative role and style was entailed by the post-independence stress on industrialisation and rural growth, the appropriate balance to be sought between institutional reform and change in the calibre and skills of service personnel was less obvious. The colonial State itself was never confined simply to a law-and-order role; it serviced one of Africa's major mining industries and, in the post-war period, helped to underpin a prosperous commercial agriculture and an increasingly sophisticated urban sector. On the other hand, the successor elite which was to control the workings of the State apparatus was qualified to a marked degree by experience rather than academic preparation; it was thus substantially conditioned by the institutional practices to which its career development had had to conform. Those veteran African cadres forming the backbone of the new Zambian public service had previously had little access to roles in which a capacity for initiative and risk-taking, and indeed for administrative leadership, might be deemed important. Many had served as teachers or in routine executive or clerical posts, while those initial groups receiving promotion into Divisions I and II after the middle 1950s had mainly worked in departments providing services to the African community – agencies which were given scant opportunity to assume responsibility for major spending programmes.

In the immediate post-independence setting, conditions in fact did prove favourable to the emergence of a disposition towards bureaucratic entrepreneurialism, as one of the authors has argued elsewhere.[111] The slow start made towards Africanising the public service, the bias towards youth in its age structure, the marked inexperience of the new top administrators (and hence their limited socialisation to service mores), the opportunities for rapid promotion, and the relative looseness of ministerial organisation combined to provide considerable scope for enterprise and innovativeness, particularly at departmental level, as individual civil servants aspired to link the success of development programmes with their own career advancement. Other tendencies, however, worked against entrepreneurialism. Particularly in the early years after independence there was difficulty in matching training facilities with the backlog of demand – a problem with clear implications for the development of individual efficacy in senior decision-making roles.[112] A survey undertaken by the National Institute of Public Administration among top administrators attending its courses between 1968 and 1970 revealed that no fewer than forty per cent felt their training to be inadequate for their current positions; of the remainder, some half expressed doubts about their own administrative capabilities.[113] Moreover, for the initial generation of senior officials at least, education attainments on the whole were modest, suggesting a comparatively narrow range of skills which key personnel would have been able to bring into the service. Though by the early 1970s the majority of permanent secretaries in the central Ministries were university degree holders,[114] the top administrators passing through NIPA courses during 1968–70 included only a third with degrees. The evidence also indicated that degrees were far less common in that pool of upper echelon public servants from among whom top administrators would be recruited in the immediate future.[115] From the late 1960s, on the other hand, increasing numbers of university graduates were becoming available to the public service. While there was considerable competition with the parastatal sector for this manpower,[116] the prospects were for substantial, if gradual, processes of change during the 1970s in the character of the experience and qualifications displayed by top-level decision-makers. These change processes again underlined the close interconnection in the Zambian context between the issues of institutional reform and manpower development.

Notes

[1]   *Manpower report* (1966), *op. cit.*, pp. 1–2.
[2]   *Public Service Commission Report for 1965* (Lusaka, 1966).
[3] The European Civil Service contained administrative, professional and technical career streams, and its personnel were of mixed territorial origin. Provision was made for 'designated' and 'non-designated' officers; the former were recruited by the Colonial Office and were subject to transfer to other British dependencies, while the latter were appointed by the Northern Rhodesian Government. Around forty-five per cent of European officials had 'designated' status in 1963.

The African Service was divided in turn into a Junior and Senior Service. The former was composed of lower functionaries like clerks, guards and district messengers; the latter of more skilled cadres, wireless operators and adult education assistants, for example. While the Junior Service had no minimum educational requirements, the Senior Service possessed three salary bands defined according to educational qualifications. However, the vast majority of the Senior Service fell in the lowest band, requiring a Standard IV education; only a very small number (under 2 per cent in 1957) were in the highest band, requiring a Higher School Certificate. The latter, of course, represented a strategic pool for possible recruitment into the European Service under the 1955 reform.

For a more detailed discussion of the racial divisions of the Northern Rhodesia public service during this period and their practical consequences, see D. L. Dresang, *The Zambia civil service: entrepreneurialism and development administration* (Nairobi, 1975), pp. 27–32.

[4]   Cited in *A report on a preliminary examination of the salaries and grading structure of the Northern Rhodesia Civil Service (including the Northern Rhodesia Police)* (The Shone Report) (Lusaka, 1960), p. 29.

[5]   The 1955 reform was linked to the Legislative Council's passage the previous year of the famous 'Moffat Resolutions', which called, *inter alia*, for an eventual end to racial representation in the legislature and the eradication of racial barriers in employment. The ambivalence of the colonial administration on the question of African advancement in the public service was attested by the Shone Report in 1960. *Ibid.*, para. 118, cited in Dresang, *The Zambia civil service, op. cit.*, p. 39.

[6]   The relatively highly-educated group admitted to the intermediate grade in 1955 was subsequently depleted as the nationalist movement gathered momentum. Peter Matoka, Elijah Mudenda, John Mwanakatwe and Arthur Wina were all members of the UNIP Government at independence, and were to have significant public careers thereafter. Though immediately following the December 1978 election only Mudenda still retained public office – as a Central Committee member and nominated MP – these four had by then accumulated Cabinet service totalling approximately forty-four years.

[7]   Establishment Circular Minute No. TS1653 of 9 September 1959, Annexure, para. 3.

[8]   Secretariat Circular B1 (TS. 42/4) of 31 January 1962; the terms were given retrospective effect to 1 April 1961, and applied only to personnel in the 'designated' category (see n. 3, above). The Scheme's general conditions were already known to many European officials, and indeed the campaign by 'non-designated' officers to gain inclusion commenced in 1960, following the first announcement of the Scheme in the British Parliament. See Dresang, *The Zambia civil service, op. cit.*, pp. 42–43.

[9]   For details of the compensation features of OSAS, see Republic of Zambia, Establishment Circular No. B 166 (TS. 94315) of 6 January 1964.

[10]   The Scheme also provided for housing at 12·5 per cent of salary and allowances for leave, travel to and from Zambia, baggage, overseas boarding school education for an officer's children, and travel expenses for children to visit their parents during one school holiday each year. See Dresang, *The Zambia civil service, op. cit.*, p. 41.

[11] The division of the African Civil Service into a Senior and Junior Service is described at n. 3, above.

[12] Division IV was abolished by stages after 1966 and its personnel were absorbed into Division III.

[13] For detailed discussion, see *ibid.*, pp. 127–42; and Tordoff and Molteno, 'Government and administration' in Tordoff (ed.), *Politics in Zambia, op. cit.*, pp. 255–64. See also chs. 4 and 8 below. Prior to 1968, there had been no attempt to adjust structures at central level, apart from the rearrangement of Cabinet portfolios in three major and three minor reshuffles.

[14] See *An outline of the transitional development plan, op. cit.*; and *FNDP, op. cit.* Fuelled by rising copper prices and other factors, government revenues climbed from K63·7 million in 1963–64 to K275·5 million in 1967, reaching K432·4 million in 1970. *Statistical Year-Book, 1971* (Lusaka, 1973), p. 124.

[15] Thus while in 1975 the Mwanakatwe Commission was 'appalled at the continuing lack of real agricultural expertise at District level . . .', it noted the need after independence to replace professional with non-professional field officers 'in the interests of Zambianisation'. Mwanakatwe Report, *op. cit.*, p. 46.

[16] Nor was this latter problem of minor consequence in its manpower implications. Shortly after Rhodesia's UDI in November 1965 there were serious racial incidents in the border town of Livingstone which prompted a two-day strike by European railway workers stationed there and expressions of 'grave concern' by European miners on the Copperbelt. In July 1966, fifteen senior expatriate Special Branch officers were sacked for allegedly transmitting secrets to the Rhodesian Government; and the following year a Rhodesian spy-ring was uncovered. See *Zambia Police, Annual Report for the Year 1965* (Lusaka, 1966), pp. 3–4; and Tordoff and Molteno, 'Introduction', in Tordoff (ed.), *Politics in Zambia, op. cit.*, pp. 22, 25.

[17] *Nat. Ass. Deb.*, 12 January 1965, quoted in K. D. Kaunda, *Zambia: independence and beyond. The speeches of Kenneth Kaunda*, ed. C. Legum (London, 1966), p. 203.

[18] Only 4 per cent of the 3,649 degree holders in Zambia at this time were Africans and, since it was illegal before 1959 to admit Africans to apprenticeships, only a fifth of the craftsmen. The only economic sector effectively Zambianised at independence was subsistence agriculture. See *Manpower report* (1966), *op. cit.*, pp. 14–15. The tables in the *Manpower Report* do not allow exact determination of the proportion of non-Zambians employed by public authorities (either national or local), but this may be estimated at between 20 and 25 per cent.

[19] After independence a network of official committees evolved to monitor Zambianisation in both the public and private sectors. Richard Jolly notes that the committee dealing with civil service manpower had authority to vet intra-service transfers as well as control the number of Zambian school leavers whom the mines could recruit each year. The Government also sought to direct many university graduates into specified public employment – especially secondary school teaching – through the use of tied bursaries which obliged them to accept stipulated jobs for a given period of years. See R. Jolly, 'The skilled manpower constraint,' in Elliott (ed.), *Constraints on the economic development of Zambia, op. cit.*, p. 35, and Nkwabilo, 'Remarks on manpower and Zambianisation,' *op. cit.*, p. 5. See also Tordoff and Molteno, 'Government and administration,' *op. cit.*, p. 270.

[20] The Mwanakatwe Commission calculated that the value of the allowances and benefits received by a top parastatal executive might exceed his annual salary. Mwanakatwe Report, *op. cit.*, p. 138.

[21] See *Times of Zambia*, 24 November 1970, quoted in Szeftel, *Conflict . . . in Zambia, op. cit.*, pp. 302–3.

[22] The Commission said that it could not ignore complaints about the fairness of appointment and promotion procedures stemming from 'senior and objective sources'. Mwanakatwe Report, *op. cit.*, p. 15.

[23] For this section as a whole, see ch. 6, below; Tordoff (ed.), *Politics in Zambia, op.*

cit., pp. 116n., 183, 282, 368, 373; Szeftel, *Conflict . . . in Zambia, op. cit.*, chs. V–VI, *passim*; and B. V. Mtshali, 'The Zambia foreign service', *The African Review*, vol. 5, No. 3 (1975), pp. 303–16. Useful case materials are provided by the *Report of the Commission of Inquiry into the affairs of the Lusaka City Council* (Lusaka, 1969), pp. 27–32.

²⁴ *Africa Research Bulletin*, political, social and cultural Series, vol. 5, No. 12 (December 1968), p. 1266.

²⁵ Tordoff and Molteno, 'Government and administration', *op. cit.*, p. 272. See also *ibid.*, pp. 259, 262; and Dresang, *The Zambia civil service, op. cit.*, pp. 131, 137–9.

²⁶ A point which Kaunda, then Prime Minister, acknowledged in Parliament, while suggesting that this reflected short-term exigencies rather than a long-term aim. After independence, however, the phenomenon remained the same, the terms changing from Africanisation to Zambianisation. There was no influx of non-African Zambian citizens into the civil service and virtually all officers on local service conditions were African. See the Hadow Report, *op. cit.*, p. 16, and Kaunda, *Zambia: independence and beyond, op. cit.*, p. 103.

²⁷ See Mulford, *Zambia: The politics of independence, op. cit.*, pp. 329–30; Molteno, 'Cleavage and conflict in Zambian politics,' in Tordoff (ed.), *Politics in Zambia, op. cit.*, pp. 62–106; and the *National Convention on the Four-Year Development Plan*, Kitwe, 11–15 January 1967 (Lusaka, 1967), p. 26. Molteno's careful analysis disentangles the complex blend of ethnicity and regionalism which has given 'tribalism' its distinctive provincial idiom within Zambian politics.

²⁸ For illustrative materials making evident this process of linkage, see Szeftel, *Conflict . . . in Zambia, op. cit.*, pp. 303–94, *passim*; and Dresang, *The Zambia civil service, op. cit.*, pp. 61–2. What perhaps had changed with the Second Republic was the greater use made of the National Assembly as an arena within which to pursue such claims and the specific structure of adversary relationships, with the earlier preoccupation with 'Bemba dominance' giving way to concern over the share which Eastern Province now seemed to hold of senior public sector appointments. See, for example, *Nat. Ass. Deb.*, Hansard No. 35, 30 January 1974, cols. 690–2; and Hansard No. 38, 30 January 1975, cols. 551–2; and *Times of Zambia*, 2 December 1977.

²⁹ The survey was undertaken by the Zambia Localised Civil Servants' Association. Questionnaires were sent to a random sample of 195 Zambian public servants stationed outside Lusaka; 154 officers completed and returned their questionnaires. For further discussion of the survey's findings on these issues, see Dresang, *The Zambia civil service, op. cit.*, pp. 62–6.

³⁰ See the Zambia Independence Order 1964, s. 16; and the Constitution of Zambia Act (No. 27 of 1973), s. 17, as amended by the Constitution of Zambia (Amendment) Act (No. 18 of 1974). The original provision required six months' notice of termination of appointment plus allowance for any leave due; the amended version removes the latter entitlement and makes it somewhat simpler for the provision to be applied.

³¹ On 25 June 1964 the Government announced the names of 38 Zambians who were to understudy European civil servants in this manner. Zambian officers with supernumerary status received 60 per cent of the salaries paid to the expatriate officers. All 38 were already civil servants, and the posts involved ranged from permanent secretary to senior principal.

³² For details see Jolly, 'Skilled manpower constraint', *op. cit.*, p. 26.

³³ For example, total secondary school enrolment was still under 14,000 in 1964; four years later it was over 42,000. See *Zambian manpower* (Lusaka, 1969), pp. 5, 31; and *Manpower report* (1966), *op. cit.*, p. 2. See also *Zambia, 1964–1974, op. cit.*, pp. 31–5.

³⁴ Officially, Government's aim was self-sufficiency by 1980 as far as possible, and the closing of any remaining gaps not long thereafter. See *Manpower report* (1966), *op. cit.*, pp. 50–52; and Nkwabilo, 'Remarks on manpower', *op. cit.*, p. 5. See also *Zambian manpower, op. cit.*, pp. 38–41, 53–55; the calculations here indicate an expected shortfall in 1980 in the case of university graduates, in some sectors (e.g. engineering,

science teaching, 'administrators and managers') a quite significant one.

[35] Now known as the National Institute of Public Administration (NIPA).

[36] See *Manpower report* (1966), *op. cit.*, pp. 39–45, *passim*, and table F18, pp. 161–4. The schemes listed do not include any teacher training programmes and understate the number of short courses overseas on which civil servants were sent; the list does, on the other hand, include courses for local government and defence force personnel.

[37] In subsequent years, the proportion of listed courses scheduled to function was always above 77 per cent.

[38] See *ibid.*, p. 42; and Jolly, 'Skilled manpower constraint', *op. cit.*, p. 40. The actual output from NIPA alone during this period was 1,830; Dresang, *The Zambia civil service, op. cit.*, p. 48.

[39] This particular training technique appears to have been often uncongenial and little productive. See Dresang, *ibid.*, pp. 49–50.

[40] *Manpower report* (1966), *op. cit.*, pp. 44. The figures on course intakes and output provided in table F18 suggest that the wastage overall from programmes of nine months or less in 1965 was no more than 10 per cent, and probably rather less (since the estimate is based on a calculation maximising the possible loss); for individual courses, however, the apparent wastage was twice or even three times this average. See *ibid.*, pp. 161–4.

[41] See Jolly, 'Skilled manpower constraint', *op. cit.*, pp. 35, 53–4; and Mwanakatwe Report, *op. cit.*, p. 91, para. 10.91.

[42] *Manpower report* (1966), *op. cit.*, pp. 43–4. However, the rural sector training programme for the 1965–69 period was not insignificant: there were 35 separate schemes – roughly one in six of the total listed – with a planned output of over 5,600 personnel, or a quarter of all cadres who were expected to be trained.

[43] See *ibid.*, pp. 4, 6; and *Zambianisation in the public service: progress report, 1975, op. cit.*, pp. vii–ix, xi–xiii; the latter tables somewhat understate the total number of Zambian staff in these divisions through the omission of reference to a number of government agencies. See also *Zambian manpower, op. cit.*, p. 5; the figure given here of 19,000 Zambians employed in Divisions I and II in 1968 is inconsistent with other data, and should be treated with reservation.

[44] For the period 1965–68, the establishment for Divisions I and II grew on average by 1,849 posts per year, and for the period 1968–75, by 553 posts per year.

[45] *Zambianisation in the public service, op. cit.*, pp. vii–ix, xi–xiii.

[46] For the grading structure used by the Zambia public service see Dresang, *Zambia civil service, op. cit.*, pp. 175–6.

[47] See Dresang, *The Zambia civil service, op. cit.*, p. 45; and *Zambianisation in the public service, op. cit., passim*. The 1975 figure is based on fifty-five government departments headed by officials of superscale rank below the permanent secretary level but above that of assistant secretary (that is, in grades S2 to S5). If the field is enlarged to include all types of government agency with a director of this seniority (thereby adding to the list two development projects, nine training institutes, and five large-scale medical units), the percentage of agencies with expatriate heads rises to 42.

[48] See *Manpower report* (1966), *op. cit.*, p. 8, table 15; and p. 169, table G3.

[49] 'Some ministries are more highly Zambianised than others. Some – like Foreign Affairs, Police and Defence – have in the national interest had to be given priority . . . This has meant that other ministries have had to be held back in Zambianisation, and this will remain true until the number of qualified Zambians increases.' *Ibid.*, p. 6.

[50] The 'strength' of an agency (or grade) is the actual number of serving officers – i.e., the establishment less any vacancies which may exist.

[51] Mulford, *Zambia: the politics of independence, op. cit.*, pp. 10–13, 48. See also Gann, *A history of Northern Rhodesia, op. cit.*, p. 346; and Davidson, *The Northern Rhodesian legislative council, op. cit.*

[52] The six comprised four European and two African members; the Executive Council also included four officials. D. C. Mulford, *The Northern Rhodesia general*

election, 1962 (Nairobi, 1964), pp. 14–15.

⁵³ The Office of the President at one stage during 1967 contained no less than seven divisions of sufficient importance to require each being headed by a permanent secretary.

⁵⁴ See Tordoff and Molteno, 'Government and administration', *op. cit.*, pp. 258–9, 263–4.

⁵⁵ See *Africa Research Bulletin*, political . . . series, vol. 15, No. 9 (September 1978), pp. 4986–7; *Times of Zambia*, 19 December 1978; and *Zambia Newsletter* (London), 4 January 1979.

⁵⁶ The figures for Education, Home Affairs and Health here include the establishments for the various specialist services – respectively, Teaching and Technical Education, Police and Prisons, and Medical and Nursing. The totals remain, however, incomplete, as their source does not include data on Division III staff. See *Zambianisation in the public service, op. cit.*, pp. vii–xviii.

⁵⁷ For the discussion here, the Offices of the President and Prime Minister have been omitted. The former, including the civil service complement within the defence establishment and the Mechanical Services Branch, was not covered by the 1975 Zambianisation survey. The latter has been left out since numerically its major component, the Provincial Administration, provides the cadres staffing the provincial Ministries, which require separate mention.

⁵⁸ Their number was increased to nine in February 1976, with the creation of Lusaka Province.

⁵⁹ As in Table 3.4, the provincial Ministries are given a single 'entry' here in view of the essentially identical nature of their personnel structure.

⁶⁰ Superscale posts as a percentage of total establishment in the exceptional cases were: Foreign Affairs, 25.7; Mines and Industry, 16.2; Health, 14.7; and the provincial Ministries, 13.8. In the first instance, the status occupied by diplomatic personnel was a major contributing factor; but in this case, as in the fourth, the figure was boosted artificially by the dearth of professional and technical posts in the ministerial establishment. In the other two cases, the relatively high proportion of superscale posts is traceable to the number of professional personnel in the superscale grades – for reasons which are specific to these two Ministries.

⁶¹ The percentage for some eight Ministries was either at or under this figure: Commerce, 2.5; Finance, 1.5; Labour and Social Services, 1.5; Education, 1.1; Foreign Affairs 0.5; Home Affairs, 0.3; Information and Broadcasting, 0.3; and the provincial Ministries, 0. The exceptional 'cases for the professional category were: Health, 29.7; Mines and Industry, 28.4; and Rural Development, 11.9.

⁶² See ch. 8, pp. 190–2, below. At this time, the technical staff for each provincial Ministry comprised a single driver; there were no professional staff.

⁶³ Mwanakatwe Report, *op. cit.*, p. 13; see also *Zambianisation in the public service, op. cit.*, p. vii. The 1975 figure given by the Mwanakatwe Report is some sixty-four posts greater than that provided by the Zambianisation report (and used earlier, in Table 3.3), presumably reflecting the establishment in the Office of the President, which the latter report omitted from its calculations.

⁶⁴ The formal break-up of the Central African Federation in December 1963 involved the handover of sections of a number of formerly federal departments.

⁶⁵ See *Manpower report* (1966), *op. cit.*, p. 7; the establishment figures used here were those for the end of April 1966.

⁶⁶ There has been over time a certain amount of interchange of units between section and departmental levels; likewise certain agencies – the Planning Office, National Guidance, and the Zambia National Tourist Bureau — have served as both Ministries and departments, the first two having shifted more than once.

⁶⁷ There were also twenty-five diplomatic missions abroad; some fifteen general and special hospitals plus the Flying Doctor Service under the Ministry of Health; and various teacher training and technical training institutions under the Ministry of

Education – to include only those units of sufficiently large scale or sufficient administrative status to merit superscale staff in their establishments.

68 Tordoff and Molteno, 'Government and administration', *op. cit.*, p. 243.

69 The nature of our source here – the annual *Financial reports* – makes precise calculation difficult. With one possible exception, no individual appears in the same post for more than four *Reports* in succession. Because no separate figures for defence expenditure have been published since 1969, this sector has been omitted from consideration. Though the provincial Ministries were established in 1969, they were only first given individual mention in the 1970 *Financial report*.

70 The provinces in question were Eastern, Northern, North-western and Western. The central Ministries were divisible into two groups: those like Home Affairs, Education and Foreign Affairs, which had experienced basic organisational continuity despite the frequent transfer of permanent secretaries; and those like Mines, Trade and Industry, Labour and Social Services, and Lands and Natural Resources, which had also been prone to periodic transfer of constituent departments.

71 Tordoff and Molteno, 'Government and administration', *op. cit.*, pp. 265n., 278.

72 See Mtshali, 'The Zambia foreign service', *op. cit.*, pp. 308–9; and Mwanakatwe Report, *op. cit.*, pp. 40–1.

73 See, for example, *Report of the Commission appointed to review the grading structure of the civil service; the salary scales of the civil service, the teaching service, the Zambia police and the prisons service; and salary scales and wages of non-civil service (industrial) employees of the government; and the pay scales and conditions of service of the Zambia defence forces* (The Whelan Report) (Lusaka, 1966), p. 3; O'Riordan Report, *op. cit.*, pp. 15, 19–20; *Report of the National Commission* (1972), *op. cit.*, p. 29; Simmance Report, *op. cit.*, pp. 35–6, 51; and Mwanakatwe Report, *op. cit.*, pp. 16–17.

74 ZIS background paper No. 77/69, 1 November 1969, quoted in Tordoff and Molteno, 'Government and administration', *op. cit.*, p. 264.

75 *Financial Times*, 15 December 1977.

76 Attention to the sharpening policy and ideological divisions in Zambian politics under the Second Republic has focused on the relations between the executive and the National Assembly. Apart from suggestive comment in some news reports, reference to intra-governmental policy divisions has been lacking – though the evidence available would indicate a relatively minor role for these in explaining the movement of senior personnel, whether administrative or political.

77 Notably with Elijah Mudenda's dismissal as Prime Minister in July 1977 and the sacking of three senior Ministers for alleged corruption and abuse of power in April and August the same year. Executive agencies coming under critical fire included the army – in April 1977 President Kaunda dismissed the officer in charge of the Mechanical Services Branch, the department which the army had been assigned to administer and 'clean up' in November 1974. See *Africa Research Bulletin*, political . . . series, vol. 12, No. 12 (December 1975); p. 3853; and *Times of Zambia*, 25 April 1977.

78 As Mtshali's study of the Foreign Service suggests, these pressures could have considerable weight as the President 'tries to satisfy various interest groups – such as party stalwarts, the trade unionists and regional elements – all of whom compete for [senior] posts.' The constant shifting of the top three officials in Zambia's diplomatic missions indicates that 'no high post abroad is the preserve of any particular interest group'. Mtshali, 'The Zambia foreign service,' *op. cit.*, p. 309.

79 Tordoff and Molteno point out further the complications for the control of expenditure which were caused by frequent governmental reorganisations. See 'Government and administration', *op. cit.*, p. 265.

80 *Times of Zambia*, 17 June 1978, quoted in *Africa Research Bulletin*, political . . . series, vol. 15, No. 6 (June 1978), p. 4881.

81 Mwanakatwe Report, *op. cit.*, pp. 40–1, 44.

82 *Ibid.*, pp. 50–1, 56.

83 Whelan Report, *op. cit.*, p. 3; and Mwanakatwe Report, *op. cit.*, pp. 35, 55. See also Jolly, 'Skilled manpower constraint', *op. cit.*, pp. 35, 53–4.

84 Mwanakatwe Report, *op. cit.*, pp. 13–14.

85 Tordoff and Molteno, 'Government and administration', *op. cit.*, p. 266.

86 Mwanakatwe Report, *op. cit.*, p. 18.

87 *Ibid.*, p. 13.

88 These figures, of course, refer to salaries and allowances alone, and do not include the many indirect costs of the civil service which appear under the 'recurrent departmental charges' heads. The figures also do not include the wages of daily-paid workers, which in recent years have added roughly four per cent to the total cost of emoluments.

89 Zambia's army has thus increased from a complement of 4,083 in 1966–67 to one of 12,800 in 1978–79 (according to estimates provided by the London-based International Institute for Strategic Studies); in the same period, the air force has grown from 355 to some 1,500 personnel. The armaments with which the military are equipped have also been greatly strengthened. Total outlays for the Constitutional and Statutory Expenditure head – under which the Government has included defence spending since deciding to cease making these figures public in 1970 – increased from K22.9 million in 1964–65, to K56.9 million in 1969 and K236.3 million in 1976; budgeted expenditure reached K321.6 million in 1979. In proportional terms, 'constitutional and statutory' expenditure rose from 18.8 per cent of actual recurrent expenditure in 1969 to 44.3 per cent of budgeted recurrent expenditure in 1979. Note should be taken that such comparisons with recurrent expenditure, while obeying budgetary convention, are here somewhat misleading: the incorporation of defence spending under this head since 1970 has entailed the annual inclusion of a capital expenditure element. Also complicating an assessment of the impact of defence spending on the recurrent budget is the fact that pension expenditure was removed from constitutional and statutory expenditure to another spending head in 1975; on the other hand, debt servicing payments, which have risen sharply over this period, remain in this category. For further details regarding constitutional and statutory expenditure, see the explanatory note following Table 3.8, p. 89, above.

90 Mwanakatwe Report, *op. cit.*, p. 14.

91 *Times of Zambia*, 29 January 1977. Other measures promised were the temporary suspension of the payment of cash in lieu of leave for civil servants; the reduction of staff in overseas missions; and a cutback in trips abroad on official business.

92 See *Zambia Newsletter* (London), 1 December 1977, pp. 11–12; and *Sunday Times of Zambia*, 4 December 1977. The parliamentary select committee noted that no figures revealing precise levels of overmanning in either the civil service or parastatal sectors had been made available, but recommended that any such redeployment of manpower should be voluntary – a condition it did not find necessary in the case of the urban unemployed – and with full retirement benefits. The infrastructural requirements and back-up services which the committee thought essential to assist redirected civil servants establish themselves in farming would have made this programme exceedingly costly to implement.

93 *Times of Zambia*, 4 March 1971, cited in Tordoff and Molteno, 'Government and administration', *op. cit.*, p. 266.

94 Mwanakatwe Report, *op. cit.*, p. 15.

95 Tordoff and Molteno, 'Government and administration', *op. cit.*, p. 266, and Mwanakatwe Report, *op. cit.*, pp. 90–1.

96 The Government accepted the Commission's recommendations, but details of their implementation have not been available to the authors. See Mwanakatwe Report, *op. cit.*, pp. 88–90; *Summary of the main recommendations of the Commission of Inquiry* (1975), *op. cit.*, p. 18; and Dresang, *The Zambia civil service, op. cit.*, pp. 126–7.

97 *Report of the Commission of Inquiry into the affairs of the Lusaka City Council, op. cit.*

98 Viz., the Central and Southern provincial operations of the African Farming

Improvement Fund. A number of civil servants were among the accused, though it was the role played by several senior political figures which commanded primary attention. See the *Report of the Commission of Inquiry into the allegations made by Mr Justin Chimba and Mr John Chisata* (Lusaka, 1971).

[99] See Public Service Commission, *Annual reports* for 1971 and 1973 (Lusaka).

[100] This and the African Farming Improvement Fund scandal are discussed in Szeftel, *Conflict . . . in Zambia, op. cit.*, pp. 273–81, 295–6.

[101] See *Times of Zambia*, 4 May 1976.

[102] Mwanakatwe Report, *op. cit.*, pp. 102, 103.

[103] See, for example, the *Reports of the auditor general* (Lusaka): 1968, p. 13; 1971, p. 13; 1972, pp. 25–6, 35; 1973, pp. 21, 22.

[104] The tightening of controls over ministerial spending, for instance, might prove yet a further source of delay in the release of funds for development projects.

[105] See Statutory Instrument No. 288 of 1973, and its successor, Statutory Instrument No. 108 of 1974.

[106] These were defined in broad terms as 'all persons in the service of' the ruling party, the Government, all local authorities, any parastatal body (including institutions of higher learning) in which the State has a majority or controlling interest, and any public commission. Anyone employed by a registered trade union or the Zambia Congress of Trade Unions at an annual salary of K2,500 or more was also affected.

[107] See ch. 8, below.

[108] The re-introduction of a senior civil servant as head of the public service was recommended by both the O'Riordan Commission in 1971 and the Chona Commission in 1972; in the second case the Government accepted the recommendation. See O'Riordan Report, *op. cit.*, p. 1; *Report of the national commission* (1972), *op. cit.*, p. 29; and *Report of the national commission . . . summary of recommendations accepted by government* (1972), *op. cit.*, pp. 14–15.

[109] See, for example, Simmance Report, *op. cit.*, pp. 27–8.

[110] Tordoff and Molteno, 'Government and administration', *op. cit.*, pp. 260, 275 and n., 276, 278–80.

[111] See Dresang, *The Zambia civil service, op. cit.*, pp. 146–60; and 'Ethnic politics, representative bureaucracy and development administration: the Zambian case', *American Political Science Review*, vol. LXVIII, No. 4 (December 1974), pp. 1605–17.

[112] The shortage of training facilities remained in the mid-1970s, though its effects were most apparent at middle and lower levels of the service. See Mwanakatwe Report, *op. cit.*, p. 16.

[113] I. Mackinson, *The development of senior administrators in Zambia* (Lusaka, n.d.), pp. 38–9. In the context of the NIPA courses, 'top administrators' comprised permanent and under secretaries, department heads, and chief executives and deputy chief executives of parastatal bodies. See *ibid.*, pp. 5–6.

[114] J. Momba and R. Nglazi, 'Permanent secretaries – a study of those serving in 1972', in R. V. Molteno (compiler), *Studies in Zambian government and administration* (Lusaka, 1973, mimeo.), pp. 38–9.

[115] Mackinson, *The development of senior administrators, op. cit.*, pp. 17–22; see also V. Subramaniam, 'The social background of Zambia's higher civil servants and undergraduates', paper presented to the University of East Africa Social Science Conference, Nairobi, December 1969.

[116] See Mwanakatwe Report, *op. cit.*, p. 134; and Directorate of Civil Service Training, *A record of Zambian graduates in government service, the private sector and quasi-government institutions* (Lusaka, 1974). Following the report of the O'Riordan Commission in 1971, there was a short-lived attempt to create a separate administrative stream at superscale level for university degree-holders. See O'Riordan Report, *op. cit.*, p. 2, and Mwanakatwe Report, *op. cit.*, p. 26.

4. The parastatal sector

Sheridan Johns

In Zambia's drive for economic transformation a major vehicle has been the parastatal agency, the quasi-autonomous governmental body outside the regular civil service structure and generally with wide latitude to conduct its own internal operations. An official Zambian study has identified three types of parastatal agency: the 'commercial' type which is incorporated like any other private company under the Companies Ordinance to pursue a commercial undertaking; the 'semi-commercial' type created by legislative statute to provide a public service on a businesslike basis; and the 'non-commercial' type, also established by legislative statute to carry out various public functions, although not necessarily with the expectation of regular economic viability.[1]

In the past fifteen years parastatal bodies of all three types have been prominent in all segments of the Zambian economy and polity. During the first six years of independence both inherited and new parastatal bodies were utilised to provide a wide range of new services to Zambia's hitherto neglected African majority, to reorient key transportation links from minority-ruled southern Africa, and to take majority ownership in the largest commercial, industrial, and mining establishments in the country, including those dominating the all-important copper industry.[2] Subsequently, the resulting jerry-built structure has been the object of increasing attention and experimentation as the country's leadership has struggled to define further the role which these now powerful bodies should play in a society to be restructured within the matrix of an evolving ideology of Humanism.

The following analysis is intended to present in broad outline the nature of the major changes which have taken place in the parastatal sector in the fourteen years since independence. The emphasis is upon identification and interpretation of the most important trends, rather than detailed description of the evolution of specific parastatal bodies. Discussion is focused upon the changing functions of parastatal bodies, the impact of efforts to reorganise the parastatal structure in line with both constant and changing priorities, and the concern upon the part of many Zambians, including President Kaunda, that parastatals do not become a device by which new privilege is entrenched at the expense of the majority of the Zambian population.

At the time of independence the main parastatal bodies inherited from the colonial regime and the recently defunct Central African Federation were 'semi-commercial' and 'non-commercial' statutory bodies created by legislative acts rather than 'commercial' state-owned corporations. Many of these bodies continued to perform functions which they had carried out previously (for example, maize marketing by the Grain Marketing Board, cattle marketing by the Cold Storage Board, milk marketing by the Dairy Produce Board), but they also moved to extend their services both to emergent Zambian farmers in the rural areas and to undertake new activities along the line of rail, particularly in supplying dairy products and meat to urban dwellers. More salient and contentious were the activities of two new statutory bodies, the Credit Organisation of Zambia (COZ) and the Zambia Youth Service (ZYS). COZ, a 'semi-commercial' parastatal body, was created explicitly to give loans to both established and prospective African farmers. From its inception it operated with large budgets as one of the main agencies pumping money toward the rural sector and thus became a focus of attention for those jockeying for the monetary fruits of independence. Curiously, however, the agriculturally important Southern Province, dominated by the opposition African National Congress (ANC), was a principal beneficiary of the COZ programme, suggesting that the latter amounted to something more than mere political patronage for supporters of UNIP, the government party, and that perhaps agricultural considerations were sometimes taken into account. ZYS, a 'non-commercial' parastatal agency, was designed initially to train unskilled and unemployed urban youth who had been one of the mainstays of UNIP. Yet it quickly became a centre of controversy in its distribution of scarce job and training opportunities and its moves towards paramilitary status. COZ and ZYS, perhaps more than any other parastatal bodies in the first years after independence, were symbolic of the determination of the UNIP Government to use not only established government ministries, but also parastatal bodies, to reorient the priorities and services of the State towards the central demands of the African electorate which had placed it in power.

Parastatal bodies, however, were also called into service to manage the accelerated disengagement from the white south set in motion by Rhodesia's unilateral declaration of independence in November 1965. Hastily Zambia moved to break up Rhodesia Railways, which had been a parastatal agency jointly owned with Rhodesia. It set up its own independent body, Zambia Railways, under most inauspicious conditions in which much of the best equipment was kept south of the border and key white Rhodesian operating employees were hurriedly replaced by Zambians previously denied skilled training or by a polyglot group recruited upon short notice from outside the country. With similar haste a national airline, Zambia Airways, was established with the dissolution of Central African Airways (in which Malawi also had been a minority participant). The Italian State airline, Alitalia, was given the initial contract to manage and operate the new 'commercial' statutory body which took over existing domestic services and was then expanded to regional and intercontinental services. Even more crucial to Zambia's existence once she was cut off from oil supplies through Rhodesia by her acceptance of sanctions imposed against the UDI rebel regime, were new companies created under joint Zambian–Tanzanian auspices, with the participation of Italian State and private capital, to bring in vital supplies more than 1,000 miles overland from the north-east through the port of Dar es Salaam. Thus, Tanzania Zambia Road Services, owned 35 per cent by Zambia, quickly grew into a major hauler of petroleum, imported goods and machinery, and copper for export, while Tazama Pipelines, owned 67 per cent by Zambia, engaged an Italian State firm which constructed in a record eighteen months a pipeline from Dar es Salaam to the Zambian Copperbelt enabling Zambia by 1969 to pump almost all her petroleum needs into the country. In this fashion parastatal bodies became even more important in the transport sector.

Zambia's major 'commercial' State corporation at independence was the Industrial Development Corporation (INDECO), set up in 1960 and reorganised shortly before independence as an investment corporation to stimulate foreign investment in Zambia. In 1965, with the selection of Andrew Sardanis, a Zambian citizen, as chairman, INDECO undertook a number of major new industrial activities in partnership with foreign capital. The projects included chemical, explosives, and tyre factories, as well as new large hotels. INDECO increasingly came to the fore as the central agency in Zambia's efforts to expand rapidly her industrial base either in areas where private capital had previously not invested or in areas of strategic importance where foreign capital was neither forthcoming nor sought.

In April 1968 President Kaunda announced Mulungushi reforms, under which twenty-six large industrial and commercial firms, concentrated in building supplies, wholesale and retail trade, beer brewing, and transportation, were invited to sell 51 per cent of their shares to the Zambian Government. INDECO was given vast new responsibilities, not only to negotiate for the acquisition of the majority shares of the designated new partners, but also to direct and oversee their operations along with those of the enterprises in which INDECO was already engaged. Thus, almost overnight, INDECO became a vast industrial corporate giant responsible for both new major enterprises which it had initiated in line with government priorities, as well as established firms which dominated selected key sectors of production and distribution.

When President Kaunda in August 1969 declared Zambia's intention of taking 51 per cent ownership of the two copper-mining giants, Anglo-American Corporation and Roan Selection Trust, and subsequently in November 1970 when President Kaunda proclaimed that Zambia would take over all insurance activities as well as majority ownership in the established banks, the INDECO model provided the blueprint for the organisational arrangements devised to implement the decisions. For the mining sector a new parastatal body, the Mining Development Corporation (MINDECO), was created. For the financial sector, from which Zambia's three largest banks were subsequently excluded in 1971 when Government reversed its decision to take majority interest in them, another new parastatal body, the State Financial and Development Corporation (FINDECO), was set up. INDECO, MINDECO, and FINDECO were then in turn made subsidiaries of an all-embracing conglomerate, the Zambia Industrial and Mining Corporation (ZIMCO), which itself was placed under the supervision of a new Ministry of State Participation. In this fashion, Zambia quickly acquired vast new industrial, mining and financial enterprises, most of which were run in co-operation with foreign partners; they were placed within a gigantic corporate entity, one of Africa's largest, which dominated the commanding heights of the Zambian economy.[3]

Although the spectacular growth of the 'commercial' parastatal giants INDECO, MINDECO and FINDECO, symbolising Zambia's determination to gain formal control of her own economy, captured the most frequent and biggest headlines, there were also significant developments in the established 'semi-commercial' and 'non-commercial' statutory bodies and smaller state corporations. In moves of reorganisation which seemed to suggest a desire to create more rationalised structures, local and regional electricity corporations and boards were amalgamated in 1969 into one national State corporation, Zambia Electricity Supply Corporation (ZESCO). In analogous fashion in the same year the Grain Marketing Board and the Agricultural Rural Marketing Board (established after independence to provide marketing services to areas off the line of rail), were combined into a new statutory body, the National Agricultural Marketing Board (NAMBOARD). The reorganisation of the agricultural marketing parastatal agency was also accompanied by new efforts to improve its services in rural areas, and by the creation of a new Rural Development Corporation, seemingly on the INDECO model, to further production in rural areas. In a related move the foundering COZ, which had dispensed millions of kwacha in loans, but had received a negligible percentage in repayment, was legislated out of existence as a statutory body.[4] Its functions were turned over to a new Agricultural Finance Company, which was made a subsidiary of the Rural Development Corporation. Zambia's other controversial parastatal agency, ZYS, also was drastically reorganised after it was placed under the newly-created Ministry of Defence in January 1971: it ceased to be a parastatal body and henceforth, as the Zambia National Service, has been directly under the Ministry of Defence. Elsewhere within the parastatal sector, and not always with full success, efforts were being made to improve efficiency and rationalise operations. Simultaneously, Zambianisation was being accelerated to the point where for the first time since independence indigenous Zambians were replacing expatriates as managing directors, although key technical and administrative posts still remained largely in foreign hands.

By the end of 1970 the profile of Zambia's parastatal sector was pronouncedly different from that visible at the time of independence. Although with uneven results, most of the parastatal bodies in existence at the time of independence were in the process of successfully being reoriented towards the new developmental priorities established by the UNIP Government. New bodies, including ones shared with the Tanzanian Government, were grappling with the consequences of Rhodesian UDI and the quickened timetable of the disengagement from the white south. Government was increasingly utilising autonomous parastatal bodies, outside the normal ministerial hierarchy, for a variety of purposes, although the changes in COZ and ZYS suggested that certain limitations were recognised with respect to 'semi-commercial' and 'non-commercial' activities. The growth of the parastatal sector was also reflected in the pattern of budgetary allocations; each year increasing government funds were earmarked for the capitalisation of parastatal bodies or for subsidies enabling them to perform otherwise uneconomic services, particularly in providing fertiliser to farmers, cheaper basic foods to all segments of the population, and transport in all sectors.

Yet unquestionably, the most striking change evident by the end of 1970 was the pre-eminence of the 'commercial' State-owned company within the parastatal sector, particularly as an instrument for the administration of existing or projected large-scale enterprises. ZIMCO, with its trinity of subsidiaries, INDECO, MINDECO, and FINDECO, spotlighted this trend, but the establishment of the Rural Development Corporation and ZESCO also provided further evidence. Yet it was not the company form, *per se*, which made the greatest impact upon the parastatal sector as a whole but rather the practices and style of the previously private companies which had only recently been brought into the 'commercial' component of the parastatal sector. The two mining companies and most of the newly-acquired INDECO subsidiaries jointly owned with foreign partners, were large profitable ongoing operations, unlike many of the statutory bodies, some of which (for example, Zambia Railways and NAMBOARD) performed vital services at losses which were covered only by government subsidies. The substantial financial resources which could be generated within the 'commercial' companies or through their foreign partners without reliance upon Government gave them additional actual and potential autonomy in contrast to the more dependent statutory agencies within the parastatal sector. Furthermore, many ZIMCO companies remained closely linked with their previous foreign owners, who, in many instances, continued to provide management service and expatriate personnel to the 51 per cent Zambian-owned companies under contracts negotiated at the time of takeover. In style of operations these established firms were deeply rooted within private business practice, rather than being oriented toward civil service mores. Within most of these companies wage and salary levels, including important fringe benefits, not only had been above those offered within the Government (and the previously established parastatal bodies), but also the gap between the salaries of managers and technical personnel (most of whom were white expatriates) and the wages of workers (most of whom were black Zambians) was generally greater.[5]

Thus, in contrast to 1964, the rapidly expanded parastatal sector of 1970 consisted of a large component of formerly private and financially powerful institutions whose style of operation was at sharp variance with that of the older previously-established parastatal bodies and the civil service. With its experience, power and resources this new component of the parastatal sector had vast potential for quickening the Government's drive for rapid economic development including rural reconstruction, as well as being a magnet for scarce and well-trained indigenous manpower seeking higher remuneration and broad responsibilities.[6] The generally broadly defined autonomy of parastatal bodies, both old and new, gave their management considerable latitude in determining salary scales as well as the modes of operation within a particular parastatal body.[7] In more narrow political terms, the expanded parastatal sector could also be viewed as the locus of potential alternative power centres within the public sector. Unquestionably, the integration of the rapidly acquired new parastatal institutions posed a multitude of problems for the Zambian leadership.

Coping with State capitalism

The challenges posed by the transformed parastatal sector have been met with a variety of strategies. Periodic reorganisations and restructuring have been utilised both to prevent the growth of mammoth corporate entities as well as to streamline the operation of the components of the sector. Further moves have been made to delimit connections with foreign partners in line with the ongoing commitment of the Government to achieve not only formal but actual control over major economic institutions. In related moves, efforts have been made to make parastatal bodies ever more responsive to national priorities, particularly in the sphere of rural development. Finally, amidst rising clamour from Zambian public opinion, key practices of parastatal organisations have been brought under scrutiny to determine their appropriateness for a society formally committed to a progressively more socialist interpretation of Humanism.

Reorganisation as a tool for control and rationalisation has been regularly utilised by President Kaunda within government.[8] Thus, it is not surprising that he also used this device for the parastatal sector. The benchmark would seem to be the major restructuring of the ZIMCO complex which he announced early in 1971 at the time that Andrew Sardanis resigned from Government to return to private business. ZIMCO, which had been centralised under

Sardanis since its inception, was fragmented with major responsibilities for oversight and operation being devolved to MINDECO, FINDECO, and INDECO. INDECO, in addition, was further divided, losing its road transportation and hotel interests to two newly created holding companies, the National Transport Corporation (NTC) and the National Hotels Corporation (NHC). In a parallel move the Ministry of State Participation, which since its inception had been directly under President Kaunda with Andrew Sardanis as permanent secretary, was abolished, and responsibilities for the now five major holding companies were distributed upon a functional basis to five Ministries (*viz.*, INDECO – Ministry of Commerce and Industry; FINDECO — Ministry of Finance and Development; MINDECO — Ministry of Mines and Mining Development; NTC – Ministry of Power, Transport and Works; NHC – Ministry of Information, Broadcasting and Tourism). By these moves concentration of power and resources within both Government and the 'commercial' component of the parastatal sector was lessened. ZIMCO was converted from an operational centre into an umbrella holding company.

The rationale for these moves was further outlined by President Kaunda in a major address in May 1971 to the UNIP National Council. Asserting that a concentration of economic power in the hands of a few within the public sector could be worse than the private capitalism which it had replaced, President Kaunda warned of the dangers of State capitalism in which large monopolistic institutions would remain insensitive to public needs and efficiency. Accordingly, he argued that decentralisation of economic institutions was necessary to ensure that they would 'take account of the economic and social needs of the public' and that they would 'compete with a view to offering Zambians the lowest cost and the best service.[9] Concentration of power and monolithic organisation within the parastatal sector were thus declared contrary to national goals.

Subsequent organisational changes have remained broadly within the pattern set by the 1971 restructuring of ZIMCO. Within ZIMCO deconcentration has continued. To the original five major subsidiaries eight others have been added, including new corporations hived off from within existing subsidiaries;[10] newly-created holding companies have amalgamated operations from diverse sources;[11] and one autonomous body outside of the regular ministerial structure has been transferred to ZIMCO – this was the TIKA Steel and Iron Corporation, a new mining and manufacturing venture initially under the authority of UNIP. With the demise of the Medical and Pharmaceutical Corporation (MEPCO) in 1977, due to operational difficulties, and the Zambia Fisheries and Fish Marketing Corporation (ZFFMC) transferred to the supervision of UNIP and then abolished also in 1977 amidst accusations of inefficiency and corruption, ZIMCO now has eleven subsidiaries and remains the largest entity within the parastatal sector.[12] Yet responsibilities for operations and management rest with the ZIMCO subsidiaries rather than with ZIMCO head office. Although perhaps in the early 1970s ZIMCO continued to operate as a device for the exercise of co-ordination, both through its quarterly board meetings which brought together the managing directors of its subsidiaries and responsible government Ministers, and through the mechanisms of its financial controller, it would seem that increasingly its component subsidiaries have operated even more autonomously without close supervision and control from the ZIMCO head office.[13]

Although thought was apparently given at one time to enlarging ZIMCO to include both statutory bodies such as Zambia Airways and the Development Bank of Zambia and hitherto strictly government agencies such as the Zambia National Tourist Bureau and General Post Office,[14] this has not taken place.[15] With the notable exception of the Posts and Telegraph Corporation (PTC), created when the General Post Office was converted into a parastatal body in 1975, entities within the governmental structure have not been transferred to the parastatal sector. Voices have also been raised urging the conversion of statutory bodies, particularly in the agricultural sector, into State corporations,[16] but this, too, has not been done. Instead, further moves towards rationalisation of both statutory bodies and State corporations have generally been made within the existing organisational structure. Specific subsidiaries have been transferred from one parastatal body to another and ministerial oversight of specific parastatal organisations has been shifted among Ministries with a view to further division of responsibility along functional lines. For example, all trading and commercial organisations in the agricultural sector, including NAMBOARD, the Cold Storage Board, and Dairy Produce Board, have been moved from the Ministry of Rural Development to the Ministry of Commerce, while the National Import and Export Corporation (NIEC) has been moved from the Ministry of Mines and Industry and placed under the Ministry of Commerce. Within specific parastatal bodies, notably INDECO and NTC, complementary and competing subsidiaries in some instances have been amalgamated in the interests of economy and efficiency.

Financial reforms to assure proper capitalisation have also been carried out, particularly within State corporations, and calls have been made that the same should be done in statutory bodies.[17] The main thrust of ongoing reorganisation through the mid-1970s has been towards a further streamlining of rapidly expanded and hastily acquired bodies in the attempt to improve the latter's potential for sound operation without losses or the need for government subsidies.

Parallel to moves to streamline the parastatal sector have been policies designed to consolidate Zambian control, particularly in enterprises acquired from foreign owners. The strategy employed has three main features: Zambianisation, acquisition of further shares from foreign partners, and the renegotiation of management agreements. Although it is recognised that many professional and technical positions will continue to be filled by expatriates recruited outside the country in the face of a continuing shortage of qualified Zambians, on-the-job and other training schemes have been written into the management contracts signed with foreign partners. Zambians have also been increasingly promoted to top management posts in a pattern similar to that within the civil service in the immediate post-independence period. To ensure an analogous Zambianisation of capital in joint enterprises where Zambia was the minority shareholder, further negotiations have been undertaken to convert the Zambian shareholding into a majority one. In addition, the minority interests of South African shareholders in industrial and commercial enterprises have been purchased to give 100 per cent Zambian control of such undertakings.

Yet the most significant policy towards the achievement of more effective Zambian control has been the renegotiation of management agreements in line with the principle of 'self management', the outlines of which became visible in 1970–71.[18] Under the takeovers negotiated by Andrew Sardanis with the foreign firms named at Mulungushi and with the two copper mining companies, the previous majority owners were generally given a management contract which allowed them to name the managing director and to continue to conduct operations for an agreed fee upon the basis of policy set by a board of directors with a Zambian majority. Yet in the unsuccessful negotiations for the takeover of the major foreign banks (conducted after the departure of Andrew Sardanis from Government), the Zambian team insisted upon new arrangements in which the previous owners would not be given a management contract but would be asked to provide management personnel and services. Although the banks refused to accede and ultimately the Zambian Government pulled back from its decision to take 51 per

cent interest in the banks, the type of arrangements advocated by the
Zambians became a pattern which was sought in the renegotiation
of existing management contracts. The new policy was most
spectacularly proclaimed with the August 1973 decision to cancel
the management contracts which had been signed with the two
mining companies and to renegotiate the terms for the secondment
of key technical and managerial personnel.[19] Yet more quietly other
management agreements have also been renegotiated to give the
Zambian side greater powers both to name management and to
gain full responsibility for the conduct of business. In this fashion
Zambia has gained latitude to push for Zambianisation at her own
speed as well as the power, if she wishes, to move away from
exclusive reliance upon the minority partner for personnel and
technical services.

Zambia's expansion of control over previously foreign-owned
enterprises did not mean a drastic reorientation from profit-making.
Indeed, the Second National Development Plan for the period
1971–76 explicitly argued that 'commercial' parastatal bodies could
most effectively contribute to development by continuing to operate
in a businesslike fashion and thus avoid reliance upon government
subsidies except when necessary to achieve government-determined
social goals.[20]

It also asserted that parastatals had a further role to play by
directing part of the profits from their activities along the line of rail
into the rural areas.[21] In addition, they were expected to hold profit
margins low on certain basic goods and to show a particular
sensitivity to certain non-economic goals such as Zambianisation.[22]
On the whole, the 'commercial' parastatal bodies operated within
these guidelines. They maintained overall profitability within most
of their established enterprises, although profits were shifted
between subsidiaries to maintain otherwise uneconomic services.
Major State corporations, including both INDECO and FINDECO,
sited new enterprises and branches in provincial centres off the line
of rail. Their practices did not represent radical changes of
priorities, but rather a readjustment within their existing substantial
resources to encourage activity within the rural areas or to achieve
other social goals without disrupting profitability and existing
operational patterns of established industrial, commercial, and
financial undertakings.

In contrast certain 'semi-commercial' and 'non-commercial'
parastatal bodies, particularly in agriculture and transport, were
generally allowed to operate with substantial government subsidies.
Although the inability of COZ to recover all but a small portion of

its loans finally resulted in its demise, its successor, the Agricultural Finance Company continued to operate at a loss, albeit on a smaller scale.[23] More spectacular were the rising subsidies granted to other agricultural parastatal bodies (for example, NAMBOARD, the Cold Storage Board, the Dairy Produce Board, and the Tobacco Board of Zambia), over sixty per cent of which were devoted to administrative costs and the subsidisation of basic foodstuffs and fertilisers.[24] Subsidies continued to be provided to Zambia Railways in its uphill battle to achieve efficiency and viability, as well as to Zambia Airways. Further escalation in the scale of subsidisation came as a consequence of both rising costs incurred in the wake of the closure of the border with Rhodesia and accelerated price rises of petroleum and other essential imported goods.[25]

Formal governmental control over the burgeoning parastatal sector has generally been exercised through established ministerial channels, except for the broadest of directives which have usually been announced by President Kaunda in the context of national policy statements. For the most part 'semi-commercial' and 'non-commercial' parastatal bodies, the majority of which are statutory agencies rather than State companies, have been individually under the wing of a specific Ministry rather than grouped within a more encompassing agency in turn responsible to a Ministry. The practice with respect to State corporations has been more varied. During the period of ZIMCO's initial heady growth in 1968–70, when it operated as a free-wheeling conglomerate, it was directly under the aegis of the Ministry of State Participation headed by President Kaunda. With the reorganisation of ZIMCO and the abolition of the Ministry of State Participation in early 1971 its components were distributed to new, but smaller, State corporations, although in Zambian terms most corporations and their subsidiaries were large-scale enterprises. There has been no move to recreate the all-embracing conglomerate structure of ZIMCO as it existed in its first period under Sardanis.[26] Instead, Government has apparently been willing to rely upon the system of supervision used for the earlier 'semi-commercial' and 'non-commercial' statutory bodies. Ministers within specific functional Ministries have been made responsible for supervision of the 'commercial' State corporations assigned to their portfolio and serve as chairmen of their boards of directors. Managing directors, appointed by President Kaunda, are responsible for the running of the corporations within guidelines established by the supervising Ministry or, perhaps more often, by the office of the Prime Minister or the President .

In the eyes of a diverse group of observers the system of control and oversight which has evolved is unsatisfactory in terms of its openness to political pressure, its lack of effective co-ordinating mechanism, and its unresponsiveness to any national central planning. Antony Martin has argued that the more centralised system within ZIMCO under Sardanis was far less accessible and susceptible to narrow political considerations as well as generally more free from bureaucratic constraints which limit imaginative management.[27] The 1974–75 Salaries Commission, headed by John Mwanakatwe, did not comment specifically in its 1975 report upon questions of political pressure, but noted with concern the varied and imprecisely defined lines of communication between government Ministries and parastatals, thereby creating friction and impairing comprehensive control.[28] From a different perspective, Ann Seidman has raised the question whether the parastatal structures themselves are not a major barrier to greater rationality. She also contends that more effective central planning controls are needed to ensure that parastatals operate more fully in accord with proclaimed national economic goals.[29] In this vein her critique dovetails with that of analysts of the Tanzanian parastatal structure in the early 1970s who decried its responsiveness to external capitalist forces rather than to an ideologically coherent socialist planning mechanism within the country.[30] Timothy Shaw has complemented this line of criticism in his characterisation of the political economy of Zambia as 'a classic case of dependence and underdevelopment' in which the pattern of economic activity and the nature of its structure have been shaped by external interests, primarily multinationals, which have their principal links to Zambia through the parastatals.[31] A Zambian commentator, Kasuka Mutukwa, finds fault with the failure to decolonise 'the minds of that management component which thrives on overdeveloped linkages to external interests'.[32] Although speaking in a different idiom, President Kaunda has also asserted that 'industrial planning has largely been undertaken without sufficient regard for the nation's real development need – that is, development of the people by the people and for the people, in the broadest possible sense'.[33]

Criticism and new reforms

Questions about planning and control, however, were not most audible in the rising crescendo of criticism of the parastatal sector which was increasingly heard in the mid-1970s. Instead, the concerns were about the apparently privileged position of parastatal management, the alleged use of parastatal bodies for ethnic patronage, the unresponsiveness of specific agencies to demands of the public, and growing inefficiency within the parastatal sector. During public hearings held by the Mwanakatwe Salaries Commission, appointed in August 1974 to review both civil service and parastatal salary scales, witnesses repeatedly pointed to the disparities between salaries in Government and those in the parastatals. In the eyes of many this contributed to the 'brain drain' from the civil service to the parastatal sector; most urged that the salaries gap between the two be narrowed or eliminated.[34] Backbenchers in Parliament asserted that top managers had used their position within particular parastatal bodies to hire predominantly from their 'own' ethnic group to the exclusion of other Zambians; Mainza Chona, then Prime Minister, confirmed that investigations of employment practices had shown that in a number of parastatal bodies the majority of employees were from the same ethnic group as that of the general manager, but he indicated that it could not be confirmed if this was the result of deliberate intent.[35] Journalists, as well as government Ministers, criticised the insensitivity of workers in parastatal bodies to their customers and national needs.[36] Widespread inefficiency, increasing subsidies, and rising administrative costs also came under attack, with President Kaunda providing some of the most damning public evidence when he cited particular examples of sharp increases in salary, entertainment, and transportation costs in four parastatal bodies.[37]

Presidential response to the sharpened criticism of the parastatal sector was outlined on 30 June 1975, in the context of the 'Watershed' speech to the UNIP National Council. Articulating the socialist thrust of Humanism further with the announcement that all freehold tenure was immediately abolished, President Kaunda delivered a wide-ranging address criticising capitalist tendencies still visible in Zambia and reiterating his determination that Zambia must advance towards the anti-capitalist goals of Humanism enunciated in party manifestos and government declarations. He noted that parastatals had been 'created to benefit the masses', but that 'a lot of them because of the attitude of our Zambian workers have earned themselves such a bad reputation that the name *Parastatal* is now virtually a derogatory term'. He contended that 'some parastatals are full of people who failed in Government and yet were still employed by parastatals at higher salaries for doing less work'. He announced that Government would move towards unified conditions of service within both the civil service and parastatal sectors. Interim uniform wage and salary scales were to be adopted for all categories in the parastatal sector and henceforth

appointments were to be made by a central service commission in
order 'to remove corruption and nepotism which is partly
responsible for high current costs and low productivity'. Individuals
resigning from government service were to be blacklisted from
subsequent employment in parastatal bodies.[38]

President Kaunda's directives were given strong support in early
July with the release of the report of the Mwanakatwe Salaries
Commission (the contents of which almost certainly were known to
President Kaunda at the time of his 'Watershed' speech). Although
the bulk of the Commission's recommendations were addressed to
questions of salaries and conditions of service in the civil service, the
Commission made very specific recommendations for the parastatal
sector. These were in line with the mandate which it had been given
to investigate and report on salaries and conditions in that sector
with a view to standardising conditions of service within parastatal
bodies and establishing 'a closer relationship between salaries,
salary structures and conditions of service in the public services and
those applicable to the staffs of parastatal organisations'.[39]

The Commission urged that salaries in the parastatal sector be
brought down to the level of those it had recommended for the civil
service with a differential of no more than five per cent in favour of
the parastatal bodies. In the more contentious matter of fringe
benefits, where the Commission reported that many parastatal
executives enjoyed a level of benefits sharply in excess of those
prevailing at comparable levels in the civil service, the Commission
recommended that the conditions of service in the parastatals should
generally correspond with the relatively more modest arrangements
prevailing in the civil service, with specific exceptions being made
where appropriate and necessary to recruit scarce technical and
professional personnel. To enforce the standardised salaries and
fringe benefits which it had recommended, the Commission
proposed the creation of a new Parastatal Bodies Service
Commission with statutory powers to approve and enforce broadly
standardised conditions of service within parastatal bodies. In
recommendations most probably designed to placate those already
employed in parastatal bodies, the Commission agreed that existing
contracts should be honoured but that upon expiry of contract,
transfer, or promotion, the new terms of service for any individual be
brought into line with the new schedule for all posts at that level.[40]

Governmental policy was detailed specifically in a white paper
published in September 1975, in response to the report of the
Mwanakatwe Salaries Commission, and subsequently in March
1976 with the enactment of the Parastatal Bodies Service

Commission Act. In its white paper the Government accepted almost all the recommendations of the Mwanakatwe Salaries Commission that conditions of service within the parastatal sector be standardised and put on a parity with those in the civil service.[41] In a minor modification it rejected the specific salary scales set out by the Commission, but explicitly asserted that minimum and maximum salaries for parastatal employees would be the same as those prevailing in the civil service. In the politically sensitive area of arrangements for those already employed as 'permanent and pensionable officers' (mostly Zambians), the Government made careful modifications seemingly designed to mitigate resentment. A three-year transitional period was established before salaries in excess of the new scales were to be reduced to the new maxima. While Government accepted that fringe benefits were to be brought in line with those in the civil service, it set no timetable for the change, merely indicating that this would be done 'when appropriate instructions will be given'. Parastatal employees on fixed contract (almost exclusively expatriates) were, however, put on notice that any renewal of contract would only be upon terms in line with the new scales. In legislating mechanisms for enforcement of its policies the Government made only very minor adjustments to the wording of the draft bill for the Parastatal Bodies Service Commission Act proposed by the Mwanakatwe Salaries Commission.[42] The legislation, which passed through Parliament in March 1976, gave broad powers to the Parastatal Bodies Service Commission to approve and enforce standardised conditions of service in line with its 'duty . . . to ensure, as far as possible, that there shall be substantial parity in the terms and conditions of service of public officers and of employees of parastatal bodies'. Yet the new legislation, following to the word the recommendations of the Mwanakatwe Salaries Commission, gave considerable latitude to both the President of Zambia and to the Parastatal Bodies Service Commission. The Chairman and the three to six other members of the Parastatal Bodies Service Commission were to be appointed by the President for three year terms and the President was empowered to give directions to the Commission as well as to take over any or all of its functions. The Commission itself was empowered not only to enforce its decisions upon all parastatal bodies, but also 'to exempt from the provisions of this Act all employees, or any particular category of employees, of a parastatal body'.[43]

The white paper, generally endorsing the recommendations of the Mwanakatwe Salaries Commission and the creation of the Parastatal Bodies Service Commission, provided a framework for potentially more co-ordination of government policy on the conditions of employment in what had come to be the largest component of the Zambian economy, generating well over half of the Gross Domestic Product and providing more than one third of all wage employment in the country.[44] The central thrust of the new policies clearly fell broadly in line with the egalitarian goals of Zambian Humanism. Notice was given that the high salaries and fringe benefits of upper and middle management within the parastatal bodies, whether inherited in the takeover from the private sector, negotiated by high level political and professional personnel upon their appointment to senior managerial positions, or obtained through the exercise of autonomous parastatal power unencumbered by civil service regulation, were to be brought generally down to the level prevailing within the civil service where the gap between highest paid and lowest paid, although large, was less pronounced than that which had prevailed within the parastatal sector. From the time that the new policies took effect the relative attractiveness of employment within the parastatal sector for those coming into the sector from the civil service — or even possibly sections of the private sector – would be less.

Yet the new machinery clearly was designed neither as a device for tight centralised control of parastatal bodies nor as a means of ensuring their adherence to party goals. In the discretion given to the President to take over the powers of the Parastatal Bodies Service Commission, as well as in the powers of the latter to exempt categories of employees of a particular parastatal body from regulations, there existed the possibility that exceptions could be made by administrative decisions in response to appeals by particular parastatal managers or other interested parties. Furthermore, Government had explicitly stated in the white paper that it accepted the recommendation of the Mwanakatwe Salaries Commission that 'the exercise of appointing and disciplinary power should remain in parastatal hands, subject to overall control',[45] thereby permitting parastatal management to continue to exercise its authority autonomously in a fashion not possible for high civil servants bound by the regulations of the Public Service Commission. Parastatal autonomy was only delimited to the extent that management and prospective employees were put on notice that the free-wheeling practices which determined conditions of service in the early 1970s, particularly for upper level management, would not generally be tolerated. But the autonomy for day-to-day operation in the parastatal sector was not threatened either by the Parastatal Bodies Service Commission or by the policies set out in the government white paper.

It is impossible to determine precisely what has been the direct impact of the policies enunciated in the government white paper and the actions of the Parastatal Bodies Service Commission. Although the chairman and members of the Commission were appointed only in early 1977, one year after the passage of the Parastatal Bodies Service Commission Act, Government had taken action earlier to implement at least certain elements of its policies. Its insistence that terms of service for expatriates signing new contracts be standardised to exclude many of the fringe benefits and salaries in excess of the new levels set by the Mwanakatwe Salaries Commission resulted both in difficulties in retaining and attracting key technical and professional personnel as well as requests that relief be given in the interests of maintaining efficiency.[46] Yet apparently employment for Zambian skilled personnel remained sufficiently attractive that the exodus to the parastatal sector from the civil service continued in the short run.[47] Undoubtedly, numerous requests have been made to Government and to the Parastatal Bodies Service Commission since the appointment of its members for exemptions which would permit particular parastatal bodies to employ individuals upon special terms. Very probably also requests have been made for exemptions which would permit the retention of existing salaries and fringe benefits for those already employed upon a permanent and pensionable basis. It is impossible to determine what has been the pattern of actions taken by the Parastatal Bodies Service Commission, yet it would seem that Dominic Mulaisho, the Commission's chairman, would not take a doctrinaire stand against exemptions since, as a former managing director of three parastatal bodies, he is on record as urging that parastatal bodies be allowed autonomy within government policy to get on with their legitimate business of 'risk-taking' without conforming to the regulations and procedure of the civil service.[48]

The actions of the Parastatal Bodies Service Commission and the policies which it was charged to oversee have been important for all employed in the parastatal sector. However, the direction taken by the sector as a whole has been especially shaped since the mid-1970s by the deteriorating economic situation faced by Zambia and the moves taken by the Government to cope with declining government revenue, shrinking foreign exchange, low copper prices, rising import costs, accentuated transportation bottlenecks, decreasing productivity and disappointing agricultural results. The extent of the seriousness of the crisis was reflected in the financial returns of the hitherto vastly profitable major mining and industrial parastatals; in 1975–76 INDECO registered a loss for the first time since its creation and both copper companies failed to show a profit. In its response to the deepening economic crisis Zambia has resorted to reduced government budgets, devaluation of the Kwacha (by 20 per cent in 1976 and an additional 10 per cent in 1978), and accelerated foreign borrowing to meet its growing external debt.

It is against this backdrop that practices of parastatals which were tolerated or even encouraged by Government in earlier years of financial affluence have been brought further into question. Parastatal bodies have been urged to shift from their predeliction for large-scale projects, involving substantial consultancy fees and finance charges, to smaller undertakings, focusing upon local, rather than imported resources.[49] Subsidies which ballooned rapidly in the early 1970s have been cut back progressively since 1975 resulting in a substantial rise in the price of basic foodstuffs including flour, bread, cooking oil, and maize meal.[50] Government spokesmen have indicated that parastatals should be permitted to raise prices to cover other increased costs, but excluded have been price increases 'to cover losses which are due to inefficiency, mismanagement, bad planning, overstaffing, and other ills now prevailing in some of our parastatals'.[51] Government statements have been counterpointed by renewed pleas from those involved in parastatal management for latitude to operate as efficient business organisations and not as vehicles for the achievement of social or other goals promoted by Government.[52] The practice of frequent shifts of top management personnel from one post to another has been criticised by senior government Ministers, and President Kaunda has stated that Government itself is to blame for giving certain positions to inappropriately qualified individuals.[53] Accusations of corruption, which was not initially seen as a major malaise within parastatal bodies, have been increasingly heard; the prosecution and conviction of the Governor of the Bank of Zambia and the managing director of NTC provided public evidence that, at least in particular instances, there had been malpractices at the top level of parastatals which Government was no longer willing to ignore. From all quarters, including parastatal managers themselves, calls have continued to come for an end to corruption within parastatal bodies and for improved efficiency of operation.

There seems to be little dispute that many parastatal bodies are not performing in the best interests of the nation. Yet there also seems to be a broad consensus that radical restructuring of the existing arrangements is not required, either through a return of parastatals to private ownership or through a further shift to the 'left' involving more explicitly socialist practices in planning, management, and labour relations. Instead, the calls are for readjustments within the *status quo*, primarily through changes in personnel or attitudes or through further rationalisation of administrative structures and practices.[54] It does not even appear that centralised co-ordinating machinery, even on the modest level which has come to prevail in Tanzania,[55] was introduced to complement the co-ordination of conditions of service envisaged with the establishment of the Parastatal Bodies Service Commission, although it is possible that such steps are now being taken in connection with the harsher retrenchment introduced in 1978.[56]

Confronted with its longest and gravest economic crisis since independence, the Zambian Government has chosen to continue reliance upon the institutions and practices which have evolved in the last decade since the enunciation of Humanism as the overarching ideology guiding Zambian development. Despite considerable diversification of trading partners and the expansion of State ownership and State-directed economic activity within the country, Zambia is dependent upon external sources for markets for copper and other products as well as for a broadened range of imports to supply both consumer needs and expanded industrial production; she has become even more intricately enmeshed in the Western-dominated international economy. Symbolic of these continuing close links are the agreements reached with the International Monetary Fund and other major Western sources in 1978 for a package of credits and grants in return for Zambia's agreement to pursue policies of retrenchment.

Yet the policy of economic retrenchment within Zambia and continued, if not accentuated, reliance upon financial support from Western sources, has not led the Zambian leadership to reverse course sharply. Zambian leaders, including President Kaunda, have repeatedly defended and advocated carefully selected links with foreign firms, including multinationals.[57] With the announcement that there were to be no further nationalisations and the passage of the Industrial Development Act in 1977 Zambia has sought to attract more foreign investment through more explicit delineation of the terms under which it will be accepted.[58] Further liberalisation was announced in 1978 under existing regulations.[59] The steps taken to create a more attractive climate for private foreign investment, however, have not been followed by any steps to decrease the role of the State in the economy or to reintroduce 'capitalism'. Indeed, in response to challengers within UNIP, led by Simon Kapwepwe, former Vice-President, who were urging much greater latitude for private enterprise, the UNIP leadership and the Government explicitly reaffirmed that Zambia would maintain her present policies and structures. Although severely constrained by the present state of development of Zambian resources and by the nature of its linkages to the international economic system, the Zambian leadership has refused to exercise the option of a drastic shift to the 'right' – a course advocated by some domestic critics and possibly also preferred by certain Western powers and major multinationals. Instead, within tightened parameters the Zambian leadership has chosen to continue with its type of mixed economy dominated by the parastatal sector.

President Kaunda has characterised the existing Zambian system as State capitalism. There is disagreement among students of the phenomenon of State capitalism in the third world over its nature as well as its potential as a means of breaking out of a neo-colonial situation.[60] For many Zambians, nevertheless, the economic reforms set in motion at Mulungushi in 1968 and the subsequent rapid growth of State ownership have placed the country on the road to economic independence and socialism. Yet in the view of President Kaunda: 'the reforms have created a form of State capitalism where tremendous power is thus concentrated in the hands of a small managerial group who have their hands on the important switches and whose elitist attitudes set social patterns far beyond their immediate realms of command . . .'.[61] It is this group, a 'new class' as President Kaunda has characterised it, that threatens to thwart the realisation of Humanism.[62] Under the prodding of President Kaunda, UNIP and the Zambian Government have proclaimed their intention of circumscribing the privileges and power of this group, while simultaneously recognising the importance of its members' skills for further economic development. Increasingly dependent upon this 'new class' not only for their skills, but also for their political support,[63] President Kaunda has not yet moved to challenge this group directly, but instead has relied upon devices such as the leadership code and the standardisation of service conditions within the civil service and parastatal bodies to contain, but not significantly reduce, inequalities in Zambian society. It is unlikely that in the immediate future President Kaunda will depart from the evolutionary approach which he has consistently followed to date. Within the strategy adopted by Zambia to cope with its economic crisis, the 'new class' has a central role to play. State capitalism, in which the parastatal sector is pre-eminent, seems firmly entrenched. Unquestionably, debate will continue over its form and its implications for further Zambian development.

Notes

[1] *Report of the committee appointed to review the emoluments and conditions of service of statutory boards and corporations and State-owned enterprises* (Lusaka, 1970), p. 5.

[2] For a survey of developments during this period see S. W. Johns, 'Parastatal bodies in Zambia: problems and prospects,' in H and U. E. Simonis (eds.), *Socioeconomic development in dual economies: the example of Zambia* (Munich, 1971), pp. 231–51.

[3] In 1973 ZIMCO was listed for the first time in the *Fortune* directory of the three hundred largest industrial corporations outside the United States in which firms are ranked according to their volume of sales. In 1973 ZIMCO ranked 123rd in the world, second in Africa behind De Beers Consolidated Mines of South Africa. *The Fortune Directory: the 300 Largest Industrial Corporations outside the U.S.* (Chicago, 1974), p. 3. In 1977 ZIMCO ranked 134th in the world, remaining the second largest firm in Africa behind De Beers Consolidated Mines of South Africa. *Fortune*, vol. 98, No. 3 (1978), p. 174.

[4] It has been estimated that during its brief existence COZ lost K20–30 million in unrecoverable loans. C. Harvey, 'Control of credit in Zambia', *Journal of Modern African Studies*, vol. 11, No. 3 (1973), p. 289.

[5] In 1970 the basic salary for a permanent secretary at the top of the civil service was K6,760 plus allowances; the maximum salary reported in the parastatal sector was K10,000. In 1971 top civil servant salaries were raised to K9,000, a limit which remained in effect until mid-1975. According to Richard L. Sklar, university graduates entering the civil service in 1970 received salaries of K1,800–1,900, an amount nearly forty per cent higher than the average income received by wage earners outside the mining sector. University graduates entering the parastatal sector received 'substantially higher' salaries. Sklar, *Corporate power in an African State, op. cit.*, pp. 195, 198. A UNESCO-sponsored survey of Zambian graduates, taken in 1974, reported that the mean salary for graduates employed in the parastatal sector was more than K100 per month higher than the mean salary of those employed in the civil service. B. C. Sanyal, J. H. Case, P. S. Dow and M. E. Jackman, *Higher education and the labour market in Zambia: expectations and performance* (Paris/Lusaka, 1976), p. 198. In 1973 Robert Molteno stated that top parastatal managers were receiving salaries of K18,500. R. Molteno, 'Zambian Humanism: the way ahead', *African Review*, vol. 3, No. 4 (1973), p. 555. While not giving specific figures the 1975 report of the Mwanakatwe Salaries Commission guardedly stated that in some cases the prescribed upper limit on Zambian salaries of K10,000 had been 'considerably exceeded'. Mwanakatwe Report, *op. cit.*, p. 151.

[6] An indication of the relative attractiveness of the parastatal sector in the eyes of prospective graduates can be found in the results of the UNESCO-sponsored survey of students in 1974 in which 36 per cent indicated that they expected to work in the parastatal sector after graduation (while 46 per cent expected to enter the civil service). Yet those expecting to enter the parastatal sector anticipated the highest salaries while those expecting to enter the civil service anticipated the lowest salaries. Sanyal *et al.*, *Higher education, op. cit.*, pp. 173, 181.

[7] For parastatal managers at the top levels an additional feature of their mode of appointment provided further advantage in negotiating salaries well above the level prevailing even elsewhere in the parastatal sector. As the 1975 report of the Mwanakatwe Salaries Commission noted: 'We must be frank and say, however, that many top-level appointments have been announced prior to any agreement on terms and conditions of employment of the persons selected to fill them. This has placed the individual in an extremely strong position to negotiate his own terms and has led, in some cases, to the prescribed upper limit on Zambian salaries of K10,000 per annum being considerably exceeded.' The report hoped that this practice would diminish as appointments in the future would increasingly be made through normal processes of recruitment, even from within the ranks of particular parastatal bodies, rather than

by transfer from Government or elsewhere. Mwanakatwe Report, *op. cit.*, p. 151.

⁸ Ministries and components of Ministries have been quite frequently reorganised. Perhaps the most significant reorganisation was the creation of Ministries for each of Zambia's provinces and the institution of District Governors for each of Zambia's districts. See ch. 8, below.

⁹ *Times of Zambia Business Review*, 28 May 1971.

¹⁰ For example, Nchanga Consolidated Copper Mines – NCCM – and Roan Consolidated Mines – RCM – separated from MINDECO; Metal Marketing Corporation – MEMACO – formed to handle the sale of copper produced by the two mining companies; National Import and Export Corporation – NIEC – formed by withdrawing all wholesale and retail trading operations of INDECO.

¹¹ Thus, the Medical and Pharmaceutical Corporation – MEPCO – incorporated subsidiaries from INDECO and NIEC, and Medical Stores from the Ministry of Health; the Zambia Fisheries and Fish Marketing Corporation – ZFFMC – comprised a small operating subsidiary of INDECO and a newly-created loan-granting agency; and INDECO's petroleum interests and the previously independent ZESCO were grouped under the Zambia National Energy Corporation – ZNEC.

¹² The subsequent reorganisation of ZIMCO, announced by President Kaunda in December 1978, is discussed at pp. 265–6, below.

¹³ In 1972 Ruth Weiss believed that the revised ZIMCO structure still did exercise considerable co-ordination over its subsidiaries, but the Mwanakatwe Report recommended in 1975 that the administrative capacity of ZIMCO for co-ordination and supervision should be strengthened. See R. Weiss, 'Anatomy of ZIMCO', *Times of Zambia Business Review*, 15 December 1972, and Mwanakatwe Report, *op. cit.*, p. 134.

¹⁴ *ZIMCO, Annual report, 1972* (Lusaka, 1973), p. 4.

¹⁵ This was true early in 1978, when this chapter was completed. For more recent changes, see pp. 265–6, below. (Ed.).

¹⁶ *Times of Zambia Business Review*, 26 May 1972, 15 September 1972. In the latter instance the then chairman of NAMBOARD, Rupiah Banda, was reported in favour of the change. Similar sentiments were expressed by one of his successors, Rajah Kunda, in 1975. *NAMBOARD, Annual report and accounts, 1974* (Lusaka, 1975), p. 2.

¹⁷ For an example, see Rupiah Banda, 'Namboard's role – an honour and a burden, says G.M.', *Enterprise* (Lusaka), October 1973, p. 3.

¹⁸ President Kaunda described the goal of the new arrangements in the following terms: 'A feature of the coming years will be an increasing localisation and direct recruitment of management so that as a (management) contract expires a company will inherit an intact management structure which will enable it to manage itself . . . These remarks apply equally to the largest and to the smallest companies in our group'. *ZIMCO, Annual Report, 1972, op. cit.*, p. 3. A critical discussion of 'self management' is to be found in Martin, *Minding their own business, op. cit.*, pp. 247–56.

¹⁹ *Address by His Excellency the President, Dr K. D. Kaunda, at the press conference on the redemption of ZIMCO bonds, State House, Lusaka, 31 August 1973* (Lusaka, n.d.).

²⁰ *SNDP, op. cit.*, p. 194.

²¹ *Ibid.*, p. 195.

²² For a discussion of INDECO's efforts with respect to Zambianisation see *INDECO, Annual report* (Lusaka), 1972, p. 7; *ibid.*, 1973, p. 9; *ibid.*, 1973–74, pp. 9–10.

²³ For reports on the performance of the Agricultural Finance Corporation in the early 1970s see *Rural Development Corporation, annual report* (Lusaka), 1973, pp. 6, 31; *ibid.*, 1974, pp. 5, 33; *Times of Zambia*, 31 July 1977.

²⁴ *Bank of Zambia, report and statement of accounts for the year ended December 31st, 1973* (Lusaka), p. 13.

²⁵ The following table indicates the rising cost of subsidies in the early 1970s:

Year	Cost	
1969	K20,714,242	(actual)
1973	K37,000,782	(actual)
1974	K33,708,450	(budget)
1975	K69,788,870	(budget)
1975	K100,000,000+	(revised)

All figures are from *Estimates of revenue and expenditure for the year 1st January 1975 to 31st December 1975* (Lusaka, 1975), pp. xvi, except for the last, which is from *Times of Zambia*, 2 July 1975 (speech by President Kaunda).

²⁶ For the reorganisation of ZIMCO announced by President Kaunda in December 1978, see pp. 265–6, below.

²⁷ Martin, *Minding their own business, op. cit.*, pp. 251–3.

²⁸ Mwanakatwe Report, *op. cit.*, pp. 130–2, 135.

²⁹ A. Seidman, 'The distorted growth of import-substitution industry: the Zambian case', *Journal of Modern African Studies*, vol. 12, No. 4 (1974), pp. 611–4, 618.

³⁰ P. C. Packard, 'Management and control of parastatal organisations', in Uchumi Editorial Board (eds.), *Towards socialist planning* (Dar es Salaam, 1972), pp. 73–91; J. Loxley and J. S. Saul, 'The political economy of the parastatals', *East African Law Review*, vol. 5, No. 1–2 (1972), pp. 9–37.

³¹ T. M. Shaw, 'Zambia: dependence and underdevelopment', *Canadian Journal of African Studies*, vol. X, No. 1 (1976), pp. 3–22.

³² K. S. Mutukwa, 'Political control of parastatal organisations in Zambia', *Zango*, 1 (1976), p. 47.

³³ Kaunda, *Humanism in Zambia, Part II, op. cit.*

³⁴ *Zambia Daily Mail*, 22 November 1974; *Times of Zambia*, 7 December 1974.

³⁵ *Zambia Daily Mail*, 29 November 1974; *Times of Zambia*, 24 and 31 January 1975.

³⁶ *Zambia Daily Mail*, 8 November 1974, 7 April 1975; *Times of Zambia*, 22 January 1975; *Sunday Times of Zambia*, 23 February 1975.

³⁷ *Times of Zambia*, 2 July 1975.

³⁸ Kaunda, *The 'Watershed' speech, op. cit.*, p. 52.

³⁹ Mwanakatwe Report, *op. cit.*, p. i.

⁴⁰ For the full text of the Mwanakatwe Report on the parastatal sector see *ibid.*, pp. 130–55. Summaries of the recommendations are found on pp. 137, 143–4, 152, 155.

⁴¹ The relevant sections of the white paper from which the above discussion is drawn are to be found in *Summary of the main recommendations of the Commission of Inquiry* (1975), *op. cit.*, pp. 26–31.

⁴² The draft version submitted by the Mwanakatwe Salaries Commission and an explanation of its text may be found in Mwanakatwe Report, *op. cit.*, pp. 197–205.

⁴³ In December 1978 President Kaunda announced that the Parastatal Bodies Service Commission was to be disbanded. See p. 266, below. (Ed.).

⁴⁴ Mwanakatwe Report, *op. cit.*, p. 134.

⁴⁵ *Summary of the main recommendations of the Commission of Inquiry (1975), op. cit.*, p. 31.

⁴⁶ For example, see *INDECO, Annual report, 1975–76* (1976), pp. 5–6; *Times of Zambia*, 2 February 1977, 17 June 1977.

⁴⁷ It was so stated by John Mwanakatwe, the Minister of Finance, in June 1977. *Times of Zambia*, 11 June 1977. Perhaps the phenomenon reflected the fact that, under the terms of the Parastatal Bodies Service Commission Act, parastatal bodies had six months within which to submit a schedule of proposed conditions of service to the Commission and an additional three month period in which to submit a revised schedule in the event that the initial schedule was refused. During this period, and

until the final ruling of the Commission upon the schedule to prevail in any particular parastatal body, it probably would have been attractive for many to try to take advantage of what might seem to have been a last opportunity to improve conditions of service.

[48] D. Mulaisho, 'INDECO: Problems and prospects', address to the Economics Club, Lusaka, 11 January 1977 (mimeo.), p. 12.

[49] Daily parliamentary debates, No. 44m, 28 January 1977, col. 1051.

[50] Simultaneously with the 'Watershed' speech, President Kaunda recommended that subsidies be cut by up to sixty per cent, The 'Watershed' speech, op. cit., p. 37. Subsequently prices were raised on basic foodstuffs, Times of Zambia, 26 July 1975. The reduction of subsidies has continued, accompanied by further increases in the prices of both basic foodstuffs and fertiliser. In late 1977 a parliamentary select committee recommended that all consumer subsidies be phased out over a period of three years. Sunday Times of Zambia, 4 December 1977. In the wake of a warning by President Kaunda, it was announced in the 1978 budget speech that the prices of certain basic commodities would be sharply increased and that subsidies would be further reduced. Times of Zambia, 3 and 28 January 1978.

[51] Daily parliamentary debates, No. 44m, 28 January 1977, col. 1051:

[52] Mulaisho, 'INDECO', op. cit., pp. 9, 12. See also the remarks of J. M. Mwanza, former managing director of both ZNEC and INDECO, in J. M. Mwanza, 'The conflict between efficiency and social gain in parastatal enterprises in Zambia', paper prepared for delivery at the joint meeting of the African Studies Association/Latin American Studies Association, Houston, November 1977.

[53] Times of Zambia, 24 March 1977, 23 April 1977.

[54] Typical of this approach have been two reports from parliamentary committees. In late 1977 a parliamentary select committee, mandated to recommend measures to bring drastic improvement in the Zambian economy, put forth the following proposals as 'long term measures' for the parastatal sector: 'As the parastatal sector is so important to the economy, the committee recommends that the sector be re-organised so as to: (i) enable organisations to generate their own surpluses or profits; (ii) reduce dependence on Government financial support; (iii) encourage production for export; and (iv) improve the general operational efficiency. In order for these bodies to achieve these objectives, the committee recommends that the Government should allow these bodies flexible pricing policies and stable management terms' (Sunday Times of Zambia, 4 December 1977). A Parliamentary Committee on Parastatal Bodies was appointed in January 1978 to examine the reports and accounts of parastatal bodies to determine whether they were being managed 'in accordance with sound business principles and prudent commercial practices'. It limited its recommendations to very specific revision of improper practices drawn to its attention by individual parastatal bodies which it visited and to observations upon the desirability of improving the capitalisation of particular parastatal bodies. Report of the committee on parastatal bodies for the fifth session of the third national assembly – appointed on the 31st January 1978 (Lusaka, 1978).

[55] For observations by two expatriates closely involved in steps taken by the Tanzanian Government in the early 1970s to co-ordinate parastatal activity through centralised fiscal and planning mechanisms, see R. H. Green, 'Historical, decision-taking, firm and sectoral dimensions of public sector enterprise: some aspects of the angles of attack for research', in Y. Ghai (ed.), Law in the political economy of public enterprises: African perspectives (Uppsala, 1977), pp. 109–12, and K. V. Svendsen, 'Development administration and socialist strategy: Tanzania after Mwongozo', in A. H. Rweyemamu and B. U. Mwansasu, Planning in Tanzania: background to decentralisation (Nairobi, 1974), pp. 25–33.

[56] In March 1978 it was announced that Government would no longer permit overseas borrowing by the mining companies and other government institutions. Africa Research Bulletin, economic, financial and technical Series, 15 March–14 April

1978, p. 4641c. With this move the Government clearly limited an important area of autonomy which permitted parastatals partially to conduct their own 'foreign policy'. For a discussion of the role of parastatals in the conduct of Zambian foreign policy, see T. M. Shaw, 'The foreign policy system of Zambia', *African Studies Review*, vol. XIX, No. 1 (1976), pp. 43–7.

[57] In 1974 President Kaunda set out the general terms under which private foreign capital is acceptable: 'Foreign capital is most welcome to Zambia provided it is made available without strings to the State or any other institutions under it, for example, the Party, central government, local government like the city, municipal or rural council, township management board, co-operatives, public corporations, trade unions, credit unions, thrift societies, etc. Individual Zambian businessmen will only be allowed to utilise new foreign capital in Zambia *with the approval of the Government*' (italics in the original). Kaunda, *Humanism in Zambia, Part II, op. cit.*, p. 78. For more recent examples of President Kaunda's views, see K. Kaunda, *Address to Parliament on the opening of the fourth session of the third national assembly* (Lusaka, 1977), pp. 7–8, and *Times of Zambia*, 3 January 1978.

[58] *Financial Times*, 5 October 1977.

[59] *Africa Research Bulletin*, economic . . . series, 15 January–14 February 1978, p. 4576C.

[60] See, for example, B. Beckman, 'Public enterprise and State capitalism', in Ghai (ed.), *Law in the political economy of public enterprise, op. cit.*, pp. 127–36; A. Mafeje, 'The role of State capitalism in predominantly agrarian economies', paper presented at the Institute of Social Studies' 25th Anniversary Conference, The Hague, December 1977; J. Petras, 'State capitalism and the third world', *Development and Change*, vol. 8, No. 1 (1977), pp. 1–17; A. Nove and J. Petras, 'State capitalism and the third world – a discussion', *Development and Change*, vol. 8, No. 4 (1977), pp. 539–48.

[61] Kaunda, *Humanism in Zambia, Part II, op. cit.*, p. 111.

[62] *Ibid.*, p. 110. Richard Sklar, in his analysis of the impact of multinational mining companies in Zambia, argues that the appropriate term to describe the 'new class' is 'managerial bourgeoisie'. For his analysis and assessment of the prospects of this group, see Sklar, *Corporate power in an African State, op. cit.*, pp. 198–216.

[63] For an analysis of the process whereby President Kaunda and the UNIP leadership have become increasingly dependent upon the 'new class' to maintain their position in the party and the polity, see I. Scott, 'Middle class politics in Zambia', *African Affairs*, vol. 77, No. 308 (1978), pp. 321–34.

5. Corporate autonomy and government control of State enterprises

George K. Simwinga

Introduction

One of the major challenges that has confronted third world countries during the last two decades has been to strike an appropriate balance between the corporate autonomy of the fast growing public enterprise sector and government control over it. Advocates of corporate autonomy argue that because public enterprises are basically business-oriented, operational flexibility is essential and that this cannot be achieved if government control extends beyond the determination of overall policy to day-to-day activities. Public enterprises (the argument continues) do not operate in a vacuum: like their private counterparts, they face competition both at home and abroad. However, their competitiveness will be severely curtailed if their budgetary and procurement procedures are subject to rigid bureaucratic controls and if their recruitment practices suffer from delays similar to those which hamper the civil service. Moreover, the public enterprises in most developing countries today correspond to the private companies of the pre-independence period and the new States' governments depend on them to generate revenue to sustain what are generally backward economies and to promote development.[1]

In principle, corporate autonomy means freedom from unsuitable government regulations and controls and a high degree of operational and financial flexibility; the freedom to borrow money, to hire and fire, and to determine the salary scales of employees; and the freedom to plan and control long-term programmes within the overall framework of general government policy.[2] In practice, corporate autonomy means that public enterprises are not subject, like government departments, to the full panoply of executive and legislative control. On the other hand, another school argues that government control must be asserted over public undertakings if public accountability is to be ensured and if these enterprises are not to pass into the hands of small, unrepresentative and (in extreme cases) self-perpetuating groups.[3] In the case of developing countries in particular it is further argued that certain projects and programmes might need to be undertaken in the national interest, even though they do not meet the commercial criteria with which business enterprises normally comply. Public enterprises, in other words, are seen as agents of change to be used by Government to fulfil social and political goals. To a large extent, this view is held in Zambia where government control has extended beyond major policy determination to the day-to-day activities of public enterprises, ostensibly in an effort to ensure that the latter serve as development agents.[4]

This paper examines the nature of government control over three Zambian public enterprises in three different areas of activity, namely investment, personnel and finance. The three companies are the Industrial Development Corporation (INDECO), the Nchanga Consolidated Copper Mines Limited (NCCM), and the Rural Development Corporation (RDC).

The nature of government control

State control over public companies in Zambia can be said to be derived in the sense that there is nothing in the Companies Act or in the memoranda and articles of the individual enterprises which specifically vests controlling power in any organ of the State, as is the case in the statutory type of public enterprise.[5] Like private shareholders in corporate enterprises, the Government derives its power of control from the rights and privileges normally vested in the shareholders. Being the sole or majority shareholder in each of these companies, the Government exerts formal control through the Governing Board of Directors, which it appoints entirely or in part, and through the management. By convention, a Board is chaired by the supervising Cabinet Minister under whose purview that particular enterprise comes, while its members are mostly high-ranking civil servants or party officials who are loyal to the Government and share its aspirations.[6] In the case of mixed enterprises the practice of block-voting has added an extra control mechanism by which the State ensures that government policies are strictly adhered to at the policy-making levels.[7]

The second formal mechanism of control is exercised through the management, which is 'captive' in the sense that the Zambian Government, as the majority or sole shareholder, has over the past few years been able to build and create managment terms in its public enterprises which are in tune with party and government aspirations. This has been accomplished through Zambianisation and the careful selection of personnel to fill top-level management positions.[8] In all cases the chief executive, and sometimes his deputy as well, is appointed by the Head of State and is required by convention to swear allegiance to the State before assuming office.[9] A majority of the chief executives up to now have been transferred from their civil service jobs to head public enterprises.[10] They have also been subject to frequent transfer from one public enterprise to another, though the reason for such moves can only be surmised – it may reflect dissatisfaction with their performance in a particular job or it may be a way of fostering loyalty among this group of employees by making them feel insecure in their posts.[11] Whatever the reason, it illustrates the extent and ease with which Government intervenes to deploy manpower in the public enterprise sector.

The close working relations between the chief executives of public enterprises on the one hand and top government leaders on the other facilitate informal control,[12] while Parliament exercises significant influence over enterprises which are financially dependent on the State.[13] The recent creation of the Parastatal Bodies Service Commission has added yet another medium through which government control can be applied since the Commission determines the conditions of service of the public enterprise sector as a whole.[14]

Government control – investment

If the principle of corporate autonomy is accepted, investment decisions should be left to the management of public enterprises, the only requirement being that they should be compatible with overall government policy objectives. However, government control over the investment of public enterprises has often extended beyond the legitimate confines of policy in order to determine the strategy by which policy is implemented. As the sole or principal shareholder, the Zambian Government has sometimes directed individual public enterprises not only to undertake specific investment projects but also to adopt a given technology. Sometimes, too, it has decided where the plant should be sited, even though this has meant overruling a decision on siting already taken by the public enterprise concerned. For example, INDECO's feasibility studies had already indicated that the production costs of its projected dry-cell battery plant could be minimised if the plant was located at Kabwe instead of Mansa, some 600 kilometres away.[15] Other studies showed that by locating a glass manufacturing plant at Kabwe instead of at

Kapiri-Mposhi, 70 kilometres away, the corporation could take advantage of economies of scale and drastically cut production costs. However, social and political considerations weighed heavily with the Government and, in spite of the distances and the ensuing high production costs, the two plants were located at Mansa and Kapiri-Mposhi respectively.[16]

Cases where the Government has determined investment locations have been especially frequent in parastatal organisations, such as the RDC, which do not have their own corporate planning sections. In these cases, the Government has both decided what projects should be undertaken and where they should be located. Between 1972 and 1976, 59 per cent of all the projects carried out by the RDC were government-mandated projects. This contrasts with 47 per cent for INDECO and 14 per cent for NCCM.[17] Though government-mandated projects for NCCM constituted only a small proportion of total projects, the figure of 14 per cent is significant: it symbolised the beginning of an era in the copper mining industry in which the Zambian Government for the first time made an inroad in directly controlling the methods and strategies employed by the copper mining companies to realise Government's predetermined goals.[18] This was made possible only with the change in 1973 of the master agreement: the revised agreement between the Zambian Government and the Anglo-American Corporation not only withdrew the sales, management and marketing contracts, hitherto vested in AAC, but also terminated the minority veto power that required the 'A' and 'B' Directors to vote separately on issues involving financial and capital programmes.

Government control – personnel

The Zambian Government, utilising both formal and informal mechanisms of control, has from time to time imposed its mandate on the personnel activities of public enterprises in areas beyond the confines of policy, thus again violating the basic canons of corporate autonomy.[19] Interference has taken various forms, including:

1. the bringing of pay, salary scales and other conditions of service into line with those prevailing in the civil service;[20]

2. the issue of directives not to lay off State enterprise workers, sometimes even after factory production has ceased; and

3. the transfer of management personnel in and out of individual public enterprises.

Prior to the establishment of the Parastatal Bodies Service Commission, public enterprises were by and large free to recruit

manpower, determine conditions of service and fix the level of
salaries of employees at their own discretion, guided only by what
each enterprise considered to be in its best interest.[21] In other words,
they enjoyed such operational flexibility as was consistent with
corporate autonomy.[22] The creation of the new Commission altered
the situation by providing the Government with yet another means
of controlling the day-to-day activities of the public enterprises.
Through the PBSC, the Government has standardised all personnel
practices and procedures, relating for example to recruitment,
appointments and promotions, throughout the entire public
enterprise sector.[23] The maximum salary that can be offered to the
highest paid parastatal employee has now been fixed and cannot be
exceeded without the prior approval of the PBSC.[24] Moreover, the
Commission is empowered to rescind any decision made by an
individual enterprise if that decision violates the conditions of service
laid down for all public enterprises.[25]

Another area in which government interference has been felt in
the day-to-day activities of public enterprises has been in the
deployment of manpower resources. During the 1972–73 financial
year many INDECO subsidiaries, including the Zambezi Saw Mills,
Kabwe Industrial Fabrics, and Kafue Textiles, were experiencing
reduced industrial activity; the three companies were subsequently
closed down. The normal business reaction would have been to lay
off workers until the companies got back on their feet. INDECO,
however, was directed by the Government to keep all the workers on
its pay-roll for the entire period of the subsidiaries' industrial
inactivity.[26]

The Government has also interfered in the transfer of high level
management personnel, though corporate autonomy requires that
individual enterprises should be allowed to deploy their own
personnel resources in a way likely to promote the organisation's
objectives. Employees holding high positions have constantly been
moved on government directives not only from one parastatal
enterprise to another, but also in and out of party and government
jobs. During the financial year 1973–74, for example, many high and
middle-level executives were moved around within and out of
INDECO on government orders.[27] The transfer of managing
directors across parastatal boundaries has been particularly
frequent, despite the fact that both the enabling company laws, as
well as the articles of association of individual public enterprises,
empower only the shareholders, acting through their elected Board
of Directors, to appoint one of the directors as the organisation's
chief executive. Thus, between January 1973 and August 1976

INDECO alone was served by six different managing directors who came to INDECO from either government Ministries or other parastatal organisations.[28] President Kaunda, using his executive prerogative as the ultimate custodian of the public interest, has appointed and transferred chief executives at will, thereby underlining the fact that the public enterprises do not possess any meaningful operational freedom in the sphere of personnel. The Government has not, as the principle of corporate autonomy requires, restricted itself to laying down broad policy, but has also concerned itself with salary levels, transfers and the deployment of manpower.

Government control – finance

Government's involvement in the financial activities of State enterprises is most evident in the pricing of goods and services. In some cases, commodity prices have been fixed at levels well below the costs of production, the objectives being to enable low income-earners to purchase essential commodities. For example, the price of a fifty kilogram bag of corn-meal which is milled and distributed by the National Milling Company, a subsidiary of INDECO, was fixed at K4.00, though the cost of production was estimated at K12.36. Similarly, a bag of fertiliser produced by Nitrogen Chemicals sold to the farmer at the government-fixed price of K80, when the average cost of production stood at K193 per bag.[29] Where a parastatal enterprise does not enjoy a monopoly position and the price of its product is fixed by the Government, there may be a glaring price differential between what the public enterprise charges and the price charged by its private competitors. For example, in April 1976 the Super Loaf Baking Enterprise, which is a subsidiary of INDECO, charged only 18n for a loaf of bread, while a private bakery charged as much as 40n for a loaf of comparable size and quality. The Rural Development Corporation is another State enterprise which has been subjected to increased government intervention in the pricing of its commodities. Thus, the price of sunflower, a leading product, has been artificially depressed by government action: it sold to consumers at K6.64 per bag along the line of rail and K7.50 in Lusaka, when the actual cost of production was K20.74. The result, inevitably, was heavy operational losses – in excess of K154,280 in the case of this particular RDC subsidiary. The Zambia Pork Products was reported to have lost over K220,000 in the same year, the main reason again being that sub-economic prices were charged at government insistence.[30]

As we saw in the section on personnel, Government's interference in the day-to-day activities of State enterprises has also been felt in the determination of wages and salaries for State enterprise employees. The PBSC imposed a uniform salary structure which allowed salaries to be increased in special circumstances. Through standardisation, the Commission sought to ensure that the whole system was not diluted by concessions to individual or group interests.[31]

Conclusions

We have argued that government control over a country's public enterprises is essential if the latter are to be accountable and responsive to the changing needs and aspirations of the society that ostensibly owns them, and this argument is reinforced in developing countries where public enterprises are regarded primarily as instruments of change. On the other hand, we have also argued that the principle of corporate autonomy and considerations of efficiency alike demand that government control should be limited to the determination of major policy issues; control should not extend to interference with everyday operational matters.

The question arises whether, in a country such as Zambia, additional considerations have to be taken into account – how far, in other words, does the principle of corporate autonomy need to be modified in certain new State contexts? The Zambian Government is committed to promoting rural development and to reducing the income disparities between the rural and urban sectors of the economy. It was in furtherance of that policy that the Government decided, for example, that INDECO's dry-cell battery plant should be sited at Mansa, the capital of the remote Luapula Province, rather than at Kabwe in the central region of the country. Again, it was because the Government was worried about the wide gap which already exists between urban and rural income levels that it felt the need to control the rate at which wages rose in the parastatal sector and was not prepared to leave such matters to the management of individual public enterprises. It is not easy to say that intervention on these lines was 'wrong', even though the practical effect of intervention has been to detract from the economic performance of the public enterprises concerned. The fact of intervention in operational matters, in defiance of the canon of corporate autonomy, draws attention to the basic dilemma facing the Zambian Government. This is whether the Government can really pursue its egalitarian and other policies through the medium of bodies which function best within a free market economy. Present indications, including the report of the special parliamentary select committee of November 1977, are that the Government will solve this dilemma by treading more of a capitalist path of development than it has done since 1968. The more 'capitalist' government policies become, the less inclined the Government will be to assert control over the management of individual public enterprises in the fields of investment, prices and personnel.

Notes

[1] The extensive literature covering these issues includes: G. C. Maniatis, 'Managerial autonomy vs State control in public enterprise. Fact and Artifact', in *Annals of Public and Cooperative Economy*, vol. XXXIX (November 1968), p. 518; O. Prakash, *The theory and working of State corporations* (London, 1962), pp. 18–19; W. I. Abraham, *Annual budgeting and development planning*, National Planning Methods Series No. 1 (Washington D. C., December 1965), p. 15; L. D. Musolf, *Mixed enterprise* (Lexington, 1972), p. 14.

[2] United Nations, *Some problems in the organisation and administration of public enterprises in the industrial field* (New York, 1954), pp. 10–11.

[3] A. H. Hanson, *Managerial problems in public enterprises* (New York, 1962), p. 133; J. Burnham, *The managerial revolution* (Bloomington, 1962 edn.), pp. 73–4.

[4] Cf. B. W. Lewis, 'Comparative economic systems: nationalized industry, British nationalization and American private enterprises: some parallels and controls', *American Economic Review*, vol. LV (May 1965), pp. 50–4.

[5] *Laws of Zambia*, Cap. 648 (1965 rev'd. edn).

[6] The chief executives of government Ministries, departments and parastatal enterprises handle policy issues and occupy politically sensitive posts which were the first to be localised at independence.

[7] M. Chaput, *Zambian State enterprise: the politics and management of nationalized development* (Ph.D thesis, Syracuse University, 1971), p. 214.

[8] B. de G. Fortman, 'Humanism and the Zambian economic order', in B. de G. Fortman (ed.), *After Mulungushi – the economics of Zambian Humanism* (Nairobi, 1969), pp. 99–101.

[9] *Times of Zambia*, 6 November 1971.

[10] All permanent secretaries and chief executives of public enterprises are Zambian.

[11] President Kaunda has attributed the frequent transfer of top managerial personnel to the paucity of Zambia's high level manpower. John Mwanakatwe, the former Minister of Finance, believed that these frequent reshuffles accounted in part for the poor performance of Zambia's public enterprises since an individual had no time to master his job before being moved to a new one.

[12] See 'President Kaunda explains his style of leadership and decision making': edited transcript of President Kaunda's press conference at State House, Lusaka, 13 December 1970; ZIS Background Paper No. 124/70.

[13] A majority of Zambia's public enterprises receive government subsidies. However, in June 1975 the Government reduced subsidies to parastatal bodies by as much as 60 per cent. See Kaunda, *The 'Watershed' speech, op. cit.*, p. 37.

[14] Mwanakatwe Report, *op. cit.*, p. 201. This Commission has subsequently been abolished; see p. 266, below (Ed.).

[15] Cited in Memo. MM1/101/24/7, vol II, dated 12 March 1974; Ministry of Mines and Industry, Lusaka.

[16] Apart from the remoteness of the sites (particularly Mansa), changes in location entailed additional costs since new housing facilities and other amenities for employees were required. These facilities were readily available at the urban sites originally chosen.

[17] INDECO and NCCM each has its own planning division which prepares development projects before submitting them to the respective Boards of Directors. As of June 1976 the RDC depended for its projects on the Ministry of Rural Development's project department.

[18] Until April 1976 the 'B' Directors of the Anglo-American Corporation, representing the minority shareholders, retained the right to veto certain key decisions relating to the financial and capital programmes of NCCM. For details, see Bostock and Harvey, *Economic independence and Zambian copper, op. cit.*

[19] *Some problems in the organisation and administration of public enterprises, op. cit.*, p. 10.

[20] *Mwanakatwe Report, op. cit.*, p. 201.

[21] The unusually high and arbitrarily determined salaries in the parastatal enterprises have been subject to periodic criticism. The 1968 *Report on the working and finances of agricultural statutory boards*, headed by Dr. A. V. R. Rao, criticised strongly 'The appointment of poorly qualified personnel at extremely high rates of emoluments'.

[22] Maniantis, 'Managerial autonomy vs. State control', *op. cit.*, p. 518.

[23] *Mwanakatwe Report, op. cit.*, p. 165.

[24] *Ibid.*, p. 201.

[25] *Ibid.*, p. 165.

[26] *INDECO, Annual report, 1973–74, op. cit.*, p. 9.

[27] *Ibid.*, p. 10.

[28] Upon leaving INDECO one managing director was retired, two were transferred back to the civil service, and two went to other public enterprises.

[29] *Economic report, 1969*, (Lusaka, 1970), p. 166.

[30] *Ibid.*

[31] Mwanakatwe Report, *op. cit.*, p. 161.

6. Party and administration under the one-party State

Ian Scott

The introduction of one-party States in Africa has occurred both under conditions where opposition to the political leadership and the ruling party has been weak or virtually non-existent and under conditions where it has been persistent and entrenched.[1] In some countries such as Tanzania and Malawi, where the ruling party was essentially the only party or where opposition had previously been dissipated, the transition from a *de facto* to a *de jure* one-party State did not immediately affect support for the party or its leaders.[2] In other countries such as Ghana and Zambia, however, the one-party State was brought into being despite considerable opposition.[3] In the case of Zambia, opposition parties were well entrenched and support for the ruling United National Independence Party (UNIP) was probably at a lower level than at any time since before independence. It is difficult not to conclude that this state of affairs significantly affected the decision to introduce the one-party State. Under circumstances where opposition parties are banned and the one-party State is introduced in spite of opposition protests, the regime is faced with the problem of establishing a new consensus for the continuance of its rule. It is now no longer electorally dependent on the political party; indeed, it may be surmised that the inability of the party to provide a solid base of support is a major factor in the decision to create the one-party State. It may decide, therefore, that, instead of relying solely on the party and perhaps driving the opposition to subversion, it will seek a rather wider base of support involving pressure groups, the army, the civil service, former opposition stalwarts and the ruling party. In this chapter, in the context of a discussion on party–civil service relations in Zambia, I shall suggest that this search for a broader base of support has resulted in the declining importance of the political party and the marked increase in power of the civil service in particular, and of what may be loosely termed the bourgeoisie in general.

For much of its recent history, Zambia has experienced considerable conflict between civil servants and the local officials of UNIP. This conflict has reflected not only differences in education, background and interests but also issues which have been central to the politics and form of the State since the achievement of independence in 1964. Should the civil service recruit on the basis of professional qualifications or long party service? Should civil servants participate in politics? If so, to what extent? Who should decide on the allocation of loans and licences? Should party officials be paid from government funds? To each of these questions, party officials and civil servants gave different answers. Together their answers formed a composite picture of the way in which they hoped the political system would evolve. The decision to create the one-party State in 1972, and the ensuing debate on the character and form of the State, gave focus to their views. It also meant that national political leaders, who were to make the ultimate decision on the nature of the one-party State, were faced with the choice in a situation where positions had hardened sufficiently to make compromise difficult. They could support either the demands of their own local level party officials or give substance to the views of the civil servants. But it was not easy in the long run to do both. The decisions on the one-party State, then, settle many of the issues conclusively. In turn, the form of the one-party State is in part a product of the relationship between party officials and civil servants.

The causes of the antagonism between party officials and civil servants lie deep in the colonial experience. The colonial civil service administered a set of laws which UNIP, and its predecessor and later opponent, the African National Congress (ANC), viewed as harsh and repressive. The party's leaders, in fashion typical of nationalist movements in British African possessions, presented the case for constitutional change and the removal of discriminatory legislation to the British Government and to those who formulated policy in the colony. They also, of course, presented the same case, in somewhat different language, to their own followers and potential recruits, portraying Africans who supported the system as traitors to the nationalist cause. As the party grew and as discontent in the country rose, resentment against those Africans identified with the colonial regime increased. In Lusaka, the party's ire was directed at the small number of Africans who held positions of authority.[4] In the districts outside Lusaka, party activists came into, sometimes violent, conflict with those who were responsible for enforcing the laws – police, chiefs and district messengers.

Despite UNIP's castigation of those Africans associated with the colonial government, party leaders soon realised that it was to their advantage to establish a close relationship with the senior African civil servants. These civil servants formed an extremely high proportion of the small educated African elite and UNIP was woefully short of the administrative skills which the educated African civil servant could provide. Further, by 1962, under the extremely complicated franchise rules of the Macleod constitution, UNIP found it necessary to appeal to the white voters on the upper and national rolls. Since these voters had been alienated from UNIP partly, it was felt, because of the party's role in the 1961 disturbances, the leadership selected candidates from among civil servants who were, at that time, clearly outside the bounds of party politics. It was hoped that recruitment from this source would help to create a new image for the party as well as to provide a pool of talent from which future Ministers might be drawn. Elijah Mudenda, John Mwanakatwe and Arthur Wina were to become the most prominent of these 'new men', but others also left the civil service to campaign as UNIP candidates.[5] For those who remained in government employment it was clear that their futures would be best served by a tacit identification with UNIP. Although the colonial regulation which forbade the participation of civil servants in politics remained in force until 1973, in practice many Lusaka-based civil servants were committed to UNIP from 1962. However, their norms were essentially derived from Britain – recruitment on merit, impartiality in the treatment of citizens and promotion on evidence of ability – and this proved an occasional but recurring point of contention with their political masters.

In retrospect, the selection of civil servants as UNIP candidates for the 1962 election may be seen as a first step towards the future integration of the national political and administrative elites. Outside Lusaka, at the district level, by contrast, relations in 1962 and thereafter were far from cordial. There was considerable resentment among local UNIP officials that not one of their number had been selected as a party candidate for the 1962 election and that civil servants, whom they felt had done very little to aid the nationalist movement, should have been selected instead. In addition, relations with local civil servants – and particularly with the police – were soured by the widespread suspicion that the civil servants were helping the ANC, UNIP's partner in the 1962–64 coalition government but arch-rival in the quest for political support in the country. For the 1964 election, the local officials were determined to ensure both the selection of members of the party organisation as parliamentary candidates and the elimination of the

ANC. They were largely successful in both respects. They were able to prevent the selection of some civil servants whom the UNIP Central Committee, the national party executive, wanted to see on the slate and were able to increase the number of party officials selected as candidates.[6] Seventeen of forty-six new candidates were full-time local party organisers and all were elected.[7] Two civil servants were selected as candidates but neither was elected. The remaining successful candidates were national politicians, trade unionists, a teacher and a number of clerks. The ANC managed to elect only ten members in the seventy-five seats at stake. The first post-independence election, in 1968, produced a very similar result. Thirty-three new UNIP candidates (of whom twenty-four were elected) were full-time party organisers. Only eight (of whom six were elected) were civil servants.[8] The district level party organisations had established themselves in a strong position on recruitment to the National Assembly, and from there to the Cabinet, and used their strength in party organs to prevent the participation of other groups, particularly civil servants, in these major national institutions.

Party–civil service relations

In the immediate post-independence period, there was conflict in many, but not all, districts between party officials and civil servants over questions of power, status and the establishment of a party-dominated patronage system.[9] A national convention on the development plan, which met in 1967, noted the following faults in relations between civil servants and party officials at the local level:

(*a*) some outdated Civil Service regulations and some deficiencies in the Civil Service structure;

(*b*) the fact that Party officials are economically worse off than civil servants and poorly housed;

(*c*) the failure of some civil servants to understand how the party can help them in their work and vice versa;

(*d*) the lack of sufficient co-ordination and communications between ministries and their field staff;

(*e*) the lack of mutual confidence and understanding between civil servants and Party officials arising from historical circumstances;

(*f*) some politicians and some civil servants have not demonstrated a spirit of patriotism and are interested only in their personal gain;

(*g*) there were some suggestions that tribalism plays a part in appointments.[10]

The convention recommended *inter alia*:

That there is a need for civil servants and Party officials to adjust their attitudes towards each other in the interests of achieving the objective of serving the common man.

That Party officials should stop criticizing civil servants from the platform and, in turn, civil servants should refrain from making derogatory remarks against the Party and its officials.

That improvements in pay and accommodation of Party officials should be made to enhance their status in the community.

That the National Convention condemns strongly any manifestation of tribalism in the Civil Service and in Industry and recommends that where such manifestations exist, they should be eradicated ruthlessly.[11]

The convention identified many of the immediate causes of friction between party officials and civil servants. A more pervasive and underlying issue, however, which the convention only referred to obliquely, was the conflict over the establishment of a party patronage system. In those areas where the party had extensive support and was well organised, party officials sought to secure loans and liquor and trading licences exclusively for party members[12] and to bring pressure to bear on civil servants to provide jobs in the civil service for the party faithful. Initially, civil servants resisted party pressure. The traditions of British colonial practice were not instantly broken. In 1965, for example, the UNIP regional secretary in Serenje, reflecting the views of many party officials, wrote to the heads of government departments that:

. . . non-employment is rife in the district . . . we appeal that before you employ anybody approach this office because as we stated 'in the party we have got many brothers and sisters who fought relentlessly to achieve what we have INDEPENDENCE'. I am sorry to say that very little response has been coming on this question since the appeal was made from this office.[13]

A further difficulty for the party was that the rural councils, a major source of local employment, were bound by the Provincial Local Government Service Boards to recruit on grounds of merit. Gradually, however, these obstacles to the establishment of a party patronage system were overcome. It soon became clear that, in their conflict with the party, rurally-based civil servants and local government personnel could expect little support from their superiors in Lusaka or from the Boards and that, in addition, the party had a variety of means to intimidate the small number of civil servants in the rural areas. In consequence, the party often asserted a dominant voice in the issue of loans and licences and the employment of locally-recruited staff such as labourers and messengers. By 1971, the conflict, especially in the rural areas where UNIP was strong, had been resolved in favour of the party.

It should be emphasised that the amount of local level patronage available to the party was limited and party officials soon found it difficult to satisfy the demands of their own number, let alone the mass of party supporters. In consequence, their demands on the civil service became increasingly parochial. They wanted the recruitment to the district level civil service to be entirely localised. This went beyond the establishment of a patronage system to the demand that civil servants who were not born in the district should resign. Two examples may serve to illustrate the kinds of tension this produced.[14] In Serenje, the Secretary to the Rural Council, who was not a local man, was the victim of a party campaign to remove all non-local people from positions of authority in the district. In a letter to the District Governor, the head of the party and civil service in the district, the Secretary said that

. . . the local M.P. for Serenje addressed a public meeting in Serenje Township to all people on the 18th April, 1970. At that meeting all civil servants and the Council Staff who came from different districts were denounced for being inefficient in their jobs and were asked to resign, based on tribal lines . . . immediately after the rally addressed by the local M.P. from Serenje, my [Rural Council] Chairman [an elected UNIP official] began to change his attitude into hostility and started cursing me in public as if I were a small boy.[15]

The Secretary had thirteen years' experience in local government and was running the rural council efficiently. Despite this, the District Governor felt that he could not risk a confrontation with the local party machine and shortly thereafter the Secretary was transferred to another district.

In the North-western province, too, party officials tried to secure the appointment of locally-born civil servants. Addressing Kaunda during his visit to the area, the Solwezi regional secretary said: ' . . . 99% of the staff [civil servants] are people from other provinces. Your Excellency, may we point out that to avoid some criticism by these power-hungry people who say there is corruption in Government, we appeal to you . . . to give your consideration to this and find ways and means of stopping it . . .'[16] In his reply, Kaunda warned the people about 'tribalistic tendencies' but refrained from comment on the regional secretary's demand. He could scarcely have done otherwise. A locally-recruited civil service would have sabotaged the entire basis of national development and would almost certainly have resulted in inefficient, and possibly disastrous, administration in those provinces and districts which were short of qualified manpower. It did considerable harm to national integration and economic development – to which the party was formally committed – to have continual friction between party officials and civil servants on the grounds that the latter were not always local men. For more immediate political reasons, too, the rise of parochialism among local party officials was an embarrassment to the national leadership. The ultimate, though unarticulated, threat of the local party officials was that, if their demands were not met, they would cease to support the Government and might, instead, choose to support one of the opposition parties.

By December, 1972, when the UNIP National Council met to consider the Government's white paper on the one-party State,[17] these developments had had marked consequences for the political system. The local party had established itself as the effective source of recruitment to the National Assembly. But, because of the lack of ministerial talent in the party organisation, Kaunda was forced to appoint his own parliamentary nominees, most of whom were former civil servants, to the Cabinet.[18] The local party had also set up its own patronage system in many parts of the country. And it was making a serious challenge for the positions held by local civil servants who were born outside the district in which they were serving. Inevitably, this had resulted in considerable friction between party officials and civil servants, although there was little doubt that the party officials were dominant in most districts. They demanded consultation on all local issues of importance, occasionally imposed vetoes on civil service decisions and in some districts even went so far as to try to 'discipline' junior civil servants.[19] They could in any event usually mobilise local opinion against the civil servants and they were able to withhold labour on government projects if they thought conditions required it.[20] Lusaka and the provincial authority exercised authority only fitfully. Yet, despite their power, party officials were far from satisfied. The amount of patronage was limited; in some districts there was insufficient to keep lower echelon officials in line. Take, for example, the complaints of a constituency chairman in Serenje:

I am now talking to the Regional Secretary of Serenje: He should try by all means to do something about this problem. If the Regional Secretary could promote me and write to the National Secretary. He could have given me some sort of job. Either [sic] he can award me something profitable. I have worked hard and you should do something to make me grateful.[21]

Morale was low. Many branch and constituency officials, especially in the urban areas, had defected in 1971 to the United Progressive Party (UPP), a breakaway faction of UNIP which enjoyed considerable, and apparently growing, support until its proscription by the Government in February 1972.[22] The local officials' demands to the December 1972 Council meeting were unequivocal. 'UNIP', telegraphed one group of officials in the Luapula Province, 'must be supreme over anything under the sun except God.'[23] Supremacy did not simply mean the elimination of the opposition.[24] It also meant that UNIP officials should be given positions in government either locally or in Lusaka, without regard to their qualifications. It meant salaries for branch and constituency officials from government funds. And it meant an official recognition of the status of party officials in the community.

The one-party State

Party officials saw in the creation of the one-party State the chance to realise these demands. Some of them spoke of it as a 'new independence', another opportunity to gain the financial rewards and status owed to them for their contributions to the nationalist movement.[25] Each of their demands, however, posed a threat to the established positions of the civil servants and, indeed, of the national political leaders. Clearly, a civil service recruited largely on the basis of party loyalty and long party service would not only mean the removal of incumbent civil servants but would also cause serious dislocation in the administration of the country. Similarly, even the payment of a nominal salary to branch and constituency officials would be an enormous drain on government funds at a time when senior civil servants were committed to holding the line on public expenditure. Finally, the demand for official recognition of the status of party officials presented the possibility that civil servants, particularly those at the local level, would have two sets of masters – the elected party officials and their own immediate superiors in the civil service. In the face of these demands, the form that the one-party State would assume was of critical significance to both groups.

For those who were responsible for the creation of the one-party State, the demands of the local party officials were only one among a number of considerations which occupied their attention. The December 1972 National Council meeting, which discussed the Government's white paper on the one-party State, was composed largely of UNIP's national leaders and four representatives from each of the fifty-three party regions in the country. They had a very different economic status from the local-level officials who believed that they were disadvantaged. Each delegate received a salary – in the case of the least well-paid, the regional officials, a sum ranging between K80 and K120 per month.[26] Moreover, the delegates had good prospects of promotion within the system. Regional officials, for example, were almost invariably either promoted to more senior positions as District Governors or as MPs or were given well-paid government jobs following the completion of their party service. Thus, the interests of those who debated the proposals for the one-party State were directed to the maintenance of the system rather than to the radical reorganisation advocated by the branch and constituency officials in the districts.

The establishment of a one-party State had been party policy since independence. Kaunda originally anticipated that it would come about through the defeat of opposition parties at the ballot box. However, the opposition proved so resilient – and UNIP was so badly fragmented by a power struggle among its leaders – that rather than declining in strength, the UPP and ANC seemed to be gaining support. By 1972, there were signs of a real threat to UNIP's dominant position. The UPP had appealed, with some success, to those groups – trade unions, students and businessmen – who, partly because of the local party's stranglehold over recruitment, had been excluded from decision-making roles. Kapwepwe, the UPP leader, was elected to the National Assembly in a by-election on the Copperbelt in December 1971. Even though the UPP lost the other five seats which it contested, the victory served to demonstrate that UNIP could no longer assume overwhelming dominance on the Copperbelt.[27] At the same time, the ANC maintained its hold over Southern Province, much of Western Province and pockets of Central Province. In each successive election after independence there was a lower percentage poll. In the end, then, expediency rather than the ballot box brought about the one-party State.

The framers of the new order hoped that the one-party State would solve many of these problems. They anticipated, correctly, that there would be a decline in the widespread political violence which had arisen from intense competition for support. They expected, too, that factionalism would cease to have the debilitating effect on party and country which it had had in the previous five years. Most important of all, they sought to provide a solution to the problem of apathy towards the political system by stressing that the one-party State would be a participatory democracy in which decision-making would be decentralised and important groups in the society would participate in the formulation of policy. The Chona Commission, which was set up in February 1972 to investigate the establishment of the one-party State, did much to improve the status of these groups in its efforts to widen the basis of support for the regime. The Commission 'did not favour the idea of exclusive party membership'.[28] Independence 'should not be attributed solely to one political party since it was a result of collective effort by all the people'.[29] The party should be open to anyone who wanted to join. The Commission also recommended institutional representation in the National Assembly: this recommendation was not accepted by the Government, though institutional representation formed a feature of the one-party constitutional arrangements adopted in Ghana in 1964 and in Tanzania in 1965. The Commission suggested means by which civil servants could participate effectively in the political process and recommended that civil servants should have ten members on the UNIP National Council. Other interest groups were also to have representation because 'it was important for the supreme policy-making body of the Party to include within its membership representatives from as many institutions and interest groups as possible in line with the principle of One-Party Participatory Democracy.'[30] By these means, national leaders hoped both to lessen the impact of the local party officials on recruitment and to reduce the potent appeal which the UPP had made to those groups excluded from the decision-making process. However, by suggesting a pluralist mode of policy-making and a society in which leaders might be recruited from all sections of the population, the national leaders also struck at one of the fundamental tenets of their own local officials. The party could scarcely be 'supreme' if it were to be only one among a number of groups which might be called upon to make policy. The debate was enjoined. Much was conceded in rhetoric to the feelings of the local officials but little of substance was given away. The notion of party supremacy, which was supported by many former local officials who had attained national positions, was eventually adopted in formal terms and even embodied in an amendment to the constitution.[31] But it was an empty phrase, devoid of meaning, a simple rationale for the often high-handed actions of minor party officials. In practice – in terms of recruitment and in significance in policy-making – the one-party State saw an enormous increase in the influence of senior civil servants, trade union leaders, parastatal managing directors, businessmen and the small professional elite.

National political leaders were concerned in two respects with the position of civil servants under the one-party State. First, there was a lingering suspicion that civil servants were not entirely loyal to the party and to its goals. There was some talk of a programme of political education for civil servants to familiarise them with the party ideology, Humanism. UNIP's policy manifesto for the decade 1974–84 stated that the party would 'launch an effective programme of political education to raise the sensitivity and the consciousness of public officers toward the people and their problems'.[32] To date, however, no programme has been put into operation. The more practical measure has been the gradual integration of the civil service into political and party life. The Chona Commission recommended this in 1972. It noted that:

A good number of petitioners submitted that civil servants should participate fully and actively in politics although a few others submitted to the contrary. After examining the submissions, we came to the conclusion that it was desirable for civil servants to participate in politics to the extent of standing for elections . . . We also felt that civil servants should be represented in the policy-making bodies of Government and the Party, as a way of enabling them to participate fully in the policies of the country.[33]

Significantly, however, the Commission did not think that '. . . they should be permitted to hold party posts as party duties might not leave them sufficient time to perform their civil service functions.'[34] Party officials were adamant that civil servants, who, they felt, had contributed little to the achievement of independence, should not gain access to their privileged positions and possibly wrest control of the party from them. However, when the one-party State went into operation, this barrier to the participation of civil servants in politics was soon removed. In May 1976, Elijah Mudenda, the Prime Minister and himself a former civil servant, reported that

members of the public service are now contributing much more to the evolution of party policy, as a result of changes which made it possible for civil servants, for instance, to become office bearers of the party. Civil servants have taken full advantage of this and at our *bomas* civil servants form, in some areas, a good proportion of the leadership at the constituency level. The effect of this has been to foster unity and co-operation in the community and to enhance accountability on the part of the public servant. He is much more accountable than in the past.[35]

The new arrangements under the one-party State essentially worked to the disadvantage of the entrenched branch and constituency officials.

By contrast, civil servants welcomed the opportunity to play a more influential role in the political system. The introduction of the one-party State effectively gave them the same rights and status within the party as long-time UNIP officials. 'We are all UNIP now', one senior civil servant remarked to me with evident satisfaction. In the 1973 general election, a number of former senior and middle-level civil servants – among whom the most prominent were former permanent secretaries J. B. Mweemba and W. B. Mwondela – were elected to the National Assembly by a procedure which required acceptance by the local party organisation. The stranglehold which the local officials had maintained over recruitment to the National Assembly since independence was broken.

The second area of concern about the role of the civil service was in the broad field of policy implementation. Throughout the First Republic (1964–72), political leaders, and Kaunda in particular, had expressed dissatisfaction at the civil service's apparent lack of ability to implement policy.[36] The leadership maintained that UNIP's policy was clear and consistent, that the party had the support of the people in its efforts to reach its objectives, and that, in consequence, its failure to reach them could only be attributed to poor and inefficient administration. The causes of poor and inefficient administration, many party leaders believed, stemmed from 'indiscipline' – a word which covered a multitude of sins ranging from drunkenness on duty to the unwillingness of middle echelon civil servants to take decisions. The solution was seen to be essentially structural; in a phrase later used by Kaunda, the civil service needed more 'organisation, control and supervision'.[37] During the First Republic, there had been some attempts to re-organise the civil service by changing the responsibilities of Ministries and by shuffling civil servants fairly rapidly between Ministries. It was an inadequate response to what was a far more pervasive problem and its main effect was a loss of morale in the civil service. In the one-party State, the emphasis was to be rather more on 'control' and 'supervision' than on re-organisation, but the ultimate result was no more successful.

Between 1964 and 1973, when the one-party State constitution was adopted, formal responsibility for policy-making and implementation lay with the UNIP National Council, the Central Committee and the Cabinet. According to the party constitution, the National Council made policy and the Central Committee implemented it. In practice, the President and the Central Committee, which was composed of the top political leaders, not only made policy but also, in their capacity as Cabinet Ministers, implemented it. The creation of the one-party State led to an attempt to separate 'the policy-formulation role of the Party from the policy-execution role of the Government'.[38] With the exception of the President, the Prime Minister and the Secretary-General of the party, membership of the Central Committee precluded membership of the Cabinet.[39] However, 'the Party shall be supreme and . . . members of the Central Committee shall take precedence over members of the Cabinet'.[40] The two bodies were expected to meet frequently but, in line with the doctrine of the supremacy of the party, it followed that 'Should any decision of the Central Committee conflict with any decision of the Cabinet on any matter of Government or party policy, the decision of the Central Committee shall prevail.'[41] This in fact occurred in November 1974 when the Cabinet decided to remove the government subsidy on the price of maize; the decision aroused such opposition that the Central Committee overruled the Cabinet. The Central Committee also remained responsible for 'the implementation of the entire policy of the Party'.[42] This was interpreted to mean that it could require individual Cabinet Ministers and, through them, civil servants to account for their actions.

In its policy-making and implementation role, the Central Committee was divided into eight (originally six) sub-committees. The sub-committees were allocated responsibilities on a functional basis and were chaired by a member of the Central Committee. Two – the appointments and disciplinary sub-committee and the strategy, elections and publicity sub-committee – dealt largely with party matters and were composed mainly of Central Committee members and MPs.[43] The remaining sub-committees – defence and security, social and cultural, youth and sports, economic and finance, rural development, and political, constitutional, legal and foreign affairs – dealt with national policy and were composed of Central Committee members, the relevant Minister(s) and MPs. Civil servants were included on relevant committees in an advisory capacity. It was expected that the sub-committees would bring party officials into contact with senior civil servants so that each institution could participate in the making and control of government policy.

The moves taken to ensure greater party control over the implementation of policy were singularly unsuccessful. The basic assumption was that control could be achieved by establishing an additional layer of politicians in a supervisory role external to the Ministries. There was no attempt to control decision-making by setting up supervisory party committees within the Ministries. In consequence, intervention by the Central Committee members in the affairs of the Ministry was soon seen as an unnecessary intrusion by the senior civil servants. They claimed, with some justice, that they could scarcely be expected to serve two masters – the sub-committee chairman, or Central Committee members of his committee, and the Minister – and that demands of Central Committee members often showed no regard for policy and could not usually be accommodated within budgetary restraints. These tendencies were exacerbated by the decision, which stemmed from a recommendation of the Chona Commission, to appoint former civil servants and 'professionally qualified persons'[44] (thus excluding most former party officials), as Cabinet Ministers. By December 1974, seven of twenty-three Cabinet Ministers were former civil servants.[45] Fourteen of the twenty-three had university degrees or their equivalent. This ensured a relatively harmonious working relationship between the Ministers and their civil servants, but it did nothing to make members of the Central Committee feel part of the policy-implementation process and there was some resentment, especially among senior members who had formerly been Cabinet Ministers, that their role had been so devalued. In 1976–77 the Committee itself was subject to increasing criticism by members of the community and by MPs in the National Assembly on the grounds that its relationship with the Cabinet involved an unnecessary duplication of effort.[46] In November 1977, a special parliamentary select committee recommended that the Central Committee should revert to a part-time basis.[47]

The influence of party personnel on policy-making was, if anything, even less significant. Constitutionally, policy matters were supposed to be decided by the Central Committee and the National Council.[48] In practice, policy decisions were taken increasingly by the President and his coterie of advisers in State House. Moreover, when outside opinions on policy matters were sought, reference was made not to the Central Committee but to the relevant civil servants in the Ministries. To their chagrin, the Central Committee and the National Council were gradually excluded from the policy-making process. In December 1975, to take a particularly critical example, the UNIP National Council meeting was told by a civil servant, who was not, strictly speaking, a member of the Council, what party policy on Angola would be. No debate was permitted. Members of the Council were indignant that their right to debate what was a highly contentious issue had been precluded by executive action. A second reason for the demise of the Central Committee and the National Council as policy-making bodies was that they were inadequately briefed. The Chona Commission had recommended that the Central Committee should be assisted by a research unit which would enable it to recommend carefully-researched policies to the National Council.[49] The research unit was duly established and a number of senior civil servants and politicians were transferred to the Central Committee to help make it work. In practice, however, the unit was as much concerned with party work as it was with researching new public policies and the inevitable result was that it was spread too thinly to influence policy greatly. Proposals to establish a parallel structure with the civil service were rejected on grounds of cost and duplication of effort.

If the expectations of central politicians that they might control the civil service more effectively under the one-party State were not realised, then, the hopes of the local politicians were also dashed. They had hoped that the one-party State would lead to a greater number of government jobs for party functionaries. There was some basis for their hope, because, under the First Republic, appointments to a number of posts had been made on the basis of political expertise rather than professional qualifications. Politicians had been appointed to civil service positions at the district level as information officers, credit advisory officers and administrators in the office of the District Governor. The only central Ministry significantly affected was the Ministry of Foreign Affairs. As Kaunda noted at the birth of the foreign service, 'the whole job is political . . .'.[50] It followed, therefore, that party activists should be appointed to the Ministry even if they had no formal training. This, in turn, resulted in conflict within the Ministry between professionally trained civil servants and the former party officials.[51] There were cases of party activists refusing to obey the commands of career civil servants and completely disregarding diplomatic protocol.

Even before the creation of the one-party State, it was clear that the precedent established in the Ministry of Foreign Affairs would not be followed. In 1971 the O'Riordan Commission, which had been appointed to review conditions of service and salaries in the civil service, recommended that 'The Foreign Service should remain a separate service with costs related to equivalent Civil Service posts and the Permanent Secretary for Foreign Affairs should be given authority over all members of the Foreign Service irrespective of whether they are Civil Service or political appointments.'[52] Government accepted the recommendation with the proviso that Ministers appointed to ambassadorial rank should have direct access to the Minister of Foreign Affairs or the Head of State.[53] A year after the O'Riordan Commission's Report, the Chona Commission noted that:

Some petitioners submitted that Service Commissions had been subjected to outside interference in the recruitment of personnel and alleged that in some instances persons had been appointed to key public offices without regard to merit. We agreed with petitioners that merit should be the only criterion to be used in the appointment of staff.[54]

Although Government, in the summary of the recommendations it accepted from the Chona Commission, did not reaffirm its commitment to recruitment on merit, there was no large-scale influx of party officials into the civil service when the new constitution came into effect in 1973. The party manifesto itself declared that 'merit continues to be the basis of appointment and promotion'.[55] And in April 1974 Mainza Chona, who was then Prime Minister, said that, as far as the civil service was concerned, 'Merit and not favouritism has always been the test'.[56] He went on to say that the Service Commissions which undertook the recruitment of civil servants were selected from all parts of the country and it was not possible, therefore, 'for any area or Province to dominate'.[57] A competitive entrance examination to the civil service (attempted by 7144 candidates in 1973) was in fact administered by the Public Service Commission.[58] In general, successful candidates were employed but, in one case in 1974 when this did not take place, the Investigator-General (the Ombudsman) decided that the candidate should be employed.[59] In the following year, the Investigator-General undertook a detailed investigation of a board within the Ministry of Labour and Social Service after receiving a complaint about appointments made on a tribal basis. In this particular instance, the Investigator-General did find evidence of tribalism in the case of one appointment. But his break-down of the tribal backgrounds of the members of the board tends to support Chona's contention that it is not possible for any area or province to control the civil service.[60]

Not only were party officials denied access to positions in the central government, but there was also some encroachment on the traditional preserves of the patronage system. First, the Credit Organisation of Zambia, which had often provided loans to farmers with greater attention to political standing than to agricultural potential, was bankrupt by 1970. Its successor, the Agricultural Finance Company, lent money on far more stringent terms and with an eye to the possibility of repayment. Second, in 1974, the Minister of Local Government introduced a new Local Government Service Act which was designed *inter alia* to prevent situations where

individual councillors . . . persuaded the councils to suspend, dismiss or discharge employees for the most trivial reasons or for reasons arising out of a clash of personality, or the converse where inefficient or dishonest employees have continued to retain their jobs because of their contacts with councillors.[61]

On 1 September 1975 the Government inaugurated a unified and transferable local government service under this Act and vested control over the new service in a Local Government Service Commission. Since the councillors were almost invariably UNIP branch and constituency officials, these steps constituted a direct attack on their control of employment opportunities on the councils.

Some attempt was made by the Central Committee to appease local-level officials by appointing a working party to examine conditions of service for full-time party workers. Although the working party, which was largely composed of civil servants, was 'to consider the present form of appointment for those holding elective constitutional offices with special reference to retirement on medical grounds and social security generally',[62] it did little to assuage the basic grievance of branch and constituency officials, which was that they were not paid a salary. The working party was essentially concerned with officials appointed by the Central Committee who were, in any event, assured of positions in the parastatals or in district-level government offices following the completion of their party tenure. The Chona Commission had recommended salaries for branch and constituency officials, [63] but Government had said that the issue needed further study.[64] By 1974, some branch and constituency officials were sufficiently incensed that they wanted to take up the issue of salaries with the Ombudsman. However, he declined to consider the matter and the case was dropped.[65] The party Secretary-General, Grey Zulu, finally killed the issue when he said that 'the Party could not afford to pay the allowances because the Government had no money'.[66]

The unwillingness of the national politicians and the civil service to provide government jobs for middle-level party functionaries and the lack of action on the Chona Commission's recommendation that branch and constituency officials should be paid allowances resulted in a considerable loss of morale among those officials. Some of their positions were taken over by civil servants and members of the growing middle class but, particularly in the rural areas, there developed an increasing hiatus between the regional party officials and the villages. This was especially serious because the Government's programme of rural development assumed that party officials would play a role in explaining government policy to villagers and – an aspiration that was never realised – in mobilising the population. Generally, party membership and support in Africa has tended to drop following the creation of one-party States. In Zambia, the party lost membership, support and some of its most experienced local officials in a very short period after the one-party State came into effect. On the Copperbelt alone, membership declined from about twenty-five per cent of the population in 1968 to around eight per cent in 1974 and had apparently declined even further by 1976.[67] In parts of the country, according to one report, 'the only card-carrying members of UNIP are those holding posts in the section, branch, constituency and regions . . . men and women entrusted with the big task of being the vanguards of the Party, and thus the revolution, are in there purely for cupboard love'.[68] The reasons for this decline in party support lie in a number of factors which vary in importance in different parts of the country and at different levels within the UNIP organisation. There was certainly a general disillusionment with UNIP's failure to live up to its promises; the attraction of the UPP on the Copperbelt and in the Northern Province; and the fact that the one-party State removed the need to maintain a party organisation for electoral purposes. The decline in party support was particularly noticeable among party officials at the branch and constituency level. The party could not satisfy the economic expectations of these officials, which it had in part created by providing relatively extensive patronage in the years after independence, and their disenchantment led to sympathy or support for the UPP or to apathy towards political activity. At the section and village level, the basic units of organisation, where party officials played an important role in the affairs of the community and where they did not expect access to patronage, the party organisation did not disintegrate so rapidly.

The difficulty of implementing party policy soon emerged as one of the major problems facing the political leadership. Not only had their expectation that the one-party State would ensure greater party control over the civil service not materialised, but the civil servants' power had actually grown as they became more involved in policy-making and as decisions were increasingly taken at State House. In addition, there was an awareness that, even if there was party control over the implementation of policy in Lusaka, the requisite party structure for rural development programmes had all but disappeared. Ironically, the decentralisation of the Central Committee in 1976 worsened the situation since its effect was to create a hierarchy of party bosses at provincial level – a Member of the Central Committee, the Cabinet Minister, and a Provincial Political Secretary.[69] It must be said, of course, that the failure of the party to exert control over the implementation of policy was only one among many reasons for the dismal record of a number of party policies. Kaunda, however, felt that it ought to be possible to correct the situation and policy-implementation became a recurring theme in his speeches in 1975 and 1976. It was referred to throughout his wide-ranging speech to the National Council in June 1975. It was the central theme of his address to the next National Council meeting in December 1975. And it was stressed again when Kaunda opened the National Assembly in early 1976.

At the December 1975 National Council meeting, he expressed his concern at the inability of the bureaucracy to implement policy. He said:

Government administration is the principal vehicle for implementing decisions of the Party and its executive organs. No matter what decisions we make, no matter how elaborate the programmes adopted by the National Council may be, the nation has to rely on fellow Zambians who individually and collectively are responsible for the management of our administrative institutions upon which development depends. The failure by our compatriots to carry out their duties leads to stagnation and retrogression, continued failure to implement decisions finally creates new contradictions in our society and compounds the problems of development. This matter worries me a lot. I know, for example, just how many decisions we have made on rural development – on water, agriculture, buildings and roads. They have not been carried out . . . The failure to complete capital projects is due to poor organisation and planning by our fellow workers in the field. We must resolve these problems. The Party must lead. It can only lead if it is well organised and strong at the grass roots level.[70]

Kaunda saw the solution to these problems in terms of hard work, better party organisation and greater consciousness of, and commitment to, the ideology of Humanism. Yet, as he also recognised, the failures of the district level government and party organisation were in part a product of inadequacies in the decision- and policy-making processes in Lusaka. Decision-making was highly centralised. Most major, and many minor, decisions were taken at State House by Kaunda and his advisers. But State House itself was overloaded[71] and the consequence was a lack of co-ordination and policy conflict. There was some policy conflict between the Central Committee and the Cabinet and an absence of political direction, long-range planning and co-ordination in the Ministries. The solution to this kind of problem was the effective delegation of authority from State House but this Kaunda seemed unwilling or unable to do.

Conclusions

The conflict between party officials and civil servants was entirely resolved in favour of the latter under the one-party State. No concessions were made to the demands of party officials that recruitment to the civil service should be based on long political service rather than formal qualifications; indeed, some regulations were tightened to ensure that merit would be the only basis of recruitment. To the annoyance of party officials, the political status of career civil servants was improved under the one-party State. They were able to participate in politics, stand for election to Parliament with greater ease than UNIP regional officials and District Governors, and even hold office in the party. Senior civil servants had greater influence over policy-making than at any time in the past. The increased powers of State House, the weakness of the Central Committee and the tendency to appoint former civil servants as Cabinet Ministers meant that the senior civil servants began to exercise an often critical influence on policy. Finally, party officials saw central government encroachment on the traditional preserves of their patronage system. A slumping copper price and the long-standing hostility of civil servants to political appointments and political influence on the distribution of resources at the district level ensured that debts to many of the 'stone-throwers' of the nationalist movement would remain forever unpaid.

There was, of course, a price to pay. Local party officials became disenchanted. The party lost members. Contact between Lusaka and the people became increasingly difficult. At the national level, the party lost much of its corporate identity which had been a product of its willingness to exclude civil servants, businessmen and some trade unionists from the ranks of its top leadership. In the Second Republic, the national party was a much more amorphous body. Civil servants, for example, could move to ministerial office or even to the party's Central Committee. In addition, Kaunda's own powers had burgeoned to the point where the party and Government's major institutions had far less decision-making power than under the multi-party system. The consequences of this were considerable. As decision-making became more centralised, implementation became more difficult. The communication of policy decisions from the district to the village level, which had been essentially a party task, became a major problem. At the district level, there was scarcely an effective institutional framework to implement policy. Policy declarations became statements of intent rather than statements of action because, as many including Kaunda himself knew, the administrative machinery to implement policy simply did not exist.

The one-party State saw the growing importance of the civil service (and of parastatal managers, businessmen and the small professional elite) which came to exercise power because the national political leadership believed that its survival depended upon them. As Kaunda put it, 'We are getting closer to the point in time when the Party will not have people who are Party faithfuls in key positions in the nation'.[72] Certainly, among the first casualties of the one-party State were the UNIP branch and constituency officials. They did not offer a feasible alternative; they were largely concerned with their own status. They did perhaps suggest a different way of dividing the spoils of government but one which had no real chance of success in view of the forces opposed to them. Without these officials, however, the Zambian Government must devise new means of implementing its policies at the local level, of communicating its message to the population and, indeed, of retaining support for its continued existence.

Notes

[1] See *Government and Opposition*, vol. 2, No. 4 (1967); A. Gupta, 'Political system and the one-party States of tropical Africa', *India Quarterly*, vol. 31, No. 2 (April–June 1975).

[2] See *inter alia* W. Tordoff, 'Tanzania: democracy and the one-party State', *Government and Opposition*, vol. 2, No. 4 (1967); P. Short, *Banda* (London and Boston, 1974), ch. 12.

[3] See *inter alia* D. Austin, *Politics in Ghana, 1946–60* (London, 1964), pp. 414–21; R. Molteno, 'Zambia and the one-party State', *East Africa Journal*, vol. 9, No. 2 (February 1972).

[4] The colonial civil service was divided into a European Civil Service, comprising the senior positions in the administration, and an African Civil Service made up of the more junior positions. In 1961, the two services were merged. By 1963, 14 per cent of administrative positions, 24 per cent of executive positions, 38 per cent of technical positions and 1 per cent of professional positions had been 'Zambianised'. See Dresang. *The Zambia civil service, op. cit.*, table 11, p. 44, and ch. 3, above.

[5] Mulford, *The Northern Rhodesian general election, 1962, op. cit.*, p. 93.

[6] Tordoff and Scott, 'Political parties: structures and policies', in Tordoff (ed.), *Politics in Zambia, op. cit.*, p. 123.

[7] Calculated from *Nshila* No. 155 (January 1964); K. G. Mlenga (ed.), *Who's who in Zambia, 1967–68* (Lusaka, n.d. [1968]); and interviews with some of the candidates. The figures given are probably conservative in respect of the local level party candidates. Mulford estimates that over a third of UNIP's sixty-five main roll candidates were regional officials. See Mulford, *Zambia: The politics of independence, op. cit.*, p. 323.

[8] Tordoff (ed.), *Politics in Zambia, op. cit.*, p. 170.

[9] Generally speaking, the degree of conflict varied in relation to the strength of the local party organisation.

[10] *National convention on the four year development plan* (1967), *op. cit.*, pp. 25–6.

[11] *Ibid.*

[12] Liquor and trading licences were granted by the local authorities.

[13] Regional Secretary, Serenje, to all Departments, 9 December 1965.

[14] The examples cited here are drawn from the Central and North-western Provinces. However, feelings within the party against the employment of non-local civil servants seem to have been strong throughout the country. Even in the Southern

Province where the party was weak, politicians accused civil servants of exercising partiality and employing people in government 'on a tribal basis' (that is, of employing people from outside the locality). *Minutes of the civil servants' seminar* held in Gwembe, Southern Province, January 1970.

[15] Secretary Rural Council Serenje to District Governor Serenje, 31 May 1970.

[16] *North-western Province (President's Tour, November 1971): Welcome address to His Excellency the President by the Regional Secretary*, Solwezi (mimeo.). The charge of corruption in government is probably a reference to a statement made by Simon Kapwepwe, leader of the UPP. It may be of some significance that the Solwezi regional secretary was 'retired' a little over a month after he made this speech.

[17] *Report of the national commission . . . summary of recommendations accepted by Government* (1972), *op. cit.*

[18] In 1971, among the five members whom Kaunda was entitled to nominate to the National Assembly were F. M. Mulikita (Minister of Power, Transport and Works), F. Chuula (Minister of Legal Affairs and Attorney General), and J. B. A. Siyamunji (Minister for Western Province). All had previously been senior civil servants.

[19] In 1966, for example, the Resident Minister in Central Province wrote to the UNIP regional secretaries that 'some District Secretaries have complained to me that you force them to give you Government accommodation or you allocate to yourselves Government accommodation. This is very *wrong* and *must* stop forthwith'. M987 – 1/13/38, 20 July 1966.

[20] In Mkushi, for example, a maize roller mill project was delayed because the local UNIP officials suspected that the official in charge of the project was an ANC supporter.

[21] Muchinka Constituency Chairman to District Governor Serenje, 9 January 1970. Many party officials reached the conclusion that their interests were better served by joining the UPP.

[22] It is difficult to assess the effect of the UPP on the UNIP organisation. Seventy-five alleged UPP supporters were restricted in September 1971. They were virtually all from the urban areas and nearly half had been District Governors, UNIP regional secretaries and constituency or branch officials.

[23] *'A nation of equals'* – *the Kabwe Declaration: addresses to the National Council of the United National Independence Party*, 1–3 December 1972 (Lusaka, 1973), p. 77.

[24] 'Supremacy of the party' clearly has different meanings for Kaunda and the local level UNIP officials. Kaunda has said that it means 'work, high productivity, discipline and self-reliance' and 'the supremacy of the party over all other institutions'. (See *The 'Watershed' speech*, *op. cit.*, pp. 3–4.) Party officials, on the other hand, have often interpreted the phrase to mean that they are entitled to special privileges.

[25] *'A nation of equals'*, *op. cit.*

[26] Tordoff (ed.), *Politics in Zambia*, *op. cit.*, p. 128. The figures quoted are for 1971–72. The salaries of regional officials have since been increased.

[27] Gertzel *et al.*, 'Zambia's final experience of inter-party elections', *op. cit.*

[28] *Report of the national [Chona] commission*, *op. cit.*, p. 42.

[29] *Ibid.*

[30] *Ibid.*, p. 52.

[31] The UNIP central political leadership was badly divided on sectional lines between 1967 and 1972. Another fundamental division, however, and one which operated here, was between former local UNIP officials who succeeded to national positions as a result of party service and those who had always occupied national positions in either the party or the civil service. In part this may be characterised as a division between 'freedom fighters' and 'intellectuals'. After the establishment of the one-party State, the 'freedom fighters' tended to lose power, position and prestige.

[32] *UNIP: national policies for the next decade, 1974–84* (Lusaka, n.d.), p. 47.

[33] *Report of the national [Chona] commission, op. cit.*, p. 29.

[34] *Ibid.*

[35] ZIS Background No. 41/76, 14 May 1976.

[36] Tordoff (ed.), *Politics in Zambia, op. cit.*, pp. 242–87.

[37] ZIS Background No. 2/76, 16 January 1976.

[38] *Report of the national commission . . . summary of recommendations accepted by Government* (1972), *op. cit.*, p. 24.

[39] By contrast, in Tanzania there is no incompatibility rule which prevents Cabinet Ministers from serving on the Central Committee of *Chama cha Mapinduzi* and in December 1977 five of them (in addition to the President and Vice-President) did so.

[40] *Ibid.*

[41] *Constitution of Zambia Act, 1973*, Schedule: UNIP Constitution, s. 12(3).

[42] *Ibid.*, s. 12(1).

[43] With the exception of the defence and security sub-committee, members of the sub-committees were listed in *Deliberations . . . of the fourth national council of the United National Independence Party, op. cit.*, p. 17.

[44] *Report of the national [Chona] commission, op. cit.*, p. 14.

[45] Calculated from National Assembly records.

[46] One critic was the Deputy Town Clerk of Lusaka. For MPs' criticism, see (for example) *Times of Zambia*, 7 December 1976 and 14 October 1977.

[47] See *Sunday Times of Zambia*, 4 December 1977. For subsequent developments, see pp. 192, 262, 272, below.

[48] *Constitution of Zambia Act, 1973*, Schedule: UNIP Constitution, s. 12.

[49] *Report of the national [Chona] commission, op. cit.*, p. 46.

[50] Quoted in Mtshali, 'The Zambia foreign service', *op. cit.*

[51] *Ibid.*

[52] O'Riordan Commission, *op. cit.*, p. 17.

[53] *Ibid.*

[54] *Report of the national [Chona] commission, op. cit.*, p. 27.

[55] *UNIP: national policies for the next decade, op. cit.*, p. 47.

[56] *Deliberations . . . of the fourth national council, op. cit.*, p. 21.

[57] *Ibid.*

[58] *Nat. Ass. Deb.*, Hansard No. 35, 12 December 1973 – 14 March 1974, col. 671.

[59] *Annual report of the commission for investigations for the year 1974* (Lusaka, 1975), p. 43.

[60] *Annual report of the commission for investigations for the year 1975* (Lusaka, 1977), pp. 23–4. The Investigator-General found that of the 126 members of staff of the board, forty-five were Bemba and thirty-one were Ngoni, while fifty were from other ethnic groups.

[61] *Nat. Ass. Deb.*, Hansard No. 37, 3–11 December 1974, col. 72.

[62] *United National Independence Party: annual report for the year 1975* (Lusaka, 1976), p. 7.

[63] *Report of the national [Chona] commission, op. cit.*, p. 51.

[64] *Report of the national commission . . . summary of recommendations accepted by Government, op. cit.*

[65] *Annual report of the commission for investigations for the year 1974, op. cit.*, p. 43.

[66] *Sunday Times of Zambia*, 28 March 1976.

[67] *Report of seminar on Humanism, part two* (Kitwe, mimeo.); *Times of Zambia*, 1 April 1976.

[68] *Sunday Times of Zambia*, 29 February 1976.

[69] See p. 192, below.

[70] United National Independence Party: 7th national council meeting, 8–12 December 1975 (mimeo.), pp. 38–9.

[71] To take one example: every decision of the Investigator-General requires the approval of the President. By June 1976, there was an eight-month backlog.

[72] *United National Independence Party: 7th national council, op. cit.*, p. 32.

7. Urban local authorities

Alan Greenwood and John Howell

At independence, Zambia inherited a fragile tradition of local government, based upon different principles of English municipal authority and colonial indirect rule. Nevertheless, this tradition served as a foundation for a relatively uniform system of representative local government councils[1] and the desirability of such a system has never been seriously questioned by the Government. On the contrary, there have been frequent protestations of support, with the devolution of financial and administrative powers part of a formal policy of 'maximum local initiative'.[2] Yet local government has survived in Zambia rather than flourished. There has been considerable encroachment upon local government autonomy and, as elsewhere in Commonwealth Africa, there has been a familiar tendency towards centralised and authoritarian policy-making.

This encroachment is not as ,straightforward a process as it appears. First, despite the general centralising trend, there have been persistent attempts to inject vitality into local councils, even at the expense of central Ministries. Secondly, there is no single pattern of centralisation and the encroachment process takes several forms. Most obviously there is the encroachment by the Ministries of Local Government and Finance representing successful attempts to limit councils' financial, personnel and functional autonomy.[3] But there is also the loss of authority to the various levels of the ruling party hierarchy which needs to exercise influence over councils as part of its own system of control and patronage. Again, there is the challenge to local government autonomy from the grid of provincial and district administration which seeks, through 'decentralising' government decision-making, to control the various agencies at a territorial level. Finally, there is the growth of various parastatal organisations whose activities at the local level further diminish the area of authority of the local councils.

This chapter examines these trends in Zambian local government and discusses some of the areas of future controversy. We begin, however, by tracing the history and structure of local government and the staffing, financing and functions of the present system of urban local authorities. Rural councils have few of the functions, or the conflicts, of urban councils: the major issue raised by rural local government lies in its relationship to district administration and it is therefore dealt with in Chapter 8.

History and structure

1. Local councils

The British Government granted a Royal Charter to the British South Africa Company in 1889 on condition that the railway was continued northwards over the Zambezi. The line reached Livingstone in 1905 and, in laying the tracks for its further progress, the railway engineers established sidings at intervals of approximately ten miles. At many of these points small communities began to develop, and initially consisted solely of railway workers' huts; but as farms, producing maize and cattle, were established in the areas adjacent to the railways, shops and stores came into being around the sidings. In the course of time small townships grew up and the seed of Zambia's municipal administration was sown.

Under its Charter, the Company was required, *inter alia*, to promote 'good government': this was established by a series of proclamations, including one which authorised the Administrator to lay down village management regulations.[4] Over the following five years the idea of representative local government was introduced,[5] with the establishment of a village management board whose main duty was to administer the regulations. These dealt with what would now be called environmental health, as well as streets and buildings.

The village management board remained the general pattern of urban administration until the late 1920s, but in the meantime significant constitutional changes had taken place. In 1924 the British Government took over the administration of Northern Rhodesia and established it as a protectorate with the full panoply of colonial institutions – a Governor, and legislative and executive councils. The new Government turned its attention to the problems arising from the rapidly developing urban communities, and passed a Municipal Corporations Ordinance in 1927, and a Townships Ordinance in 1928. Livingstone emerged as the first municipal corporation (1928), closely followed by Ndola, the administrative centre of the Copperbelt area, in 1932. These two authorities remained the only municipal corporations for over twenty years, until a number of other urban communities (having served a lengthy apprenticeship as township councils) also achieved municipal status.[6]

The Municipal Corporations and Townships Ordinances must be considered in the light of British colonial policy in the 1920s. The Colonial Government introduced the doctrine of 'indirect rule' for the first time in 1924 and applied it to the rural areas; it was not appropriate for urban communities. Local administration, therefore, developed on two distinct lines until the passage of the Local Government Act, 1965. The Government was content to leave the development of the urban communities in the hands of the municipal and township councils, and the Ordinances of 1927 and 1928 gave these councils wide discretionary powers. The Municipal Corporations Ordinance, for example, allowed councils to establish markets, parks, slaughterhouses, sewerage systems, refuse disposal services, and water and electricity supplies. To enable the authorities to finance these undertakings, the Ordinance introduced property rating which applied to all lands and improvements within the municipal councils.[7] The councils were also expected to maintain order within their communities, and their duties extended to control over such matters as firearms, rubbish disposal, trespass, and prostitution. During this twenty-five-year period of development, however, there was a change of emphasis in functions as the Government passed general legislation on, for example, a penal code and public health. The urban local authorities became less concerned with good order and personal behaviour, and concentrated more upon the development of services. After 1965, these included a wide range of functions such as environmental health and sanitation, roads, building control and town planning, libraries, distribution of electricity, water supplies, fire services, housing, liquor undertakings and community development, but excluded education and medical services.

2. Mine townships

The rapid development of the mining industry was responsible for the introduction of a novel form of local authority outside the scope of the Municipal Corporations and Townships Ordinances. The companies developing the mines were obliged to provide houses for their employees and services for the townships because there was no other authority capable of doing so. The Mine Townships Ordinance of 1933 made special provision for these new units of administration,[8] which were formally established by the Governor at the request of a mining corporation.

From the outset, it was the intention of the Government to establish mine township boards as local authorities for the maintenance of public health and the preservation of good order and government, with powers and duties similar to township management boards set up under the Townships Ordinance. The legislation provided the Government with adequate safeguards in that the Governor (and later the Minister of Local Government) could direct that an area should cease to be a mine township; he could refuse to accept the mining corporation's nomination of a member of the board; and, since the Public Health Ordinance made the mine township a health authority, the board had certain statutory obligations to maintain a reasonable standard of public health. At the same time, the Government was relieved of any financial responsibility since the funds were provided by the mining corporations. The latter, for their part, accepted the financial responsibility, but the amount of the funds provided to the management board was, and still is, at their discretion. Services could therefore be developed at whatever pace suited the corporations, which took the profitability of mining operations into account in calculating the funds that could be allocated to township administration.

Under the terms of the Mine Townships Ordinance, the management boards were expected to conduct their business along orthodox local government lines: for example, they adopted by-laws for the conduct of meetings which were in almost the same form as standing orders of municipalities and townships. There were, however, significant differences. In particular, the mine township boards were not concerned with the raising of revenue or collection of rates and personal levy; the amount of money they could spend depended upon the size of the grant from the mining corporations; the membership of the boards was not representative, and they had no responsibility to an electorate. The boards were unlikely to take any decisions which would not have the approval of the corporations. Moreover, the main services – such as water, electricity, roads and sanitation – were the direct responsibility of the mining corporations through their professional and technical staffs.

The main concern of the boards has, therefore, been chiefly in the field of the welfare of the mine employees – community development, recreational facilities, clubs and liquor undertakings. These concerns encouraged the mine management to introduce a

degree of local worker–management communication in the mine
townships through the establishment of 'township councils', elected
through wards. These councils are unofficial bodies (for which there
is no provision in the Ordinance), whose function is to advise the
management on various township affairs. In some mines, the
'councils' are authorised to engage staff to carry on the business of
retailing liquor, administering clubs and community centres, and
normally the council will deal directly with the mine management
rather than with the statutory mine township management boards.

The significance of the mine township management board as a
form of local authority becomes apparent when it is realised that five
of the city and municipal councils adjoin mine townships, and in two
instances the population of the latter is twice that of the former.
Some two hundred thousand inhabitants (the great majority of
whom are on the Copperbelt) have no representation on local
government councils, and no direct responsibility for the raising of
revenue or for the expenditure of funds on services provided for
them.

The Zambian Government and the mining corporations are
agreed in principle on the desirability of integrating mine townships
into the adjoining municipalities; and in 1976 the Government
received a report on the feasibility of integration. For their part, the
mining corporations wish to divest themselves of responsibilities
both as local authorities and housing authorities, so that they can
devote their energies entirely to the business of mining. Integration
has been the subject of discussion between the two parties over
several years, but there are a number of practical problems still
unsolved. Although the mine workers have no vote in local
government elections, under the present arrangements they enjoy a
standard of services comparable with, and in some cases better than,
that provided by the municipalities. In addition, they pay less rent
for their houses than they would do for similar accommodation in a
local government authority; they receive from the mining
corporation certain 'fringe benefits' which the local authorities could
not maintain; and in practice they have a more ready access to
'higher authority' for complaints and grievances than they would
under a local authority. No doubt the desirable aim of integration
will ultimately be achieved, but the present state of affairs seems
likely to continue for some time yet. The report referred to above had
failed to elicit any response from Government over a year after its
submission.[9]

3. 'Peri-urban' areas

Cities and municipalities have assumed responsibility for the 'peri-urban' areas, thereby adding substantially to the development problems which face them. Until the late 1960s each municipality had a 'peri-urban' area surrounding its boundaries, outside the jurisdiction of any local authority. The term owes its origin to a provision in the Municipal Corporations Ordinance whereby the Minister of Local Government could declare an area adjacent to a municipality to be an urban district, and authorise the council to exercise within the urban district all or any of the powers of the councils. Several such urban districts were declared, but this particular provision was repealed, *inter alia*, by the Local Government Act of 1965. That Act made no mention of urban districts and assumed that the territory in question would be in the area of rural councils. Immediately, however, this was not so. The areas of jurisdiction of rural councils are based upon those of the former native authorities and the latter did not include the urban districts. After 1965, therefore, the peri-urban areas became isolated. They were not administered by any local government authority and their inhabitants were deprived of a vote at the local government elections. Legally, these pockets came under the jurisdiction of the District Secretary who collected personal levy and issued certain licences, but provided no services. On the other hand, many people chose to live in these areas rather than within the municipal boundaries. Residents had access to urban amenities and often secured employment in the towns; but they were not, of course, obliged to pay property rates.

The administrative problem of peri-urban areas varied in complexity according to the circumstances of each particular municipality. The peri-urban area surrounding Lusaka, for example, comprised the former urban district outside the municipal boundary established under the Municipal Corporations Ordinance. This district was of irregular shape, varied in depth some two to five miles from the city boundary and adjoined the townships of Chelston, Roma and Kabulonga. It included some substantial residential development and land in private ownership, laid out in building plots with light and water provided by the landlords. But it also contained five settlements, unplanned and uncontrolled, where some fifty to sixty thousand people lived in overcrowded conditions without basic services. This township and peri-urban area was eventually incorporated in the city boundaries in 1970. This is much tidier administratively but the problem of providing 'Greater Lusaka' inhabitants with basic essential services has been greatly increased.

In the Copperbelt, the two cities of Kitwe and Ndola and the three municipalities of Luanshya, Mufulira and Chingola all had peri-urban areas adjacent to their boundaries. The areas beyond municipal authority covered some 2,800 square miles and had an estimated population of over sixty thousand. However, of the 2,800 square miles, over nine hundred were covered by forest reserves, controlled under the Forestry Ordinance, and a further 509 square miles were mining special grant areas.[10] The remaining part of the Copperbelt contained many uncontrolled and unauthorised settlements, accounting for the greater proportion of the total population. In 1965, proposals for the administration of the Copperbelt peri-urban areas suggested the inclusion of all the latter within the jurisdiction of a single rural authority. However, this solution presented considerable operational difficulties. Given the geographical position of the urban settlements, the forest areas and the mining special grant areas, the truly rural territory is fragmentary and in widely separated pockets. It was felt that a rural authority established in these circumstances would lack cohesion. A step towards rationalisation was taken in 1970 when the boundaries of the five cities and municipalities were enlarged to include both adjacent local government townships and peri-urban areas (but not the mine townships). Thus, Chingola absorbed Chililabombwe and Kasompe; Kitwe absorbed Chambisi, Chibuluma, Garneton and Kalulushi; Luanshya absorbed Fisenge; Mufulira absorbed Kansuswa; and Ndola absorbed Twapia. This created political animosity however and by 1977, Chililabombwe and Kalulushi had been allowed to secede in furtherance of government policy which prescribes that every administrative district should have its own council.[11]

Councillors and officers

The present structure of representative local government is based upon the English pattern: with single-member wards[12] and (since 1976) mayors and chairmen elected by the councillors. The 1965 Act requires any council consisting of more than six councillors to appoint a finance committee, and allows any council to appoint such other standing and occasional committees as may be necessary for the discharge of its functions. The Act also allows non-council members to be appointed to council committees except in the case of a finance committee, and provided that not fewer than two-thirds of the committee are council members.

The finance committees and a number of other standing committees, such as public health and social services, normally meet once a month, although in the three larger authorities – the cities of Lusaka, Kitwe and Ndola – the committee responsible for considering building plans often meets twice monthly. In addition to these committees, there are *ad hoc* committees for particular purposes; and there is a considerable variation between authorities in the distribution and grouping of committee subject matters. Normally, chief officers present written monthly reports to committees and these often include recommendations for action on matters requiring a decision by the committee. The effectiveness of this procedure depends in large measure on the personal relationships between chief officers and councillors, but in general there is a problem of municipal councillors expecting to have recommendations, particularly on technical matters, clearly formulated with fairly comprehensive supporting information. Officers, for their part, are frequently lacking in the experience and self-assurance to steer the work of the committees and sometimes are unwilling to take the initiative, particularly in sensitive matters such as housing, rents and commercial undertakings.[13]

The committee system also involves delays in arriving at decisions. For example, a housing committee decision on maintenance will have to wait for the full council for approval but will then be passed to the finance committee for further discussion on resources. These delays are exacerbated by the tendency for councils to avoid decisions by referring back contentious (or insufficiently presented) matters for further consideration by the committee concerned. Councillors, of course, are amateur administrators serving the council in their spare time, and therefore are often ill-equipped to take decisions on major issues where a large capital outlay is at stake. As a result, important and costly projects are sometimes approved without adequate consideration because councillors cannot comprehend the issues involved, whereas relatively minor, routine matters are hotly debated because they are within the councillors' own personal experience. Councillors are often party officials at the constituency or ward level and are expected by their constituents to exercise some influence in the council. On, and outside, the housing committees, councillors are particularly active on questions relating to evictions and waiting lists. The allocation of market stalls and the issue of licences for, say, hawkers or day nurseries are further examples of lively councillor interest.

Unlike the role of councillors, the position of local government officers has undergone a significant change in recent years. Just before independence, officers came under an Ordinance[14] which empowered councils to employ and dismiss their own staffs, subject to the final authority of a Local Government Service Commission only in the case of dismissal or suspension of a small group of 'specified officers' such as town clerk or city treasurer.[15] The Commission did, however, have responsibility for determining salaries and conditions of service.

Councils were heavily dependent on expatriate manpower and this involved them, as employing authorities, in a lengthy recruitment process and meant that they experienced a high turn-over of contract staff. In 1970, the Minister of Local Government ordered local authorities to stop recruiting staff from overseas and set up a Centralised Recruitment Panel to do the job for them. The Panel aroused the hostility of the councils (which had previously sent their own recruitment teams overseas) and it had a short and uncertain career with appointment procedure, composition and relationship to other government recruitment agencies[16] proving particularly intractable.

The difficulty of overseas recruitment was however relatively unimportant compared to the wider problems of staffing local government. These problems were partly due to the regular loss of staff to better-paid central government and parastatal posts, particularly as there was no accepted system of training and promotion within the local government service. The part-time Commission and Provincial Boards proved incapable of handling the large number of disciplinary, salary and conditions of service cases presented to them; and among the councils there were wide disparities of staffing levels and recruitment procedures, with 'local politics and personal connections' influencing decisions.[17]

The Local Government Service Act of 1974 was a response to these problems. It repealed the 1963 Ordinance and created a new Local Government Service Commission which was eventually empowered to recruit, appoint, transfer, promote and dismiss all local authority staff.[18] The Commission was also charged with creating a new career structure in local government with uniform conditions of service and a co-ordinated training scheme. However, the most immediately important task was in redeploying staff, partly to prop up poorly-endowed township councils but also, it was felt within the local government service, to break up what came to be colourfully known as 'tribal mafias' in particular councils.

The period since the establishment of the Commission in 1975 has been particularly controversial for local government officers. The

Commission itself has worked under difficult circumstances: it is inexperienced and inadequately staffed; it inherited a mass of detailed cases from the defunct Commission and Provincial Boards; and it has been faced with a critical difficulty in recruiting expatriate staff.[19] Against this background, the priority given to establishing a 'transferable' local government service has created unusually high demands on the morale and loyalty of officers, with their professional association attempting to resist regular transfers.[20] The Chairman of the Commission has defended the level of transfers on the grounds of past 'indiscipline' (a euphemism for suspected corruption or nepotism) and the wide disparities between councils.[21] Complaining officers have received support from MPs who have charged the Commission in Parliament with politically-motivated interference and 'bulldozer' tactics,[22] and have asked the Government to amend the 1974 Act. In some cases, councillors have joined in the unsuccessful resistance. The Kitwe City Council, for example, temporarily 'rejected' the Commission's appointment of a deputy town clerk, claiming that there was a stronger candidate already working in the Council.[23]

On the part of the Ministry itself, there has also been concern at the operations of the Commission. Part of this concern reflects the disappointing recruitment record of the Commission and the problems of morale created by the frequent transfers. However, by 1977 there was a more fundamental point of contention. The Commission argued that a uniform and transferable service meant that differential salary grades between councils should be abolished (regardless of the size of the authority). The Ministry was unwilling to accept the substantial increase in cost that this would imply – especially with the existing levels of transfers. The matter remained unresolved, while the work of councils suffered from the inevitable confusion created by a transferable staff system without an agreed salary structure.[24]

Finance and functions

The external influence exemplified by the creation of the Local Government Service Commission is in fact only a small part of a widespread trend towards central interference in Zambian local government. This interference is seen most clearly in the areas of sources of revenue and the exercise of functions.

There is, of course, a degree of central financial control through the system of grants and the statutory powers of the Minister to approve estimates of expenditure on scheduled functions. The latter aspect of central control also extends to the issue of instructions on priorities for capital expenditure.[25] However, the only significant grants are the specific grants – most notably that for public health – and the grants in lieu of rates (as local authorities do not levy rates on government property). The rate grant is not tied to specific expenditure but it is not a particularly reliable source of income. In 1974 the rate due was reduced unilaterally by 33 per cent by the Government[26] and in 1977 the Permanent Secretary warned that only 80 per cent of the grant might be paid.[27] Other grants have now been abandoned, including the Block Grant, in 1971, and the Unit Grant (a rent subsidy) in 1974.

The central financial control does not therefore simply represent the power of the purse-string. On the contrary, the main sources of income for the larger urban councils are generated locally, particularly through the property rate, personal levy, rents,[28] and licence fees and charges.[29] The local authorities have a dismal record in exploiting sources of revenue in their commercial undertakings (of which more later), yet the major constraint upon the growth of local revenue has certainly been the reluctance of the central government to allow the introduction of higher charges. Rate increases require the approval of the Minister and in most councils, rates in 1977 were at around five ngwee in the kwacha,[30] still at their 1969 levels.[31] The rate of personal levy was also last raised in 1969. Like licence fees, the personal levy is determined by Parliament and reaches its limit (K20 per annum) at the low income level of K1,000. (The question of rents is closely tied to housing policy and this is dealt with below.)

In one important area, the central government has in fact taken over an important source of local revenue. Under the 'head-lease' system, city and municipal councils could lease State land.[32] This was abandoned in 1973 – partly as a consequence of accusations of council corruption and profiteering[33] – in favour of a 'direct lease' system which vested authority in the Commission of Lands.[34] However, the new arrangement has led to frequent accusations of long delays (and even corruption) in the allocation of plots and a slowing down of urban development.[35]

The weak financial position of councils, and the reluctance of the central government to bale them out, had led by the mid-1970s to a greater emphasis on the 'self-reliance' of councils. This, together with Presidential directives on the removal of 'landlordism', seemed to create a new climate for local councils as agents of public enterprise, particularly in the field of housing and commercial undertakings. In practice, however, the constraints have been formidable.

The functions of urban councils are mainly centred upon the provision of services, excluding the most important services of health, education and policing. However, the councils are not simply refuse collectors, street lighters, market managers or water suppliers: they also have the authority to establish commercial undertakings, to build, acquire and let property, and to establish transport services.

Until the late 1970s the commercial aspect of local authority work was rarely emphasised. Apart from running rather unprofitable enterprises such as filling stations, rest houses or plant nurseries, the main initiative was in the brewing and selling of traditional beer. 'Liquor undertaking' profits were, at least in theory, considered an important source of revenue for the housing accounts of local councils.[36] However, since around 1970 there has been a rapid decline in profits and in Lusaka, for example, there have been persistent (and – in 1974 and 1975 – heavy) *losses* on the liquor undertakings.[37] Part of the explanation appears to lie in corruption for which councillors (some of whom have interests in bars) may bear some responsibility. However, it is the central government which controls prices and it has been reluctant to raise prices on basic commodities such as maize, cooking oil – and beer.

Since 1975 councils have been encouraged to extend significantly their commercial activities, despite the dismal record on liquor. This encouragement came after President Kaunda's June 'Watershed' speech which, on the face of it, suggested a new era of local council influence.[38] The policy of assuming local control over foreign business went back to the late 1960s but by 1975 there was still a large number of foreign-owned concerns, especially in the service sector. Local authorities were therefore given loans to buy such businesses, particularly shops and small industrial concerns such as tailoring which supply uniforms to schools and government departments. By the end of 1977, however, this policy had been largely abandoned. This was partly because of the severe economic depression in the country. But some of the management problems of running businesses had also led to a reappraisal of the capacity of councils. In some cases, such as the take-over of supermarkets in Lusaka, the council had simply become the owner of the business with the previous owners remaining as managers.[39] However, elsewhere councils inherited businesses such as Strand Tailors in Kitwe where, after less than a year of council management, the Council had to ask the Ministry for a loan of K250,000 to save the company from liquidation.[40] The problems of poor investment and inept management undermined government confidence in councils,[41] but the councils themselves were seriously under-staffed and had not devised any institutional structure to accommodate such business interests.[42]

The other major expansion of local council influence in 1975 was the acquisition of flats, with councils being instructed by the President to prepare lists of flats and rented houses which would then be acquired by the councils over a period of years. This instruction had all the makings of a major political row since landlords reportedly refused to negotiate with the councils.[43] However, the councils were given neither the necessary legal powers nor the commitment of funds to support such wide-ranging measures and by the end of 1977 the issue had seemingly been forgotten, much to the relief of council housing departments which already had urgent problems managing their own property.

At independence, urban councils were already responsible for dwellings within the designated African Housing Areas and in the period after independence there was an acceleration in building, to rather higher standards than the earlier sun-dried brick dwellings with pit latrines and communal taps. The problem with much of the new 'low-cost' housing[44] was that economic rents were often well beyond the earning capacity of Zambia's low-income groups;[45] and low rents – subsidised by central government grants – were introduced as a matter of policy. With the additional recurrent costs created by the house construction programme – such as for electricity, water, sanitation, roads and public transport – this meant a heavy burden on both the central government and local authorities and by 1971 the policy of council building had been abandoned. In 1974, councils were once again permitted to build houses, but there has been a severe lack of capital available and only a few hundred houses had been completed by 1978 and these were all built for sale.

It has been impossible to meet the demands of the rapidly-growing urban population and, in response to the unacceptable cost of providing sufficient low cost housing, a programme of site-and-service provision was given priority. The councils provided serviced plots and credit for building materials, and individuals were responsible for house construction and maintenance.[46] As with other aspects of local government functions, the site-and-service schemes have been open to abuse. Plots have been allegedly sold to residents, and there have been reported cases of non-residents acquiring plots and building several houses for rent.[47]

Yet, from the councils' perspective, the most serious problems have been not in housing development but in deriving income from their existing stock. This is only partly due to low rents; even more important is 'rent-dodging', which has become a minor art form in Zambia. Even a relatively small council such as Mufulira was owed nearly K1 million in 1977 and the figures for Lusaka and Kitwe were well in excess of this figure.[48]

The 'rent problem' – and its history – is particularly illuminating in the context of local government autonomy. Prior to the 1972 Rent Act, councils could evict tenants who were in arrears, although in theory they needed a court order to do so.[49] Under the 1972 Act,[50] however, a court order became obligatory, thereby greatly lengthening the period of eviction proceedings, and in practice it was relatively easy to delay action further, for example by evading the court bailiff. By 1973, rent defaulting had become a national issue and the President suggested that the tenants who used the Act to their own advantage were committing 'daylight robbery'.[51] As a result, the Rent (Amendment) Act was passed in March 1974 giving the councils statutory powers to evict, after notice, tenants who were three months in arrears. There was an immediate surge in payment. In Lusaka alone there were over 3,300 tenants 'eligible' for eviction notices in 1974, and more money was collected in one week than would normally be collected in two months.[52] However, in their zealous pursuit of revenue, the councils quickly aroused public hostility, and the Government became alarmed at the political impact of widespread evictions. In May, the Minister suddenly ordered local authorities to suspend their eviction plans,[53] and convened a meeting of town clerks, treasurers, housing directors and mayors. Addressing this group (at the Chalimbana Local Government Training Centre),[54] the Minister recognised the councils' authority in evicting rent defaulters but suggested that there was a corresponding 'duty to act in as Humanistic way as possible'.[55]

In due course new regulations – the Rent (Local Authorities and National Housing Authority) (Defaulters Eviction) Regulations, 1974 – were issued but these were not substantially different from the existing procedure based on the old Township Regulations. Legally, therefore, the autonomy and authority of the councils was confirmed: yet in practice the combination of local party officials, on the one hand, and of politically-sensitive central government leaders, on the other, has meant that councils cannot embark upon the policy of strict enforcement which they feel is essential. Furthermore, councils lack the necessary ministerial support to embark upon the even less acceptable policy of increasing house rents. Meanwhile, councils do not have sufficient revenue to build new houses and the poor maintenance of existing stock does not inspire civic loyalties among their tenants.[56] In 1976, the Minister ordered councils to raise revenue by selling houses to sitting tenants,[57] but the survey and conveyancing work required of the councils has proved even more formidable a task than the collection of rents and by late 1977 it appeared unlikely that house sales would make any substantial difference to council housing accounts.

Local authorities and national government

The housing and rent issues discussed above illustrate a not unfamiliar pattern in Africa of administrative control and political interference from the centre. The Ministry (of Local Government and Housing) is obviously an important vehicle of this control. It is through the Ministry that central government controls the estimates of revenue and expenditure for each council and issues instructions on spending levels and priorities. Yet this formal budgetary control is a relatively minor part of much wider, and often informal, pressures upon local authorities to conform to central policy directives (for example, on the responsibilities for running clinics or the take-over of clothing firms) where local authorities have not been consulted on fundamental changes in their *modus operandi*. Councils are also subject to more short-term influence. For example, in Lusaka in 1976 it was the Central Committee member for the province who ordered the closure of the – strictly illegal – caravan snack-bars[58] which the city council, sensitive to the high demand for cheap lunch-time foods, had previously allowed to operate.[59] On a more trivial level the Town Clerk of Lusaka was summoned to a meeting of the Central Committee after a council employee had removed reserved parking notices (for Central Committee members) in Lusaka's main thoroughfare.[60]

Directives such as these are not, of course, part of day-to-day administration. On the contrary, the work of councils is largely disregarded at the centres of policy-making. This is partly because so many decisions affecting local communities are dispersed among several government and quasi-government agencies (as we explain below). It is also because the Zambian policy-makers are ambiguous on the role of local councils in the system of government as a whole. The policy of 'decentralisation' has been directed towards strengthening provincial and district administration, inevitably at the expense of local government. In 1976, provincial Central Committee members were appointed, thus adding further to the uncertainty of local government officials, particularly in the large cities, where already they could be subject to the demands of Provincial Cabinet Ministers, Provincial Political Secretaries, District Governors and UNIP Regional Secretaries.[61] Provincial and district development committees have not as yet assumed a significant role in development planning, but their establishment indicates that councils are not considered a suitable investment of local-level planning. In 1972 the Government received a report suggesting the merger of district administration and rural and township authorities into a new·system of district councils.[62] There have also been occasional intimations of support for a uniform system of local administration based upon districts rather than the irregular and quasi-autonomous system of rural, town, municipal and city councils. For example, in 1976, at a Local Government Association meeting, the UNIP Secretary-General advocated 'an integrated system of administration under which the local authorities would be like departments of the central government'.[63] However, any major reform would involve a massive amount of administration and legal energy and it seems unlikely that priority will be given to such a task in the foreseeable future. On the contrary, the Government appears to be committed to the continuation of local councils. From time to time, new councils are created – albeit extremely poor and poorly-staffed rural councils – and the Government has not reneged on its stated policy of transferring additional functions to councils.[64]

However, the lack of importance of local authorities in the national system of government cannot be explained solely as central interference – or central neglect. Central–local relations have not changed greatly since the 1965 Act and it is hardly surprising that there should be central influence on questions such as sources of revenue (particularly rents) and the appointment of senior staff. The most significant development affecting local authorities since independence has been the growth in importance of various parastatal agencies concerned with urban development and the provision of services.

In the case of major public utilities such as water supply and electricity, there is a clear rationale – on technical and spatial grounds – for authorities larger than the individual councils. Urban councils do in fact remain responsible for the management of water, including revenue collection, although the development of urban water supplies is the responsibility of a national Water Development Board. Electricity supply, on the other hand, is entirely the responsibility of the Zambia Electricity Supply Corporation (ZESCO), although at independence councils were responsible for revenue collection under a less uniform system of local power bodies.

Urban transport is also outside the area of council authority. When the privately-owned Central African Road Services was taken over after independence, a United Bus Company of Zambia (UBZ) was established – subsequently with a financially disastrous (and now defunct) Zamcab division. Apart from the much-maligned UBZ town service (its inter-city services are generally reliable), the sprawling Zambian cities are served by privately-owned taxis. Councils regularly announce plans for mini-bus services – and even tramways – but UBZ remains the recipient of government public transport investment.

However, it is in housing and town planning that the councils have found their influence declining most markedly. Formally, urban councils have been planning authorities since 1962, although in practice it is the Department of Town and Country Planning (or Ministry-appointed consultants) which prepares the statutory development plans. Housing schemes and designs are the responsibility of the National Housing Authority established in 1971. It is the NHA which has subsequently been responsible for most of the major housing developments, though other parastatal bodies such as ZESCO and Zambia Airways also develop their own housing schemes, and the Zambia National Building Society (ZNBS) also funds housing development. Indirectly, all such developments are government sanctioned and in the 1972–76 National Development Plan councils were explicitly excluded from the house building programme.

The most important housing development in recent years has been the K26 million squatter-upgrading programme; half the cost of the first phase, which started in Lusaka in 1974, is met by a World Bank loan. The administration of this programme is formally under the Lusaka City Council, but there is a largely autonomous Housing Project Unit. In the second phase, it is intended that a national co-ordinating agency should be established, with existing council departments responsible for implementation. But whatever the precise form of implementation, it is evident that the basic policy considerations of squatter-upgrading will continue to be taken nationally, with considerable influence exerted from Washington.

Another major initiative since independence has been the industrial development at Kafue. Housing was the responsibility of the Industrial Development Corporation (INDECO) through its Kafue Estates subsidiary. Negotiations for the transfer of assets to the Kafue Township Council began in 1973 but over four years later there had been no agreement after reports of 'deadlock' over

INDECO's K5 million evaluation. [65]

As with the case of the mine townships, there is a lack of confidence in the ability of councils to administer effectively major housing undertakings. Neither the Ministry of Local Government nor the Ministry of Finance seems likely to press for the grants that councils will need if they are to become anything other than impoverished landlords for a diminishing stock of low-cost houses.

Against this background of the declining importance of local government in national development, the President announced, in June 1975, the intention to transfer to councils responsibility for running primary schools and clinics; 1 January 1977 was to be the transfer date. However, when the Ministry finally communicated with the councils, it asked them for their own proposals and did not clarify the crucial questions of finance and personnel. [66] Personnel questions are particularly important since teachers, doctors and nurses are subject to their own recruitment procedures and conditions of service. [67] However, the Chairman of the Local Government Service Commission felt that 'given the support of the controlling ministries and the service commissions concerned, no problem should be encountered'. [68] This optimism was not shared by the Secretary-General of the Zambia Congress of Trade Unions (ZCTU) who opposed the transfer, claiming that the management of local authorities was in 'terrible ruins' and 'had failed to run even eating places'. [69] Furthermore, neither the Ministry of Local Government nor the Ministries of Education and Health expressed any particular enthusiasm for the decision.

In the event, the take-over of primary schools was indefinitely postponed after the publication by the Ministry of Education of a document on *Education for Development* in June 1976. [70] This proposed a new system of education partly designed to break down the pyramidal structure of diminishing opportunity (for which primary schools provided the base). The take-over date for clinics had twice been postponed and 1 January 1978 passed without substantial progress. The problems are not insurmountable in fact. Already, councils have their own Departments of Health [71] with clinics assisted by part-time (i.e. 'visiting') Medical Officers (from local hospitals). Organisationally, even difficult issues such as medical supplies, staff housing, ambulance services and recruitment could be resolved eventually. The main problem is the lack of confidence in the ability of councils to run health services efficiently. This lack of confidence is most evident in the Ministry of Health and the medical profession, but councils themselves have not sought such important new functions, and there has been no public demand for the transfer of clinics. On the face of it, such a transfer seems a somewhat arbitrary 'decentralisation' initiative on the part of the President and in due course may be quietly forgotten.

The issue of new local government functions complicates the already difficult position of urban authorities. Zambia's municipal authorities have achieved a relatively high standard of services – in this respect, the country bears comparison with any recently independent State in Africa. Yet the maintenance of these standards presents a major problem. It is necessary to bear in mind what is involved. First, there is the impact of development projects. All authorities have embarked upon ambitious schemes since independence for the extension of services such as sewerage, water supplies, roads and housing and street lighting. Once completed, development projects require maintenance and, as services expand, the burden of maintenance, both financially and in terms of manpower, becomes progressively more onerous. Secondly, in addition to the completion of major development projects and their subsequent maintenance, one of the urgent tasks facing the authorities is the extension and improvement of services and amenities in areas which have been neglected in the past. This 'levelling-up' operation is necessary in view of the disparity in the quality of services provided in the spacious residential suburbs as compared with other parts of the urban areas. The main reason for the disparity is historical. Colonial government policy was to accord a great measure of autonomy to the developing municipalities. Until 1963, the council members were predominantly, if not entirely, expatriate; they favoured the areas in which they lived rather than what were then known as 'African housing areas'. Though the housing needs of the African population were not ignored – in comparison with other territories, considerable progress was made in housing – the disparity in services and amenities was very wide. Formally, it is Zambian government policy that residential development should conform to the 'integrated community' concept, so that citizens of different backgrounds and financial resources can live in the same areas, instead of being segregated. A corollary is that all sections of the community shall enjoy services and amenities of a similar standard. It follows that as the levelling-up process continues, the burden of maintaining all-round standards will increase. In the third place, because municipal boundaries have been extended to include peri-urban areas and small township authorities, the municipalities are required to provide urban services and amenities in areas where they have not previously operated. The problem has been to provide for this expansion, while at the same time maintaining at a high level services within the former municipal boundaries. In the event, they have done neither. Services in the established areas have gradually deteriorated, while in the new areas residents complain that the level of services (virtually non-existent in some places) does not justify their payment of property rates. While financial resources are so limited, and technical and administrative capacities so restricted, the immediate objective of municipalities must be to consolidate their resources and expand existing services. At present, the acquisition of new functions is not in the long-term interests of local government in Zambia.

Notes

[1] Established by the *Local Government Act, 1965.*

[2] *UNIP: national policies for the next decade, op. cit.*

[3] In December 1978 President Kaunda announced the abolition of the Ministry of Local Government and Housing; Local Government is now constituted as a division within the Prime Minister's Office (Ed.). See p. 201, below.

[4] Proclamation No. 1 of 1907.

[5] Proclamations No. 6 of 1911, No. 11 of 1913, and No. 48 of 1913.

[6] Broken Hill (now Kabwe), Luanshya, Mufulira, Kitwe, Lusaka, all in 1953; and Chingola in 1954. Lusaka, Kitwe and Ndola are designated 'cities', but this is a title of honour and does not affect their powers and duties.

[7] The powers and duties under the Municipal Corporations and Townships Ordinances were substantially alike, so that when the six other towns attained municipal status, there was in fact no material change in their functions. Instead of a chairman there was a mayor, while a town clerk replaced the secretary to a Township Management Board.

[8] Eight mine townships came into being during the period 1932–35.

[9] This was largely due to fears of political opposition on the Copperbelt. When the working party on integration was taking oral evidence, miners threatened 'a struggle on the lines of the fight against Federation' if integration was imposed against their will. *Zambia Daily Mail*, 24 January 1976.

[10] Areas in which the mining corporation has certain concessions, and which are used for prospecting and development of new seams.

[11] The secession came at a time of growing financial crisis for local authorities and the Kalulushi township secretary complained that the council was 'crippled' by transport and staff problems. *Times of Zambia*, 31 August 1977.

[12] One obvious difference however is the 'primary' system in which an electorate of party members is allowed to narrow the field of candidates to three. All candidates must be approved by the party hierarchy.

[13] In condemning 'sectional cliques' and 'lack of integrity' in Kitwe City Council, the Minister of Local Government complained at the ease with which council chairmen could influence officers. *Times of Zambia*, 14 April 1977.

[14] *Local government (officers) ordinance, 1963.*

[15] In the case of rural councils, Provincial Local Government Service Boards had wider powers, including those of appointment.

[16] In 1972, for example, candidates awaiting confirmation of appointment by individual councils were interviewed by the National Housing Authority and many were offered posts. For an account of the recruitment panels, see G. M. Pelekamoyo, 'Local autonomy and central control in Zambian urban authorities' (M.A. thesis,

University of Zambia, 1977), pp. 141–53.

[17] Statement by the chairman of the Local Government Service Commission: *Times of Zambia*, 22 October 1976.

[18] Ministry of Local Government and Housing Circular No. 67/75, 26 August 1975.

[19] This has been exacerbated by the loss of Zambian staff, to parastatals particularly, after their training was completed. City Treasurer, Lusaka: *Times of Zambia*, 29 November 1976.

[20] *Zambia Daily Mail*, 26 October 1976.

[21] *Times of Zambia*, 23 May 1976.

[22] *Zambia Daily Mail*, 17 February 1977.

[23] The reaction to this dissent was illuminating. The Chairman of the Commission (quite correctly of course) invoked the authority of the President, and the government newspaper reminded the Council of the Minister's powers to dissolve any council which refused to take orders. *Ibid.*, 14 January 1977.

[24] For further elaboration of this point, see pp. 200–1.

[25] Ministry of Local Government and Housing Circular No. 15/74, 28 May 1974. This advised a limitation on projects and the following order of priority: water, sewerage, housing, roads, fire services, office and public buildings, street lighting, miscellaneous.

[26] Ministry of Local Government and Housing Circular No. 27/74, 30 September 1974.

[27] *Zambia Daily Mail*, 29 August 1977.

[28] In practice, rents are a source of revenue only in a technical sense as there is a large deficit (around K15 million by 1978) on council housing accounts.

[29] These include such things as trading and cinema licences and market stall fees, but only a small fraction of vehicle, driving and liquor licences which are collected on behalf of the central government.

[30] In Lusaka as low as 3.85 ngwee, and this was paid on a 1971 valuation. Furthermore, the shortage of valuation officers meant that many new developments were not on the valuation roll.

[31] This problem was exacerbated by long delays in preparing valuation rolls. In 1977 at least three township councils were still without any valuation roll at all.

[32] Formally, sites leased at nominal rates to councils for ninety-nine years and then sub-leased at a substantial profit.

[33] Pelekamoyo, 'Local autonomy and central control', *op. cit.*, pp. 120–8.

[34] Ministry of Lands and Natural Resources Circular No. 1/73, 28 March 1973.

[35] Among the critics was the Secretary to the Local Government Association of Zambia, *Times of Zambia*, 11 May 1976.

[36] J. R. Malik, J. Branston and J. H. Barraclough, 'The history and finance of local government' in N. R. Hawkesworth (ed.), *Local government in Zambia* (Lusaka, 1974), pp. 27–32.

[37] Pelekamoyo, 'Local autonomy and central control', *op. cit.*, p. 108. In Lusaka a K125,130 profit in 1970 had become a K265,244 loss in 1975.

[38] In addition to taking over primary schools and clinics (discussed below), councils were to inherit the properties of flat-owners and other privately-owned housing.

[39] An arrangement which often suited expatriate businessmen, given the insecure business environment.

[40] *Times of Zambia*, 29 September 1976.

[41] The Minister of Local Government, for example, attacked 'glaring inefficiency' and warned that he would not approve council applications to take over businesses unless he was fully satisfied of the ability of councils to run them efficiently. *Zambia Daily Mail*, 9 October 1976.

[42] In some cases they came under the City Treasurer, in others under departments

responsible for liquor undertakings.

⁴³ *Zambia Daily Mail*, 27 October 1976.

⁴⁴ In Lusaka, this included Chilenge South, New Kabwata and Libala.

⁴⁵ Richard Martin in 'Housing in Lusaka' (Hawkesworth (ed.), *Local government in Zambia, op. cit.*, p. 88) suggests that many Lusaka residents are 'over-housed' in the sense that their employers, due to a shortage of appropriate accommodation, have provided housing which is beyond the reasonable needs of their employees. Subsidised accommodation is, of course, an accepted feature of public sector employment in Zambia, especially at the senior levels. For those in the middle and high income brackets, this was a period when there was a massive growth in high cost housing, with the accommodation demands of central government, parastatals and the private sector sustaining the boom.

⁴⁶ There was an imaginative extension of this self-help housing strategy in 1974, when work began on a massive programme of upgrading Lusaka's squatter compounds through a combination of external financing and community organisation. The success of the programme has led to plans for its replication in other Zambian towns, starting in 1978.

⁴⁷ *Zambia Daily Mail*, 23 June 1975: this report particularly mentioned 'corrupt council officials' in Kitwe and Lusaka's Kaunda Square area.

⁴⁸ *Ibid.*, 21 August 1977.

⁴⁹ The procedure followed was that laid down in the Townships Regulations, although the particular regulation (No. 139) had been revoked by the 1965 Act. However, the tenancy agreements gave the councils the sanction of common law. See also Pelekamoyo, 'Local autonomy and central control', *op. cit.*, ch. IV: 'The Rent Act, 1972', pp. 63–91.

⁵⁰ The Act itself was passed largely in response to charges of exploitation by private landlords.

⁵¹ Address to the Local Government Association of Zambia: *Times of Zambia*, 27 July 1973.

⁵² Pelekamoyo, 'Local autonomy and central control', *op. cit.*, p. 82.

⁵³ *Zambia Daily Mail*, 20 May 1974. A Lusaka local government officer told one of us that the Revenue Hall of the City Centre was fairly busy early on that day; when the *Mail*, reporting the Minister's statement, arrived, the place was 'deserted within minutes'.

⁵⁴ The training at the Centre is largely confined to clerical and junior executive grades. Professional courses for senior local government administrators take place – rather irregularly – at the National Institute of Public Administration in Lusaka.

⁵⁵ *Zambia Daily Mail*, 23 May 1974. The headline read 'Matoka [the Minister] orders more time for defaulters'.

⁵⁶ In 1976 the Minister at the time (Alexander Chikwanda) accused the councils of taking four months to repair windows and ten years to repaint council houses in need of redecoration. *Ibid.*, 20 March 1976.

⁵⁷ *Ibid.*, 20 August 1976.

⁵⁸ As holders of hawkers' licences, the caravan-owners are required to be mobile.

⁵⁹ *Ibid.*, 30 September 1976.

⁶⁰ The employee had, in fact, misunderstood his instructions which were to remove *other* illegal reservations. This (unreported) incident occurred in August 1977.

⁶¹ For the detailed complaints of duplication and uncertainty from a Town Clerk, see *ibid.*, 24 November 1976.

⁶² Simmance Report, *op. cit.*

⁶³ *Zambia Daily Mail*, 8 May 1976.

⁶⁴ The primary school and clinic issues are discussed below.

⁶⁵ *Ibid.*, 3 January 1976.

⁶⁶ Ministry of Local Government and Housing Circular No. 4/76, 12 January 1976.

[67] There is a further personnel problem, of course, in the establishment of new council departments to run these services.

[68] *Times of Zambia*, 19 March 1976.

[69] *Zambia Daily Mail*, 10 November 1976.

[70] *Education for development: draft statement on educational reform* (Lusaka, 1976).

[71] Concerned mainly with promotive and preventive – rather than curative – health.

8. Rural administration

William Tordoff

One of the Zambian Government's most urgent tasks in 1964 was to transform the inherited structure of provincial administration[1] – the focal point of the colonial system of government – into an instrument of economic development. The transformation proceeded on lines already mapped out in Tanzania, which to some extent served as a model for Zambia.[2] Many of the duties formerly performed by officers of the provincial administration devolved on the police and Ministries; the Ministry of Local Government, for example, became responsible for supervising the rural local authorities through its own cadre of Local Government Officers (LGOs). Although Zambia did not follow Tanzania's lead in increasing the number of provinces (there continued to be eight until Lusaka Province was created in 1976), each province was headed, as in Tanzania, by a politically appointed representative called in turn Under-Minister, Resident Minister, and Minister of State. Unlike the Regional Commissioner in Tanzania, the Minister of State did not hold any party office in the province – UNIP did not (and still does not) have any party organisation at the provincial level. Nevertheless, the machinery of State was used to underpin the party in the district; this was achieved through the appointment to each province of one or more presidential public relations assistants[3] and up to four political assistants, paid out of public funds. Administratively, the Minister of State was served by a resident secretary and a supporting staff of a reduced size and quality – priority was given to filling key posts in the central Ministries.[4] He presided over a provincial development committee (PDC), which met on average every three months to consider ministerial progress reports and to identify and resolve difficulties which had arisen in implementing a centrally-formulated National Development Plan which was broken down into regional programmes.

Zambia did not take early steps to politicise the district

administration and the pattern of administration established in the districts (initially forty-four, and now fifty-five) was somewhat closer at first to that of Kenya than Tanzania. Each district was administered by a (civil service) district secretary who, like the resident secretary above him, was responsible to the Provincial and District Government Division of the President's Office. In June 1966 district secretaries were charged by the President with being 'the chief Government co-ordinating officers in their ... districts with particular reference to the work of economic development'.[5] However, the ability of the district secretary to perform this role was seriously undermined a year later when he was replaced as chairman of the district development committee (DDC) by the full-time, centrally appointed regional secretary of UNIP; he was made secretary instead. The DDC was of course the counterpart at district level of the PDC: its functions included watching the progress of district projects; anticipating, analysing and trying to solve obstacles and problems; and stimulating self-help schemes. It was not regarded, as in Tanzania, as a committee of the rural council (the predominantly elected local authority in the district) and it was to the latter rather than to the DDC that subordinate development committees, notably ward development committees and village productivity committees, were primarily responsible.

The chief defect of these arrangements was that departmental heads worked vertically out of the district or province in which they were stationed, the district head to his provincial boss and the latter to ministerial headquarters. Decision-making was highly centralised in Lusaka, giving rise to local feelings of frustration in dealing, for example, with development matters. 'Up to now', stated the Minister of State for the Eastern Province in a memorandum written eight months after the First National Development Plan (1966–70) was launched,

... I see nothing but confusion. Some heads of departments have no idea about what is supposed to be done. While some centralisation is good, I think that after the plan has been accepted the decentralisation will greatly facilitate the implementation of the plan. I am convinced there are capable men and women in the provinces to carry out development projects. Why, for instance, should we wait for money for a good one year for a simple health centre, a small house for a court messenger, etc.? Let money be released and let us in the provinces see to the building programme. The bottleneck in the four-year plan is Lusaka and if this tendency goes on what we intend to accomplish will in the actual fact be thrown in our faces.[6]

In 1967 certain steps were taken to remove these frustrations and strengthen PDCs. Each province was given a block vote of K50,000 primarily in order to speed up the execution of a project that was being delayed through lack of immediate funds; plans were made to re-establish the provincial accounting services which were wound up at the end of 1965, thus facilitating the control of expenditure at provincial level; and an administrator on the staff of provincial and district government was designated provincial development officer. However, these were palliatives and did not go to the root of the problem which was, in President Kaunda's words, 'the snail-like speed with which the wheels of the bureaucratic machinery of Government turn in the formulation of policy and the transmission of policy decisions to the field operators for execution.'[7]

In November 1968 President Kaunda announced 'decentralisation' measures which involved the posting of a Cabinet Minister and a permanent secretary to each province and the politicisation of district administration through the appointment of a District Governor to each district.[8] These changes in personnel were important, but the structural change entailed in this reorganisation was limited and mainly resulted from the merger at all levels of officers of the Provincial and District Government Division of the President's Office and the separate cadre of LGO (but not PLGO).[9] These reforms paralleled those made in Tanzania in 1965; in general, the situation was modified, but not transformed.[10] A few District Governors wrongly assumed that the focus of development had indeed shifted to district level. Thus, the vigorous District Governor of Namwala, an opposition area in the Southern Province, made a valiant attempt in 1969 to assert local autonomy by reducing reference by district departmental heads to higher authority at Choma (on the line-of-rail) and the provincial headquarters at Livingstone:[11]

DG: '. . . you deal with that in the office of the DS [district secretary], not in Choma. We can't play. Get the best team you can to go and finish that building. Namwala–Choma–Livingstone–Lusaka is in the rubbish basket! That is finished, now it is Namwala, Namwala, *Namwala!*' (Applause).[12]

On another occasion, the Governor blamed district officers for laziness in failing to penetrate the remote parts of the district and 'condemned the Land Rover way of explaining Government policies in Rural Areas'.[13] However, without the backing of his political superiors, the District Governor's challenge to bureaucratic procedures, which were identified as a hangover from the colonial administration, could not be long sustained and the external vertical links (and blockages) were re-established. Other newly-appointed District Governors showed such little understanding of their new role that the rural economy seemed unlikely to become 'a dynamic force in the development of the country'.[14] This was still the case after 1970 when, under the Provincial Investment Programme, funds for specific programmes and projects initiated by the provinces were voted each year by Parliament and were controlled by provincial permanent secretaries.[15]

After a trial run of nearly three years it was decided that the system of 'decentralised' administration should be critically reviewed. In December 1971 the Secretary General to the Government[16] therefore appointed an official Working Party, under the chairmanship of Mr A. J. F. Simmance, Staff Development Adviser in the Cabinet Office, to undertake the review and 'to identify those aspects of it that are not operating smoothly and to make recommendations for such further changes as may be necessary'.[17] In its report submitted in May 1972,[18] the Working Party judged the framework of decentralised administration to be sound; only in local government were radical changes needed. However, the decentralised system was not working because executive authority remained firmly at the centre and must be transferred for the system to succeed. The provincial Cabinet Minister should be given more power and should exercise portfolio responsibility, and the permanent secretary, as executive head of the provincial secretariat, should control the provincial budget, transport and staff. An 'essential feature of decentralised administration', said the Report,

must be the preparation by the province of its own capital and recurrent estimates for all the activities of sectoral ministries and departments which will now come under provincial rather than Lusaka-based control. This is one of the most important – perhaps the most important – measures by which true decentralisation can be achieved.[19]

The Working Party recommended that the post of District Governor should be retained, though a new impetus should be given to his role by making him chairman of the district council, a predominantly elected body to be formed out of the merger of the rural and township councils in every district where they co-existed.[20] Like the provincial Minister above him, he should be subject to less frequent transfer. The district secretary, who would be council secretary, should remain the senior civil servant in the district, but the calibre of this officer needed to be improved – about half the district secretaries had no more than primary schooling, while the bottom of the barrel had been scraped in recruiting assistant district secretaries. The Working Party was critical of the performance of

PDCs and DDCs; each committee should have a revised and reduced membership and should be provided with effective executive support. At present, the provincial development officer was little more than 'a routine administrator with a fancy name';[21] an economist or professional planner should be recruited to this post.

Before the Working Party had completed its assignment, the Chona One-Party State Commission was appointed; however, Mr Simmance and his colleagues were convinced that, apart from minor adjustments, their recommendations would be valid 'whatever constitutional pattern may emerge under a One-Party Participatory Democracy'.[22] In the event, relatively few of the Working Party's recommendations have been implemented. Though not relegated to 'the waste-paper basket', as was at one time feared, the Report has been allowed to gather a thickish layer of dust on government office shelves. Why this has happened, and despite the existence since March 1973 of a committee of senior officials appointed to implement recommendations of the Simmance Report acceptable to Government, is a matter for surmise; one reason is probably the strong vested interests of the central Ministries in retaining their powers. In this they have been largely successful, even though some of the main recommendations of the Simmance Working Party were echoed in 1974 by a World Bank Survey on the Agricultural and Rural Sector. 'If decentralisation is to be successful', stated the Survey, 'supervisory powers for planning, finance and personnel must be granted to the province', and professional and technical specialists should be transferred from the centre.[23] Again, little happened and in 1975 the Mwanakatwe Commission observed: 'Effective decentralisation of the decision-making process has not yet been achieved, but is vital to the morale and efficiency of the [public] service'.[24] Against this background, we review the position as it existed in December 1978, *prior to* the President's announcement on 18 December that the post of provincial Cabinet Minister had been abolished and that the local government portfolio was being transferred to the Prime Minister's Office, a step that involved dissolving the Ministry of Local Government and Housing.[25]

The provincial Cabinet Minister

The provincial Cabinet Minister's statutory powers were not significantly increased in the post-Simmance period – it was to the PLGO, for example, rather than to the provincial Minister that the Minister of Local Government and Housing delegated his powers over the local authorities – and he still lacked precise portfolio responsibilities for his province's affairs at the time of his disappearance from the scene. He had next to no control over national projects and (through his permanent secretary) over the recurrent expenditure in his province of departments other than the Provincial Administration Division.[26] Table 8.1 indicates the very small share of the provinces in the Government's annual capital and recurrent expenditure.

Table 8.1: Provincial capital and recurrent expenditure allocations, 1973–77

Year	Provincial allocation (K m)		Total national allocation (K m)		Provincial allocation as % of total	
	Capital	Recurrent	Capital	Recurrent	Capital	Recurrent
1973	10·13	4·14	113·87	241·05	8·9	1·7
1974	13·82	4·54	158·27	274·83	8·7	1·6
1975	15·65	4·85	240·08	332·96	6·5	1·5
1976	12·37	5·70	133·27	382·58	9·3	1·5
1977	12·88	5·64	159·42	386·82	8·1	1·5

Note
Constitutional and statutory expenditure figures have been omitted from the Table.

Source: Estimates of revenue and expenditure: 1973, 1974, 1975, 1976 and 1977 (Lusaka), and compiled into Tables 1 and 2, covering capital and recurrent expenditure respectively, by John Howell, 'Planning the provinces: another look at decentralisation in Zambia', *Zango*, No. 3 (Lusaka, August 1977). Dr Howell's figures for 1976 and 1977 have been corrected from *Estimates*, 1977, pp. 6 and 223.

Table 8.1 shows that the Government has reacted to the acute economic difficulties facing Zambia since 1975 by slashing capital expenditure; recurrent expenditure, by contrast, has continued to increase annually, though the provincial share, as a percentage of the total, has remained constant over the three year period. What the figures do not show is that about eighty per cent of the total provincial capital expenditure goes on education (30 per cent), rural development (27), and power, transport and works (22),[27] and that actual capital expenditure falls short in a majority of provinces, and therefore overall, of planned expenditure.[28] Again, it is not apparent from Table 8.1 that most provincial projects are very small, valued at under K20,000, and that no criteria exist for distinguishing between central Ministry and provincial projects, with the result that there is needless overlapping (water supply projects, for example, are included in both the national and provincial budgets) and that small and simple central Ministry projects may be supervised direct from Lusaka.[29] The figures also do not reveal that certain Ministries – notably Education (with 25·4 per cent of the total recurrent expenditure in 1976), Rural Development (19·3), Health (11), and Home Affairs (8·6) [30] – spend within each province sums often far in excess of the funds allocated to the provincial administration.

Table 8.1 also does not give the distribution of funds between provinces. Table 8.2 shows that capital expenditure is highest in the 'cinderella' provinces – Western and North-western – and lowest in the new Lusaka Province and in the Central and Copperbelt Provinces, though of course most national projects are concentrated in these three line-of-rail provinces. This suggests a modest attempt by Government to correct regional imbalances in the economy.[31] On the recurrent side the Western, Southern and Northern Provinces are the principal beneficiaries.[32] Table 8.2, in turn, does not reveal the unevenness of development spending *within* individual provinces, the major urban centres benefiting the most: thus, in 1975 Lusaka had 65·8 per cent of all the capital expenditure in the

Table 8.2 Capital and recurrent expenditure allocations by province, 1976 and 1977

Office of the cabinet minister	Capital		Recurrent	
	Authorised expenditure		Total authorised estimate expenditure	
	1976	1977	1976	1977
Lusaka Province	370,000	577,000	105,400	341,701
Copperbelt Province	1,225,000	1,230,000	734,101	649,001
Central Province	1,020,000	1,187,000	667,792	595,401
Northern Province	1,601,000	1,597,000	814,380	771,401
Western Province	1,668,000	1,767,000	746,602	825,901
Eastern Province	1,587,000	1,650,000	624,897	659,401
Luapula Province	1,612,700	1,632,000	666,902	673,502
North-western Province	1,660,000	1,679,000	661,602	667,702
Southern Province	1,624,000	1,565,000	788,602	802,501
Provincial totals	12,367,700	12,884,000	5,810,278	5,986,511
National totals	133,272,415	159,424,200	382,580,844[1]	386,820,228[1]

Note
[1] Total estimates of voted expenditure, i.e. constitutional and statutory expenditure excluded.

Source: Estimates of revenue and expenditure, 1977, op. cit., pp. 6 and 223.

Central Province, while 58·3 per cent went to Solwezi in the North-western Province.[33]

Not only were the powers of the provincial Minister limited, financially and otherwise, but his position was also eroded by the appointment to each province in 1976 of a Member of the Central Committee (MCC). Because UNIP is constitutionally supreme, the MCC outranked the Minister, though by presidential direction the latter still presided over the PDC. There was no clear-cut division of responsibilities between them, and the wastage of manpower and duplication of effort entailed in this arrangement both in the province and at the centre were increasingly the subject of critical comment in the National Assembly;[34] in November 1977 a parliamentary select committee recommended that membership of the Central Committee should once again be tenable on a part-time basis.[35] Nor is this all: though the post of provincial Minister of State was abolished in the 1968–69 reorganisation, a provincial political secretary now serves in each province to deal primarily with political (i.e. party) matters. The existence of this top-heavy political hierarchy meant that the provincial permanent secretary had to cope with three bosses and the UNIP regional secretary with four (the three above and the District Governor)! A premium was placed on good working and personal relations between the provincial MCC and the Minister, and in view of this it is intriguing to note that one MCC (Mr M. Liso) and two provincial Ministers (Mr M. Mumbuna and Mr N. Mundia) in November 1977 were prominent ANC members until the one-party State was created in December 1972. The ex-ANC leaders did not serve in their provinces of origin or in the provinces (mainly Southern and Western) where ANC was formerly strong.[36] It continued in fact to be the normal practice for senior politicians to be posted outside their 'home' areas. Table 8.3 shows that in November 1977 no one province was unduly favoured or discriminated against in the distribution of provincial MCC and Cabinet posts. All provinces had one 'son' serving in each capacity except Northern (two MCC posts), North-western (three provincial Minister posts) and Lusaka Province, created in 1976 (no posts in either category).[37] Of the total of eighteen provincial MCCs and Ministers, four were former civil servants – a lower proportion than for members of the Central Committee and Cabinet at the centre, where there was also a substantially higher number of graduates: some six out of fifteen on the Central Committee and ten in the Cabinet, including Mr Mainza Chona, then Prime Minister and Secretary-General of UNIP since mid-June 1978, in each case.[38]

Table 8.3: Provincial MCCs and ministers, November 1977 (the first-named in each group is Provincial MCC, the second Provincial Cabinet minister)

Province where stationed	Name	Province of origin	Points of interest
Central	A. B. Mutemba	Northern	Former Minister of State
	M. Mumbuna	Western	Ex-education officer; Ex-UP; Ex-ANC
Copperbelt	S. J. Soko	Eastern	Ex-local government officer
	S. M. Chisembele	Luapula	Former parliamentary secretary
Lusaka	D. M. Lisulo	Western	Also minister of legal affairs
	R. Kunda	Central	Ex-head teacher
Western	S. C. Mbilishi	North-western	
	S. K. Tembo	Eastern	
Northern	A. K. Shapi	Luapula	Ex-provincial cabinet minister
	M. Ngalande	North-western	Former diplomat
North-western	B. F. Kapulu	Copperbelt	
	N. Mundia	Western	Ex-UNIP cabinet minister; Ex-UP; Ex-ANC
Southern	S. Sikombe	Northern	
	W. R. Mwondela	North-western	Ex-permanent secretary
Luapula	M. Fulano	Central	Ex-UNIP women regional secretary
	R. C. Sakuhuka	North-western	
Eastern	M. Liso	Southern	Ex-ANC
	J. C. Mutale	Northern	Former minister of State

The provincial permanent secretary

As the Simmance Working Party pointed out, the responsibilities of the provincial permanent secretary derive naturally from those of his political superior.[39] Since most capital and recurrent funds do not come directly under provincial jurisdiction, his responsibilities are correspondingly diminished. The current provincial budgeting procedure is that in consultation with the provincial and district development committees, the provincial permanent secretary prepares annual and five-year capital estimates for both on-going and new development projects. This is a difficult task because of the lack of firm guidelines from Lusaka. After the estimates, which hitherto have been presented by the provincial Minister, receive parliamentary approval, the permanent secretary can implement the development projects without interference from the central Ministries. Here again he will face difficulties both because of the late release of funds – which will mean that projects do not start until late in May or June – and the need to observe bureaucratic Tender Board procedures.[40]

The permanent secretary heads a provincial secretariat and communications from and to the centre are supposed to be channelled through it, but departments at provincial level operate more independently than is possible in any one of Tanzania's twenty regions.[41] The permanent secretary is supported by an under-secretary as well as an assistant secretary, but not by a personnel officer with the professional competence envisaged by Simmance. Moreover, the provincial development officer continues to be a general administrator lacking the expertise of a trained and experienced planner; there is an acute need for a well-staffed planning unit at each provincial headquarters. A provincial accounting control unit exists, though individual Ministries, such as Education, retain their own accounting services. The organisational chart for the Central Province is typical of all the provinces. See Fig. 8.1, facing p. 212.

As 'responsible' officer in terms of the Public Service Commission (Amendment) Regulations, 1970, the permanent secretary is said to exercise the same control over the provincial staff as the central permanent secretary does over staff within his Ministry. However, except for the staff of the Provincial Administration Division, the parallel is not, and cannot be, exact since departmental officers serving in a province necessarily retain some responsibility to their parent Ministry. The latter, in respect of promotion for example, has the major say in judging professional competence, even though the confidential reports of departmental officers now pass through permanent secretaries for comment. The permanent secretary exercises some, though not complete, control over provincial transport. He operates a small pool of vehicles purchased out of the provincial capital expenditure vote,[42] but other vehicles are still bought from departmental funds and are specifically allocated to departments.

Provincial and district development committees

The permanent secretary, like the former Minister and the MCC, exercises a co-ordinating role. The main institution through which they work is the PDC. A weakness of this body in the past has been that it served as 'a talking shop', without control over any funds and lacking executive authority.[43] Has the PDC now become a more effective organ of development? Available evidence suggests that there has been little change.

The PDC remains 'abnormally large' and does not therefore have 'the necessary effect on the implementation of projects'.[44] An ineffective attempt to tackle the problem was made in June 1976 by the Cabinet:[45] its instructions were ignored or side-stepped from the outset in most provinces. Thus, the Cabinet's strange ruling that rural and township councils should be represented on the PDC by their chairmen and municipal councils by their mayors, to the exclusion of chief officers of councils, seemed 'wrong or an omission' to the Southern PDC, while the Permanent Secretary of North-western Province commented: 'Experience has shown that some of the Council Chairmen completely fail to answer fairly simple queries.'[46] In fact, council secretaries continued to serve or were quickly restored (unofficially) to the PDC. As a result of this and other breaches of the Cabinet's instructions, a PDC meeting today might still be attended by a hundred or more,[47] including provincial heads of departments, local MPs, District Governors, and local authority representatives, as well as the three main officials from each UNIP region. A compensating advantage of the PDC's large size is that representatives of (say) parastatal bodies, whom the Cabinet had proposed to exclude, may be present when matters affecting them are discussed,[48] while district representatives cannot convincingly disassociate themselves subsequently from decisions on the allocation of development projects reached in the PDC.[49] Moreover, much of the preliminary work of the PDC in drawing up the provincial capital expenditure programme and scrutinising ministerial progress reports is done by its planning and implementation sub-committee.[50] It is as the dominant members of this body, which normally meets monthly under the chairmanship of the provincial permanent secretary, rather than as members of the full PDC that civil servants can make their voices felt.

The items discussed by the Eastern PDC, at its meeting on 19 and 20 October 1976, included the production of cotton; the proposed railway link to Chipata and the tarring of the Chipata-Lundazi road (both national projects); the shortage of tractors; and cattle ranches and marketing fees.[51] The lack of transport and the shortage of farm implements, especially tractors, was a recurrent theme in the discussions of all PDCs:

' . . . the problem of tractors was so critical', said the District Governor for Chipata in December 1976, 'that the matter should immediately be looked into by the Central Committee if Zambia were to develop its agricultural industry fully . . . it served no useful purpose talking about the agrarian revolution when farming implements were not available'.[52]

Some matters, such as the permissible size of individual landholding for agricultural purposes, were referred to the PDC by the DDC,[53] while other issues were ventilated first in the PDC before being passed downwards – an example was the use of foreign labour in border farms in the Eastern Province, rendered necessary because the local people were found to be lazy and unreliable 'due to most services being free'.[54]

The minutes of some committees suggest confusion over what constitute national, as distinct from provincial, projects; thus, in December 1976 the MCC for Luapula Province sought to mollify PDC members by suggesting that the probable reason why the provincial agricultural officer had not been consulted over the change of site of a sugar estate from one district to another was that this was a national project directed from Lusaka.[55] There was a clear determination to assert provincial rights against central encroachment. Take, for example, the reaction of the Northern PDC in April 1977 on hearing that the UNIP Central Committee had over-ruled its decision that the Industrial Development Corporation should establish a mill in Kasama: 'The members felt that the decisions of the Provincial Development Committee should be respected, and that in future ... those over-ruling the Provincial Development Committee's decisions will be called upon to give reasons why they over-rule the Provincial Development Committee.'[56] Members of the North-western PDC were similarly frustrated when they learned in July 1977 that the pineapple canning factory established by RUCOM Industries Ltd. at Mwinilunga had stopped functioning because the company lacked cans and, due to foreign exchange restrictions, had not been able to obtain an import licence to replenish their stocks from Kenya. At the end of the meeting the chairman – the provincial political secretary on this occasion – felt the need to assure members that 'it is not the intention of UNIP Government to treat this Province as a Sub-Province'; the policy of the party and Government was to develop all parts of the country.[57]

What conclusions, then, can be drawn? To say of PDCs that 'they have failed'[58] is perhaps unduly harsh. In relation to provincial capital expenditure the PDC can and does make meaningful decisions and provincial heads of department are required to carry them out; to this limited extent, the committee has both control of funds and, through the MCC and his staff, executive authority. Its weakness derives from the continuing absence of a comprehensive provincial budget and from departmental control over recurrent expenditure.

The district development committee (DDC) is the counterpart at district level of the PDC. Though smaller in size (thirty to forty is a rough average), this committee also includes civil servants, who constitute its dominant element, UNIP regional officials, representatives of the local authority or authorities in the district, and parastatal organisations and other interest groups. The District Governor is chairman of the DDC, which is encouraged to meet quarterly, and the district secretary is its secretary and executive officer. There is of course a wide variation in the problems which districts face, but a number of them are common and are ventilated at DDC meetings. They include the shortage of finance, manpower (especially technical), and staff accommodation; the lack of transport, farming implements – even hoes were in short supply in 1976–77 – and spare parts; the unreliability of some contractors and the periodic non-arrival of essential materials to complete a particular project.

The DDC has not, as the Simmance Working Party recommended,[59] been reconstituted as a committee of the rural council and works independently of that body over which an elected chairman, as distinct from the District Governor *ex-officio*, presides. On the other hand, the rural council acts as the channel through which development projects put forward by ward development and village productivity committees reach the DDC. These projects are assessed and incorporated in a district capital expenditure programme which is then forwarded to the PDC. Decisions of the DDC are therefore subject to review by this higher body and the only funds at the disposal of the DDC are those released by the province for the implementation of approved development projects. Thus, the DDC is a somewhat weak link in the chain from village to province and, overall, has a marginal impact on development. Not surprisingly, many DDC members feel frustrated and press the need for further decentralisation to district level.[60]

The district governor

The severe constraints within which the DDC is obliged to operate hamper the work of the District Governor: only where he combines energy with intelligence and ability can he make of the DDC something more than a blunt instrument for development. Since June 1971, when District Governors attended a workshop in Lusaka and their functions and duties were more fully defined in a Cabinet Office circular, they have a better understanding of their role as 'economic and social development agents'.[61] There is less abuse of power than formerly and relations between Governors and

district secretaries have considerably improved. It is claimed
officially – by the Provincial Administration Division of the Prime
Minister's Office – that District Governors are less subject to
transfer than in the past, enabling them to become more conversant
with the problems facing their district, and that merit has become
the principal determinant of appointment.

In appointing District Governors, President Kaunda has drawn
predominantly from the ranks of politicians, especially regional
secretaries of UNIP and former political assistants;[62] however, he
has also called upon a number of civil servants. As at 1 October 1977
there were fifty-five District Governor posts, divided (unequally)
between the nine provinces.[63] Some eight of the Governors were
former civil servants, one was a minister of religion, and two were
women. Very few Governors served in their 'home' district and at
least three-quarters of them served also outside their province of
origin. The main exceptions to this pattern were the Eastern
Province, where three out of the six Governors were Easterners, and
the Northern Province, where as many as six out of the eight
Governors were Northerners. In the case of the Northern Province at
least this is unlikely to be accidental; it probably represents an
attempt by the President to woo support in an area which has felt
itself politically disadvantaged since 1969.

While District Governors have made some gains – the provincial
permanent secretary, for example, now normally consults the
Governor over staff transfers affecting his district – there has been
little change in other respects from the position as described by the
Simmance Working Party in 1972. Only in a loose sense can the
District Governor be said to be 'the leader of a united district team,
responsible to the Minister in the province for his district's affairs'.[64]
For, despite the stated intention in 1968, it is the province rather
than the district which remains the focus of development: the
province has the funds and determines their allocation to district
level,[65] and provincial and district departmental heads are still
linked through what are effectively independent channels of
command. The district secretary is a pale shadow of his Tanzanian
counterpart – the district development director – and only
exceptionally is a graduate.[66] He lacks adequate machinery for the
administrative control of district departments and, though he can
recommend to his permanent secretary that a particular officer
should be suspended or interdicted, he cannot himself take
corrective action. He is not supported by a development planning
officer and has virtually no control over transport; moreover, district
accounting units have still not been established in many districts. He

has no legal powers over the rural council in his district, but one of his two assistants may hold a watching brief over council activities.[67]

Rural councils

Sixty-seven local authorities have been established under the Local Government Act, 1965, and of these twenty-four are urban authorities. Our concern is with the remaining forty-three rural councils, of which nine were created as recently as 1 August 1977.[68] Most councillors are elected, but the Minister of Local Government has used his powers under the 1965 Act to nominate additional members (normally five), often representative of the traditional interest. Today, in the one-party State, all elected councillors necessarily belong to UNIP. Regional party officials are debarred from standing, but constituency, branch and section officials, all of whom are unpaid, are frequently returned. The last elections were held in 1975, and like the parliamentary elections in 1973 and 1978, took place in two stages – a primary party election followed by a final popular election. In the latter 640,114 votes were cast (of which 594,100 were valid) out of a registered electorate of 1,664,047, giving a 38·47 per cent poll. There were 1855 validly nominated candidates, but 351 of the 966 wards were not contested.[69] The turnout was highest in Luapula Province (48·79 per cent) and lowest in North-western Province (22·39 per cent), closely followed by Western and Northern Provinces. However, the proportion of uncontested seats was easily highest in the Northern Province (103 out of 164); North-western Province came next with 46 uncontested wards out of 86. Among the successful candidates were several former ANC councillors – four of them at Namwala in the Southern Province,[70] ANC's traditional stronghold where over 36 per cent of the people voted. In addition, many of the new councillors had formerly belonged to the ANC. Since all candidates had been screened by UNIP before the popular election was held, no barrier was placed in the way of ex-ANC members being elected to office as council or committee chairmen. Thus, Mr Enoch Shooba, a former ANC MP, was elected chairman of the Mumbwa Rural Council. Nor were nominated members debarred: Chief Mukumbi has for several years been chairman of the finance and general purposes committee at Solwezi.

The finance committee (often broadened to include 'general purposes') is the only standing committee which is statutory, though most councils also have works and development committees. The Ministry of Local Government advised that all councils should form

education and health committees, preparatory to their assuming
responsibility for primary education and rural health centres on 1
January 1977; however, the Government eventually decided that, on
staffing and other grounds, it was premature for councils to assume
these new responsibilities.

Each rural council has three senior officials – a secretary, a
treasurer, and a public works officer; the main weakness in staffing
is on the technical side. Until 1975 senior staff of rural councils were
appointed by statutory Provincial Local Government Service
Boards, of which there was one for each province comprising five
members and presided over by the provincial permanent secretary.
Each Board operated independently of the employing authorities in
handling disciplinary cases and working out conditions of service;
council officers were therefore given some sense of security. On 1
September 1975 the Government inaugurated a unified and
transferable local government service (a step taken by Tanzania as
early as 1963) under the Local Government Service Act, 1974.[71]
Control over the new service is vested in a Local Government Service
Commission. The latter superseded both the Provincial Boards and
the part-time Local Government Service Commission which had
previously dealt with qualifications for, and the grading of, certain
senior posts in municipal and township government. Conditions of
service are still being worked out, but the Commission and the
(recently dissolved) Ministry of Local Government and Housing
were in sharp disagreement over the salary scales which should
apply to the unified service. Whereas the Ministry wanted to retain
its former grading schemes, which differentiated between different
types of authority according to size and resources, the Commission
argued that since administrators of all authorities received the same
training and had identical qualifications, they should be given the
same rates of pay, tied to civil service scales, irrespective of the size
or wealth of the authority. For the Commission's proposals to be
adopted, the central government will have to undertake to foot the
bill – rural local authorities do not collect property rates out of
which they can pay their officers substantially increased salaries. In
the meantime, and to the frequent distress of the Ministry, the
Commission has effected many transfers across all authorities,
including the transfer of officers from rural councils to township and
municipal councils, often without determining in advance what
salary the officer was to receive in his new post. (No difficulty has
arisen over transfers on promotion.) These transfers have taken
place for one of three reasons, or a combination of them: at the
request of individual officers, on the recommendation of a particular

township or rural council secretary, and on the initiative of the Local Government Service Commission itself. In the Commission's view, many officers have grown stale in the employment of a particular council and would benefit from a move; some have been at loggerheads with the council, while others have become immersed in local politics. The Chairman of the Commission would like to see officers transferred from one authority to another once every three years.

As he recognises, one way of resolving the present difficulties, as well as making optimum use of available manpower, would be to follow Ghana's lead in merging the various services which now exist – the civil, local government, teaching, police and prisons services – into a single unified public service, divided into different sections.[72] However, given the present attachment to the principle of local government autonomy, such a merger is not in prospect; nor is the more modest proposal of the Simmance Working Party that, following the creation of a new district council, the staff of the former rural and township councils should be absorbed into the civil service where possible, or allowed to retire.[73] The irony of the situation is that the *de facto* autonomy of rural councils is already small; it will remain so until councils can recruit better staff and raise more revenue from local sources.

At present the main sources are a graduated personal levy, subject to a maximum individual payment of K20 per annum,[74] licences and fees. Commercial activities such as the opening of beer taverns, the erection of houses for rental, and the provision of school uniforms are often undertaken, though the loss at Mazabuka in 1977 of some K150,000 on the purchase of out-dated uniforms underlines the riskiness of entering into commercial ventures without the advice of cost accountants and proper managerial supervision. The yield falls well short of council expenditure and rural councils remain heavily dependent on the central government, as Table 8.4 shows. The Local Government Division of the Prime Minister's Office imposes tight financial controls on the way in which council revenue is spent. These controls are exercised in each province by the PLGO, who is an employee of the Division. He is assisted by a team of financial advisers, including auditors, in checking the estimates of the councils within his province, auditing their books, and supervising generally their finance and administration. These arrangements mean that the rural councils operate largely independently of the district administration and that an integrated approach to development at district level is lacking.

Table 8.4: Finances of rural councils, 1976

1976 total beer surtax payments	1976 estimates expenditure	1976 estimates income (excluding beer surtax funds)
K7,029,000	K11,089,599	K4,296,430

Notes

The beer surtax payment acts as a deficiency grant and is paid to all rural councils, even where no *chibuku* (local beer) is brewed. Allocation is made according to two criteria – needs, determined by the shortfall of a council's income over expenditure, and population, based on the number of voters registered for parliamentary elections within the council area.

In addition to the beer surtax payment, rural councils receive a small health grant from central government.

The table is based on thirty-four rural councils; the number of councils was increased to forty-three on 1 August 1977. The expenditure and income (excluding beer surtax) totals include approximations for Kawambwa and Samfya Rural Councils.

Source: Ministry of Local Government and Housing, Lusaka.

Sub-district level

At sub-district level, ward development committees (WDCs) and village productivity committees (VPCs) have had a chequered existence since President Kaunda first encouraged their formation in 1967. Their functions are outlined in a pocket manual published in 1971.[75] Each elected councillor is expected to form a ward committee representative of all sections of the local community. Committee membership varies from ward to ward, with a typical committee having some twelve members. Among them will normally be the chairmen and secretaries of the VPCs within the ward area, most of whom are also UNIP constituency or branch officials.[76] Government staff who work locally, such as the Community Development Assistant, will be invited to attend. At what (if it is active) may be a monthly or bi-monthly meeting, the committee receives reports from the VPCs in its area, decides what development projects to sponsor and, as an informal agent of the Agricultural Finance Company, recommends which farmers should be given agricultural loans. The last function, assumed only in recent years, has given a boost to WDCs, many of which were moribund.[77] So, too, has the practice adopted in some rural councils, such as Mumbwa in the Central Province, of assigning WDCs the task of interviewing applicants for trade licences on the council's behalf.

Some districts also have a ward council, comprising WDC members and the chairmen and secretaries of VPCs within the ward (if they do not already belong to the WDC). At Mumbwa, for example, the council normally meets twice a year to review the work of the WDC and keep the VPCs informed of what is happening. The VPC is the basic institutional link in the development chain: its miscellaneous functions may include settling minor disputes, encouraging food production, controlling the illegal brewing of beer, and concerning itself with security arrangements, house improvements, village regrouping and Parent Teacher Association activities.[78] But it is a somewhat weak link, tending to be active only spasmodically – for example, in pressing a particular local demand, perhaps for a school or additional classrooms. Among its (ten or so) members will normally be the village headman, probably as chairman, the literate members of the community such as the local schoolteacher or agricultural demonstrator, and local farmers. When it comes to electing farmers to both the VPC and WDC, the tendency is for the well-to-do, progressive farmer to be chosen – as one politician explained, the poor farmer can only understand problems up to the level that he has himself attained. But he was emphatic that wealth would never be the sole criterion of election; the farmer should also be impartial and have sound judgement.

At both ward and village levels, the party organisation is supposed to communicate government policy and assist the committees in mobilising the people for development. However, UNIP has declined in both vigour and effectiveness since the one-party State was declared in December 1972 and could only muster a 39·8 per cent poll in the general election a year later. As Ian Scott has pointed out, one reason for this is that up-country party officials are demoralised and disgruntled: their expectation that the creation of the one-party State would constitute 'a "new independence"', another opportunity to gain the financial rewards and status owed to them for their contributions to the nationalist movement' have not been realised.[79] UNIP's decline may not however be irreversible: if the economy should revive, money would again become available for distribution as patronage to the lower reaches of the party organisation.

The rural economy[80]

The decentralised system of administration seems to have had little impact on the rural economy. Since 1968 economic policies directed towards rural development have not significantly increased the growth of marketed agricultural or industrial output. Co-operative farming has largely failed and in recent years has been de-emphasised in favour of individual and family farming;[81] the experiment with Intensive Development Zones (IDZs) in the Eastern and Northern Provinces has not been successful,[82] and both they and the State farms and ranches established elsewhere have required heavy capital inputs. The agro-based industries sited in the rural areas (such as the pineapple canning factory at Mwinilunga in the North-western Province) have mostly had disappointing results. These policies have also not noticeably reduced the urban-rural gap or improved the incomes and social conditions of the poorest section of the rural population (Table 8.5).

Table 8.5: Approximate distribution of households according to income levels in 1972

	Urban	Rural[1]	Total
High income (over K125 a month)	85,000	15,000	100,000
Middle income (K40–K125 a month)	170,000	90,000	260,000
Low income (less than K40 a month)	40,000	620,000	660,000
		Total	1,020,000

Note [1] Rural non-cash income has been valued using urban prices in order to make comparison with urban income.

Source: Reproduced from David Evans, 'The "mix" of policy objectives in rural development', paper presented to the Economics Club, Lusaka, November 1977. (Estimates from the *Report of the ILO/JASPA Mission*, Geneva, 1977.)

Faced with a situation of economic crisis, which was precipitated by a sharp drop in the price of copper and increased production costs, President Kaunda has launched a programme of 'production for one self and export' throughout the country.[83] His other proposals were studied by a parliamentary select committee, which reported at the end of November 1977. Though the select committee did not address itself specifically to the question of income distribution, it did recommend that a three-year emergency plan should be launched in 1979; the plan should be 'primarily rural-oriented' and should place emphasis on employment generation.[84] It remains to be seen whether this interest in promoting agricultural development will be sustained should the price of copper increase dramatically from 1980 and the national economy revive. For, as James Finucane has pointed out, the general' decline in copper prices in 1968–70 'occasioned an increased interest in national agricultural development as the import bill was being examined for ways and sectors in which foreign exchange could be conserved'.[85] The result, at that time, was the IDZ programme. However, the leadership's commitment to agricultural development lessened in 1973, as the price of copper reached a record level.

Conclusions

1. *Participation versus control*

In 1972 steps were taken to establish a one-party *participatory* democracy. Among the institutions providing avenues for participation are PDCs and DDCs, rural councils, and WDCs and VPCs. Of these probably the most important are the PDC, with its large membership, and the rural council, which remains a predominantly elected body. However, the PDC lacks executive powers of its own and the rural council both performs a limited range of functions and is tightly controlled, both financially and otherwise, by the Local Government Division of the Prime Minister's Office. That the decentralised system of administration, taken as a whole, is subject to firm central control is consistent with what President Kaunda stated in announcing the administrative reforms in 1968. He then stressed the need to

decentralise in centralism. I define this decentralisation in centralism as a measure whereby through the Party and Government machinery, we will decentralise most of our Party and Government activities while retaining effective control of the Party and Government machinery in the interests of unity. In short, you decentralise to avoid regionalism ... we should integrate more the Party and Government activities.[86]

Popular participation remains something of a myth; it provides a cloak for the vigorous assertion of central control.

2. *The extent of decentralisation*

Decentralisation, understood as the political devolution of power by the (legally supreme) central government to subordinate authorities, is limited. It will remain so as long as executive authority is concentrated at the centre, the provinces are granted only a very small share in the Government's annual capital and recurrent expenditure, and rural councils operate within a context of 'central control and local impotence', yet independently of a hierarchical system of provincial and district administration.[87] Further changes are said to be impending, and in December 1978 a Minister of State for Decentralisation was appointed in the Prime Minister's Office. The fact that both provincial administration and local government are now under that Office may lead to some change in the relationship of the institutions at district level.

Decentralisation, understood as the deconcentration of authority, has been more meaningful, especially on the political side. Within the narrow limits of the provincial budget, provincial MCCs and District Governors exercise fairly wide discretionary powers in implementing provincial and district development projects. For administrative purposes, each province has a permanent secretary and an under-secretary and, in these respects, equates with a central Ministry. Overall, however, the post-independence trend of withdrawing the most competent officers from the field and transferring them to Lusaka has not been reversed. The new central Ministries created since 1968 have had to be staffed,[88] and key manpower has frequently been side-tracked into the parastatal sector with adverse effects on all Ministries, including the Provincial Administration Division of the Prime Minister's Office. Except at the highest level of provincial administration, there is an almost complete absence of graduates; thus, no economist or professional planner is available on a regular basis to guide either the PDC or DDC. The contrast with Tanzania in staffing the decentralised administrative system is very marked.[89]

3. 'Bureaucratic dominance'?

While the bureaucracy at sub-national levels appears strong in relation to the party, which at present is demoralised and ineffective, it is doubtful whether any talk of 'bureaucratic dominance' is warranted.[90] On the basis of admittedly limited observation, I would argue that the bureaucracy has suffered from too much rather than too little political control, exercised until recently by three (and now by two) political bosses at provincial level and by the District Governor especially at district level. The result is that many civil servants seem to lack initiative and a sense of purpose. The position may well differ at the sub-district level where the bureaucrat does not labour constantly under direct political supervision.

4. *Rural development*

Rural development has been a major commitment of the Zambian Government since at least 1968 and was enshrined as the central theme of the Second National Development Plan, which took effect on 1 January 1972. Government assistance to the rural areas has taken a variety of forms, ranging from the establishment of co-operatives, and the provision of marketing facilities, rural credit and tractors, to the introduction of new administrative structures. Unfortunately, the record of achievement so far has not been impressive: the agricultural (non-commercial) sector of the economy has been stagnant or in decline since 1964; the people have become increasingly dependent on government support, not least for the supply of mechanical equipment which is often beyond their competence to maintain;[91] and urban advance has been at the expense of the rural sector, with the result that while the rural population makes up nearly two-thirds of the total population, it receives only about one-third of the national income.[92] According to one writer, 'the division of income in Zambia is among the most unequal in the world'.[93]

The present emphasis in government policy is on the need to save and earn foreign exchange through increased agricultural output; this may result in giving added incentives to the commercial farming community.[94] Economically, such a policy can be expected to yield better dividends than the continued underpinning, largely on ideological grounds, of co-operative farming or the pumping of vast sums of money into large, capital-intensive schemes, such as the Intensive Development Zones. However, the social consequences of pursuing a particular economic policy must be considered in view of the need also to expand rural employment opportunities[95] and to reduce income disparities between the rural and urban sectors and within the rural sector itself. As Professor Evans has pointed out, if a 'mix' of economic and social policy objectives in rural development is to be achieved that is compatible with Zambia's Humanist philosophy, the case for making a substantial policy-shift in favour of the traditional farming community is very strong.[96] In turn, this will mean giving the provinces and districts more responsibility in planning and implementation, transferring to them well-qualified staff from the central Ministries, and giving them a substantially increased share in the Government's annual capital and recurrent expenditure.

Notes

[1] A generic term referring to government at all levels except the centre.

[2] For details, see W. Tordoff, 'Provincial and district government in Zambia', Parts I and II, *Journal of Administration Overseas*, vol. VII, No. 3 (July 1968), and vol. VII, No. 4 (October 1968).

[3] The full title of this officer was 'Special Presidential Public Relations Assistant to the Minister of State'. He was often referred to (incorrectly) as the 'Assistant Minister'.

[4] Whereas at the beginning of 1964, Provincial and District Government had a staff of 227 administrative officers of whom eighteen were Zambians, by the end of 1966 there were only seventy-five administrative officers of whom fifteen were expatriates. Zambian officers mostly lacked training and experience.

[5] President Kaunda's directive of 19 June 1966, reproduced in *Annual report of the provincial and district government, 1966* (Lusaka, 1966), p. 1.

[6] Quoted by C. Hesse, 'Some political aspects of development planning and implementation in Zambia with particular reference to the Eastern and Luapula Provinces' (mimeo.), p. 7; paper presented to the University of East Africa Social Science Conference, January 1968.

[7] Seminar of Ministers, Permanent Secretaries and District Governors, Lusaka, 30 December 1968; ZIS Press Release No. 2223/68, 30 December 1968, p. 9.

[8] President Kaunda's Speech to UNIP delegates at Mulungushi, 9 November 1968, ZIS Background No. 84/68, 8 November 1968.

[9] At first the PLGO became administrative officer (local government) in the provincial permanent secretary's office, but was soon allowed to resume his old title in order to comply with the requirements of the Local Government Act, 1965, s. 107 (1).

[10] For a fuller discussion, see W. Tordoff, 'Provincial and local government in Zambia', *Journal of Administration Overseas*, vol. IX, No. 1 (January 1970).

[11] Namwala was one of the smallest districts in the country and not all departments were manned by senior heads with direct access to provincial headquarters; some had only junior heads, who came under district-level officers resident at Choma.

[12] Minutes of the District Development Committee, Namwala, quoted in R. J. Fielder 'Government and politics at district level: case study of an opposition area' (Lusaka, 1970, mimeo.).

[13] *Ibid.*

[14] This was stated to be the main intention of the administrative reforms. ZIS Press Release No. 2223/68, *op. cit.*, p. 4.

[15] M. Chilczuk, 'Increased provincial share in plan implementation: an outline' (Lusaka: Ministry of Development Planning, October-December 1975, mimeo.), p. 3.

[16] The head of the civil service and a Minister of Cabinet rank (created February 1969).

[17] Simmance Report, *op. cit.*, preface.

[18] *Ibid.*, pp. 1–130.

[19] *Ibid.*, pp. 65–6.

[20] Mazabuka and Kafue Townships were excluded from these merger proposals. *Ibid.*, p. 103.

[21] *Ibid.*, p. 68.

[22] *Ibid.*, p. 3.

[23] *Republic of Zambia: agricultural and rural sector survey* (3 vols., 1974), vol. II, Annex 6: 'organisation for rural development', p. 7.

[24] Mwanakatwe Report, *op. cit.*, p. 20.

[25] President Kaunda's Address to the National Assembly, *Times of Zambia*, 19 December 1978, *op. cit.* No details are yet available, but one assumes that the powers and functions of the provincial Minister will be assumed by the provincial Member of the Central Committee.

[26] The latter was already part of the Prime Minister's Office, to which (as noted above) local government has now been transferred. Parliament first voted recurrent funds to the provinces in 1973; however, the amount was both small and confined to recurrent expenditure of the provincial administration. Chilczuk, 'Increased provincial share in plan implementation', *op. cit.*, p. 3.

[27] 'Provincial capital budget, 1972–76', in Chilczuk, *ibid.*, p. 9, table 4.

[28] Assuming that the provincial capital budget for 1976 would be more or less the same as for 1975, Chilczuk calculated that provincial performance was likely to be 81 per cent of the Second National Development Plan outlay. The rate of spending in the provinces is much better than at the national level. *Ibid.*, pp. 7–8, 17.

[29] *Ibid.*, pp. 10–14.

[30] J. Howell, 'Planning the provinces: another look at decentralisation in Zambia', *Zango*, No. 3 (Lusaka, August 1977), p. 24.

[31] *Estimates of revenue and expenditure*, 1977, *op. cit.*, p. 223. However, if figures for the 1972–75 period are also included in the table, the only consistent pattern to emerge is the discrimination in favour of Western Province.

[32] *Ibid.*, p. 6.

[33] Chilczuk, 'Increased provincial share in plan implementation', *op. cit.*, p. 12.

[34] See, for example, *Times of Zambia*, 7 December 1976 and 14 October 1977.

[35] See *Sunday Times of Zambia*, 4 December 1977.

[36] However, Mr M. Mumbuna, a former UP/ANC leader, was the Cabinet Minister for Central Province, where ANC had strong pockets of support.

[37] As noted above, the central Ministries (rather than the provincial Ministries) were the key Ministries to hold in the sense that they determined the allocation of national resources. See p. 15, above.

[38] In November 1977 the Central Committee had twenty-five members, including the President, the Secretary-General of UNIP, and the Prime Minister. Of the nine provincial MCCs, one (Mr D. M. Lisulo, who was also Minister of Legal Affairs and Attorney General until he was made Prime Minister in June 1978) served also at party headquarters. Two central positions were vacant. The Cabinet had twenty-nine members, including the three key office-holders named above; twenty served at the centre and nine in the provinces. In December 1978, when the post of provincial Minister was abolished, the size of the Cabinet was reduced to twenty; a Minister of State, Decentralisation, was appointed to the Prime Minister's Office. 'New Cabinet line-up', *Zambia Newsletter*, 4 January 1979.

[39] Simmance Report, *op. cit.*, p. 38.

[40] Chilczuk, 'Increased provincial share in plan implementation', *op. cit.*, p. 4.

[41] In Tanzania's decentralised system, development Ministries are integrated under the Regional Development Director at the regional level and under the District Development Director at the district level; both these officers have substantial powers in relation to departmental 'functional managers'.

[42] The sub-head for the purchase of vehicles in the 1977 estimates varied from K24,000 in Lusaka Province to K100,000 in Western Province; the average for the nine provinces was K52,444. *Estimates of revenue and expenditure*, 1977, *op. cit.*, pp. 259–75.

[43] Simmance Report, *op. cit.*, p. 89.

[44] Permanent Secretary Provincial Administration to Permanent Secretary

Southern Province, 1 December 1976; Conf. Policy Matters, PA/72/10/9, Provincial Administration Division, Prime Minister's Office, Lusaka.

⁴⁵ Cabinet Circular Minute No. CO. 101/4/54 of 7 September 1976, *ibid.*

⁴⁶ The Secretary to the Cabinet reacted angrily to the observations of the Southern PDC, but to no effect. Minutes of the 39th Meeting of the PDC, Southern Province, 21 November 1976; Secretary to Cabinet to Permanent Secretary, Provincial Administration, 29 November 1976; and Acting Permanent Secretary North-western Province to Secretary to Cabinet, 4 August 1977. PA/72/10/9, *op. cit.*

⁴⁷ Examples are the PDC meeting in the Northern Province on 13–14 April 1977 (115) and that in the Eastern Province on 16 June 1977 (100). Northern Province: File No. PAN GC 72/10/6, and Eastern Province: File No. PA/72/10/2; Provincial Administration Division, Prime Minister's Office, Lusaka.

⁴⁸ Thus, the acting general manager of the Eastern Co-operative Union Ltd. attended the Eastern PDC meeting on 31 March 1977 when the shortage of maize meal in the province was discussed. File No. PA/72/10/2, *op. cit.* Conversely, the absence of a parastatal representative can be inconvenient. At the Luapula PDC on 21 December 1976 there were 'roars and murmurs' deploring the situation at the provincial diary farms when there was no market for the milk produced, but 'as there was no representative from the Dairy Produce Board the sad information was merely noted'. File No. PA/72/10/8, Provincial Administration Division, Prime Minister's Office, Lusaka.

⁴⁹ Nevertheless, they might try to do so, as did two DDCs in Copperbelt Province. *Times of Zambia*, 7 August 1976.

⁵⁰ A different title is used in some provinces.

⁵¹ File No. PA/72/10/2, *op. cit.*

⁵² Minutes of the meeting of the PDC, Eastern Province, 21 December 1976; PA/72/10/2, *op. cit.*

⁵³ *Ibid.*, 31 March 1977.

⁵⁴ *Ibid.*, 16 June 1977.

⁵⁵ Minutes of the meeting of the PDC, Luapula Province, 21 December 1976; PA/72/10/8, *op. cit.*

⁵⁶ Minutes of the meeting of the PDC, Northern Province, 13–14 April 1977; PAN GC 72/10/6, *op. cit.* The PDC again resolved that INDECO should establish a mill in Kasama, but with what results is not known.

⁵⁷ Minutes of the meeting of the PDC, North-western Privince, 21 July 1977; PA/72/10/1, Provincial Administration Division, Prime Minister's Office, Lusaka.

⁵⁸ Simmance Report, *op. cit.*, p. 90.

⁵⁹ *Ibid.*, pp. 103–4.

⁶⁰ Thus, frustration at not being allowed to buy locally spare parts for government vehicles and at the lack of a district accounting unit was expressed at the meeting of the DDC, Mumbwa, on 31 August 1977: items 19/7 (f) and 25/7 (h); DDC Minutes, Office of the District Governor, Mumbwa.

⁶¹ 'The role of a district governor', Address by President K. D. Kaunda on opening the District Governors' Workshop, Lusaka, 2 June 1971, and C.O. 101/20/16 issued from the Cabinet Office, Lusaka, on 7 June 1971.

⁶² These, together with the public relations assistants, disappeared in the 1968–69 reorganisation.

⁶³ In addition, a small number of District Governors served at the centre. Southern Province had nine Governors, followed by Copperbelt and Northern with eight each; except for Lusaka Province with three, the rest had five or six. Four posts were vacant, three of them in Southern Province. 'District governors, district secretaries as at 1 October 1977', Provincial Administration Division, Prime Minister's Office, Lusaka. What follows is based on discussions with officers in that Division.

⁶⁴ Simmance Report, *op. cit.*, p. 48.

65   However, local authorities within districts have funds of their own.

66   In Tanzania it is exceptional for the DDD not to be a graduate.

67   This was the intention when LGOs disappeared as a separate cadre; much depends on the interest of the officer concerned.

68   Government policy is that every administrative district should have its own council so that the area of the council exactly corresponds with the boundary of the administrative district.

69   From returns prepared by the Elections Office, Lusaka. (The figure for validly nominated candidates has been corrected – from 1853 to 1855.)

70   Namwala was one of four rural councils in the Southern Province controlled by ANC following the elections of August 1970; there were also two councils in Western Province with ANC majorities.

71   This section is based on discussions with the Chairman of the Local Government Service Commission and officials of the Ministry of Local Government and Housing.

72   *Report of the commission on the structure and remuneration of the public services in Ghana* (The Mills–Odoi Report) (Accra, 1967), p. 4, para. 30.

73   Simmance Report, *op. cit.*, pp. 103–4.

74   The maximum is payable on an income of K1,000 or more, while anyone with an annual income of less than K120 is exempt. The Ministry of Local Government and Housing wanted the present scale extended progressively beyond K1,000 to K5,000, with the maximum levy payable raised to K50.

75   *Village productivity and ward development committees: a pocket manual* (Lusaka, 1971).

76   The number of VPCs will vary from one ward to another. A study of Ward 19, Serenje District, conducted in 1974, showed that there were five registered VPCs in the ward, each with an average of twenty villages, and mostly established in 1972 and 1973. There was found to be 'a very high degree of overlap in membership of local organisations'. 'Government machinery at the grass-root level: an area study of Ward 19 of Serenje District', Administrative Studies in Development No. 11 (Lusaka, National Institute of Public Administration, March 1974).

77   The assumption is that WDCs will know which farmers are credit-worthy and can be relied upon to repay the loans; but, as Bratton points out, WDC involvement in credit distribution may contribute to further economic stratification in the rural areas. See minutes of the meeting of Namwala Rural Council, 28 March 1977, LGH 102/6/51, vol. IV, Ministry of Local Government and Housing, Lusaka; and ch. 9, below. The Administration for Rural Development (ARD) Research Project applauds the ward system of agricultural credit and recommends that more government agencies should invest authority in WDCs despite their organisational weakness. *Organisation for participation in rural development in Zambia* (Lusaka and Amsterdam, January 1977, *mimeo.* – draft report), p. 94.

78   'Governmental machinery . . . Ward 19 of Serenje District', *op. cit.*

79   See p. 146, above.

80   In this section I have drawn upon the paper 'The "mix" of policy objectives in rural development' by Professor David Evans, University of Zambia, presented to the Economics Club, Lusaka, in November 1977.

81   Co-operative membership had unanticipated social consequences: for example, members of a society which acquired a tractor by means of a government loan were helped in their bid to solidify their position as a rural elite. See Quick, 'Bureaucracy and rural socialism', *op. cit.*, ch. VI.

82   The IDZ programme was capital-intensive and heavily dependent on external funding and personnel; it was launched in 1969–70, though implementation was delayed. For a useful account, see J. Lühring, *Rural development planning in Zambia: objectives, strategies and achievements* (Tangier, April 1975), pp. 35–44. See also ch. 10, below.

83   Address by President Kaunda to the First Emergency Meeting of the National

Assembly, Lusaka, 11 October 1977; ZIS Background Paper No. 93, 11 October 1977.

[84] *Sunday Times of Zambia*, 4 December 1977.

[85] Finucane, 'Intensive and experimental approaches to rural development: Zambia's IDZ's', *op. cit.*

[86] ZIS Background Paper No. 84/68, 8 November 1968, *op. cit.*, p. 19. By 'regionalism' the President was referring to the sectionalism which plagued UNIP both during and following the Central Committee elections at Mulungushi in August 1967.

[87] Review by John Howell of Hawkesworth (ed.), *Local government in Zambia, op. cit.*, in *African Social Research*, No. 23 (June 1977), pp. 242–4.

[88] Initially, in 1968–69, the size of the Cabinet was not increased as a result of the posting of eight Ministers to the provinces. However, some of the 'omnibus' Ministries at the centre (such as Rural Development) proved unwieldy and new Ministries were created. In November 1977 the Cabinet had twenty-nine members; its size was reduced to twenty after the December 1978 general election. See p. 15, Guidelines) in 1971.

[89] In Tanzania the RDD, DDD, Regional Planning Officer and District Planning Officer are normally graduates.

[90] As, for example, occurred in Tanzania with the issue of *Mwongozo* (the TANU Guidelines) in 1971. Cf., however, p. 234, below.

[91] 'The District Governor Lundazi informed the Committee that the people in his district had responded very well to the call of 'go back to the land' but the set-back was the lack of modern farming equipment such as tractors.' Minutes of the meeting of the PDC, Eastern Province, 19–20 October 1976; PA/72/10/2, *op. cit.*

[92] 'Narrowing the gaps: planning for basic needs and productive employment in Zambia', *Report of the ILO/JASPA Mission* (Geneva, 1977), p. 288, quoted in Evans, 'The "mix" of policy objectives', *op. cit.*

[93] 'While 60 per cent of the total population have to share as little as 27 per cent of gross national income, a 5 per cent elite monopolizes as much as 37 per cent.' Lühring, 'Rural development planning in Zambia', *op. cit.*, p. 14.

[94] Cf. the emphasis placed on the private sector in the report of the parliamentary select committee, *Sunday Times of Zambia*, 4 December 1977.

[95] Necessary also because the absorptive capacity of the urban sector is strictly limited.

[96] Evans, 'The "mix" of policy objectives', *op. cit.*

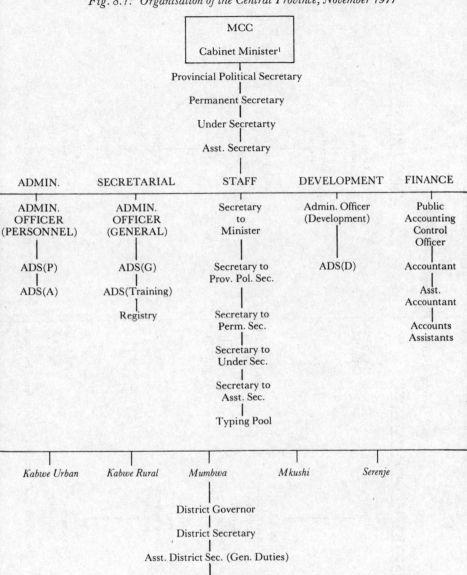

Fig. 8.1: *Organisation of the Central Province, November 1977*

MCC

Cabinet Minister[1]

Provincial Political Secretary

Permanent Secretary

Under Secretarty

Asst. Secretary

ADMIN.	SECRETARIAL	STAFF	DEVELOPMENT	FINANCE
ADMIN. OFFICER (PERSONNEL)	ADMIN. OFFICER (GENERAL)	Secretary to Minister	Admin. Officer (Development)	Public Accounting Control Officer
ADS(P)	ADS(G)	Secretary to Prov. Pol. Sec.	ADS(D)	Accountant
ADS(A)	ADS(Training)			Asst. Accountant
	Registry	Secretary to Perm. Sec.		Accounts Assistants
		Secretary to Under Sec.		
		Secretary to Asst. Sec.		
		Typing Pool		

Kabwe Urban   *Kabwe Rural*   *Mumbwa*   *Mkushi*   *Serenje*

District Governor

District Secretary

Asst. District Sec. (Gen. Duties)

Asst. District Sec. (Local Govt.)

Note   [1]The post of provincial Cabinet Minister was abolished in December 1978.

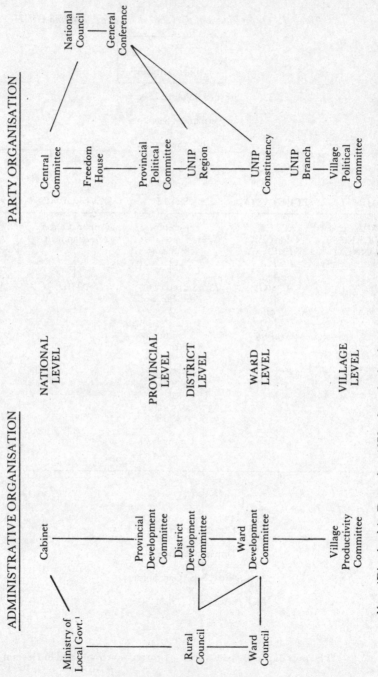

Fig. 9.1: Organisation of Party and State in Zambia

ADMINISTRATIVE ORGANISATION

Cabinet

Ministry of Local Govt.[1]

NATIONAL LEVEL

PROVINCIAL LEVEL — Provincial Development Committee

DISTRICT LEVEL — District Development Committee — Rural Council

WARD LEVEL — Ward Development Committee — Ward Council

VILLAGE LEVEL — Village Productivity Committee

PARTY ORGANISATION

National Council — General Conference

Central Committee

Freedom House — Provincial Political Committee

UNIP Region

UNIP Constituency

UNIP Branch

Village Political Committee

Note [1]Dissolved in December 1978 when the local government portfolio was transferred to the Prime Minister's Office.

9. The social context of political penetration: village and ward committees in Kasama District

Michael Bratton

A primary assumption for the political economy of administration is that policy decisions and policy implementation are coloured by the structure of the society in which the State apparatus is located. As Saul has said, 'institutions cannot be viewed or assessed independently of the social structure that sustains them and influences their activities'.[1] In practice, the actual development trajectory that a State follows is determined by the interaction of intended strategies with the interests of powerful social groups. Group interests make themselves felt at the policy formulation and policy implementation stages and at the international, national and local levels. This chapter focuses on the interplay between an emergent local social structure and the implementation of one aspect of the Zambian strategy for rural development. The locality chosen for case study is Kasama District, Northern Province, an area characterised by a long history of outward labour migration and subsistence agricultural production. The aspect of State development strategy chosen is that of local-level institution-building or, in other words, political penetration.

Empirical studies of political penetration usually seek to determine whether State performance is 'effective', but rarely ask 'effective at what?' or 'effective for whom?'.[2] Local-level institutions can be effective in institutionalising inappropriate production techniques, inequality and even repression. Political penetration can lead to a wide or narrow diffusion of development benefits. It can lead to increased local participation but it can also lead to increased central control. Thus the question of 'who benefits?' is as pertinent to political penetration and local institution-building as it is to any aspect of the rural development process.

The Zambian Government was faced at independence with the need to construct an infrastructure of political–administrative institutions to penetrate the rural areas. There was a need not only to consolidate the hold of the State on the ethnically and sectionally diverse periphery, but also to increase and spread development benefits that had not reached the countryside under colonial rule. Inasmuch as rural development received planning attention in the first ten years of independence, it was predicated on the creation of a political–administrative organisation linking the centre with all localities. Ideologically, the new regime was committed to mass participation and mass mobilisation. A 'participatory–democratic' rather than a 'bureaucratic–authoritarian' mode of penetration was favoured in the quasi-socialist ideology of Zambian Humanism.

The most difficult question was how to translate ideology into organisation. Creating an organisation to link centre with periphery completely *de novo* was a difficult task given the vast rural periphery of Zambia. One alternative to creating an organisation from scratch was to adapt existing organisations to new functions. But a striking feature of the rural areas in 1964 was the absence of any viable organisation that could be used for political participation or political control. One possibility might have been for the centre to use the colonial administrative apparatus as the Kenyan Government had chosen to do. The dissolution of the colonial provincial administration and the reduction in the number of field-level administrators after independence in Zambia, however, had left an 'institutional vacuum' at district level and below.[3] Linkages between the district bomas and the villages were severed with the abolition of the Native Authorities and the withdrawal of powers from the traditional chiefs. In other words, the organisation used by the colonial administration was largely dismantled at the grass-roots level. Alternatively, there was the Tanzanian strategy of using the political party as the prime organisational link with the locality. The United National Independence Party (UNIP) was the only non-colonial national institution with a significant grass-roots presence in 1964. UNIP suffered, however, from an uncontrolled membership and an organisation and ethos better suited to national liberation than national construction. Over time, UNIP lost peasant support and branch organisation. Moreover, UNIP's own penetration was in doubt in those areas of Zambia where opposition political parties were popular.

Hence the design that Zambian penetration strategy finally took was a compromise, with resemblances to both the Kenyan and Tanzanian models. The Zambian 'development front' is a patchwork organisation of government, party and traditional institutions. Cliffe and Saul have pointed to the difficulties of implementing a coherent penetration strategy when the machinery

for penetration is an uncoordinated array of development bodies.[4] In
Zambia the 'development front' comprises at the district level the
Office of the District Governor, field agencies of central government,
local authorities and co-operative unions. Each has a different
emphasis with reference to the overall tasks of inducing mass
participation and economic mobilisation and each has a different
measure of contact and linkage with peasants at village level. In an
attempt to rationalise the activities of this unintegrated development
front the Zambian State established a framework of development
committees, from provincial to village level. This organisational
framework was aimed at providing horizontal linkage among all
government agencies in the locality and vertical linkage between
national centre and local periphery. As such, development
committees are at the crux of the Zambian strategy for penetrating
the rural localities.

Provincial and district development committees were introduced
as regional planning units at the time of the First National
Development Plan (1966), but are not of central concern to this
study. Local-level development committees for village and ward
were established under the Registration and Development of
Villages Act (1971) and a pocket manual was published in order to
convey to peasants the details and intent of the new organisations.
Together these committees were to extend the central State
apparatus to the point where it touched and mobilised every adult in
Zambia (see Fig. 9.1, facing p. 213). Every village would have a
village productivity committee (VPC) and every local government ward a
ward development committee (WDC). These elected committees would
provide a forum both for the expression of local demands and for the
enforcement of central policies. VPCs and WDCs were linked to the
State apparatus via local authorities and the office of the District
Governor. They were intended to fill the institutional vacuum at the
sub-district level and to be woven into the fabric of local social life.

It has been estimated that a total of 25,000 village productivity
and 1,500 ward development committees are needed for the task of
rural penetration in Zambia.[5] The conventional wisdom concerning
these committees is that most of them are 'not working'. A national
newspaper, for example, stated in an editorial that 'there are signs
that in some areas, perhaps the larger part of the country, the
productivity committees exist on paper only'.[6] President Kaunda
expressed the view in 1971 that the 'administrative machinery must
become one with the people so that they can see it as their own and
as part and parcel of them'. This chapter analyses the performance
of VPCs and WDCs and the recruitment of local leaders in one rural

locality. The perspective of analysis is consistent with the hope expressed by the Zambian President in the sense that administrative organisation and society are viewed as overlapping structures. The outcome of the policies of political penetration cannot be fully understood in terms of organisational considerations alone but must be related to the social context of implementation.

Village productivity committees

There were 496 VPCs in Kasama District by the end of 1974. The vast majority of these, 447, were created as part of the registration of villages exercise in 1972. The composition of registration teams determined who were to be the 'penetrators' in the crucial task of organising the villages. Students from the University of Zambia were recruited as registration officers and were accompanied on tour by the chief of the area, the ward councillor and regional party officials.[7] In other words, Zambia's organisation for penetration consisted of a 'front' of traditional, administrative and party elements. The registration exercise called for the touring team to arrive in a village, prepare a register of inhabitants and for the chief then to summon a meeting in order to elect a VPC. The newly-elected VPC would in turn choose one of its members to accompany the headman to gatherings of the ward council, a large plenary body composed of representatives of every village in the ward. Once the VPC was elected, the touring team would leave for the next village.

The way that village registration was conducted in Kasama District had an important influence on the make-up of village and ward committees. The most striking feature of village registration was the extent to which it was a purely administrative exercise. The political party was only marginally involved. Ward councillors and other UNIP branch and constituency officials did little mobilising on behalf of village registration. Of the twenty-three ward councillors in Kasama District only two eventually agreed to accompany the registration teams on their tours of the villages; the remaining twenty-one did not assist in registration or the formation of VPCs.[8] Their lukewarm response can be attributed to the condition in which the local party found itself in 1972. The previous year had witnessed the formation of the United Progressive Party (UPP). Though few UNIP officials came out openly in support of UPP, significant numbers at branch and constituency levels, including ward councillors, harboured sympathies for the new party. In the highly charged atmosphere of the aftermath of the banning of UPP, people in Kasama were suspicious of any registration exercise that required the disclosure of personal information. Moreover, councillors were probably reluctant to associate themselves with any national project at a time when popular support for the political centre was at a low ebb.

In the absence of the party the path was cleared for other leadership groups, particularly traditional leaders, to exercise undue influence over the formation of village committees. The exercise 'progressed smoothly thanks to the chiefs who played a major part ... inclusion of the traditional leaders on tour made it possible to meet no opposition from the villages except in isolated cases concerning Watchtower adherents'.[9] Peasants, when asked about village registration two years later, often recalled that the chief's *kapasu* and the university student were in their village but only rarely did they mention the district messenger or the party official. Some even spoke of the register as the 'chief's register'.

Traditional leaders thus used the opportunity presented by the registration of villages to enhance their own positions of authority. Under the Chiefs Act of 1965, which had decapitated the traditional social structure by removing the judicial powers of the chief, the Government reserved the right to delegate new powers to the chiefs as and when it saw fit. The first of these powers were delegated in 1971 under the Registration and Development of Villages Act; they included the chief's right to grant recognition to villages for purposes of registration, call a VPC election, attend VPC and WDC meetings, and provide a communications link between the House of Chiefs and District Governor on the one hand and the villagers on the other.[10] Chiefs therefore had an interest in making themselves visible during the registration procedure. Like headmen, they stood to be the immediate beneficiaries of the Government's patchwork strategy for penetrating the rural areas. They stood to regain some of the power lost after independence to elected local government councillors. From the very outset the strategy for penetration was captured by the most socially institutionalised group at the village level. Party cadres were not the 'penetrators'. Far from representing a balanced institutional mix, the task of penetration gave rise to a working alliance between representatives of central administration and traditional leaders.

Registration of villages, after a promising start, proved to be a difficult policy for the centre to implement in Kasama. By the end of the three-month registration period, villages were registered and VPCs formed in only three of the six chiefs' areas. Blame was attributed to a scattered settlement pattern, although undoubtedly the low enthusiasm of the party was also an important factor. As a result, a supplementary registration period had to be set up for Kasama and four other districts in the Northern Province. After an extra three months of village touring in late 1972 a halt was called to registration in Kasama with a total of 628 villages registered and 447 VPCs formed on paper. Yet additional VPCs continued to be formed for some time after the departure of the registration teams – forty-one during 1973 and eight during 1974. In some wards the majority of VPCs were created after the registration exercise was halted; in others, the number of VPCs actually declined over time due to the regrouping or breaking up of small villages. Many individual settlers residing outside a village community also escaped registration. Thus Kasama District was not fully 'penetrated' after village registration, even though the District Secretary could report the establishment of a large number of VPCs and provide membership lists to prove it.

In addition, fewer than ten per cent of the 496 VPCs in Kasama District were 'active' by 1974–75. That is, fewer than ten per cent began to fulfil the functions of popular participation and control of the local economy for which they were intended. Fewer than ten per cent had a communal village project underway. The remaining 90 per cent had never met since the VPC members were first elected. The figure of one-tenth activation of VPCs is based on interviews with forty-four village headmen in Kasama District. Headmen were not selected according to a systematic sampling formula but rather in terms of access afforded to certain villages. Nevertheless, an attempt was made to obtain a representative spread of villages in the district according to criteria of size, remoteness and level of development. Only four villages had active VPCs. A significant minority of headmen, thirteen out of forty-four, particularly in small or outlying villages, were unaware of the requirement to have a VPC. And many of those who were aware had never seen the pocket manual, or could not read or understand it.

There is one contradiction in the organisation of VPCs that may account for their poor performance. Because VPCs are adapted from the traditional social structure they may be unsuited to the development tasks expected of them. Traditional leaders can use VPCs to bolster their own authority rather than to initiate change. In the absence of any other established local leadership cadre or institution in 1971, the State was forced to choose village headmen as chairmen of VPCs. The disadvantages of the State's pragmatic choice of village headmen as grassroots leaders and mobilisers is evident in the performance of VPCs in Kasama.

Take the recruitment of membership of VPCs, for example. In most cases the election of VPC members did not disturb existing power relationships at the village level. Since elections were conducted by means of a public show of hands at a village meeting, the voters were subject to social pressures to defer to the headman's choice of VPC members. Almost invariably, village elders or the headman's traditional advisers were chosen. The general rule was that older males acceded to the VPC, but any person with literacy skills, regardless of sex or age, was included in the VPC if there was no adult male with these qualifications. In sum, however, the make-up of the VPCs did not represent a break with the leadership patterns of the past. The headman and his advisers were still able to make most village decisions. They were sometimes challenged by educated youths or UNIP branch officials or women, but these were not changes that were directly attributable to the introduction of VPCs.

The persistence of tradition was also observed in the functions of VPCs. The frequency and content of meetings was determined more by the occurrence of social disputes among peasants than by the need to plan village productivity systematically. In most VPCs there was no regular schedule of meetings; they were held in response to the ebb and flow of village life. On average, an active VPC thus met once every three or four months when village problems had become too aggravated to ignore; as one headman put it, 'we meet when there is a complaint or a quarrel'. Much VPC time was devoted to witchcraft accusations; the minor cases were settled in the village but the most serious cases were conveyed to the chief in accordance with traditional practice. Where headmen still performed ritual functions, such as choosing a site for a new village or constructing ancestor shrines, they were also likely to air such matters at village meetings. These meetings, while nominally meetings of the VPC, were little different from traditional village meetings. There was public discussion of village issues and the headman, with the assistance of his advisers, interpreted the popular consensus and announced a decision. The settlement of social disputes and vigilance for the welfare of the village community have always been the responsibility of the village headman. The survival of these aspects of the headman's role has been encouraged by the introduction of VPCs.

So, at minimum, village productivity committees provide continuity with the past by conducting the traditional business of the village. That is all that many VPCs do. Of twenty-three ward councillors interviewed, sixteen confirmed that VPCs in their wards still concerned themselves with traditional cases; one said that they did not; and six had no idea what their VPCs did, if anything.

Nevertheless, some exceptional VPCs have begun to make the transition from traditional social matters to the functions of social and economic innovation for which they were intended. For example, the following items were discussed at a meeting of one of the active VPCs in Kasama District in mid-1974:

1. The headman/chairman announced that now that the dry season had arrived, and in accordance with instructions from the Rural Council, fire breaks should be burnt around the village, and bush fires controlled;

2. The headman/chairman also requested that trees should not be cut for the purposes of *citemene* cultivation on a certain side of the village because all villages in the region were experiencing a shortage of construction timber;

3. Every household must have a pit latrine;

4. People should come together to widen the road to the village bar on a self-help basis 'so that we don't have to walk along (in single file) like women in the forest';

5. Every household must have a vegetable garden. Those with seeds should share them with their neighbours;

6. The village must be 'organised'. Rather than quarrelling among themselves, villagers should 'be of one mother'. One man, the UNIP branch chairman, had been igoring the greetings of his fellows. The headman would have a word with him.[11]

Some VPCs were therefore beginning to take on a multi-purpose character. Village disputes continued to receive attention (item 6), but the above VPC meeting was largely devoted to village development (items 1, 2, 3, 4, and 5). The items concerning bush fires, pit latrines and vegetable gardens were aspects of Government policy for village development and here the headman acted as spokesman for the centre. Not all of these items were followed up: for example, few households began growing more than the familiar dietary items of beans and spinach despite the headman's remonstrations. VPC minutes revealed that this was not the first time the chairman had appealed for vegetable growing. The timber shortage and bar road items illustrate a VPC devising local solutions to local problems. In the active VPCs this sort of self-reliant policy-making was increasingly common.

Active VPCs in Kasama have had their greatest impact in the construction and maintenance of villages. Screened and roofed pit-latrines are a common sight and villages with active VPCs have a clean well-swept appearance. The mass construction of permanent housing with sun-dried or burnt brick has resulted in part from VPC dissemination of information and encouragement of house-building. On occasion VPCs have combined to undertake larger projects that affect more than one village; access roads, small bridges and wells have been built with communal VPC labour in Kasama. Larger scale projects such as schools and clinics, however, are beyond the scope of VPC action and are left to the WDC to plan and implement.

Nor have VPCs contributed to the expansion of production. Kasama village economies are of a subsistence or sub-subsistence standard with heavy peasant reliance on income remissions from relatives in urban employment. With the exception of the planting of village fruit orchards, agricultural innovation appears to be a matter of individual rather than VPC initiative. VPCs have not transformed villages into the 'effective production units' envisaged in the pocket manual. As far as village planning is concerned, some active VPCs have evolved their own differentiated organisation to handle development tasks: responsibility for supervising brickmaking, water supply, cleanliness and agriculture was assigned to leading VPC members. In the most active of VPCs regular weekly meetings were held and members presented progress reports. In these villages, peasants as a community were aware of the existence of the VPC and even referred to the headman as 'chairman'. Often, however, VPC activity was mere bureaucratic procedure consisting of meetings, minute-writing and the sending of resolutions to the ward councillor. What was lacking even in active VPCs was the actual mobilisation of local self-help resources on productive village development projects.

To summarise, the record of VPC performance in Kasama District is not an encouraging one. Villages with active VPCs remain the exception rather than the rule. Undoubtedly, there are formal organisational and procedural considerations that partly account for poor VPC performance. But these are not the central concern of this essay; instead, consideration is given to the implications of the central State decision to entrust development tasks to leadership elements from traditional society – to attempt, in other words, political penetration without social transformation.

A main argument presented here is that traditional leaders have used VPCs in Kasama as a vehicle for pursuing their group interests. We have seen how the membership and functions of VPCs have been tilted towards reinforcing the status of chiefs and headmen. Traditional leaders have also attempted to exceed the limited authority granted them in the committee organisation to regain lost powers, for example of legal arbitration. Village meetings which have been called to discuss local disputes have ended with the headman imposing a fine on the guilty party in the name of the VPC.[12] Fines have been imposed not only for a variety of civil cases such as adultery and violation of the demarcation of plots for village gardens, but even for criminal cases such as theft of livestock. All cases should have been handed over to the local courts for arbitration. In the most celebrated case of this kind in Kasama, a chief tried unsuccessfully to use a VPC to sentence a peasant with whom he had a personal dispute to a one-year prison term. In the pre-colonial Bemba State the authority of local leaders rested squarely on the sanctions which they were able to impose on their followers. The transfer after independence of judicial functions to government officers in the Ministry of Legal Affairs damaged the already dwindling credibility of chiefs and headmen among their own people. In Kasama the VPCs have become one of the only arenas available to traditional leaders who wish to reassert their powers of legal arbitration.

A second indicator of the way in which the committee organisation has benefited traditional leaders as a group is in the location of development projects. From the point of view of peasants, among the most urgent development problems are the provision of a year-round clean water supply and access to health-care facilities. Of the six piped water schemes in Kasama District, three were located at the headquarters of a chief. Of the seven government (i.e., non-mission) health centres in the district, four were located at the headquarters of a chief. And again, of the seven villages first selected by the DDC for 'intensive village regrouping', three were the headquarters of a chief. In part, this pattern of project location is attributable to the concentration of population at these places, but it also indicates the ability of traditional elements to use the committee organisation to secure preferential option on the limited central resources that percolate down to the local level.

Thirdly, certain chiefs and headmen can be seen to benefit from the committee organisation, not simply by virtue of traditional group membership, but as individuals, or by virtue of other group criteria. Richards noted as early as 1957 that certain 'go-ahead' chiefs had used their government allowances to pay labourers engaged in traditional tribute labour and to buy trucks, thereby becoming 'successful market gardeners'.[13] A contemporary example can be given to corroborate and extend Richards's account. The chief in question was an appointed councillor on Kasama Rural Council. He led the mobilisation of scattered villages into regrouped settlements and reaped the credit for the provision of government services that followed. He was also able to enlarge his following, and thereby his prestige, by attracting settlers, some even from neighbouring Mporokoso District, to his own regrouped village. Thus this chief skilfully utilised the State apparatus (development committees) and a national policy (regrouping) to entrench his own power position. It is significant that this chief was a successful farmer who hired agricultural labour and marketed sufficient surplus to afford to run a private motor vehicle. His area was also chosen by the Tobacco Board of Zambia as the site of a virginia tobacco settlement scheme; he secured one of the first plots on the scheme on which construction of his second private house was undertaken. The social background of this type of leader, which often contains some secondary education and paid employment, is atypical of purely 'traditional' elements. If there is any group interest to be discerned it is not an uncomplicated case of 'tradition' asserting itself, but of the emergence of a wider group of 'progressive' or 'bourgeois' interests whose presence at village level is still rare and recent.

In conclusion, the composition and performance of VPCs in Kasama indicates that traditional leaders have captured village-level leadership positions in the administrative apparatus of the State, but that the decline in traditional authority, first noted by Richards,[14] has not thereby been stemmed. Chiefs have in general been more effective than headmen in grasping opportunities offered by committee formation. The great majority of headmen either have no VPC or are unable to use a VPC to attract central resources or initiate self-help projects. The apparatus of the State has only sparse presence at village level. Notwithstanding the relative powerlessness of traditional leaders, however, chiefs and headmen still enjoy a more institutionalised following at village level in Kasama than does the UNIP machine. The only practical choice open to the Zambian Government in 1971 was to rely on the leadership structure of the past and thereby provide a partial continuity with the colonial strategy for rural penetration. By recruiting traditional patrons to formal leadership positions, the State stood to garner the support of at least some peasant followers too. Older peasants and women still hold esteem for traditional leaders and these groups are prominent in Zambia's rural demographic profile. If anything, since 1971, the central government has placed even greater reliance on traditional leaders for the implementation of policies like village regrouping, voter registration, and the recovery of agricultural loans.[15] The Zambian State thus acknowledges a low capacity to replace even severely weakened traditional institutions and accepts the likelihood of minimal village-level social mobilisation and economic development.

Ward development committees

At the level of the local government ward, the formation and operation of development committees has proceeded further than at the village level. A higher proportion of WDCs than VPCs has survived since initial formation and WDC activities have had concrete results in the form of actual rural development projects. The claim that WDCs exist on paper only is decidedly untrue for Kasama.

At the same time, however, WDC performance in Kasama also illustrates a continued dependence of local institutions on central government resources, an overbureaucratisation of the local decision-making process, and the emergence of powerful local interests. Like VPCs, WPCs have not yet brought about a mass mobilisation of local material and manpower or even a fairly equitable diffusion of central resources to the mass of the peasant population. Like VPCs, WDCs have been merged with the social structure of the locality and have provided an opportunity for ambitious elements to dominate the resource distribution process. The principal beneficiaries of participation in development committees at ward level are necessarily different from those at village level. Above the village, traditional leaders have given way to new leadership groups. The nature of the new rural social structure and its relation to the local-level apparatus of the State is the main concern of the present analysis of WDC performance.

In 1967 President Kaunda called for the creation of ward and village committees in *Humanism, Part I*. According to this early formulation, ward committees would engage in such basic economic functions as allocating and enforcing agricultural production targets, supplying farmers with fertilisers, credit and marketing facilities, and planning economic investment for the ward. They were urged to meet monthly and 'in terms of the policy of self-help ... should as far as possible, resolve most of their [own] problems'.[16]

The ward councillor was permitted wide discretion in composing a ward committee. The only guideline provided was that the councillor would be chairman; the make-up of other members would vary according to local circumstances, and should include 'representatives of all sections of the community' by which was meant farmers, businessmen, headmen and field-level civil servants.[17] In 1969 responsibility for committee formation was formally vested in the hands of District Governors. But even then central supervision and standardisation were difficult to enforce because most District Governors were preoccupied with the problem of carving out positions of authority from the preserves of the district secretary and UNIP regional secretary. Thus recruitment to local-level office was in 1969, and still remains, a matter of predominantly local concern. Central government in Zambia has never enjoyed the capacity to supervise and control fully the building of local institutions.

An opportunity was thus presented to peasants to take advantage of a flexible State strategy for penetration by forming ward committees from below. Not unexpectedly, however, the formation of early development committees at the ward level in Kasama did not reflect a broad-based participation. Instead, the power-wielders in the local social structure made their influence felt. Local notables took control of the selection of committee members. The District Governor in Kasama abdicated all responsibility to local government councillors to pick 'ten people in your ward as your henchmen' (sic).[18] The first group to be recruited to the WDC were prominent party men. Councillors utilised their freedom of selection to assemble committees of compatriots from UNIP with whom they were accustomed to working. This is not to say that ward committees were immediately and fully integrated into a vigorous party organisation, but rather that nominal holding of UNIP office was the easiest criterion for claiming membership of a WDC. Automatic accession of party officials to WDC office was part of the process whereby UNIP at the local level made the transition from protest party to ruling party.

Furthermore, the first Humanism document suggested that the new committees would oversee the distribution of development benefits in the locality. Hence, councillors and other local party leaders perceived an opportunity to gain patronage rewards both for themselves and their party followers. Ex-freedom fighters who retained UNIP office naturally felt that first option on the fruits of independence was rightfully theirs. A second group also made itself visible early in the committee formation process. These were ambitious farmers who pressed the councillors for places on the WDC because they wanted credit from the government'.[19] To some extent the two groups overlapped. The bulk of UNIP's early support in Kasama had come from subsistence cultivators; market-oriented farmers were attracted to the Watchtower and Lenshina movements. With the advent of WDCs, however, the latter group found a common interest with party officials in using the new committees to extract resources from the centre. Thus from their inception, WDCs were grafted on to the UNIP patronage machine like the agricultural co-operative and Credit Organisation of

Zambia programmes before them. And a precedent was set that membership and resources of WDCs were open to control by patrons within the local-level party.

Against this historical background, the nature of the present local power structure in Kasama in 1974–75 can be more readily appreciated. The patronage pattern of recruitment to WDC office and of distribution of development benefits at the ward level has not fundamentally altered since the structure of local institutions was formalised in law. This finding is partly confirmed by the results of a social background survey conducted among the members of WDCs in Kasama District in 1974.[20] WDC membership was chosen as the target population on the assumption that any local leadership group seeking access to State resources was likely to find its way on to the local-level State apparatus. It was further assumed that from a survey of this population a social profile of local leadership could be drawn. In other words, the question 'who are local leaders?' could be tentatively answered.

WDC membership is predominantly *middle-aged* and *male*. The average age of members is forty-seven years in a range from youngest to oldest of twenty-three years to eighty-five years. They are recruited from the same generation, and often are the same individuals, as the 'freedom-fighters' of fifteen years earlier. There has been little refreshment of local-level leadership cadres since the nationalist phase. Only three WDC members are women, that is, women scarcely enjoy token representation. Even at ward council meetings where attendance is often thrown open, fewer than 15 per cent of those attending are women.

WDC membership in Kasama is also *ethnically homogeneous*, being 96 per cent Bemba. An even higher percentage (97 per cent) take ChiBemba to be their mother tongue. This striking homogeneity is an indication partly of the location of Kasama District at the heart of the traditional Bemba State, but also of a sectional solidarity in Kasama that makes 'Bembaness' a *sine qua non* of election to local or national office. This characteristic of WDC membership can also be interpreted, not so much as a sign of ethnic solidarity, but as *localism*. Eighty-one per cent of WDC members now live and were elected to leadership positions in the same chief's area in which they were born. To have one's self and one's family known in the locality is an asset in achieving a position of committee leadership.

Relatively few WDC members are drawn from among traditional leaders in distinct contrast to the dominance of these elements at village level. Only 19 per cent claim to be headmen. In most wards there are only one or two headmen on the WDC. However, in some wards where party organisation is weak and there are few branch officials, headmen can form up to half the committee. Of the traditional Bemba clans, none has undue representation on WDCs, a measure both of the declining importance of kinship to politics and of the inability of the royal clan (*bena n'gandu*) to continue to claim office ascriptively. The general impression to be gained is that at the ward level, unlike the village level, a break has occurred with the leadership patterns of the past.

At first glance WDC members appear to be characterised by relatively *low formal education*. The average length of primary schooling is four years. A mere 11 per cent have had the advantage of post-primary education. This educational pattern is also partly reflected in the figure of 35 per cent who speak English, the official language of government and business in Zambia. Nevertheless, these figures disguise the fact that in a predominantly illiterate society even minimal formal education is an important criterion for recruitment to leadership position. Kasama WDC members do represent a relatively privileged group who have had access to limited educational resources.

In terms also of other socio-economic indicators, WDC membership can be seen to be drawn from the relatively privileged stratum in the locality. The majority of WDC members engage in relatively *'well-to-do' occupations*. Nineteen per cent have paid employment. This category includes State functionaries such as primary school teachers and agricultural demonstrators. It also includes carpenters and bricklayers who enjoy a regular income from hiring themselves out to private individuals and co-operatives. Nine per cent describe themselves as 'businessmen'; their businesses are usually in the petty retail trade. Thirty-eight per cent, by far the largest group, can be described as 'emergent farmers', in the sense that their farming activities are oriented towards production of a marketable surplus. Together the three well-to-do groups of salaried employees, businessmen and emergent farmers account for 66 per cent of WDC membership. Only one-third of WDC membership is drawn from the largest stratum of the rural population, that is, from among subsistence peasants.

Almost without exception WDC members claim *UNIP membership* (99 per cent). Only one man answered 'no' to the survey question on this topic. This high response, however, must be regarded with caution. WDC members have nothing to lose and much to gain by claiming party membership in a single-party State. If party membership was measured by the payment of annual party dues, the figure would be far lower. Party organisation and committee organisation are better integrated at ward than at the village level. Almost half (42 per cent) of WDC members hold a party office within UNIP. There is also a large overlap between WDC leadership and leadership in other local institutions. Again, nearly half (45.9 per cent) are members of a co-operative, a credit union, or a parent–teacher association, and 17 per cent hold office in these institutions. This significant overlap of leaders points to a recruitment pattern in which leadership is limited to a small local elite.

Recruitment to local leadership in Kasama is thus a closed rather than an open affair. Two sets of recruitment criteria can be distinguished. First, there are certain minimum social attributes of sex, age, ethnicity, religion and localism without which candidacy for leadership is virtually impossible. But other secondary criteria must be present to ensure recruitment. Certain social attributes, which are unevenly distributed in the locality, endow particular groups with advantage in the leadership recruitment process. The key secondary recruitment criteria for access to WDC position in Kasama are *well-to-do occupation* and *UNIP party office*.

Social background data on leadership is alone insufficient to describe the distribution of development benefits in the locality. It must be linked to the performance of WDCs in actual policy-making and project implementation. Of twenty-three WDCs in Kasama rural area, twelve can be said to be active (see Table 9.1). For the purpose of this chapter, an active WDC was taken to be one which both held regular meetings and undertook self-help projects involving the participation of residents of more than one village.

The scheduling of WDC meetings is haphazard. WDCs are supposed to meet every three months but few in Kasama do so. Most meet on the VPC pattern, that is, when a local issue arises. A seasonal water shortage, the non-availability of farm requisites, or an impending visit of the District Governor have triggered WDC meetings in Kasama. In half the wards in Kasama there is no written record of WDCs ever having met. In some cases this is a result of poor record-keeping by the WDC secretary, but in many cases the WDC does not in fact meet. Under such circumstances the scant knowledge of members about the purposes of a WDC, and their own place within it, is predictable and was found to exist by this researcher.

The WDC is supposed to act as the executive body in the ward by implementing policy decisions taken by the ward council. In practice the WDC, where active, is both the formulator and implementer of local plans. The distinction between ward council

Table 9.1: Development projects of ward development committees in Kasama District, 1973–74

Ward	WDC Active[1]	Capital projects using central resources[2]	Self-help projects using local resources[3]
1		piped water scheme	village regrouping; school
2	Yes	piped water scheme; health centre	group housing; bridge
3			
4			
5			
6		settlement scheme (coffee)	school; group housing
7	Yes	piped water scheme; settlement scheme; health centre	village regrouping; school; group housing
8	Yes	piped water scheme; health centre; post office	group housing; maize production
9	Yes	piped water scheme; health centre	school; rest house
10			
11		IDZ rice scheme	Note: no schools in this ward!
12	Yes	secondary school	schools; maize production
13	Yes	Rural Council HQ; settlement scheme; Farm Training Inst.; secondary school; health centre etc.	schools; maize production
14	Yes	brickfield	school
15	Yes	Rural Reconstruction Camp; bridge	schools; bridge
16	Yes	piped water scheme (for township)	
17			bridge
18		hydro-electric scheme (for township); ZNS camp	group housing
19	Yes		group housing
20	Yes		group housing
21		bridge; settlement scheme (tobacco)	schools
22			group housing
23	Yes	dairy	sewing project

Notes

[1] Based on evidence independent of the ward councillor's own account, i.e., minutes of meetings, observation of WDC meetings, and/or accounts from disinterested third parties. One meeting or more in the period 1 January 1973 – 31 December 1974 was deemed sufficient to describe a WDC as 'active'.

[2] This category includes projects financed and executed under the supervision of the Kasama Rural Council or central government departments, and in which the planning decisions were usually out of the hands of the WDC. It excludes wells and roads built by the central government which can be found in almost all wards. It also excludes mission-aided projects.

[3] This category includes projects implemented by communal peasant labour, projects financed by village collections, and projects financed by central government grants-in-aid with a local self-help component.

and WDC is not rigorously observed in the day-to-day operations of these committees in Kasama. Instead, one general-purpose ward-level committee has tended to emerge with a regular attendance of anywhere between eight and eighty persons. That this committee is popularly acknowledged to be a 'ward development committee' does not necessarily mean that it conforms in membership to the WDC as laid down in the pocket manual.

Contrary to conventional wisdom WDCs, 'properly' constituted or not, are beginning to make an impact on the locality. A representative picture of routine WDC business can be gained from the following summary of issues discussed at a WDC meeting in Ward 13 of Kasama Rural Council in early 1973:

1. The councillor/chairman explained to the members of the WDC that they would be meeting three more times in the year and reminded them of the necessity of regular attendance and of the duties of WDC members.

2. The committee discussed the increase of maternity cases in the ward and called on the Ministry of Health to station a midwife permanently at Mungwi Clinic. They also requested the building of an extension to the clinic, or, alternatively, the conversion of another government office into a maternity wing.

3. The committee considered requests from the VPCs of James village, Kabula village and Fundiboma village for piped water extensions. The WDC instructed the residents of the villages to start a self-help fund and, if sufficient money was collected, then an approach to the Rural Council would be made.

4. The councillor/chairman and visiting works officer from the Kasama Rural Council advised that agricultural loans would not be given unless farmers cultivated two hectares of land and unless farmers managed to find fertiliser on their own.

5. Complaints concerning the poor condition of bridges at Chisapa and Kananda over the flooded Chibile stream were brought to the committee's attention. In both cases people from the ward had begun repair work but were hampered by the lack of motor transport to bring logs and gravel to the bridge sites. The WDC resolved to ask the Kasama Rural Council to provide a truck to do this work once the rainy season had ended.

6. The VPC at White Chiti village reported that 126 children were unable to gain primary school enrolment. The councillor advised that government policy forbade the building of a new school within two miles of an existing school. He also told WDC members that elsewhere in the ward there were 513 children without school places. The WDC resolved that the only solution was to request a double stream at all schools in Ward 13 and a letter was written to the Local Council of Education to this effect.

7. A petition was presented from several villagers alleging abusive and arrogant behaviour on the part of the Senior Medical Assistant at Mungwi Clinic. The WDC decided to report this government officer to the District Governor, Kasama, for discipline or removal.[21]

By involvement in a wide range of health, education and welfare matters, WDCs in Kasama are becoming institutionalised as agencies of innovation at the local level. But clear limits to WDC effectiveness have also become apparent. First, the majority of their upward demands are unsuccessful; for example, the peasants from Kabula and White Chiti villages (items 3 and 6) were making identical demands for piped water and double-stream primary schools at a WDC meeting 15 months later.[22] At a public meeting in 1975, a speaker in the crowd was still able to elicit cheers for a demand to 'remove these incompetent people at the clinic'.[23] Indeed, by early 1975 not one of the requests for central intervention made at the above meeting had been met.

Second, WDCs are, like VPCs, designed as part of the control mechanism of the State. While the two 'control' issues raised at the above meeting (items 1 and 4) clearly do hold developmental benefits for the locality, issues can nevertheless be found in other WDCs where central and local interests come into conflict. The most common issue of this type is that of *citemene* cultivation, which from a local viewpoint is a rational response to a poor agricultural environment, but from a central viewpoint is a 'malignant cancer on the nation's natural resources'.[24] *Citemene* continues to be practised in every ward in Kasama against the express control attempts of councillors and government extension agents. These latter officials view WDCs primarily as an instrument for the implementation of State policy from above. WDCs do offer an opportunity for rapid downward communication in otherwise isolated rural areas, but they can also be all too easily used for a bureaucratic-authoritarian mode of policy implementation.

Third, the conception of planning held by WDC members is merely that of demanding resources from the centre. According to the widespread 'shopping list' approach, as many projects as possible are demanded in the hope that one or two will prove acceptable to the centre. No consideration is given to the practical problems of implementation or to the availability of scarce central resources. At the Ward 13 meeting, of the five items that concerned pressing local issues, only two (items 3 and 5) were deemed soluble by self-help techniques and even these two items also involved requests for assistance from the centre.

The finding that local planning has definite limitations was reinforced by a general review of the performance of active WDCs in Kasama District. Analysis of the frequency and content of WDC demands revealed that the local development strategy sought by WDC members emphasised social welfare above economic productivity.[25] Over three-quarters (79 per cent) of the issues raised at WDC meetings concerned social welfare, that is schools (21 per cent), roads (18 per cent), domestic water supplies (18 per cent) and health facilities (14 per cent), all of which bear at best an indirect relationship to economic productivity. Issues such as fertiliser availability (7 per cent), the formation of co-operatives (1 per cent) and other economic matters accounted together for less than one-quarter (21 per cent) of WDC planning activity. Significantly, issues such as provision of seed, tractor hire and marketing facilities did not occur in councillor reports.

Thus, only if development is defined broadly to include the provision of social facilities as well as the inducement of the growth of production can WDCs be said to have a development orientation at all. Yet within this limited framework WDCs do perform in the active rather than passive mode. Of items discussed at WDC meetings, 70 per cent were concerned with the initiation of new projects and 30 per cent with the care and maintenance of existing projects (see Table 9.2). Earlier impressions of WDC reliance on central resources were confirmed by the general survey of active WDCs. Almost three-quarters (73 per cent) of WDC demands were accompanied by requests for government funding; only one-quarter (27 per cent) explicitly designated self-help resources. Finally, the notion that WDCs function to reinforce central control as well as local participation was also confirmed. 'Upward' communications at WDC meetings outnumbered 'downward' communications in a ratio of two to one, but a far higher ratio might have been expected given the sheer numerical majority of peasants over central representatives at such meetings.

Among the main conclusions to be reached about WDC performance to date is that, like VPCs, WDCs have yet to mobilise local material and manpower resources for agricultural and other production. Instead, they tend to act as a demand forum in which a share from national economic surplus is sought. The meagre surplus that does trickle down for the use of WDCs is usually invested in non-productive social trappings of modernisation. WDCs reflect the economic dependence of rural localities in that they have yet to embark upon the accumulation and reinvestment of local surplus. They offer symbolic but not effective local participation in the national planning process.

Table 9.2: Content of selected WDC meetings, Kasama District, 1972–75[1]

Ward	Date	Develop-ment item	Care & mainten-ance item	Self-help resources	Government resources	Commun-ication up	Commun-ication down
7	23.9.72	1	–	2	1	2	2
13	31.1.73	8	2	4	5	9	2
2	25.2.73	1	–	–	1	1	1
2	8.5.73	2	–	–	2	2	2
15	19.5.73	4	3	3	4	4	4
7	9.1.74	6	–	2	6	4	5
14	2.2.74	3	2	2	2	2	–
2	30.3.74	8	2	–	8	6	8
7	8.4.74	2	4	1	3	2	5
13	17.4.74	7	–	–	7	10	5
15	18.4.74	25	7	7	22	29	2
7	19.5.74	3	2	–	3	3	2
14	8.6.74	7	2	2	7	8	2
15	13.7.74	9	1	2	6	9	3
2	24.7.74	1	1	–	3	3	4
7	25.8.74	5	1	2	4	4	2
4	5.10.74	–	3	1	–	–	3
2	12.10.74	4	4	3	4	6	5
16	17.11.74	4	1	3	2	3	3
7	26.3.75	3	1	–	3	3	1
	Total	103	36	34	93	110	61
	percentage	70	30	27	73	64	36

Note
   [1] Based on items discussed at twenty WDC meetings between 23 September 1972 and 26 March 1975, as filed on minutes with Kasama Rural Council or as recorded by this researcher.

The distribution of benefits

The performance of WDCs has so far been examined with little reference to social context. As argued earlier, the form taken by local institution-building is determined by the interaction of the objectives of the State with the interests of local leadership groups. For this reason it is necessary to ask the question 'who benefits?' from WDC activity and to trace the nature and extent of the diffusion of development benefits in the locality. Three local leadership groups dominate the resource distribution process in Kasama: field-level civil servants, ward councillors and WDC members. The impact of the interests of each will now be briefly examined.

The rejection of WDC projects or the delay in implementing projects is sometimes attributable, not to poor WDC planning, but to poor civil service implementation. In 1972, at the end of the financial year, Northern Province had to return to Lusaka K66,000 in development funds that provincial and district level civil servants had failed to spend.[26] Until 1974, the first year in which the provincial Cabinet Minister as chairman of the PDC was able to ensure the expenditure on time of all development funds, inefficiency in project implementation made the return of unspent funds from Northern Province a regular occurrence. Numerous cases can be cited where WDC projects in Kasama suffered from non-performance or delays on the part of field-level civil servants. For example, the 1972 Ministry of Rural Development estimates provided funds for a village water supply. The funds were not used by the Department of Water Affairs in that year and their benefit was lost to villagers.[27] Another case concerned the pollution of a village river which, notwithstanding vocal WDC representation, went uncorrected for three years despite the allocation of K35,000 for a borehole and pipes under the Second National Development Plan.[28] Peasants in that ward became sceptical that the WDC could do anything for them and attendance at WDC meetings declined as a consequence.

Bureaucratic bottlenecks can in part be traced to the shortage of experienced manpower, transport, and delegated authority experienced by provincial and district officers of government. There is ample evidence, however, that civil servants regard a devolution of real policy-making power to local-level committees as a threat to their own interests. The obstructive attitudes and actions of local officials to the growth of WDCs have been documented in Mkushi District.[29] In Kasama, district officials were unwilling to tour the villages or to attend WDC meetings when invited, but readily expressed disdain for the calibre of ward- and village-level leadership. A 'commandist' style in administrative communication was predominantly adopted by district level officials at those few WDC meetings they did attend. Moreover, civil servants in Kasama were poorly informed about the activities of WDCs and gratuitously spread the inaccurate rumour that WDCs existed 'on paper only'. The formation of what has been called a bureaucratic bourgeoisie in Zambia since independence finds its expression at the local level in the jealous guarding of administrative power and economic privilege against devolution to participatory institutions.

A second social group whose actions and interests account for the performance of WDCs are the ward councillors. As chairmen of

WDCs ward councillors occupy the top formal leadership posts on local committees. The extent to which they utilise their key role of linking central and local State apparatus determines to a large extent whether or not the local committee system is activated. Councillors are often the only connection between people in distant villages and the State. A councillor who frequently tours his ward and maintains personal contact with his constituents is able to mobilise VPCs into regular meetings. He can also ensure that WDC development projects are implemented. But if a councillor neglects this part of his job he is likely to be faced with dormant committees. Of the twenty-three councillors in Kasama Rural Council, only five initiated systematic programmes for ward touring and for quarterly WDC meetings. Peasants in Kasama often complained that they did not know their councillor because he did not visit their villages. Complaints of this type were particularly common in large or outlying wards throughout the district and close and regular contact between councillor and constituents was the exception rather than the rule.

If the downward communication through councillors was sparse and sporadic so, too, was upward communication. WDC initiatives are futile if they are not conveyed by the councillor to the appropriate higher authorities or if the councillor lacks influence at the rural council and regional UNIP headquarters. Part of the routine process of upward communication in Kasama is the provision to the rural council of councillor monthly reports; only three of the twenty-three councillors provided reports with any regularity. In addition, councillors ensured that WDC minutes were written and communicated upward to the rural council in only eight out of twenty-three wards. WDC minutes for only two wards could be found on file at the District Governor's office. Since formal channels of upward communication are underutilised, councillors instead rely heavily on informal personal contacts. Almost all councillors (twenty-one out of twenty-three) personally brought development requests from their wards to the attention of the District Governor or UNIP regional secretary and success was related to rank in the local-level party. Thus party office is not only a criterion for recruitment to WDC leadership position, as documented earlier, but also a determinant of the allocation of development resources in the locality. Peasants and WDC members alike acknowledge that top local party officials, many of whom were appointed councillors, acted consciously as a group to take first option on the central development resources.[30]

The influence of a third and final leadership group can be seen in the performance of WDCs in Kasama. As noted previously, WDCs recruit predominantly from among party officials, emergent farmers and other well-to-do elements. Together this group also stakes a claim to the development benefits that WDCs have at their disposal. WDC members perceive WDC membership as a means of satisfying personal and group interests, sometimes through preferential access. An example can be given concerning access to agricultural credit afforded to WDC members. In the 1974–75 farming season the Agricultural Finance Company launched an experimental programme to decentralise agricultural credit facilities. Loan applications were to be vetted by the WDC, meeting in conjunction with field extension workers of the Department of Agriculture. A tentative indication of WDC resource distribution patterns was gained from the first lists of loan applicants that were submitted to AFC Kasama in 1975. Two facts were clear. First, WDCs acted to enforce the selective national strategy of isolating the 'emergent farmer' as the main agent of agricultural innovation. AFC instructions to WDCs were replete with references to the farming background, credit-worthiness, 'willingness to hire labour' and other measures of the 'character, ability and industry' of the applicant.[31] Ward councillors in Kasama unanimously agreed that only the best farmers should get loans and WDC recommendations to date have not deviated from the notion of 'building on the best'. The WDC procedure is undoubtedly reaching more prospective farmers than before; 353 loans were approved in Kasama for 1975–76, up from 222 in 1974–75. But given the Government's current strategy to assist individual family units, as opposed to mass-mobilising the peasantry and granting credit co-operatively, WDC involvement in credit distribution contributed to further economic stratification in the rural areas. WDCs also assisted in the selection of tenants for the settlement schemes in Kasama District with the same result.

The second indication of how WDCs distributed resources was found in the high incidence of WDC members using their positions to recommend themselves for loans. An analysis of the 1975 lists of WDC-recommended loan applicants showed the names of one-third (32 per cent) of the WDC members in Kasama District.[32] Names of councillors and WDC secretaries were included. The remaining applicants were those emergent farmers and local party officials who did not sit on the WDC but who were close to it in terms of the local party organisation. For example, of the twenty-two applicants recommended by one WDC, two were ward councillors, four were members of the WDC, and fifteen were branch and constituency

officials of the party.[33] Thus as WDCs gained more central
resources, so they became integrated into the patronage machine
that supervised the distribution of resources in the locality. The
primary beneficiaries were those who were recruited by virtue of
emergent farmerhood or party office into positions of WDC
leadership.

Conclusions

The formation of local-level participatory institutions in Zambia has
not altered the uneven distribution of development benefits and the
dependent character of rural economies inherited from colonial rule.
The development trajectory of rural Zambia is the product of a State
development strategy that emphasises political control above
political participation, the resources of which are mediated by local
leadership groups.

Analysis of the recruitment and performance of local-level
participatory institutions in Kasama suggests that the Zambian
Government has achieved a modicum of penetration and
administrative control over the rural periphery. The creation of an
all-inclusive and viable body politic remains, however, an unfinished
task. The State penetrates so far and no further. Development
committee organisation is firm at provincial and district levels,
partial at ward level, and peters out almost completely at village
level. At both ward and village levels, development committee
organisation has become intertwined with local social structure but
with contradictory results for development. VPCs have in some cases
performed to bolster the powers of traditional leaders, but have not
universally filled the 'institutional vacuum' in the village. WDCs,
where active, have embarked on local development projects; the
decentralised AFC credit procedures have been particularly
valuable in giving WDCs something to do. In general, however,
WDCs have failed to secure more than a selective or truncated
diffusion of benefits with regard to local social structure.

In a national context, the impact of development committees on
policy-making in Zambia is negligible. First, WDCs and VPCs are
not consulted about major industrial or infrastructural projects, of
which the Tanzam railway and industrial plants in Kasama are
good examples. The only control exercised over State expenditure is
over the location of water schemes or rural health centres, although in
the case of schools even this limited control is denied. Second, local-
level committees are able to make little or no expenditures of their
own. Funds allocated by the rural council to each ward are

invariably tied to specified projects and the WDC is allowed no leeway in adjusting even the choice of technique by which a project is implemented. Third, the State has not placed resources behind self-help as the strategy for rural development in Zambia. Repeated observations in Kasama indicated that peasants were willing to organise themselves into local-level committees and to provide labour on community projects if the State met their efforts with capital resources. The absence of funds for self-help, however, has often resulted in a demobilisation of popular energies and a withdrawal of support for the centre. National ideological commitment to devolution and participation through WDCs has not been matched with a commitment of material resources. There is little 'trust in the masses' in the Zambian strategy for rural development.

The fact that the quality of peasant life has not improved markedly is due not only to the choices made by national planners, but it is due also to a hierarchical local social structure in which certain leadership groups are able to influence the pattern of resource distribution. Some of these groups, namely field-level civil servants, local party officials, and emergent farmers, have been identified. A stratum of leaders that has benefited from development resources has aligned itself with the centre and has become an instrument of State policy. Intermediate leaders manage and contain peasant demands on behalf of the centre through the medium of the State administrative apparatus, the lowest echelon of which is composed of WDCs. Intermediate local leaders are, in Saul's words, 'those actors – their, interests and goals – who define what government actually represents' in the locality.[34]

Notes

[1] J. S. Saul, 'Class and penetration,' in L. Cliffe and J. S. Saul (eds.), *Socialism in Tanzania: an interdisciplinary reader* (Dar es Salaam, 1973), vol. I, p. 122.

[2] See L. Cliffe, 'Penetration and rural development in the East African context' (University of Dar es Salaam, 1973, mimeo.).

[3] C. J. Gertzel, 'Institutional developments at district level in independent Zambia' (University of Zambia Political Science Workshop, 1972, mimeo.).

[4] L. Cliffe and J. S. Saul, 'The district development front', in Cliffe and Saul (eds.), *Socialism in Tanzania, op. cit.*, vol. I, pp. 302–28.

[5] Simmance Report, *op. cit.*, p. 107.

[6] *Times of Zambia*, 23 April 1975; see also 'Village groups are a failure', *ibid.*, 17 March 1975.

[7] Circular No. 5 of 1972, Office of the Permanent Secretary, Northern Province.

[8] *Registration and development of villages* (report compiled by E. B. Chituta), p. 2; Office of the District Secretary, Kasama.

[9] *Monthly progress report on registration of villages*, 30 April 1972; Office of the

Permanent Secretary, Northern Province.

[10] *Registration and development of villages Act, 1972*, part VI.

[11] James Mwilwa, VPC meeting, 13 June 1974.

[12] Minutes of Ward Council Secretaries' meeting, Mungwi, 1 October 1974; confirmed in interviews with District Governor, Assistant District Secretary and numerous headmen and councillors.

[13] A. I. Richards, 'A changing pattern of agriculture in East Africa', *Geographical Journal*, vol. 124, No. 3 (1958), p. 311.

[14] A. I. Richards, 'The political system of the Bemba tribe', in M. Fortes and E. Evans-Pritchard, *African Political Systems* (London, 1941).

[15] 'Help us recover loans': report on address by Minister of Rural Development to House of Chiefs, *Times of Zambia*, 25 September 1975.

[16] Kaunda, *Humanism in Zambia and a guide to its implementation, op. cit.*, p. 43.

[17] *The councillors' handbook* (Lusaka, 1966).

[18] Address by District Governor to Kasama Rural Council, 22 September 1971; minutes of 30th ordinary meeting.

[19] Interview, Councillor, Ward 17, 25 November 1974.

[20] With twenty-three wards in the Rural Council area of Kasama District and a formal membership of 10 on each WDC, there were 230 potential respondents. The total population was surveyed by means of a self-administered questionnaire. A satisfactory response rate was achieved: of 230 questionnaires circulated, 204 were recovered, a response rate of 88·7 per cent.

[21] Minutes of WDC meeting, Ward 13, Rural Council Welfare Hall, Mungwi, 31 January 1973.

[22] Noted at WDC meeting, Ward 13, Council Chamber, Mungwi, 17 April 1974.

[23] Noted at meeting for MP for Kasama, Mungwi, 25 April 1975.

[24] See President Kaunda's speech commemorating World Forestry Day, *Times of Zambia*, 22 March 1976.

[25] Analysis is based on 103 councillor reports on the content of WDC meetings between November 1973 and May 1974, Kasama Rural Council, File LG/KA/1/4.

[26] S. Kalulu, member of the Central Committee, public meeting at Buseko Hall, Kasama, 24 May 1974.

[27] Interview, Councillor, Ward 20, 27 November 1974.

[28] Minutes of WDC meeting, Ward 14, 2 February 1974.

[29] H. McEnery, 'The village productivity committee system and production targets in Mkushi District' (Lusaka, August 1974, mimeo.).

[30] For a fuller analysis of the mechanics of party patronage based on a prestige-rating study, see M. Bratton, 'Peasant and party-State in Zambia: political organisation and resource distribution in Kasama District' (Ph.D. dissertation, Brandeis University, 1978), chs. 4 and 6.

[31] AFC Instructions Nos. 410 1A and 1B, April 1974.

[32] Based on provisional figures for new and existing customers for 1975–76 provided by AFC, Kasama. The percentage may well be higher, given that loan applicants sometimes used names different from those appearing on WDC membership lists. Moreover, a study of the AFC procedure in Mpika, Mumbwa and Mazabuka Districts revealed a higher proportion of WDC members among loan applicants than in Kasama. Only 20 per cent of those receiving credit in Kasama were WDC members, whereas the figure averaged 40 per cent for the other three districts. J. Due, 'Agricultural credit in Zambia by level of development' (Urbana-Champaign: University of Illinois, Agricultural Economics Staff Paper, 1978), p. 26.

[33] Interviews, UNIP branch officials, Nseluka village, 22 April 1975.

[34] Saul, 'Class and penetration', *op. cit.*, p. 119.

10. Two case studies in rural development

Cherry Gertzel

The two case studies presented in this chapter describe two separate rural development programmes adopted by the Zambian Government in the early seventies.[1] The first, the Task Force, was limited in scope to Western Province (formerly Barotseland). It proved a minor affair and might best be described as an *ad hoc* attempt to deal with the particular development problems of that province with a minimal outlay of resources. Set up in 1971, it was abandoned little more than a year later. The second programme was more substantial. The Intensive Development Zones (IDZs) were conceived as a national strategy and presented in the Second National Development Plan (SNDP) as a major innovation in rural administration which would require substantial resources of both capital and personnel. The programme, however, was discontinued after only three years, before the SNDP had run its course. Both programmes might therefore, in view of their brief life, best be viewed as failures. Nevertheless, each had been introduced, in the first place, as an important innovation in rural development. It is for this reason that they deserve consideration: although both disappeared within a short period of time, their experience focuses attention upon some of the constraints upon rural development in these years and the administration as an agency for rural change.

The background: the nature of the rural development problem

The background to both these programmes was Zambia's continuing search for a viable rural development strategy. The colonial period had left the country's rural areas seriously disadvantaged in every way in comparison with the urban areas along the line of rail, and especially the industrialised Copperbelt.[2] UNIP had committed itself, when it assumed power, to redress that rural-urban imbalance, and both First and Second National

Development Plans accorded priority to rural development. After independence the resources available for agriculture were considerably greater than they had been in the colonial period, and a good deal of money was invested in the rural sector in the sixties. At the same time, the Government embarked upon a series of programmes designed to transform agriculture so as to overcome the inherited dualism between the small, expatriate-dominated, modern 'commercial' agricultural sector, and the great mass of Zambia's so-called 'traditional farmers', the bulk of whom still farmed at subsistence level.[3] In 1965 the President launched a major co-operatives and credit programme; and in 1967 the Government established an enlarged Credit Organisation of Zambia (COZ) to rationalise credit to small farmers. The sixties also saw attempts to introduce a massive mechanisation scheme, land clearance, and a variety of settlement schemes. A succession of administrative reforms attempted to overcome the weaknesses inherited from the colonial years as well as the serious deficiencies in staff. The most important of these were introduced in 1968–69 when President Kaunda proposed a significant measure of decentralisation to provincial level. Directed at the improvement of the rural administration as an agency of development, these reforms emphasised the role of province and district, and the responsibilities of provincial and district development committees, in the development process. Subsequently, in 1971, a Village Regrouping Act provided a legislative basis for the village regrouping and resettlement proposed as early as 1965 as a measure to increase grass roots participation in the same process.[4] In 1969 a major ministerial reorganisation brought together all those departments involved in rural development into a new Ministry of Rural Development; the latter provided a central focus for rural development organisation.[5] In 1969 also the marketing bodies were reorganised into the National Agricultural Marketing Board (NAMBOARD). On a different plane the Land Acquisition Act in 1969 sought to break traditional control over land use.

None of these measures, however, produced any substantial improvement either in the rural areas or in agriculture. On the contrary, the terms of trade turned further against the agricultural sector and the rural dweller was worse off in 1970 than he had been in 1964.[6] There were, it is true, some positive achievements in this period. A great amount of expenditure was incurred on schools, hospitals, clinics and other social services, and the major road communications across the country substantially improved. Nevertheless, the diversification of the rural economy had certainly not proceeded at the pace envisaged in the FNDP. The co-operative policy failed to produce a viable co-operative movement, and COZ by 1969 was in serious difficulties as a result of the massive non-repayment of loans.[7] The mechanisation programme proved premature. The material standard of living of the bulk of rural dwellers, who gained their livelihood from agriculture, had scarcely changed, as the accelerated migration to the urban areas demonstrated: in 1971 they could still be said to farm at the subsistence level with occasional sales of produce in a good season. The great majority of the 767,000 holdings in the traditional sector were small holdings; nearly half of them comprised less than 2·5 acres, and three-quarters less than 4·5 acres. Many small-holders, especially in the northern parts of the country, still used forms of shifting cultivation. Most lived in small villages, almost half of which had no more than fifty inhabitants. Dispersed settlement patterns thus remained a serious constraint upon the provision of both services and the economic infrastructure that was a necessary prerequisite for agricultural development.[8] Moreover, notwithstanding the priority accorded rural development and the increased expenditure over the FNDP period, 82 per cent of actual capital expenditure in the FNDP went to the three 'line of rail' provinces (Southern, Central and Copperbelt), leaving the remaining 18 per cent to be shared among the other five provinces.[9] The economy, finally, remained overwhelmingly dependent on copper.

The failure to achieve any substantial change in the rural condition was a major source of government and presidential comment as the sixties drew to a close. The starkness of the rural–urban imbalance and the plight of the rural dweller were highlighted by the *Report on Incomes, Wages and Prices* presented to Government by Professor Turner in 1969[10]. This report formed the basis of discussions at the Kitwe Convention on Rural Development held in December of that year.[11] It was Kaunda himself, however, who earlier in August had most forcibly acknowledged the country's failure to achieve any rural transformation and who had warned the UNIP National Council that Zambia might well become a country with two nations in one: the one rural and the other urban.[12] It was, moreover, the President who took the initiative in seeking new ways to foster rural development.

It is against this background that we must consider the two rural development programmes to which we now turn.

The Western Province task force

The Western Province at independence presented Zambia's most acute problem of rural underdevelopment. It is the country's second largest province, with the smallest population, whose main economic activity is raising cattle. In the colonial period the region had served as a labour reserve, from which Lozi migrants went steadily backwards and forwards to the South African mines, their remittances being one of the province's major sources of income. The latter-day efforts of the former colonial government to halt the province's long term economic decline failed. The province's development problems were complex, exacerbated by its isolation from the country's main national infrastructure, the marginal nature of much of its soils, and the particular ecological problems of the Zambezi floodplain. The special position that had been accorded the traditional Lozi Kingdom in the colonial period had also left a legacy of severe political tension between the traditional leadership and the UNIP Government, and this presented a further severe constraint upon integration already made difficult by the province's geographical isolation.[13]

Capital expenditure in Western Province increased significantly after independence, in comparison with expenditure by the Barotse Government during the colonial period. Nevertheless, the amount spent was still modest and only a limited amount of development activity was initiated. In the FNDP period the major change was in the provision of social rather than economic infrastructure, and few new economic opportunities became available. Moreover, an outbreak of foot and mouth disease in 1969 seriously affected the economy. Equally significant was the fact that in 1966 the Government took the decision to prohibit migrant labour to South African mines, at a time when no alternative means of employment within the province was available. This meant a serious loss of income for a significant section of the population. At the same time, the Government also went a long way to dismantling the traditional authorities which still enjoyed substantial popular support, but which were in conflict with the ruling party. The combination of changes in traditional authority and failure to achieve any real economic improvement combined to produce a strong sense of grievance at grassroots level. That sense of deprivation cost the UNIP Government a good deal of its earlier support in the 1968 general election, in which the party was overwhelmingly defeated.[14]

The initiative for the Task Force came from President Kaunda. Impressed by what he had seen on a visit in the middle of 1969 to the successful Kafubu Settlement Scheme on the Copperbelt, the President requested the Israelis to provide a technical assistance team to survey Western Province and advise on its development. He was specifically concerned with the possibility of applying the Kafubu experience to the Western Province, as his statement on the Province in August 1969 made clear. 'I want', he said, ' . . . to see the development in the Kafubu Block to be repeated in Western Province. To this effect I have already started considering possible projects for Western Province, using the Kafubu Block development experience and I will be announcing them as soon as possible . . .'[15] The Israeli team which visited the province in November 1969 did not however adopt this approach. Its report, submitted in July 1970, in fact emphasised the need to devise a development strategy that took cognisance of the province's particular circumstances. First, the team suggested that the varied conditions across the province necessitated a project approach to development, with specific projects located and connected as far as possible with a (improved) provincial road network. Second, it recommended a number of specific projects which would repay further attention, including an abattoir at Mongu (the provincial headquarters) and an extension of summer grazing. Third, the Israelis suggested that the complex ecological constraints upon development required a special investigatory team of professional officers able to identify and test new projects. They therefore recommended the creation of a central professional Task Force, located in Lusaka and responsible directly to the Office of the President, to work on the long-term development problems that faced the region.[16]

This report was considered by a special inter-ministerial committee (of representatives from the Ministries of Rural Development, Finance and Planning, and from State House) set up by Kaunda for that purpose; the committee met under the chairmanship of the State House member in November 1970. The Israeli recommendations were substantially accepted, although the committee concluded that the Task Force, to consist of eight professional officers, should be based in Mongu rather than Lusaka and should be responsible not to the President's Office but to the Ministry of Rural Development. The President accepted these recommendations. The abattoir became the responsibility of the Cold Storage Board which proceeded independently from that point; it was completed two years later. The responsibility for the establishment of the Task Force was handed to an inter-ministerial committee, composed of senior civil servants from Rural Development and Finance and Development Planning, with the

Permanent Secretary, Rural Development, as chairman. State House, at this point, passed out of the picture.[17]

The co-ordinating committee, however, found itself responsible for a proposal for which there were no funds. The following six months were therefore spent in searching for finance and housing for the Task Force; most of this work fell to a senior expatriate adviser in the Ministry of Rural Development, working to the Minister and having also, it seemed, a liaison role with State House. Although the committee, when it met in April 1971, suggested that in view of the presidential interest in the project the Minister for Rural Development might if necessary appeal to State House for financial support, no such appeal appears to have been made. In the event, the Ministry provided K25,000 (originally allocated for land use work in Western Province) and agreement was reached with the provincial permanent secretary to transfer to the Task Force K60,000 allocated to Western Province for a vegetable production scheme. This K85,000 enabled the committee to proceed. Two officers were appointed in July and took up residence in Mongu in September in borrowed housing, but with their own landrovers.

Although the original plan had envisaged a team of eight professional staff, no additional appointments were made. In Mongu the two officers received some assistance from one of the agricultural officers at the Agricultural Research Station. Otherwise the Task Force, from September 1971, consisted only of themselves: the Team leader, who had formerly been a provincial planning officer, and the other officer, an agriculturalist. The Team leader, as we shall see, left in April 1972, after which the other officer remained alone, until the end of 1972, when the experiment was drawn to a close.

In Mongu, the two Task Force officers proved unable either to establish a valid role for themselves within the province's development programme, or to justify the notion of a special investigatory team as a necessary part of that programme. While it was true that they were hampered by lack of funds and supporting staff, a more fundamental constraint arose from the fact that neither showed himself equipped to initiate a programme of fundamental research. While the Team leader drew up a list of projects on which he thought the Task Force should embark, all of these were part of on-going departmental programmes. The result was that he laid himself open to the charge of duplication, and of interference in established departmental activity. Moreover, the Lusaka co-ordinating committee had its own ideas as to the functions of the Task Force, which it regarded as an opportunity to overcome existing difficulties — the livestock industry, which had been seriously affected by the outbreak of foot and mouth disease, was regarded as the primary objective of Western Province development. From the point of view of Lusaka's Chief Animal Husbandry Officer, the crucial need in 1971 was to revive cattle sales and so to concentrate upon improved marketing facilities. Since transport was a severe constraint upon departmental action, the co-ordinating committee proposed that three of the Task Force landrovers should be used immediately to assist with the construction of cattle holding grounds. The Task Force leader disagreed with this order of priorities, arguing that prior consideration should go to extension work.

Whatever activities the members of the Task Force engaged in, however, it was crucial for their success that they co-operate with existing departmental officers. It was therefore unfortunate that within a very short time of their arrival the Team leader had clashed with one after another of the provincial departmental heads. The reasons for this soon became obvious. On the one hand, provincial officers had not originally been consulted about the Task Force, which was additional to the provincial programme and bound to compete for scarce resources of funds and staff. It was not therefore surprising that these officers were somewhat doubtful about the programme. On the other hand, the central issue between Task Force and provincial officers as the conflict grew in the following months was the insistence of the former that the Task Force was independent of the provincial authority, and the leader's claim to be directly responsible only to the Ministry in Lusaka. Such claims challenged the whole notion of decentralisation to which so much emphasis had been given, and which was over these same months the subject of a government inquiry.[18] The Provincial Rural Development Officer (responsible for the co-ordination of all rural development programmes in the province) quickly asked his permanent secretry in Lusaka to clarify who was 'boss'. The provincial permanent secretary was equally disturbed, and the PDC, theoretically responsible for development in the province, found that it apparently had no control over the Task Force or influence upon its activities. The Task Force seemed to duplicate rather than to supplement existing programmes, in a situation of acute shortage of both funds and staff. Its landrovers, with their own distinctive markings (purchased, it must be remembered, with funds originally allocated for an agricultural project) in a province chronically short of transport, acutely symbolised the competition. The Task Force was in a position to lend transport to other departments. Yet the record suggested that its only positive achievement at the end of 1972 had been support, with funds and transport, for a series of research sub-stations set up by the Agricultural Research Station, for the maintenance of which the latter had no recurrent funds.

Relationships were undoubtedly soured further by the personal indiscretions of the Task Force leader. Mongu was a small community in which such behaviour, especially on the part of expatriate officers, was bound to result in social tension. Nor were matters improved by the boast that the Task Force enjoyed direct access not only to the Ministry in Lusaka but also to State House. The boast was an empty one, but it was nevertheless tactless, particularly of an expatriate officer.

After a difficult three months the PDC, at its January 1972 meeting, recorded its loss of confidence in the Task Force leader who appeared to them to spend more time in the local hotel than in his office.[19] In March the provincial permanent secretary requested his transfer on the grounds that he was unsuitable for the post. In April, he was moved back to Lusaka, having himself decided not to renew his contract.

Nevertheless, personality was not the only cause of local opposition to the Task Force, which fared no better with the change of leader after April 1972. The provincial permanent secretary attempted, later in the year, to rescue the situation by reviving the original notion of the Task Force as a research unit, and making it responsible to a sub-committee of the PDC set up to oversee its activities. By that time, however, the Task Force funds were exhausted, and the 1973 estimates included no more than a token K10,000. At the end of the year therefore he recommended, and the permanent secretary in the Ministry agreed, that in view of the lack of finance the Task Force should be wound up, and its equipment (the landrovers) and the subordinate staff (the drivers) absorbed into existing departments. We can only surmise the discussion that must have taken place when the permanent secretary from the Ministry visited Mongu at the beginning of the new year. Both men were sensitive to the political and social circumstances that had originally been responsible for the decision to create the Task Force. Neither believed, however, that the Task Force had made any contribution to economic progress. Both were also aware that there appeared to be no commitment to the project either in the Ministry in Lusaka or in the provincial departments in Mongu. Bureaucratic opposition to the continuation of the Task Force was scarcely in doubt. It was also apparent, however, that the Task Force had no political support either in the province or at the centre. The provincial Cabinet Minister had shown no interest in it and there was no popular involvement or support. The only political support had come from President Kaunda, whose attention was by this time transferred elsewhere, and who had shown no significant concern about the project on the occasion of his visit to the Western Province provincial development committee in September 1972.

Quietly, therefore, in the course of the regular budgetary proceedings, the Task Force was abandoned. No one questioned this decision, and the project disappeared into oblivion, the only reminder being the specially marked landrovers left in Western Province.

Intensive development zones

The Intensive Development Zone (IDZ) strategy, which Zambia adopted with the SNDP, was in keeping with ideas on integrated rural development fashionable with planners in the sixties. An FAO/IBRD mission in 1965, an ILO mission in 1969 and a further FAO mission in 1970 had all suggested such an area focus for consideration.[20] The idea was however by no means new to Zambia, since the colonial government, in the late 1950s, had attempted such an approach in the Northern and Luapula Provinces.[21] Moreover, some of Zambia's civil servants considered that the intensive development strategy had evolved out of the ideas and experiences of the Land Settlement Board and the settlement schemes established since independence.[22] The programme that went into the SNDP, however, undoubtedly received its real impetus within Zambian government circles from the President, who raised the idea on four different occasions between March 1969 and March 1970.[23] On the fourth of these occasions, in March 1970, he delivered a major policy speech to a senior civil servants' seminar on rural development in Lusaka, in the course of which he outlined what he saw as the ten principles of his new rural development strategy, including village regrouping and IDZs. Village regrouping, he argued, would be essential in many cases if rural development was to take place; the Ministry of Rural Development would, therefore, be confronted with the task of demarcating those areas where natural conditions allowed rapid expansion of economic activities as Intensive Development Zones, and of encouraging people to move to those areas. 'The identification, demarcation and development of planned Intensive Development Zones is necessary in order to bring a measure of consistency into long term planning and to avoid the continuous wastage of scarce resources . . .[24] A month later the Commissioner for Land Settlement announced at the annual meeting of the Local Government Association of Zambia that the Government proposed to embark upon an IDZ programme.[25] By November 1970 the Ministry of Rural Development had produced a memorandum on organisation and implementation, and during 1971 an FAO/SIDA[26] Report on Rural Development suggested *inter alia* an outline programme and criteria for the selection of zones. The IDZ proposals were also considered in the course of the preparation of the SNDP during 1971, especially in the committee on rural administration and development. A special memorandum on IDZs was submitted to the committee by a UN adviser on administration, and the views of the University and the Government's own National Institute of Public Administration were also sought.[27] In October 1971 an Inter-Ministerial Committee was created to draw up an IDZ programme, the committee consisting of the permanent secretaries of the Ministries of Rural Development and Development Planning and National Guidance; the Director and Deputy Director of Planning, from Development Planning and National Guidance; the Under Secretary in the Ministry of Rural Development (who was the same technical assistance officer responsible for the liaison on the Task Force over the same period); and an IDZ Working Group of professional economists, drawn from the two Ministries and including also a representative from the UNDP team resident in Lusaka.[28] This Working Group was made responsible to the Inter-Ministerial Committee for the preparation and planning of the IDZ programme.

The SNDP, published at the end of 1971, committed the Government to the IDZ approach as a 'major new strategy' which would substantially improve both the institutional and economic services to the rural areas. It proposed that one IDZ should be established in each province by the end of the Plan period, 1976. These would be set up in two phases, with priority given to the remote provinces, and the first phase selection being completed by March 1972. The Plan envisaged a tentative investment of K17·5 million over five years, with supplementary funding of investment and personnel from external aid donors.[29] At that stage, however, no detailed planning had been carried out. This became the responsibility of the Working Group, which throughout 1972 was engaged in the preparation both of proposals for budget and staff and of a lengthy exposition of the criteria for the selection of IDZs. These were incorporated in a policy paper presented to Cabinet by the Minister for Rural Development in January 1973. During 1972 the Ministry was also engaged in discussions with potential donors and the Working Group proceeded with identification of IDZs.

Notwithstanding the stated intention to give priority to the remote areas, in January 1972 the Ministry of Rural Development announced that the first IDZ would be established in Eastern Province.[30] The Eastern Province IDZ, which in March the PDC decided should be located in Chipata District, therefore claimed the greater part of the Working Group's attention during the year. None the less, the team also visited Northern and North-western Provinces for which IDZs were planned in this first phase, and drew up recommendations for each PDC to consider. In addition, and in response to the decision by the Inter-Ministerial Committee to pursue work in Luapula Province, it met the PDC in Mansa.

By the end of 1972 three IDZs had been agreed upon, in Eastern, Northern and North-western Provinces. Only the first two took further shape in the course of the next two years, the Eastern Province IDZ being established first. After several months of preliminary work by the Working Group, Swedish technical assistance staff arrived in Chipata in September 1972 to form the basis of the Eastern resident planning team. In the following February a team co-ordinator arrived, at which point the first or experimental stage of the programme began. Progress was made on staff housing in Chipata during 1973, and a number of rural projects were embarked upon.

In December 1972 an economist from the Ministry of Rural Development Planning Unit was seconded to the Northern Province for six months to organise the collection of data, and in July 1973 the first IDZ officer arrived in the province to begin planning the experimental phase. By the beginning of 1974 there were four Danish officers in Kasama as the nucleus of the IDZ team and a modest rural programme was begun.

The IDZ operations from the end of 1972 therefore involved the Lusaka Working Group and the two provincial teams. At the beginning of 1973 the Working Group was reorganised as the IDZ Central Unit within the Ministry of Rural Development, responsible to an enlarged Inter-Ministerial Committee, and with a Zambian instead of an expatriate civil servant as chairman. Virtually all IDZ staff otherwise were technical assistance personnel, both in the Central Unit and in the provincial teams. The Central Unit was responsible for the supervision of the programme and for the budget and recruitment. Each provincial team came under the control of a team co-ordinator who was in turn responsible directly to the Central Unit in Lusaka. In addition, there was in each province a provincial IDZ co-ordinating committee under the chairmanship of the provincial permanent secretary, and composed of departmental heads, the District Governors and district secretaries of the districts involved in the IDZ, and the chairman of the rural council. The IDZ co-ordinator was secretary.

The IDZ operation in Chipata was altogether a larger affair than that in Kasama, not least because it received the bulk of the IDZ vote in both years. Thus in 1973, when the total IDZ budget was K400,000, K300,000 went to Eastern Province. Both teams however developed a similar programme, though Kasama's was on a smaller scale. Both embarked at the outset on a building programme to provide staff housing, and both commenced a number of small-scale rural development projects within the general framework of this first experimental phase. The Chipata team began construction of a Rural Development Centre which was intended as the central focus of its proposed extension project; assisted the tsetse control programme with bush clearing; took the first steps to establish a mechanisation centre; and carried out a soil survey. In Eastern Province also a research team from NIPA and another from the Rural Development Bureau at the University, in association with the IDZ, carried out additional survey work, and a good deal of relevant information was collected in this way.

The Kasama group was able to draw upon a major provincial survey recently completed by a research team from the Land Resources Division of the British Foreign and Commonwealth Office,[31] but it also became involved in data collection as a basis for planning. After considerable discussion it agreed with the co-ordinating committee on three projects on which to focus attention: coffee development at Ikumbi in Isoka District; assistance to the Agricultural Department's rice scheme; and an improved farming programme in an identified area. More generally, it sought to support departmental activity with supplementary resources – for example, it provided the Agricultural Department with transport. Every agricultural assistant in that small part of the district on which the IDZ team concentrated its efforts to improve farming techniques had a Honda at the end of 1974.

Both IDZ teams thus proceeded along lines in keeping with the conventional wisdom on integrated development. Both teams were enthusiastic, committed to the development programme, and had a good deal to offer in terms of professional competence and experience as well as enthusiasm. They were aware of the need for local participation and anxious that the provincial co-ordinating committee should work; and were pleased at the rapport they appeared to have established within a short time with provincial officers. They also sought to involve local leaders, and especially councillors, in the programme and encouraged these leaders to accompany them on their visits.

Nevertheless progress was slow, and the SNDP's timetable had soon proved unrealistic. One constraint was undoubtedly financial. Notwithstanding the SNDP promise of substantial capital investment, the IDZ received only a fraction either of the sums originally proposed or of the budgetary needs subsequently calculated by the Working Group and the provincial teams. Authorised expenditure in 1972 was K208,000, in each of 1973 and 1974 K400,000, and in 1975 K230,000, although the estimated total cost of the programme for 1973 alone had been originally K10,000,000.[32]

The Government thus refused to make the substantial investment originally proposed, or to provide the necessary personnel. This presumably reflected the inability of the Minister of Rural Development to win the full support of his Cabinet colleagues, especially the Minister of Finance, for the programme. It also suggested internal disagreement within his own Ministry, where the IDZ programme had to compete with other projects from the development budget – the SNDP had laid down that the planning and investigation costs of the IDZ programme would be borne within the current budgets of the executive Ministries. The financial constraints under which the IDZs began were also a consequence of the Government's failure to obtain the expected technical assistance which had been seen as necessary for the success of the programme. Notwithstanding the strong interest expressed at the outset in the IDZs by a number of potential donors, aid proved difficult to obtain. In the event, potential donors refused to commit themselves without a more substantial commitment on the part of the Zambian Government. The only external assistance that in consequence eventuated was limited support from SIDA, as well as from the Danish Government which provided the salaries of the four Danish staff posted to Kasama.

The IDZ teams also encountered difficulties at the provincial level as they sought to establish a role for themselves as part of the provincial development programme. In the first place, the intense competition between local leaders, including MPs and District Governors, to have IDZ projects located in their own areas imposed a severe strain on IDZ planning; it also inhibited general provincial support. Local leaders were well aware that if the IDZ was to be the focal point for the concentration of rural development resources, then ·

areas outside the zone, once it had been decided upon, stood at a disadvantage. In the second place, the teams quickly discovered that the village and ward committees through which they proposed to establish communications with the grass roots level were far less established than they anticipated. They also found the party of limited help. They were moreover frustrated in their efforts to establish local contacts and to create a local awareness of the programme by their inability to speak the local language; they had therefore to rely on interpreters. The dominance of expatriates in both IDZ teams was a further disability in building grass roots rapport.[33]

At the level of the administration, the arrival in the province of the IDZ team with its independent means carried with it the potential at least for resentment on the part of departmental officers who were themselves constantly constrained by limited resources. While both IDZ teams, for example, embarked upon a building programme to provide their own staff housing, Government had at that time imposed severe restrictions on the construction of new civil service housing. In a world of chronic shortage of transport, the IDZ vehicles might also prove a source of envy and tension.

Although the IDZ programme had its own budget, the IDZ projects were also competing for scarce resources. Yet in some cases at least they appeared to duplicate existing departmental programmes. The Chipata IDZ, for example, soon ran into difficulties when it tried to integrate its new Rural Development Centre into the Agricultural Department's extension programme. It was not easy to justify the establishment of two centres, even though the courses to be offered were directed at different clienteles.[34]

A more fundamental weakness so far as the administration was concerned was the centralisation of control in the Lusaka IDZ Central Unit, at a time when provincial officers had been told that the Government was committed to decentralisation. The problem emerged at an early stage in Eastern Province, where provincial staff were in the first place enthusiastic about the IDZ in which they assumed they would be deeply involved, and where the Permanent Secretary immediately set up a Chipata Working Group to plan and co-ordinate action. In May 1972, however (before the IDZ was off the ground) at a joint meeting of provincial and Ministry staff, the Permanent Secretary, Rural Development, made it clear that direction of the programme was to come from Lusaka.

This centralisation in Lusaka, which was later to be criticised by the Chipata IDZ team as well as the provincial administration, undoubtedly slowed down activity. The Lusaka Working Group itself proved to be a weak body, without sufficient staff and hesitant in providing leadership, notwithstanding its insistence on retaining control. While the IDZ programme was originally the joint responsibility of the Ministries of Rural Development and of Development Planning and National Guidance, the two Ministries disagreed at an early date on how to implement it, so that gradually Rural Development become solely responsible. The Working Group, restricted to that Ministry, suffered from continuing changes in membership. From mid-1972 it consisted of only three Rural Development economists. All expatriates, they were enthusiastic but highly secretive and strongly paternalistic in their approach, and this attitude undoubtedly inhibited co-operation with other Ministries, and indeed within Rural Development itself.

Lusaka's dominance over the provincial level was demonstrated in a number of ways. Although the PDC was responsible for the decision on the IDZ location, its choice was made from a series of alternatives drawn up and presented to it by the Lusaka Working Group. Although a provincial IDZ co-ordinating committee was set up, with the provincial permanent secretary as chairman, the IDZ co-ordinator controlled the funds and was responsible directly to Lusaka. While this same committee was responsible for decisions on particular projects, again the planning of those projects was directed from Lusaka. The provincial staff therefore found themselves assigned to a subordinate role in the IDZ programme. Not unexpectedly, they questioned this 'planning from the top' rather than the bottom, especially since it conflicted with the whole principle of decentralisation and provincial participation.[35] Although the IDZ team believed that it had won support from provincial departmental heads, the co-operation of departmental officers in local projects was not always forthcoming. The Cabinet Ministers in both provinces were, it seemed, able to some extent to influence the IDZ planning. On the one hand, the Cabinet Minister for Eastern Province intervened to influence the choice of Chipata as the IDZ, though this had not been the Working Group's first recommendation. On the other hand, the Cabinet Minister for Northern Province decided that he himself would chair the co-ordinating committee, on the ground that it should be a high-powered body. The Northern Province Minister and his permanent secretary were also quick to appreciate the opportunities that the IDZ offered them of access to an expertise which they were unlikely otherwise to find available at provincial level (where there were as yet no professional planning officers) and they did not hesitate to exploit that expertise where possible in connection with other provincial programmes.[36] Nevertheless, direct access to the Cabinet Minister did not necessarily ensure support for the IDZ itself; nor did it establish the need for the IDZ as an organisational focus for the province. It was the latter question that the Minister and his staff doubted. While they valued the expertise, they believed that the IDZ would be more advantageously located within the existing departmental organisation rather than as a separate body. Moreover, the ability of the provincial administration to provide the organisation for rural mobilisation was demonstrated in the Northern Province in 1974 when the Cabinet Minister initiated a successful drive for increased agricultural production, not through the IDZ, but through an *ad hoc* committee of departmental officers, chaired by himself; the committee set out to ensure simply that seed and fertiliser should reach the farmers in good time. Opinion in the province was later generally agreed that this plan, which the Minister called his Northern Province Agrarian Revolution, had been a success, as demonstrated by the increased maize production that season. Opinion was also agreed (certainly within the administration) that this success was due primarily to the Minister's leadership. And while this undoubtedly suggested past inadequacies on the part of the administration, it also suggested that the answer could be found, given leadership, within the existing administrative machinery as much as in a new development organisation.[37]

By this time, however, events had suggested more widespread doubts about the programme. At a time of growing economic crisis and increasing financial difficulty, the IDZ strategy had failed to produce any significant results. At the end of 1974 the Mid-Term Review of the SNDP concluded that it was difficult to say whether even the Eastern Province IDZ, which had received the more substantial assistance, had as yet got off the ground; and it concluded of the programme as a whole that: 'The achievements so far are not in any case commensurate with the efforts put in. There is thus a need to have a fresh look at the programme as a whole.'[38] It also warned of the need for Zambia to husband her limited resources, especially of administrative personnel. An IBRD mission in 1974 had also proposed changes in the programme, and a simpler administrative approach, and when at the beginning of 1975 a Central Committee member publicly questioned the utility of the IDZs as a basis for rural development,[39] it was clear that the whole programme was under review.

While Cabinet discussion on the issue is by its nature not available, we may infer from other events the disagreement over the future of the IDZs that had developed over the past year. There had been disagreement within the bureaucracy from the outset as to whether the IDZ programme was the most appropriate strategy for rural development. Early inter-ministerial disagreement as to the implementation of the IDZs had, as we have seen, left the Ministry of Rural Development as the only Ministry seriously involved in the programme, and other Ministries appear to have failed to take the IDZs into account in their own planning. Thus, in 1973, the Ministry of Development and Planning carried out a study of development along the corridor of the new Tanzam railway in Northern Province without reference to the IDZ in that province. In addition, the separate identity of the programme was emphasised by the IDZ structure and style of operations which had isolated it from the central administration as a whole. The Central Unit in the Ministry of Rural Development had operated independently to a large extent, and information and discussion about its activities and IDZ progress had been restricted. The expatriate dominance in the Unit as well as the provincial teams meant that few Zambians were involved and few were committed to the notion of IDZs.

The debate in the National Assembly in 1974 indicated that the politicians did not support the programme. In their view, the IDZs were much too long term in their perspective and also favoured some districts over others. What they wanted was a scheme that offered some immediate results and which also provided a more equal distribution of development resources over the country as a whole.[40]

The critical weakness of the IDZs therefore was that they failed to maintain political support. The Minister of Rural Development, who was responsible for the IDZ programme when it was first initiated and had himself been fully committed to it, left the Ministry at the end of 1973. The programme's key supporter was thus removed. Much more significant than the change of Ministers, however, was the change of governmental and party organisation that occasioned it; this followed the introduction of the new one party constitution in 1973, which established a Central Committee superior to the Cabinet. There followed a period of political wrangling and argument focused on the position of Central Committee member and Minister and the relationship between the two; for a time at least, this seriously strained the machinery of government. Whether or not in 1974 the new Minister of Rural Development (who was a former civil servant and now a nominated Member of Parliament) was as enthusiastic about the IDZ programme as his predecessor (who was now a member of the Central Committee and chairman of its rural development sub-committee), he faced a new set of political constraints upon departmental decision-making. His Ministry's programmes were now subject to the questions not only of fellow Ministers in the Cabinet but also of Central Committee members who were seeking to identify their role and functions and to assert their power over policy-making; the former Minister apart, members of the Central Committee were not apparently in favour of the IDZs. Moreover, the President, the programme's original backer, had developed an interest in another programme: early in 1975 he announced a new Rural Reconstruction programme under the direction of the National Service, which would set up a rural reconstruction camp in each district.[41] By the end of 1975 the IDZs had been largely abandoned, although the strategy of concentrating investment and services in selected areas of relatively high agricultural production potential once again received government support with the term 'rural growth areas' being employed in the Third National Development Plan.[42]

Conclusion

We may conclude with some justification that neither the Task Force nor the IDZ was given a sufficient opportunity to demonstrate its potential as an instrument for rural development. Neither was established as originally conceived, and neither at any time enjoyed the full support of the bureaucracy. Nevertheless, it is necessary to set these two experiments against the broader political environment within which the bureaucracy had to operate. The period from 1969 was in Zambia one of increasing political and economic tension focused, on the one hand, on the intra-party conflict that finally split UNIP in 1971 and, on the other, on the deteriorating economic situation that resulted from fluctuating copper prices and the international energy crisis in 1973. The efforts to introduce a viable and successful rural development programme had to take into account Zambia's increasingly difficult budgetary position, in a situation of intense competition for scarce development resources. Rural development, moreover, had to be considered in the light of Zambia's industrial development and the consequent political power of the line of rail and Copperbelt populations. In this situation political support was essential for any programme ultimately to succeed.

We must also bear in mind the extent to which both programmes had been associated at the outset with President Kaunda, who had since independence deliberately developed the role of the presidency as innovator, so that presidential initiative had become a characteristic feature of the Zambian political system. A prime weakness in this situation, however, derived from his inability to ensure commitment to his ideas from either political colleagues or bureaucracy. In a situation where the presidency played a crucial innovating role, there were no institutional links between State House and administration to ensure such commitment. State House was in a very real sense, and notwithstanding the power of the President, isolated from the machinery of government. Hence, once presidential attention moved elsewhere, as was bound to be the case, there was the potential for a loss of political support and direction. It is therefore impossible, in seeking to understand the failure of each programme, to separate administrative and political arenas.

Notes

[1] The material on which these case studies are based is drawn from field research carried out in Zambia over the period 1970 to 1975. I am grateful to those members of the administration who assisted me, and so freely gave their time to discuss the issues involved; also for access to selected government materials. The conclusions drawn here are of course my own.

[2] The most succinct analysis of the rural–urban imbalance in relation to the allocation of resources is D. Rothchild, 'Rural–urban inequalities and resource allocation in Zambia', *Journal of Modern African Studies*, vol. 10, No. 3 (1972). See also Baldwin, *Economic development and export growth, op. cit.*, and the Seers Report (1964), *op. cit.*

[3] See Elliott (ed.), *Constraints on the economic development of Zambia, op. cit.*; C. S. Lombard and A. H. C. Tweedie, *Agriculture in Zambia since independence* (Lusaka, 1972); and S. Quick, 'Rural socialism in Zambia', *Journal of Modern African Studies*, vol. 15, No. 3 (1977).

[4] See Dresang, *The Zambia civil service, op. cit.*; Tordoff, 'Provincial and district government in Zambia' (1968), *op. cit.*, and 'Provincial and local government in Zambia' (1970), *op. cit.*

[5] This remained so, although in September the Ministry of Lands and Natural Resources was re-established as a separate Ministry.

[6] C. E. Young, 'Rural–urban terms of trade', *African Social Research*, No. 12 (December 1971); and Maimbo and Fry, 'An investigation into the change in the terms of trade', *op. cit.*

[7] SNDP, *op. cit*, pp. 4, 169; Quick, 'Rural socialism in Zambia', *op. cit.*

[8] Ministry of Rural Development, *Crop reporting programme, 1968–69*, p. 13. Also *Census of agriculture, 1970–71, first report, op. cit.*

[9] SNDP, *op. cit.*, p. 167.

[10] International Labour Office, *Report to the government of Zambia on incomes, wages and prices in Zambia: policy and machinery* (The Turner Report) (Lusaka, 1969).

[11] *Report of the second national convention on rural development, incomes, wages and prices in Zambia: policy and machinery*, Kitwe, December 1969 (Lusaka, 1970).

[12] *Towards complete independence* (Lusaka, 1969), pp. 44–5.

[13] On Western Province see *inter alia*, G. L. Caplan, *The elites of Barotseland, 1878–1969: a political history of Zambia's Western Province* (Berkeley and Los Angeles, 1970), and 'Barotseland: the secessionist challenge to Zambia', *Journal of Modern African Studies*, vol. 6, No. 3 (October 1968).

[14] Tordoff (ed.), *Politics in Zambia, op. cit.*, and Gertzel *et al.*, 'Zambia's final experience of inter-party elections', *op. cit.*

[15] *I wish to inform the nation* (Lusaka, 1969).

[16] A preliminary report was presented in November 1969, and the final report in July 1970.

[17] Memo., Task Force: WP/DEV. 1/2/3; Office of the Permanent Secretary, Mongu.

[18] At that time a Working Party had been set up by the Secretary General to the Government to carry out a review of the decentralised administration. See Simmance Report, *op. cit.*

[19] *Minutes of provincial development committee*, Mongu, 6 January 1972.

[20] FAO = Food and Agricultural Organisation; IBRD = International Bank for Reconstruction and Development; ILO = International Labour Organisation.

[21] See Baldwin, *Economic development and export growth, op. cit.*, pp. 201ff.

[22] Lombard and Tweedie, *Agriculture in Zambia, op. cit.*, pp. 62–3.

[23] Those occasions were the UNIP National Council, March 1969; the Kitwe Convention, December 1969; his address to the National Assembly in January 1970; and his address at the opening of the Rural Development Seminar, Lusaka, March 1970.

[24] Address to the Rural Development Seminar, Lusaka, 23 March 1970.

[25] *Times of Zambia*, 24 April 1970.

[26] SIDA = Swedish International Development Agency.

[27] Fourteen committees, of civil servants, other public leaders, and academics, were set up in 1971 to draw up recommendations for the SNDP.

[28] UNDP = United Nations Development Programme.

[29] *SNDP, op. cit.*, pp. 180–1.

[30] *Times of Zambia*, 11 February 1972.

[31] *Land resources of the Northern and Luapula Provinces, Zambia: a reconnaissance assessment* (London, 1973).

[32] *Estimates of expenditure*, 1973–75 (Lusaka).

[33] See, for revealing comments, President's Citizenship College: *Tour report of IDZ project in Eastern Province* (Kabwe, 1975, mimeo.).

[34] *Ibid.*

[35] *Minutes of Northern Province provincial IDZ co-ordinating committee*; Office of the Cabinet Minister, Kasama.

[36] Thus, one of the team produced a report on the Northern Province Co-operative Marketing Union and assisted with the Minister's special agrarian revolution programme.

[37] See the *Northern Province: Department of Agriculture, annual report*, 1974, and memo. by the Cabinet Minister, Kasama, on 'Agrarian revolution, Northern Province' (1974, mimeo.); Office of the Cabinet Minister, Kasama.

[38] *Mid-term review of the Second National Development Plan* (Lusaka, December, 1974), p. 45.

[39] At a UNIP Seminar in Kitwe in January.

[40] See, for example, National Assembly debates, January 1970.

[41] See his speech to the National Assembly.

[42] *Third national development plan, 1979–83* (Lusaka, October 1979).

11. Conclusion

William Tordoff

Zambia is today[1] facing a grave economic crisis: not only is the copper industry operating at a loss, but the industrial sector as a whole is working under capacity; foreign exchange reserves are depleted and there is an external debt of some £250 million;[2] the level of inflation is estimated at over forty per cent, unemployment is rising, and basic commodities, such as maize meal (the staple diet), are in short supply; the social services, including public health and eduction, are badly hit by the shortage of funds, while hoarding and black marketeering are on the increase.[3] Some of these difficulties can be explained by the sharp decline in copper revenue since mid-1974, the continuing adverse consequences on the Zambian economy of the Rhodesian UDI, and the fact that armed conflict in Southern Africa has spilled over three of Zambia's borders, most seriously that with Rhodesia.[4] But other difficulties are of Zambia's own making. A development strategy based substantially on the external infusion of capital has failed to mobilise internal resources.

In 1978 the Zambian Government took a number of tough measures: in an austerity budget in January it cut government spending, slashed food and fertiliser subsidies, and froze public employment; and in March it devalued the Kwacha by 10 per cent in order to avoid mine closures and extensive redundancies.[5] However, Zambia's basic problem remained the over-dependence of the economy on a single export commodity (copper). Though the Government had sought from time to time to diversify the economy, initiatives – such as the Intensive Development Zones, studied in this volume by Dr Gertzel[6] – tended to be taken by the President himself without the firm commitment to them of either his political colleagues or the bureaucracy, and were not therefore long sustained when the President's attention shifted elsewhere.

Following the series of economic reforms initiated in April 1968, the State itself has become the main agent of development and in consequence, as Sheridan Johns demonstrates, the parastatal sector has expanded at a phenomenal rate.[7] Unfortunately, however, the record of performance of many statutory boards and State-owned companies has been disappointing (the mining companies were an exception until the price of copper plummeted). A parliamentary select committee, whose report was tabled in August 1978, drew attention to the inefficiency of many parastatal bodies, citing instances of poor management, theft and corruption.[8] Many State-owned companies operated at a loss because they were constantly subject to political pressure and could not be run on business-like lines; some were also hit by the shortage of qualified manpower. Uneconomic pricing (examples of which are given by Dr Simwinga), and government delays in approving price increases, resulted in certain companies incurring heavy losses.[9] The consequences for the National Agricultural Marketing Board of Zambia were serious since it was 'experiencing extreme difficulties in collecting debts, particularly from parastatal organisations and millers, which are its largest customers'; these debts amounted to over K22 million in March 1978.[10] In general, the State farm sector has proved a costly failure, while the group made up of the National Transport Corporation of Zambia Ltd. and its five wholly-owned subsidiaries 'has never made a profit since it was established in 1972 and the losses have been rising from year to year'.[11]

Inevitably, economic failure and decline have political and administrative repercussions. One effect has been to reduce further the amount of patronage available to UNIP constituency and branch officials who, as Ian Scott points out, were already disenchanted by their failure to share the fruits of independence.[12] The resultant weakness of the party organisation at district level is reflected in the inability of party officials to take up the development functions assigned to them by the President in 1967. Village productivity committees – for which, together with ward development committees, these officials were responsible – have a poor record of performance; in his study of Kasama, Michael Bratton suggests that the fact that they have been adapted from the traditional social structure (and are used by traditional leaders to bolster their own authority) may mean that they are unsuited to the development tasks expected of them.[13] WDCs have a rather better record of performance: in Kasama District, for example, they have undertaken some rural development projects, though the chief beneficiaries of their activities have been the party officials, emergent farmers and other elements from which committee membership has been recruited. Civil servants have been reluctant to devolve real policy-making powers to local-level committees, with the result that WDCs 'offer symbolic but not effective local participation in the national planning process'.[14]

Central government control has been a more obvious characteristic of the development committee structure as a whole than local participation – thus, the over-large provincial development committee, which stands at the apex of this structure, is effectively dominated by civil servants through their membership of the PDC's planning and implementation sub-committee. Moreover, in the absence of comprehensive provincial budgets and in view of departmental control over recurrent expenditure, the experiment in decentralisation – launched with such fanfare by President Kaunda in November 1968 – has had a minimal impact.[15] Despite the confusing presence of both a Cabinet Minister and a Member of the Central Committee at each provincial headquarters – an arrangement which lasted until December 1978 when the post of provincial Cabinet Minister was abolished – substantial political power has not been devolved from the centre. Though some deconcentration of administrative authority has taken place and is reflected in the posting of senior staff to the rural areas, an 'imaginative management approach to the operation of field agencies' has been entirely lacking.[16] Relying on 'a patchwork organisation of government, party and traditional institutions',[17] the Government has also failed to secure mass mobilisation, though such mobilisation is essential if Zambia is to shape 'a future without copper' by growing more food both for local needs and for export.[18] Ill-conceived policies (or policies embarked upon but not sustained) and institutional weakness together account for the failure of successive government plans to reduce the rural–urban gap and to provide employment opportunities.

Urban residents, who make up nearly forty per cent of the population, feel no less disadvantaged than their rural counterparts. Urban growth, averaging some eight per cent a year, has given rise to huge slums, soaring crime rates, and escalating demands for housing, services and jobs which are beyond the capacity of either the central government or the urban authorities to satisfy. The latter, as Alan Greenwood and John Howell show, face a major problem both in maintaining the standard of services within the former municipal boundaries and of extending those services to the peri-urban areas and small township authorities now incorporated within those boundaries.[19]

There are also political dimensions of the urban problem and these are particularly marked on the Copperbelt. What Cherry

Gertzel wrote of the mid-seventies remains true in late 1978: ' . . . the most glaring characteristic of Copperbelt society . . . is the inequality of wealth, not only between African and European, but also within the African community.[20] If Michael Burawoy is right to assert that class has become an important determining factor in industrial relations and in workers' reactions to government policy, the rank and file of the Mineworkers' Union of Zambia may, in a deteriorating economic situation, be less amenable than ever to union leaders whom they see as part of a new Zambian élite.[21]

Widespread discontent among all sections of the Zambian population made the UNIP leadership nervous of the outcome of the 1978 presidential election. The latter, like the parliamentary election held at the same time, took place in two parts: a party election followed by a popular election. According to the Constitution of Zambia, the members of the UNIP general conference 'shall elect a person to be the President of the Party, and such person shall be the sole candidate in an election to the office of President . . .'.[22] In September 1978 the general conference adopted amendments to the UNIP constitution whose effect was to ban Simon Kapwepwe, Harry Nkumbula and a third aspirant (Robert Chiluwe, a Lusaka businessman) from contesting the nomination.[23] President Kaunda was therefore re-elected unopposed as party president and, as such, became the sole candidate for the national presidency. This doubtful political tactic was taken on the initiative of the UNIP national council, possibly against Dr Kaunda's own wishes.[24]

Again, political considerations – notably, Kapwepwe's earlier promise, in his election manifesto, that if he became President he would reopen the border with Rhodesia and buy goods from South Africa – must be set alongside economic factors, such as the desperate need for fertiliser for the farms, in persuading the President to announce, in October 1978, that Zambia was reopening her border with Rhodesia and would again use Rhodesia Railways.[25] However, this step made less convincing Zambia's hitherto brave posture of defiance to the Smith regime in Rhodesia and, predictably, was unpopular with her 'front-line' allies.[26] The President's humiliation was complete when, in the same month, his defence forces were shown to be powerless to prevent Rhodesian air strikes at refugee camps only some twelve miles from Lusaka, the Zambian capital.[27]

Contrary to the predictions of a number of observers, who expected Dr Kaunda merely to scrape 51 per cent of the vote in a low poll, the President won comfortably: though the 'no' vote increased by a third, he still carried 80 per cent of the vote on a 67 per cent

turnout.[28] Perhaps voters responded to the basic campaign message
'that Zambia will be plunged into chaos if President Kaunda isn't
re-elected';[29] unhappy with the poor state of the economy and
deeply concerned at the acute shortage of maize meal, it is unlikely
that they were impressed by the recital during the campaign of past
government achievements.[30] None the less, Zambia's record of
performance, under Dr Kaunda's leadership, since independence in
October 1964 is in many respects impressive and helps to shade a
little light into the gloomy picture painted above.

Achievements

As James Fry shows in his chapter on the economy,[31] there was
rapid economic expansion in the period up to 1970 when the price of
copper was high: manufacturing output almost doubled, total
employment expanded fast, and employed workers enjoyed a
considerable rise in their standard of living. The economy's
performance did deteriorate thereafter, though this was partly as a
result of factors beyond the Government's control: thus, allowing for
the effects of inflation, there were only two years (1973 and 1974) of
the 1971–77 period when copper prices were high enough to earn the
mining companies, which became 51 per cent government-owned in
1970, a reasonable return. Taking the post-independence period as a
whole, however, Fry finds that 'the Zambian economy has
progressed considerably since 1964' – it is more diversified than it
was; Zambians have assumed positions of responsibility in key
sectors; and even the agricultural sector is 'showing encouraging
signs of sustained growth'.[32]

Another major achievement has been the expansion of Zambia's
economic infrastructure, first as a means of reducing her inherited
dependence on the white-ruled territories to the south, and secondly
to benefit the rural areas by constructing roads and providing
amenities such as pipe-borne water and electricity. Important, too,
in the economic sphere was the progress made in localising
manpower, a problem examined in this volume by Dennis Dresang
and Ralph Young.[33] In the key sector of the mines, safety factors
were an additional consideration determining the pace at which
Zambianisation could proceed. But here, too, progress was achieved
and the size of the expatriate work force was reduced by 50 per cent
between December 1964 and December 1970.

A significant milestone in Zambia's post-independence history
was the State's assumption of ultimate control over all major
sections of the economy, with the exception of large-scale

commercial agriculture and the banks. This was achieved by a series of economic measures, beginning with the Matero reforms of April 1968. Of course, the management contracts usually given to the companies taken over, together with the continuing acute shortage of local managerial and professional manpower, tended to reduce in the short run the reality of public control; in the mining sphere, this problem persisted even after the contracts were terminated in 1973.[34]

In his address to mark the official opening of the first session of the fourth National Assembly in December 1978, President Kaunda announced changes to be made to the machinery of government – the abolition of some Ministries and of the posts of provincial Cabinet Minister, the creation of new Ministries, and the transfer of a number of departments from one Ministry to another[35] – and other measures to revitalise the economy, notably the reorganisation of the Zambian Industrial and Mining Corporation (ZIMCO).[36] The latter directly or indirectly controls over 90 companies, many with substantial foreign minority interests and including the Nchanga Consolidated Copper Mines (NCCM) and Roan Consolidated Mines (RCM), though the mining companies themselves are not affected by the changes. The intention is to improve the running and performance of the State-owned industrial and commercial sector by conferring increased responsibility on the various companies brought under the ZIMCO umbrella.

The President stated that all ZIMCO sub-holding corporations except for the Industrial Development Corporation (INDECO) and the National Import and Export Corporation (NIEC) would be abolished and that all the subsidiaries of the National Transport Corporation (NTC), the Finance and Development Corporation (FINDECO) and the Mining Development Corporation (MINDECO) would become direct operating subsidiaries of ZIMCO – the status already enjoyed by NCCM and RCM. Organisations which were at present unprofitable but which could be made self-supporting and profitable, would become members of ZIMCO; among them were Zambia Airways, Zambia Railways, the Posts and Telegraph Corporation, and the Rural Development Corporation (less certain of RDC's constituent units which would revert to direct ministerial control). A ZIMCO board of directors, to be chaired by the Prime Minister, would be responsible for the appointment of all managing directors, general managers or chief executives of subsidiary companies and corporations. ZIMCO would determine the prices of the products of its subsidiaries except for those essential products (maize meal, stock-feed, petroleum products, cooking oil, bread, salt, sugar and flour) which require government approval. It would also assume the functions of the Parastatal Bodies Service Commission which, though pronounced to have been successful, was to be disbanded.[37] The object of these various changes is not to extend further State control over the economy, but to increase the commercial viability of the large number of enterprises brought under State control as a result of the first leg of post-independence economic reforms.

The second leg of those reforms was a series of measures to increase the participation of Zambians in the remaining private sector. Beginning again in 1968, they were dramatically extended on 1 January 1972, after which date no foreigner could obtain a retail or wholesale licence anywhere in the country. The result was to create massive new opportunities for citizen entrepreneurs; these opportunities may be extended if the Industrial Development Act of 1977 is successful in attracting to Zambia foreign investors who will be looking for partners in the State or private sectors.[38]

In its social policy the Government has made equally significant strides both by removing those elements of institutionalised and overt racialism which remained from the settler past and by progressing towards a welfare State.[39] Inevitably, however, the expansion in both the range and scale of social services – thus educational expenditure rose from K13 million in 1963–64 to an authorised amount of over K108 million in 1977[40] – has been at the expense of investment in more directly productive, job-generating sectors and has placed an additional burden on a civil service which has lost top-level manpower to both the parastatal and private sectors.

On the political front, there has also been some success. Above all, in a continent where military take-overs have become commonplace, it represents a considerable achievement on President Kaunda's part to have maintained civilian rule in an atmosphere of peace and relative stability. Until December 1972, when the constitution was amended to allow a phased transition to a one-party State, that rule was practised within a multi-party framework and, particularly before the emergence of the UPP in 1971, with regard for democratic principles. Elections were supervised by an independent and impartial commission presided over by a judge, freedom of debate prevailed in the National Assembly, the press was not muzzled, trade unions retained considerable operational autonomy, merit remained the main criterion of civil service recruitment, and the independence of the judiciary was respected except on those rare occasions when the interests of the executive were directly involved.[41] Moreover, notwithstanding occasional lapses,[42] these principles have been substantially upheld under the Second Republic's one-party constitution, enacted in August 1973.

Finally, we turn to achievements in the foreign sphere. A difficulty here is that assessment of Zambia's record tends, more obviously than in respect of domestic policy, to vary according to the ideological bias of the observer. Those who write from a Marxist or neo-Marxist perspective tend to be highly critical of the initiatives taken in Southern Africa by President Kaunda and see his primary objective as being the entrenchment in Rhodesia, as in Angola in 1974–75, of a black bourgeois regime underpinned by Western capitalism. Thus, Timothy Shaw draws upon dependency theory to argue that Zambia's 'bureaucratic bourgeoisie' is so bent on maintaining its own dominance, as the lackey of foreign companies, that the Zambian Government has been lukewarm in its support of Southern African liberation movements.[43]

On the other hand, Douglas Anglin, who adopts a liberal–democratic standpoint, finds class analysis of limited help in explaining Zambia's foreign policy: 'Class interest is undoubtedly present in Zambia, and growing. What is so surprising is that, at least to date, it has been so impotent in diverting the government from its liberationist goals'.[44] This, he believes, is due above all to the character of President Kaunda, who 'was, if anything, more radical than either his cabinet colleagues or the attentive public generally'.[45] Richard L. Sklar, himself a radical scholar, argues in his study of Zambia's response to the Rhodesian UDI that 'revolutionary idealism has a powerful claim of its own upon the Zambian government.' The latter 'has always been willing to accept the economic and military risks of participation in collective action against Rhodesia, if they are realistically designed to dislodge the white minority regime . . . This mixture of liberationist principle and realpolitik displeases the doctrinaire proponent of either persuasion'.[46]

Since independence in October 1964 Zambia has been constantly in the forefront of the struggle to liberate Southern Africa. She is therefore entitled to claim some credit for the fact that Guinea-Bissau, Mozambique and Angola are now established as independent States and that independence for Rhodesia and Namibia is in prospect. It may well be that President Kaunda made certain tactical mistakes in his Southern Africa policy – perhaps in establishing direct contact with Portugal when Caetano succeeded Salazar as Prime Minister in 1968;[47] in seeking to establish a government of national unity in Angola in 1974–75; and in working

with Mr Vorster, the former Prime Minister of South Africa, for a
negotiated settlement in Rhodesia. But the assertion of Shaw and
Mugomba that Zambia's diplomacy in Southern Africa reflected the
interest of her new ruling class in maintaining 'its own affluence and
control' has not been empirically validated.[48] If that assertion had
been true, Zambia would have collaborated outright with the rebel
regime in neighbouring Rhodesia in order (for example) to secure
for herself both cheaper imports than she could obtain elsewhere
and a cheaper, quicker and more reliable outlet for her copper than
was provided by northern routes through Tanzania, the
construction of which constituted a heavy drain on the Zambian
exchequer. Certainly, some of Zambia's political leaders thought
that Zambia was paying too high a price for her principles and
wanted to put Zambia's national interest first. Thus, as far back as
August 1966 Harry Nkumbula, the leader of the African National
Congress, told the National Assembly that Zambia was going too far
in her 'attempts to end the rebellion in Rhodesia . . . we must be
careful not to commit suicide ourselves . . . £31 million that we have
so far spent on U.D.I. is not a joke . . . Apart from our Republic
other member states of O.A.U. have done nothing practical to end
the illegal Smith regime.'[49] However, Kaunda, with at that time
substantial backing from his party and Government, refused to shy
away from a policy of confrontation with the white minority regimes.
That remains his own position, but it is one which has been
increasingly difficult to maintain since 1975 in the face of mounting
economic difficulties at home and the political capital being made
out of these difficulties by his rivals for the presidential nomination
in 1978, notably Kapwepwe and Nkumbula; hence, Kaunda's recent
decision to reopen Zambia's border with Rhodesia.

In sum, though it might well be the case that President Kaunda
would like to see a moderate, non-Marxist African government
established in an independent Zimbabwe, it is irrefutable that
Zambia has made greater sacrifices in her efforts to topple the Smith
regime than any other country in Africa. In retrospect at least,
Zambia's contribution to the liberation of Southern Africa is likely
to be regarded as substantial.

In all these achievements, President Kaunda's own contribution
has been pre-eminent. This is not accidental. The effect of the one-
party State constitution was to increase further his already
considerable powers as executive President and Dr Kaunda has used
his powers to the full. Though he has not sought to reproduce in
Zambia the situation in Republican Ghana where Dr Nkrumah's
Ministers were reduced to being 'little more than presidential

secretaries who represent the leader in departments of state',[50] State House has become increasingly the focus of major decision-making. Evidently convinced of the rightness of his own solutions to the problems facing Zambia, President Kaunda not only formulates government policy on a very broad front, but also concerns himself with its implementation. But presidentialism, which is now enshrined as the dominant feature of Zambia's governmental system, has its drawbacks.[51] It has meant that key policies – such as the 1968–69 decentralisation measures, the Intensive Development Zones, and the Rural Reconstruction programme – which have either been directly initiated by Dr Kaunda or received his strong backing, have not been subject to sufficiently close scrutiny before they have been launched. Another consequence, already mentioned, is that the success of a project might well depend on the President's continuing commitment to it.[52]

Nevertheless, despite his wide powers, President Kaunda is far from being a dictator; such a position would violate the Humanist principles to which he is deeply attached and which he is seeking to inculcate into Zambian Society. A gentle and humane person, though with a tough underlying streak, he has already succeeded, against considerable odds, in instituting some of the basic values of Zambian Humanism. Though the materialist ethic remains strongly entrenched in Zambia and Humanism is not a sufficiently powerful ideology to effect the institutional transformation to which Fred Burke draws attention,[53] Kaunda's constant references to Humanism has at least led thinking Zambians to question themselves about the kind of society they want. Even the leadership code, despite its limited application, may have served to prevent the grosser forms of abuse on the part of those holding high public office.[54]

The public service

The achievements outlined above would not have been possible without the administrative support of the public service. The latter's ability to adapt the inherited structure and organisation to meet the new demands that independence placed on it,[55] was itself a remarkable achievement, particularly in view of Zambia's dismal administrative legacy. The statement that 'the colonial polity was essentially bureaucratic'[56] tends in general to discount the attention given to economic and social development by an administration that became increasingly functionally specific in the terminal period of British (and French) colonial rule.[57] However, Northern Rhodesia, as a member of a Central African Federation that was geared to promote Southern Rhodesian interests, was atypical in this respect, so far at least as African development was concerned. Moreover, membership of the Federation also meant that at independence Zambia, whatever the position in other new States, certainly did not constitute an 'overdeveloped' State on the lines projected by Hamzat Alavi and John Saul.[58] As Colin Leys said of Tanzania, the Zambian State was not 'very strong in relation to its tasks'.[59]

Until the eve of Zambia's independence, senior and most middle-level bureaucrats were Europeans and Asians, and not Africans. The result was that in experience and training, as well as in formal education, the Zambian civil service was ill equipped to meet the needs of a Government which, in October 1964, had at its disposal vast copper revenues out of which to finance development. Administrative training was provided, especially at the National Institute of Public Administration, though the relevance of this training for development administration has been questioned.[60] Not only did the civil service grow in size, but manpower had also to be found to service the growing parastatal sector. In these circumstances, Richard Jolly was right to point to 'the ways in which the scarcity of skilled and educated manpower has held back development' and to argue that 'growth, though rapid, was not as rapid as would have taken place if skilled manpower had been in optimal balance with other resources, instead of in shortage and relative scarcity'.[61]

The shortage of skilled manpower has had other consequences. First, it has contributed to that horizontal and vertical mobility within both the civil service and parastatal sector which has been such a marked feature of President Kaunda's administration;[62] this mobility has been extended in recent years to the unified local government service.[63] The result has been detrimental to government performance and to the unity and cohesion of the public service. The latter has also suffered from a lack of social cohesiveness. What Goran Hyden wrote of the Kenyan civil service in 1972 was true of the Zambian public service under the First, and probably also under the Second, Republic: 'The civil service today is to a significant extent a mirror of the Kenyan society at large; the individualistic ambitions, the social obligations to the extended family and the tribal inclinations are characteristics of civil servants as of any other category in the population.'[64] In the Zambian context, where there has been some interchange between politicians and civil servants at the highest levels, power in society has tended to cut 'across the boundaries of formal institutions'.[65] Not only have former civil servants become Ministers, but senior administrators in both the civil service and parastatal sector have had a major impact on policy. Examples are the important part played by Andrew Sardanis when, as permanent secretary, Ministry of State Participation, he negotiated majority shareholding for the State in the copper industry; the continuing role of Mark Chona, special assistant to the President, in shaping policy towards Southern Africa, and that of his colleague, Dominic Mulaisho, in redefining the performance criteria for the parastatal sector; the success of A. J. Adamson, permanent secretary, Ministry of Local Government and Housing, in resisting the further encroachments on local government autonomy implicit in the Simmance Committee recommendations;[66] and the part played by P. A. Siwo, permanent secretary, Ministry of Education, in watering down the far-reaching proposals for educational reform made in 1976.[67] Nevertheless, despite such clear indications of Zambian bureaucrats exercising political functions[68] and despite the decline under the one-party State of such rival power structures as UNIP and the trade union movement, the Zambian bureaucracy is not all-powerful. The boundaries between politics and administration have probably been permeated less in Zambia than in either Kenya or Tanzania,[69] and Chambers's argument that 'the present style of administration is not bureaucratic enough' loses some, if not all, its force when applied to Zambia.[70] Paraphrasing Michael Lofchie, we can say of the Zambian bureaucracy that its power is indirect, being exerted on the political leadership; it has no source of legitimacy independent of the political system as a whole; and its internal divisions, principally between a civil service and a parastatal sector, and its fragmentation along functional lines mean that it lacks a unified structure.[71] As Hyden commented in a different context: that the ruling party 'is weak is no proof that the civil service is powerful'.[72]

A second consequence of the shortage of manpower has been that so much energy has been absorbed in keeping the State machinery going that fundamental administrative reform has not been undertaken. The nearest approach to such reform came with the 'decentralisation' of government in 1968–69. Though in 1972 the Government recognised the need to review the working of the decentralised system of administration and set up the Simmance Committee, it has subsequently failed to implement most of the Committee's major recommendations.[73] In the event, centre–periphery relations have not been vitally affected, local participation has been sacrificed to central control, and system maintenance has been preferred to innovative development administration. Like its colonial predecessor, the Zambian public service remains essentially hierarchical; as a result of the Mwanakatwe Commission recommendations of 1975, it is also well-paid and elitist at senior levels.[74]

Policy-making

Despite the strong influence exerted by individual public servants and the good working relationship which usually exists between Ministers and their civil service advisers, authoritative leadership at the centre, and in the provinces and districts, has stemmed from the politicians rather than the bureaucracy. Paradoxically, 'bureaucratic dominance' – which was condemned in *Mwongozo* (the TANU Guidelines) in 1971[75] – has been more a feature of Tanzanian than of Zambian administration.[76] However, the political voice in Zambia has itself been muted through the existence of two parallel and sometimes competing structures – the Cabinet and the UNIP Central Committee – each of which detracts from the other's role. Though the Cabinet is in practice the more important policy-making organ,[77] the overall result has been to enhance the position of President Kaunda as Zambia's key decision-maker.

That such divisions exist within the political leadership is itself an argument for following Szeftel in distinguishing between the different elements of the 'managerial bourgeoisie', notably the political, bureaucratic and entrepreneurial elements. [78] An additional reason is the position of the business community which, despite strong links with both politicians and bureaucrats, is dependent on the State for public subsidies and loans. The entrepreneurial bourgeoisie wants to maintain good working relations with the political and State bureaucracy; it needs a climate in which private enterprise can prosper and favours government policies that will advance the individual and collective interests of businessmen. By the same token, both through its representatives in the National Assembly and elsewhere, it vigorously opposes policies which seem detrimental to those interests.[79] Take two examples, both of which are examined in full by Morris Szeftel. When, in 1975, the Government declared in force that clause in the Industrial Relations Act, 1971, which made provision for workers' councils, the effect was to unite (for the first time) in noisy opposition 'all strata and sections of the bourgeoisie', both domestic and foreign.[80] Though the Government did not capitulate to this storm of protest, it did not press workers' participation upon an unwilling management. The second instance occurred early in 1976 when

Arthur Wina, the leading parliamentary spokesman of the business community,[81] criticised the Rural Reconstruction programme whose purpose was to train and discipline unemployed youth for a rural and co-operative future. He argued that, instead of wasting money on such an ill-planned venture, the Government should provide incentives to the commercial farmers to grow more, for 'It is not groups of people who are going to feed the nation but individuals'.[82]

From another perspective, given that Zambia *has* adopted an external infusion strategy and that international capitalism is firmly entrenched within the Zambian economy, one can talk meaningfully of an undifferentiated 'managerial bourgeoisie', all the elements of which are pulling in the same direction and leading to the same outcome – the continuance of Zambia's external dependency. To that extent, 'the national bourgeoisie is the local wing of a transnational class', though it is 'normally nationalistic'.[83] However, President Kaunda still talks of reaching Humanism through socialism,[84] and this would involve reducing the links with external capital which at other times he seems to favour. The reality is a good deal different: Kaunda has instituted in Zambia a regime which combines socialist, populist and State capitalist strands.[85] The socialist strand – the desire for greater social equality – which Kaunda himself embodies and the populist strand, which is uppermost within UNIP, moderate the starkness of State capitalism. It is perhaps because Zambia's development strategy has to reflect these different elements that it has tended to lack consistency and to result in unexpected shifts in public policy.

Ultimately, that is to say, policy-making in Zambia is a composite process in which Kaunda, the chief policy-maker, has to accommodate demands from the party, the State bureaucracy and the business community. In view of the weakness of UNIP, the poor state of the economy, and the 'overlap of public position and private interests' to which we referred in the Introduction,[86] Zambia seems to be moving away from socialist solutions to the difficulties which she now faces. Under her present leadership she is likely, at least in the short term, to retain a State capitalist economy, with an increasing share of the market being cornered by the private sector. Though the indigenous entrepreneurial bourgeoisie will accept links with foreign companies willing to invest in Zambia, it will also continue to display a strong sense of economic nationalism. In the longer term, the continuing process of embourgeoisement can be expected to sharpen existing class divisions and, perhaps, lead to a struggle for power between a rural-urban proletariat and the managerial bourgeoisie. However, at a time when such a struggle is not in prospect, it is too early to try and forecast its effects upon the Zambian administration.

Notes

[1] I.e., late December 1978.

[2] The reduction of public indebtedness was one of the conditions laid down by the International Monetary Fund (IMF) in making available to Zambia a short-term loan of US$390 million in March 1978. Despite this IMF package, Zambia's aid requirements remained substantial and in November 1978 the World Bank accorded her 'poor country' status to enhance aid prospects. R. A. Young, 'Zambia', in H. V. Hodson (ed.), *The annual register: world events in 1978* (London, 1979 forthcoming).

[3] Comments by John Borrell and Alan Rake, 'The world today', *BBC World Service*, 12 December 1978.

[4] Young, 'Zambia', *1978, op. cit.*

[5] *Ibid.*

[6] See ch. 10, above.

[7] See ch. 4, above.

[8] *Report of the committee on parastatal bodies* (1978), *op. cit.*, pp. 1–17.

[9] *Africa Confidential*, vol. 19, No. 23 (17 November 1978); *Financial Times*, 21 December 1978. See ch. 5, above.

[10] *Report of the committee on parastatal bodies* (1978), *op. cit.*, p. 8. For NAMBoard see also *Quarterly Economic Review of Zambia*, 4th quarter 1978 (London, 1978), pp. 11–12.

[11] *Report of the committee on parastatal bodies* (1978), *op. cit.*, p. 4.

[12] See ch. 6, above.

[13] See ch. 9, above.

[14] See p. 232, above.

[15] See ch. 8, above.

[16] Cf. R. Chambers, *Managing rural development: ideas and experience from East Africa* (Uppsala, 1974), p. 31.

[17] This phrase is used by Bratton at p. 214, above.

[18] Recommendations of the parliamentary special select committee, *Sunday Times of Zambia*, 4 December 1977.

[19] See ch. 7, above.

[20] C. J. Gertzel, 'Labour and the State: the case of Zambia's Mineworkers Union – a review article', *The Journal of Commonwealth and Comparative Politics*, vol. XIII, No. 3 (November 1975), p. 298.

[21] M. Burawoy, 'Another look at the mineworker', *African Social Research*, No. 14 (December 1972), pp. 261–7, 276ff. Even if the development of an urban proletariat on the Copperbelt is less advanced than Burawoy assumes, the prospect is no more encouraging for the Government: given the down-turn in the copper industry and the consequent threat of massive unemployment, the miners' leadership may no longer be amenable to government control and may elect to identify itself more closely with the rank and file than it has done in recent years.

[22] *Constitution of Zambia Act*, No. 27 of 1973, *op. cit.*, s. 38 (3).

[23] For Kapwepwe, see p. 8, above, and Nkumbula, p. 268, below. Subsequently, Kapwepwe and Nkumbula unsuccessfully challenged the amendments' legality in the Lusaka High Court.

[24] *Africa Confidential*, vol. 19, No. 22 (3 November 1978); interview with President Kaunda, 'Tonight', *BBC Television*, 11 December 1978.

[25] *The Guardian*, 7 October 1978.

[26] Tanzania, Mozambique, Angola and Botswana.

[27] See L. Pintak, 'Dr Kaunda says Rhodesia attack would be suicide for Zambia', *The Times*, 24 October 1978.

[28] Young, 'Zambia', *1978, op. cit.* In the parliamentary elections (for 125 National Assembly seats), voters rejected twenty-four sitting MPs, including ten serving or former Ministers; the UNIP Central Committee had earlier disqualified twenty-eight contestants, including several active backbench critics of government policy in the outgoing Assembly. *Ibid.* See also J. Borrell, 'Kaunda increases his support', *The Guardian*, 15 December 1978.

[29] J. Borrell, *BBC World Service*, 12 December 1978, *op. cit.*

[30] *Ibid.*; *The Guardian*, 11 December 1978.

[31] See ch. 2, above.

[32] See p. 65, above.

[33] See ch. 3, above.

[34] See p. 27, above.

[35] For details, see pp. 82, 189, 209 n. 38, above.

[36] President Kaunda's address is reported in *Times of Zambia*, 19 December 1978, *op. cit.*

[37] *Ibid.*

[38] See pp. 27–8, above. Towards the end of 1977 a parliamentary special select committee recommended that 'in addition to improving the performance of the parastatal sector, the Government should take measures to encourage private investment from within and outside the country especially now that legislation has been passed to this effect – the Industrial Development Act'. *Sunday Times of Zambia*, 4 December 1977.

[39] See p. 28, above.

[40] Divided between K92,810,751 recurrent and K16,029,000 capital expenditure. *Estimates of revenue and expenditure for the year 1st January 1977 to 31st December 1977* (Lusaka, 1977), pp. 5 and 222.

[41] For one exception, see Tordoff (ed.), *Politics in Zambia, op. cit.*, p. 368.

[42] In October 1978 the Supreme Court overturned the conviction in July 1974 of four men charged with treason for recruiting Zambians for secret military training by South Africans in Namibia; the four, including a former Mayor of Livingstone and a former MP, were immediately detained. Young, 'Zambia', *1978, op. cit.*

[43] See, for example, Shaw, 'Zambia's foreign policy', *op. cit.*

[44] Anglin, 'Zambian versus Malawian approaches to political change in Southern Africa', *op. cit.*, p. 31.

[45] *Ibid.*

[46] Sklar, 'Zambia's response to the Rhodesian unilateral declaration of independence', in Tordoff (ed.), *Politics in Zambia, op. cit.*, p. 362.

[47] See D. G. Anglin, 'Confrontation in Southern Africa: Zambia and Portugal', *International Journal*, vol. XXV, No. 3 (summer 1970).

[48] Shaw and Mugomba, 'The political economy of regional detente', *op. cit.*

[49] An expanded version of this extract appears in Tordoff (ed.), *Politics in Zambia, op. cit.*, p. 204.

[50] J. M. Lee, 'Parliament in republican Ghana', *Parliamentary Affairs*, vol. XVI, No. 4 (1963), p. 382.

[51] For a good discussion of presidentialism see B. O. Nwabueze, *Presidentialism in Commonwealth Africa, op. cit.*

[52] See ch. 10, above.

[53] See p. 1, above.

[54] It is possible that the suspension in 1977 of Mr Aaron Milner, a Cabinet Minister upon whom President Kaunda relied heavily, for alleged violation of foreign exchange control regulations, has had a salutary effect on other public officeholders.

[55] See A. L. Adu, *The civil service in Commonwealth Africa* (London, 1969) for a general discussion of this issue.

[56] B. B. Schaffer, 'The concept of preparation: some questions about the transfer of systems of government', *World Politics*, vol. XVIII (October 1965), p. 52.

[57] See J. M. Lee, *Colonial development and good government: a study of the ideas expressed by the British official classes in planning decolonization, 1939–1964* (Oxford, 1967).

[58] H. Alavi, 'The State in post-colonial societies: Pakistan and Bangladesh', *New Left Review*, No. 74 (July-August 1972), and J. S. Saul, 'The State in post-colonial societies – Tanzania', in R. Miliband (ed.), *The socialist register* (London, 1974).

[59] C. Leys, 'The "overdeveloped" post colonial State: a re-evaluation', *Review of African Political Economy*, No. 5 (January-April 1976). However Leys may have overdrawn this aspect of Alavi's argument. He also probably underestimates the task facing the post-colonial State of subordinating pre-capitalist social formations. This issue is dealt with extensively by Goran Hyden in *Peasants and underdevelopment in Africa: the Tanzanian experience and beyond* (London and Berkeley–Los Angeles, forthcoming).

[60] See G. D. Wood, 'Administrative training in Zambia: a study in institutionalisation and change' (M.Phil. thesis, University of Sussex, 1971).

[61] R. Jolly, 'Skilled manpower as a constraint to development in Zambia', *Communications Series No. 48* (Institute of Development Studies, University of Sussex, January 1970), pp. 11 and 34.

[62] One commentator recently described this process in graphical terms: 'Ministers, top civil servants, diplomats, and senior officials in the state corporations are like so many peas in a drum, to which Kaunda gives a vigorous shake every few months'. *Africa Confidential*, vol. 19, No. 22 (3 November 1978), p. 2.

[63] See p. 200, above.

[64] G. Hyden, 'Social structure, bureaucracy and development administration in Kenya', *The African Review*, vol. 1, No. 3 (January 1972), p. 123. See pp. 74–5, above.

[65] *Ibid.*, p. 124.

[66] See p. 188, above.

[67] *Education for development* (1976), *op. cit.* These proposals testify to the social impact of Zambian Humanism. President Kaunda's 'exposition of the Philosophy of Humanism has given the conceptual framework for the type of society that our educational system should build', said the Minister of Education in his foreword to the draft statement.

[68] Cf. F. W. Riggs, 'The context of development administration', in F. W. Riggs (ed.), *Frontiers of development* (Durham, N.C., 1970), p. 79, whose view is 'not only that bureaucrats do exercise political functions, but that they must, and that a significant (but not overwhelming) degree of bureaucratic power is functionally requisite for the organisation of a developed system of government'.

[69] In Kenya one thinks particularly of the position of civil service Provincial and District Commissioners. In Tanzania, the incompatibility rule which forbade public officers, including civil servants, to become constituency MPs has been relaxed and backbenchers are now encouraged to be associated with government-owned or controlled companies. See H. Kjekshus, 'Perspectives on the second parliament, 1965–70', in the Election Study Committee, University of Dar es Salaam, *Socialism and participation: Tanzania's 1970 national elections* (Dar es Salaam, 1974), pp. 81ff., esp. p. 89.

[70] R. Chambers, 'Planning for rural areas in East Africa: experience and prescriptions', paper read at the Conference on Comparative Administration, Arusha, 25–8 September 1971, quoted in Hyden, 'Social structure, bureaucracy and development administration in Kenya', *op. cit.*, p. 126.

[71] M. F. Lofchie, 'Representative government, bureaucracy, and political development: the African case', *Journal of the Developing Areas*, vol. 2 (October 1967).

[72] Hyden was writing on Kenya: 'Social structure . . . Kenya', *loc. cit.*, p. 124.

[73] See ch. 8, above.

[74] Cf. Bernard Schaffer, who writes of 'the major themes of inheritance . . . preparation, training and the salary race disguised as administrative reform . . .': B.

B. Schaffer, 'Administrative legacies and links in the post-colonial State: preparation, training and administrative reform', *Development and Change*, vol. 9 (1978), p. 197.

[75] The unanticipated reaction of urban workers to *Mwongozo* is examined in I. G. Shivji, *Class struggles in Tanzania* (London, 1976).

[76] Cf. Finucane: 'The administrative or bureaucratic approach to development has dominated in Tanzania'. J. R. Finucane, *Rural development and bureaucracy in Tanzania: the case of Mwanza Region* (Uppsala, 1974), p. 184. Zambia has no counterpart, for example, to the powerful Regional and District Development Directors in Tanzania and the political role of public officers is more narrowly circumscribed in Zambia than in Tanzania. See p. 276, n. 69, above.

[77] See Szeftel, 'Conflict . . . in Zambia', *op. cit.*, p. 395.

[78] Szeftel identifies two broad categories of the bourgeoisie – State personnel and private entrepreneurs. *Ibid.*, pp. 414–15. There is a strong argument for sub-dividing the 'State personnel' category into its component political and bureaucratic elements since their interests do not always coincide.

[79] See pp. 32–3, above.

[80] Szeftel, 'Conflict . . . in Zambia', *op. cit.*, p. 443.

[81] Arthur Wina, a former Cabinet Minister of great ability, was one of twenty-eight UNIP parliamentary candidates who were debarred from standing for election in December 1978 by the party Central Committee. *Financial Times*, 12 December 1978.

[82] Szeftel, 'Conflict . . . in Zambia', *op. cit.*, p. 442.

[83] Sklar, *Corporate power in an African State, op. cit.*, p. 201.

[84] He repeated this assertion in a BBC television interview featured in 'Tonight', 11 December 1978.

[85] I am indebted for this formulation to Professor Richard L. Sklar.

[86] See p. 31 above; Szeftel, 'Conflict . . . in Zambia', *op. cit.*, p. 425.

Bibliography

The Bibliography is limited to documents cited in the text.

1. Manuscript sources

(a) Agricultural Finance Company, Lusaka

Instructions Nos. 410 1A and 1B, April 1974.

(b) Cabinet Office, Lusaka

'Ministerial reorganisation: division of the office of the Pesident', Cabinet Office circular No. 91 of 1967, 18 December 1967.
  C.O. 101/20/16, 7 June 1971.

(c) Central Ministries

(1) *Ministry of Lands and Natural Resources*
  Circular No. 1/73, 28 March 1973.
(2) *Ministry of Local Government and Housing*
  Circulars Nos. 15/74, 28 May 1974; 27/74, 30 September 1974; 67/75, 26 August 1975; 4/76, 12 January 1976. Minutes of the meeting of Namwala Rural Council, 28 March 1977, in File No. LGH 102/6/51, vol. IV. Estimates of the revenue and expenditure of rural councils, 1976 (*mimeo.*).
(3) *Ministry of Mines and Industry*
  Memo. MMI/101/24/7, vol. II, dated 12 March 1974.
(4) *Ministry of Rural Development*
  Crop Reporting Programme, 1968–69.
  'Review of the working group' (Lusaka: 1977, mimeo.).

(d) Elections Office, Lusaka

Local government elections, 1975–returns.

(e) Offices of District Governors/Secretaries

Public meeting at Buseko Hall, Kasama, 24 May 1974: speech by S. Kalulu,

member of the UNIP central committee.
'Registration and development of villages' (report compiled by E. B. Chituta), Kasama District.
Minutes of the meeting of the district development committee, Mumbwa, 31 August 1977.

(f) *Offices of provincial cabinet ministers/permanent secretaries*

Resident Minister Central Province to UNIP regional secretaries, 20 July 1966, M 987–1/13/38; Kabwe, Central Province.
Circular No. 5 of 1972: 'Monthly progress report on registration of villages', 30 April 1972; Kasama, Northern Province.
Minutes of Northern Province provincial IDZ co-ordinating committee; Kasama, Northern Province.
Northern Province: Department of Agriculture, annual report, 1974; Kasama, Northern Province.
'Agrarian revolution, Northern Province': memo. by Cabinet Minister, Kasama, Northern Province (1974 mimeo.).
Memo., Task Force: W.P./DEV.1/2/3; Mongu, Western Province.
Minutes of provincial development committee, 6 January 1972; Mongu, Western Province.

(1) *Kasama*
Meeting for M.P. Kasama at Mungwi, 25 April 1975.
Minutes of 30th ordinary meeting of the rural council, Kasama: address by District Governor, 22 September 1971.
Minutes of village productivity committee meeting, 13 June 1974.
Minutes of ward council secretaries' meeting, Mungwi, 1 October 1974.
Minutes of ward development committee meetings, Ward 13, Mungwi, 31 January 1973 and 17 April 1974.
Minutes of ward development committee meeting, Ward 14, 2 February 1974.
Rural Council File No. LG/KA/1/4: ward development committee meetings, September 1972 – March 1975.

(2) *Serenje*
Secretary Rural Council Serenje to District Governor Serenje, letter of 31 May 1970.

(g) *Office of the Prime Minister, Lusaka – Provincial Administration Division*

'Confidential policy matters': file No. PA/72/10/9.
'District Governors, District Secretaries as at 1 October 1977'.
'Eastern Province': file No. PA/72/10/2.
'Luapula Province': file No. PA/72/10/8.
'Northern Province': file No. PAN GC 72/10/6.

'North-western Province': file No. PA/72/10/1.

(h) *Personnel Division, Lusaka*

'Review of establishments and personnel work' (Lusaka: Establishment Division, 1967, mimeo.).

(i) *United National Independence Party*

UNIP regional secretary Serenje to all departments, letter of 9 December 1965.

'Address by his Excellency Dr Kenneth D. Kaunda, President of the Republic of Zambia, to the Mulungushi conference and a guide to the implementation of humanism in Zambia', presented to the annual general conference at Mulungushi, 14–20 August 1967 (Lusaka: Government Printer, n.d. [1967]).

Muchinka UNIP constituency chairman to District Governor Serenje, 9 January 1970.

North-western Province (President's tour, November 1971): welcome address to his Excellency the President by the regional secretary, Solwezi (mimeo.).

A nation of equals – the Kabwe declaration: addresses to the national council of the United National Independence Party, 1–3 December 1972 (Lusaka: Zambia Information Services, 1973).

The constitution of the United National Independence Party, schedule to the Constitution of Zambia Act, No. 27 of 1973 (Lusaka: Government Printer, 1973).

'The leadership code and responsibilities of the leadership in the creation of a new social order' – Address by his Excellency the President, Dr K. D. Kaunda, to the national council on 2 December 1972 (Lusaka: Zambia Information Services, 1973).

UNIP: national policies for the next decade, 1974–84 (Lusaka: Zambia Information Services, n.d. [1973]).

'Deliberations, proceedings and resolutions of the fourth national council of the United National Independence Party held in Mulungushi Hall, 20th–25th April 1974' (Lusaka, n.d.).

United National Independence Party: 7th national council meeting, 8th–12th December 1975 (mimeo.).

United National Independence Party: annual report for the year 1975 (Lusaka, 1976).

The 'Watershed' speech: President Kaunda's address to the UNIP national council, Lusaka, 30 June 1975 (Lusaka: Government Printer, 1976).

Communocracy (a strategy for constructing a people's economy under humanism) – addresses by his Excellency the President, Dr K. D. Kaunda, to the leadership seminar and the ninth UNIP national council held at Mulungushi Rock, Kabwe; 14–24 September 1976 (1976).

2. *Printed primary sources*

(a) *Northern Rhodesia/Zambia publications* (by. the Government Printer, Lusaka, subject to the exceptions and additions shown. Entries are listed by year, and alphabetically within each year).

Establishment circulars/minutes, 1959–1964 (Lusaka: Establishment Division).

A report on a preliminary examination of the salaries and grading structure of the Northern Rhodesia Civil Service (including the Northern Rhodesia Police), A. B. Shone, Chief Establishment Officer (The Shone Report), (Lusaka, February 1960).

Monthly Digest of Statistics, 1960–77 (Lusaka: Central Statistical Office).

Government Gazette, 1964–68.

Report of the Commission appointed to review the salaries and conditions of service of the Northern Rhodesia public and teaching services and of the Northern Rhodesia army and air force (The Hadow Report), (Lusaka, 1964).

An Outline of the Transitional Development Plan (Lusaka: Central Planning Office, 1965).

Economic Report, 1964 (Lusaka: Ministry of Finance, 1965).

Establishment registers, 1965–69 (Lusaka: Establishment Division).

Annual report of the provincial and district government, 1966 (1966).

First National Development Plan, 1966–70 (Lusaka: Office of National Development and Planning, July 1966).

Manpower report: a report and statistical handbook on manpower, education, training and Zambianisation, 1965–66 (1966).

Public Service Commission: annual reports for 1965, 1966, 1969–75.

Report of the Commission appointed to review the grading structure of the civil service, the salary scales of the civil service, the teaching service, the Zambia police and the prisons service, the salary scales and wages of non-civil service (industrial) employees of the Government and the pay scales and conditions of service of the Zambia defence forces (The Whelan Report) (1966).

Report of the Commission of Enquiry into the mining industry, 1966 (The Brown Report) (1966).

Zambia police: annual report for the year 1965 (1966).

National convention on the four-year development plan, Kitwe, 11–15 January 1967 (1967).

Financial Reports, 1968–76.

Reports of the Auditor General, 1968, 1971–73.

Report on the working and finances of agricultural statutory boards, under the chairmanship of Dr A. V. R. Rao (1968).

Government directory, April 1969–1978 (Lusaka: Cabinet Office).

International Labour Office, *Report to the government of Zambia on incomes, wages and prices in Zambia: policy and machinery* (The Turner Report), (Lusaka: Cabinet Office, 1969).

Report of the Commission of Inquiry into the affairs of the Lusaka City Council (1969).

Zambian Manpower (Lusaka: Development Division, 1969).

Economic Report, 1969 (Lusaka: Ministry of Finance, 1970).

Report of the Committee appointed to review the emoluments and conditions of service of statutory boards and corporations and state-owned enterprises (Lusaka: Cabinet Office, 1970).

Report of the Second National Convention on rural development incomes, wages and prices in Zambia: policy and machinery, Kitwe, December 1969 (Lusaka: Zambia Information Services, 1970).

Report of the Commission appointed to review the salaries, salary structure and conditions of service of the Zambia public service (including the Zambia police) and the defence force (Government paper No. 1 of 1971), (The O'Riordan Report), (1971).

Report of the Commission of Inquiry into the allegations made by Mr Justin Chimba and Mr John Chisata (1971).

Second National Development Plan: January 1972–December 1976 (Lusaka: Ministry of Development Planning and National Guidance, December 1971).

Village productivity and ward development committees: a pocket manual (1971).

Report of the national commission on the establishment of a one-party participatory democracy in Zambia (1972).

——, *Summary of recommendations accepted by government* (Government paper No. 1 of 1972) (1972).

Report of the Working Party appointed to review the system of decentralised administration (The Simmance Report), (Lusaka: Cabinet Office, May 1972).

Annual estimates of revenue and expenditure, 1973–77.

Statistical year-book, 1971 (Lusaka: Central Statistical Office, 1973).

A record of Zambian graduates in government service, the private sector and quasi-government institutions (Lusaka: Directorate of Civil Service Training, 1974).

Census of Agriculture, 1970–71: First Report (Lusaka: Central Statistical Office, May 1974).

Mid-term review of the Second National Development Plan (Lusaka: Development Planning Division, Ministry of Planning and Finance, December 1974).

Zambia, 1964–74: ten years of achievement (Lusaka: Zambia Information Services, n.d. [1974]).

Annual report of the Commission for Investigations for the year 1974 (1975).

Budget address by the Minister of Planning and Finance, the Hon A. B. Chikwanda, M.P. (January 1975).

Report of the Commission of Inquiry into the salaries, salary structures and conditions of service of the Zambia public and teaching services, the Zambia police and prisons service, the defence forces and staffs of local authorities, including casual and daily-paid employees, and of personnel employed by statutory boards and corporations and by companies in which the state has majority or controlling interest, Volume I: the public services and the parastatal sector (The Mwanakatwe Report) (1975).

Summary of the main recommendations of the Commission of Inquiry into the salaries, salary structures and conditions of service, together with the party and government reactions to the recommendations, Volume I: the public services and the parastatal sector (Government paper No. 1 of 1975) (1975).

Zambianisation in the public service: progress report, 1975 (Lusaka, n.d., mimeo.).

A humanist handbook: how to understand and practice humanism (Lusaka: Freedom House, November 1976).
Education for development: draft statement on educational reform (Lusaka: Ministry of Education, 1976).
Humanism in Zambia, with narration by President Kenneth Kaunda (Lusaka: Zambia Information Services, n.d.).
The year ahead: a look at some of the problems we face – how they arose and how to deal with them (Lusaka: Zambia Information Services, 1976).

Annual report of the Commission for Investigations for the year 1975 (1977).
Economic Report, 1976 (Lusaka: Ministry of Finance, 1977).

Third National Development Plan, 1979–83 (Lusaka: National Commission for Development Planning, Office of the President, October 1979).

(b) Zambia: parastatal sector
Zambia Industrial and Mining Corporation, annual report, 1972 (Lusaka, 1973).
Zambia Industrial Development Corporation, annual reports, 1972, 1973, 1973–74, 1975–76 (Lusaka).
Bank of Zambia, report and statement of accounts for the year ended December 31st., 1973 (Lusaka, 1974).
Rural Development Corporation, annual reports, 1973 and 1974 (Lusaka).
National Agricultural Marketing Board, annual report and accounts, 1974 (Lusaka, 1975).
Report of the committee on parastatal bodies for the fifth session of the Third National Assembly – appointed on the 31st January 1978 (Lusaka: Government Printer, 1978).

(c) British government publications
Land resources of the Northern and Luapula provinces, Zambia: a reconnaissance assessment (London: Foreign and Commonwealth Office, O.D.A. Land Resources Division, 1973).

(d) Ghana government publications
Report of the Commission on the structure and remuneration of the public services in Ghana (The Mills–Odoi Report) (Accra: Ministry of Information, 1967).

3. *Printed secondary sources*
Abraham, W. I., *Annual budgeting and development planning*. National Planning Methods Series No.1 (Washington, D.C.: National Planning Association, December 1965).
Adu, A. L., *The civil service in Commonwealth Africa* (London: George Allen & Unwin, 1969).
Alavi, H., 'The state in post-colonial societies: Pakistan and Bangladesh', *New Left Review*, No. 74 (July-August 1972).
Anglin, D. G., 'Zambia and the Angolan civil war' (April 1977, mimeo.).
—, 'Confrontation in Southern Africa: Zambia and Portugal', *International Journal*, vol. XXV, No. 3 (summer 1970).
Austin, D., *Politics in Ghana, 1946–60* (London: Oxford University Press, 1964).
Baldwin, R. E., *Economic development and export growth: a study of Northern Rhodesia, 1920–60* (Berkeley and Los Angeles: University of California Press, 1966).
Bancroft, J. A., *Mining in Northern Rhodesia* (London: British South Africa Company, 1961).
Banda, R., 'Namboard's role – an honour and a burden, says G.M.', *Enterprise* (Lusaka), October 1973.
Barber, W. J., *The economy of British central Africa: a case study of economic development in a dualistic society* (Stanford: Stanford University Press, 1961).
Bates, R. H., *Unions, parties, and political development: a study of mineworkers in Zambia* (New Haven: Yale University Press, 1971).
—, *Rural responses to industrialisation: a study of village Zambia* (New Haven: Yale University Press, 1976).
Baylies, C., and Szeftel, M., 'Control and participation in the 1973 Zambian one-party election', in Gertzel, C. J. (ed.), *Zambian Politics* (forthcoming).
Beckman, B., 'Public enterprise and state capitalism', in Ghai, Y. (ed.), *Law in the political economy of public enterprises: African perspectives* (Uppsala: Scandinavian Institute of African Studies and the International Centre for Law and Development, 1977).
Bond, G. C., *The politics of change in a Zambian community* (Chicago: University of Chicago Press, 1976).
Bostock M., and Harvey, C. (eds.), *Economic independence and Zambian copper: a case study of foreign investment* (New York: Praeger, 1972).
Burnham, J., *The managerial revolution* (Bloomington: Indiana University Press, 1962 edn.).
Caplan, G. L., *The elites of Barotseland, 1878–1969: a political history of Zambia's Western Province* (Berkeley and Los Angeles: University of California Press, 1970).
—, 'Barotseland: the secessionist challenge to Zambia', *Journal of Modern*

African Studies, vol. 6, No. 3 (October 1968).

Chambers, R., *Managing rural development: ideas and experience from East Africa* (Uppsala: Scandinavian Institute of African Studies, 1974).

Chilczuk, M., 'Increased provincial share in plan implementation: an outline' (Lusaka: Ministry of Development Planning, October-December 1975, mimeo.).

Clegg, E., *Race and Politics: partnership in the Federation of Rhodesia and Nyasaland (London: Oxford University Press, 1960).*

Cliffe, L., *'Penetration and rural development in the East African context' (University of Dar es Salaam 1973, mimeo.).*

—, and Saul J. S. (eds.), *Socialism in Tanzania: an interdisciplinary reader*, 2 vols. (Dar es Salaam: East African Publishing House, 1973).

—, and Saul, J. S., 'The district development front', *ibid.*, vol. I.

Davidson, J. W., *The Northern Rhodesian Legislative Council* (London: Faber & Faber, 1948).

Dotson, F. and L. O., *The Indian minority of Zambia, Rhodesia and Malawi* (New Haven: Yale University Press, 1968).

Dresang, D. L., 'Ethnic politics, representative bureaucracy and development administration: the Zambian case', *American Political Science Review*, vol. LXVIII, No. 4 (December 1974).

—, *The Zambia civil service: entrepreneurialism and development administration* (Nairobi: East African Publishing House, 1975).

Due, J., 'Agricultural credit in Zambia by level of development' (Urbana-Champaign: University of Illinois, Agricultural Economics staff paper, 1978).

Dumont, R., with Mazoyer, M. (translated by Cunningham, R.), *Socialisms and development* (London: Andrë Deutsch, 1973).

Elliott, C., 'The Zambian economy' (Lusaka, 1968, mimeo.).

— (ed.), *Constraints on the economic development of Zambia* (Nairobi: Oxford University Press, 1971).

Epstein, A. L., *Politics in an urban African community* (Manchester: Manchester University Press, 1958).

Faber, M. L. O., and Potter J. G.., *Towards economic independence: papers on the nationalisation of the copper industry in Zambia* (London: Cambridge . University Press, 1972).

Fielder, R. J., 'Government and politics at district level: case study of an opposition area' (Lusaka: Institute of African Studies, University of Zambia, 1970, mimeo.).

Finucane, J., 'Intensive and experimental approaches to rural development: Zambia's IDZs', University of Zambia correspondence lecture No. 41, PA 410/73/26 (Lusaka: 1973, mimeo.).

—, *Rural development and bureaucracy in Tanzania. The case of Mwanza region* (Uppsala, Scandinavian Institute of African Studies, 1974).

Fortman, B. de G., 'Humanism and the Zambian economic order', in Fortman, B. de G. (ed.), *After Mulungushi – the economics of Zambian humanism* (Nairobi: East African Publishing House, 1969).

Fry, J., *Employment and income distribution in the African economy* (London:

Croom Helm, 1979).

Gann, L. H., *The birth of a plural society: the development of Northern Rhodesia under the British South Africa Company, 1894–1914* (Manchester: Manchester University Press, 1958).

—, *A history of Northern Rhodesia: early days to 1953* (London: Chatto & Windus, 1964).

Gertzel, C. J., 'Dissent and authority in the one-party state: parliament, party and President in the Zambian one-party participatory democracy' (mimeo., 1975).

—, 'Institutional developments at district level in independent Zambia' (University of Zambia Political Science Workshop, 1972, mimeo.).

—, Mutukwa, K., Scott, I., and Wallis, M., 'Zambia's final experience of inter-party elections: the by-elections of December 1971', *Kroniek van Afrika*, vol. 2 (June–July 1972).

Green, R. H., 'Historical, decision-taking, firm and sectoral dimensions of public sector enterprise: some aspects of and angles of attack for research', in Ghai, Y. (ed.), *Law in the political economy of public enterprises: African perspectives* (Uppsala: Scandinavian Institute of African Studies and the International Centre for Law and Development, 1977).

Gupta, A., 'Trade unionism and politics on the Copperbelt', in Tordoff, W. (ed.), *Politics in Zambia* (Manchester: Manchester University Press, 1974).

—, 'Political system and the one-party states of Tropical Africa', *India Quarterly*, vol. 31, No. 2 (April–June 1975).

Hailey, W. M., *An African survey* (London: Oxford University Press, 1957).

Halcrow, M., *Intensive rural development plans for Northern and Luapula provinces, 1957–61* (Lusaka: Government Printer, 1958).

Hall, R., *The high price of principles: Kaunda and the white south* (London: Hodder and Stoughton, 1969).

Hanson, A. H., *Managerial problems in public enterprises* (New York: Asia Publishing House, 1962).

Harvey, C., 'Control of credit in Zambia', *Journal of Modern African Studies*, vol. 11, No. 3 (1973).

Hawkesworth, N. R. (ed.), *Local government in Zambia* (Lusaka: Lusaka City Council, 1974).

Hellen, J. A., *Rural economic development in Zambia, 1890–1964* (Munich: Weltforum-Verlag, 1968).

Howell, J., 'Planning the provinces: another look at decentralisation in Zambia', *Zango*, No. 3 (Lusaka: University of Zambia, August 1977).

—, Review of Hawkesworth, N. R. (ed.), *Local Government in Zambia* (Lusaka: Lusaka City Council, 1974) in *African Social Research*, No. 23 (June 1977).

Hyden, G., 'Social structure, bureaucracy and development administration in Kenya', *The African Review*, vol. 1, No. 3 (January 1972).

—, *Peasants and underdevelopment in Africa: the Tanzanian experience and beyond* (London: Heinemann, and Berkeley and Los Angeles: University of California Press, forthcoming).

Johns, S. W., 'Parastatal bodies in Zambia: problems and prospects', in

Simonis, H. and U. E. (eds.), *Socio-economic development in dual economies: the example of Zambia* (Munich: Weltforum-Verlag, 1971).

—, 'Parastatal bodies in Zambia: a survey' (mimeo.).

Jolly, R., 'The Seers report in retrospect', *African Social Research*, No. 11 (June 1971).

—, 'Skilled manpower as a constraint to development in Zambia', *Communications Series No. 48* (Institute of Development Studies, University of Sussex, January 1970).

—, 'The skilled manpower constraint', in Elliott, C. (ed.), *Constraints on the economic development of Zambia* (Nairobi: Oxford University Press, 1971).

Kasfir, N., 'Prismatic theory and African administration', *World Politics*, Vol. 21, No. 2 (January 1969).

Kaunda, K. D., *Zambia: independence and beyond. The speeches of Kenneth Kaunda*, (ed.) Legum, C. (London: Nelson, 1966).

—, *Humanism in Zambia and a guide to its implementation* (Lusaka: Government Printer, n.d. [1967]).

—, *Zambia: towards economic independence* (Lusaka: Government Printer, 1968).

—, *I wish to inform the nation* (Lusaka: Government Printer, 1969).

—, *Towards complete independence* (Lusaka: Government Printer, 1969).

—, *Address at the opening of a seminar on rural development, Lusaka, 23 March 1970* (Lusaka: Zambia Information Services, 1970).

—, *Take up the challenge* (Lusaka: Government Printer, 1970).

—, 'The role of a District Governor', address on opening the District Governors' workshop, Lusaka, 2 June 1971 (Lusaka: Zambia Information Services, 1971).

—, *Address at the press conference on the redemption of ZIMCO bonds, State House, Lusaka, August 31 1973* (New York: Permanent Mission of the Republic of Zambia at the United Nations, n.d.).

—, *Humanism in Zambia, Part II* (Lusaka: Government Printer, 1974).

—, *Address to Parliament on the opening of the fourth session of the third National Assembly* (Lusaka: Government Printer, 1977).

—, *Address to the first emergency meeting of the National Assembly, Lusaka, 11 October 1977* (Lusaka: Zambia Information Services, 1977).

—, *Address at the official opening of the first session of the fourth National Assembly, Lusaka, 18 December 1978*, as reported in *Times of Zambia*, 19 December 1978.

Keatley, P., *The politics of partnership: the Federation of Rhodesia and Nyasaland* (Harmondsworth: Penguin, 1963).

Kirkman, W., *Unscrambling an empire – a critique of British colonial policy, 1956–66* (London: Chatto & Windus, 1966).

Kjekshus, H., 'Perspectives on the second parliament, 1965–70', in Election Study Committee, University of Dar es Salaam, *Socialism and participation: Tanzania's 1970 national elections* (Dar es Salaam: Tanzania Publishing House, 1974).

Lee, J. M., 'Parliament in Republican Ghana', *Parliamentary Affairs*, vol. XVI, No. 4 (1963).

—, *Colonial development and good government: a study of the ideas expressed by the British official classes in planning decolonization, 1939–1964* (Oxford: Clarendon Press, 1967).

Lewis, B. W., 'Comparative economic systems: nationalized industry, British nationalization and American private enterprises: some parallels and controls', *American Economic Review*, vol. LV (May 1965).

Leys, C., 'The "overdeveloped" post-colonial state: a re-evaluation', *Review of African Political Economy*, No. 5 (January–April 1976).

—, and Pratt, C. (eds.), *A new deal in central Africa* (London: Heinemann, 1960).

Libby, R. T., and Woakes, M. O., 'Nationalization and the displacement of development policy in Zambia' (Lusaka: November 1977, mimeo.).

Lofchie, M. F., 'Representative government, bureaucracy, and political development: the African case', *Journal of the Developing Areas*, vol. 2 (October 1967).

Lombard, C. S., *The growth of co-operatives in Zambia, 1914–71* (Institute for African Studies, University of Zambia, Zambian Papers No. 6. Manchester: Manchester University Press, 1971).

—, and Tweedie, A. H. C., *Agriculture in Zambia since independence* (Lusaka: Neczam, 1972).

Loxley, J., and Saul, J. S., 'The political economy of the parastatals', *East African Law Review*, vol. 5, no. 1–2 (1972).

Lühring, J., *Rural development planning in Zambia: objectives, strategies and achievements* (Tangier: CAFRAD, April 1975).

Mackinson, I., *The development of senior administrators in Zambia* (Lusaka: National Institute of Public Administration, mimeo., n.d.).

Malik, J. R., Branston, J., and Barraclough, J. H., 'The history and finance of local government', in Hawkesworth, N.R. (ed.), *Local government in Zambia* (Lusaka: Lusaka City Council, 1974).

Maniatis, G. C., 'Managerial autonomy vs state control in public enterprise. Fact and artifact,' in *Annals of Public and Co-operative Economy*, vol. XXXIX (November 1968).

Maimbo, F. J. M., and Fry, J., 'An investigation into the change in the terms of trade between the rural and urban sectors of Zambia', *African Social Research*, No. 12 (Lusaka: Institute for African Studies, University of Zambia, December 1971).

Martin, A., *Minding their own business: Zambia's struggle against Western control* (London: Hutchinson, 1972).

Martin, Richard J., 'Housing in Lusaka', in Hawkesworth, N. R. (ed.), *Local government in Zambia* (Lusaka: Lusaka City Council, 1974).

Martin, Robert, 'The Ombudsman in Zambia', *The Journal of Modern African Studies*, vol. 15, No. 2 (1977).

McEnery, H., 'The village productivity committee system and production targets in Mkushi District (Lusaka: August 1974, mimeo.).

Mlenga, K. G. (ed.), *Who's who in Zambia, 1967–68* (Lusaka: Zambia Publishing Co. Ltd., n.d. [1968]).

Molteno, R., 'Zambia and the one-party state', *East Africa Journal*, vol. 9,

No. 2 (February 1972).

—, 'Cleavage and conflict in Zambian politics: a study in sectionalism', in Tordoff, W. (ed.), *Politics in Zambia* (Manchester: Manchester University Press, 1974).

—, 'Zambian humanism: the way ahead', *The African Review*, vol. 3, No. 4 (1973).

—, and Scott, I., 'The 1968 general election and the political system', in Tordoff, W. (ed.), *Politics in Zambia* (Manchester: Manchester University Press, 1974).

Momba, J., and Nglazi, R., 'Permanent secretaries – a study of those serving in 1972', in Molteno, R. V. (compiler), *Studies in Zambian government and administration* (Lusaka: University of Zambia, 1973, mimeo.).

Mtshali, B. V., 'The Zambia foreign service', *The African Review*, vol. 5, No. 3 (1975).

Mulford, D. C., *The Northern Rhodesian general election, 1962* (Nairobi: Oxford University Press, 1964).

—, *Zambia: the politics of independence, 1957–64* (London: Oxford University Press, 1967).

Musakanya, V., 'The role of rural development in national development', paper presented to seminar on Rural Development and Zambian Economic Progress, University of Zambia, May 1970, and reproduced in Geza, S.(ed.), *Rural development papers*, vol. 2 (Lusaka: University of Zambia, February 1973, mimeo.).

Musolf, L. D., *Mixed enterprise* (Lexington: Heath & Co., 1972).

Mutukwa, K. S., 'Political control of parastatal organisations in Zambia', *Zango*, 1 (1976).

Mwanakatwe, J. M., *The growth of education in Zambia since independence* (Lusaka: Oxford University Press, 1968).

Nkwabilo, K. H., 'Remarks on manpower and Zambianisation' (Lusaka: University of Zambia, 26 June 1969, mimeo.).

Nove, A., and Petras, J., 'State capitalism and the third world – a discussion', *Development and Change*, vol. 8, No. 4 (1977).

Nwabueze, B. O., *Presidentialism in Commonwealth Africa* (London: C. Hurst & Co., in association with Nwamife Publishers, Enugu and Lagos, 1975).

Packard, P. C., 'Management and control of parastatal organisations', in Uchumi Editorial Board (eds.), *Towards Socialist Planning* (Dar es Salaam: Tanzania Publishing House, 1972).

Petras, J., 'State capitalism and the third world', *Development and Change*, vol. 8, No. 1 (1977).

Pettman, J., *Zambia – security and conflict* (Lewes: Julian Friedmann Publishers Ltd., 1974).

Prakash, O., *The theory and working of state corporations* (London: Allen and Unwin, 1962).

Quick, S., 'Rural socialism in Zambia', *Journal of Modern African Studies*, vol. 15, No. 3 (1977).

Rasmussen, T., 'The popular basis of anti-colonial protest', in Tordoff, W.

(ed.), *Politics in Zambia* (Manchester: Manchester University Press, 1974).

Richards, A. I., 'A changing pattern of agriculture in East Africa', *Geographical Journal*, vol. 124, No. 3 (1958).

—, 'The political system of the Bemba tribe', in Fortes, M., and Evans-Pritchard, E., *African political systems* (London: Oxford University Press, 1941).

Riggs, F. W., *The ecology of public administration* (London: Asia Publishing House, 1961).

—, *Administration in developing countries: the theory of prismatic society* (Boston: Houghton–Mifflin, 1964).

—, 'The context of development administration', in Riggs, F. W. (ed.), *Frontiers of Development* (Durham, N.C.: Duke University Press, 1970).

Roberts, A., *A history of Zambia* (London: Heinemann, 1976).

Rotberg, R. I., *The rise of nationalism in central Africa: the making of Malawi and Zambia, 1873–1964* (Cambridge, Mass.: Harvard University Press, 1965).

Rothchild, D., 'Rural–urban inequalities and resource allocation in Zambia', *Journal of Modern African Studies*, vol. X, No. 3 (1972).

Sanyal, B. C., Case, J. H., Dow, P. S., and Jackman, M. E., *Higher education and the labour market in Zambia: expectations and performance* (Paris/Lusaka: UNESCO Press/University of Zambia, 1976).

Saul, J. S., 'Class and penetration', in Cliffe, L., and Saul, J. S. (eds.), *Socialism in Tanzania: an interdisciplinary reader*, 2 vols. (Dar es Salaam: East African Publishing House, 1973).

—, 'The state in post-colonial societies – Tanzania', in Miliband, R. (ed.), *The socialist register* (London, 1974).

Schaffer, B. B., 'The concept of preparation: some questions about the transfer of systems of government', *World Politics*, vol. XVIII (October 1965).

—, 'The deadlock in development administration', in Leys, C. (ed.), *Politics and change in developing countries: studies in the theory and practice of development* (London: Cambridge University Press, 1969).

—, 'Administrative legacies and links in the post-colonial state: preparation, training and administrative reform', *Development and Change*, vol. 9 (1978).

Scott, I., 'Middle class politics in Zambia', *African Affairs*, vol. 77, No. 308 (1978).

Seidman, A., 'The distorted growth of import-substitution industry: the Zambian case', *Journal of Modern African Studies*, vol. 12, No. 4 (1974).

Shaw, T. M., 'The foreign policy system of Zambia', *African Studies Review*, vol. XIX, No. 1 (1976).

—, 'Zambia: dependence and underdevelopment', *Canadian Journal of African Studies*, vol. X, No. 1 (1976).

—, 'Zambia's foreign policy', in Aluko, O. (ed.), *The Foreign Policies of African States* (London: Hodder and Stoughton, 1977).

—, and Mugomba, A. T., 'The political economy of regional détente: Zambia and Southern Africa', *Journal of African Studies*, 4 (Winter, 1977).

Shils, E., 'The concept and function of ideology', a reprint from vol. 7 of *International Encyclopedia of the Social Sciences* (New York: Macmillan and

Free Press, 1968).

Shivji, I. G., *Class struggles in Tanzania* (London: Heinemann, 1976).

Short, P., *Banda* (London and Boston: Routledge & Kegan Paul, 1974).

Sklar, R. L., 'Zambia's response to the Rhodesian unilateral declaration of independence', in Tordoff, W. (ed.), *Politics in Zambia* (Manchester: Manchester University Press, 1974).

—, *Corporate power in an African state: the political impact of multinational mining companies in Zambia* (Berkeley and Los Angeles: University of California Press, 1975).

Svendsen, K. V., 'Development administration and socialist strategy: Tanzania after Mwongozo', in Rweyemamu, A. H., and Mwansasu, B. U., *Planning in Tanzania: background to decentralisation* (Nairobi: East African Literature Bureau, 1974).

Tordoff, W., 'Tanzania: democracy and the one-party state', *Government and Opposition*, vol. 2, No. 4 (July–October 1967).

—, 'Provincial and district government in Zambia', *Journal of Administration Overseas*, vol. VII, Nos. 3 and 4 (July and October 1968).

—, 'Provincial and local government in Zambia', *Journal of Administration Overseas*, vol. IX, No. 1 (January 1970).

—(ed.), *Politics in Zambia* (Manchester: Manchester University Press, and Berkeley and Los Angeles: University of California Press, 1974).

—, 'Zambia: the politics of disengagement', *African Affairs*, vol. 76, No. 302 (January 1977).

—, 'Residual legislatures: the cases of Tanzania and Zambia', *Journal of Commonwealth and Comparative Politics*, vol. XV, No. 3 (November 1977).

—, and Molteno, R., 'Government and administration', in Tordoff, W. (ed.), *Politics in Zambia* (Manchester: Manchester University Press, 1974).

—, and Scott, I., 'Political parties: structures and policies', in *ibid*.

Weiss, R., 'Anatomy of ZIMCO', *Times of Zambia Business Review*, 15 December 1972.

Young, C. E., 'Rural–urban terms of trade', *African Social Research*, No. 12 (Lusaka: Institute for African Studies, University of Zambia, December 1971).

Young, R. A., 'Zambia', in Hodson, H. V. (ed.), *The Annual Register: World Events in 1974* (London: Longman, 1975).

—, 'Zambia', in *ibid.*, *1975* (London: Longman, 1976).

—, 'Zambia', in *ibid*, *1978* (London: Longman, 1979 forthcoming).

4. *Miscellaneous*

(a) *Anonymous publications*

The councillors' handbook (Lusaka: Ministry of Local Government and Housing, 1966).

Government and Opposition, vol. 2, No. 4 (July–October 1967): special issue on 'Political conflict in Africa'.

'Governmental machinery at the grass-roots level: an area study of Ward 19 of Serenje District', Administrative Studies in Development No. 11 (Lusaka: National Institute of Public Administration, March 1974).

The Fortune directory: the 300 largest industrial corporations outside the U.S. (Chicago: Fortune Magazine, 1974).

Tour report of IDZ project in Eastern Province (Kabwe: President's Citizenship College, 1975, mimeo.).

Administration for Rural Development (ARD) Research Project, *Organisation for Participation in rural development in Zambia* (Lusaka: National Institute of Public Administration, and Amsterdam: Free University January 1977, mimeo., draft report).

Quarterly Economic Review of Zambia, 4th Quarter 1978 (London: Economic Intelligence Unit Ltd., 1978).

(b) Conference papers etc.

Anglin, D. G., 'Zambian versus Malawian approaches to political change in southern Africa', paper presented to the conference on African responses to colonialism in Southern Africa, California State University, Northridge, 10 January 1976.

Apedaile, P. L., 'Intensive development zones – some theoretical aspects', paper presented to the Economics Club, Lusaka.

Burke, F. G., 'Public Administration in Africa: the legacy of inherited colonial institutions', paper presented at the World Congress of the International Political Science Association, Brussels, 18–23 September 1967.

Chambers, R., 'Planning for rural areas in East Africa: experience and prescriptions', paper presented to the Conference on Comparative Administration, Arusha, 25–28 September 1971.

Evans, D., 'The "mix" of policy objectives in rural development', paper presented to the Economics Club, Lusaka, November 1977.

Hesse, C., 'Some political aspects of development planning and implementation in Zambia, with particular reference to the Eastern and Luapula Provinces', paper presented to the University of East Africa Social Science Conference, Dar es Salaam, January 1968.

Kaunda, K. D., Address at the opening of a seminar on rural development, Lusaka, 23 March 1970.

Mafeje, A., 'The role of state capitalism in predominantly agrarian economies', paper presented at the Institute of Social Studies' 25th anniversary conference, The Hague, December 1977.

Minutes of the civil servants' seminar held in Gwembe, Southern Province, Zambia, January 1970.

Mulaisho, D., 'INDECO: Problems and Prospects', paper presented to the Economics Club, Lusaka, 11 January 1977.

Mwanza, J. M., 'The conflict between efficiency and social gain in parastatal enterprises in Zambia', paper prepared for delivery at the joint meeting of the African Studies Association/Latin American Studies

Association, Houston, November 1977.
Report of seminar on humanism, Part Two (Kitwe, *mimeo.*).
Subramaniam, V., 'The social background of Zambia's higher civil servants and undergraduates', paper presented to the University of East Africa Social Science Conference, Nairobi, December 1969.
Van Donge, J. K., 'Independence at the grass roots and dependency theory: a case study in decolonisation and privilege from Mwase Lundazi, Zambia', graduate research seminar paper, University of Manchester, 17 May 1979.

(c) *Legislation*

Cap. 648 of *The Laws of Zambia* (1965 edition).
Constitution of Zambia Act, No. 27 of 1973 (Lusaka: Government Printer, 1973).
Constitution of Zambia (Amendment) Act, No. 18 of 1974 (Lusaka: Government Printer, 1974).
Statutory Instruments Nos. 288 of 1973 and 108 of 1974.

(d) *Media*

United Kingdom:

BBC Television, 11 December 1978: 'Tonight'.
BBC World Service, 12 December 1978: 'The World Today'.
Financial Times, 1977–78 (London).
The Guardian, 1978 (London and Manchester).
The Times, 1978 (London).

Zambia:

Sunday Times of Zambia, 1974–77 (Ndola).
Times of Zambia, 1970–78 (Ndola).
Times of Zambia Business Review, 1971–72 (Ndola).
Zambia Daily Mail, 1974–77 (Lusaka).
Zambia Information Services (Lusaka):
    Background papers, 1968–77.
    Press releases, 1965–1968.
    Nshila, No. 155 (January 1964).
Zambia Newsletter, 1 December 1977 and 4 January 1979 (London: Zambia High Commission).

(e) *Parliamentary records*

Zambia:

Daily parliamentary debates, 1977 (Lusaka).
National Assembly debates, Hansard Nos. 5–38, 1965–75 (Lusaka).

(f) Research bulletins

Africa Confidential (London), 1978.
Africa Research Bulletin (Exeter), political, social and cultural series, 1968,
1975, 1978, and economic, financial and technical series, 1978.

(g) Theses

Bratton, M., 'Peasant and party-state in Zambia: political organisation and
resource distribution in Kasama District' (Brandeis University: Ph.D.,
1978).
Chaput, M., 'Zambian state enterprise: the politics and management of
nationalized development' (Syracuse University: Ph.D., 1971).
Mubako, S. V. S., 'The presidential system in the Zambian constitution'
(University of London: M.Phil., 1970).
Pelekamoyo, G. M., 'Local autonomy and central control in Zambian urban
authorities' (University of Zambia: M.A., 1977).
Quick, S., 'Bureaucracy and rural socialism: the Zambian experience'
(Stanford University: Ph.D., 1975).
Szeftel, M., 'Political conflict, spoils and class formation in Zambia'
(University of Manchester: Ph.D., 1978).
Wood, G. D., 'Administrative training in Zambia: a study in insti-
tutionalisation and change' (University of Sussex: M.Phil., 1971).

(h) United Nations

*Some problems in the organisation and administration of public enterprises in the
industrial field* (New York: United Nations, 1954).
United Nations Economic Commission for Africa, *Economic survey mission on
the economic development of Zambia: report of the UN/ECA/FAO mission* (Ndola:
Falcon Press, 1964).
Report of the ILO/JASPA Mission (Geneva—1977).

(i) International Bank for Reconstruction and Development

Republic of Zambia: agricultural and rural sector survey (3 vols., 1974): vol. II,
Annex 6: 'organisation for rural development'.

Index